Russian-American Dialogue
on the History of U.S. Political Parties

Russian–American Dialogues

on United States History

Volume 4

General Editors

Eugene F. Yazkov

Louis W. Potts

Russian-American Dialogue

on the History of U.S. Political Parties

Edited by Joel H. Silbey

☆
☆
☆
☆
☆

University of Missouri Press

COLUMBIA AND LONDON

Copyright © 2000 by
The Curators of the University of Missouri
University of Missouri Press, Columbia, Missouri 65201
Printed and bound in the United States of America
All rights reserved
5 4 3 2 1   04 03 02 01 00

Library of Congress Cataloging-in-Publication Data

Russian-American dialogue on the history of U.S. political parties / edited by Joel H.
  Silbey.
       p.   cm.—(Russian-American dialogues on United States history ; v. 4)
     Includes bibliographical references (p.   ) and index.
     ISBN 0-8262-1276-X (alk. paper)
     1. Political parties—United States—History.   I. Silbey, Joel H.   II. Series.
  JK2261.R87   2000
  324.273'09—dc21   00-036462

⊗™ This paper meets the requirements of the
American National Standard for Permanence of Paper
for Printed Library Materials, Z39.48, 1984.

Designer: *Elizabeth K. Young*
Typesetter: *Bookcomp, Inc.*
Printer and binder: *Thomson-Shore, Inc.*
Typefaces: *Times, Boton*

To *Theodore K. Rabb*
and the memory of
N. V. Sivachev

Contents

Joint Preface

This is the fourth published volume in a series originally conceived by historians in Russia and the United States in 1986. The series was largely the product of three key developments: 1) the growth of American Studies in the Soviet Union from its inception in the 1930s to its blossoming in the 1970s, especially in the Department of Modern and Contemporary History at Moscow State University, the Institute of General History, and the Institute of U.S. and Canadian Studies; 2) the maturation of the Fulbright program from 1974 forward, which enabled outstanding American scholars to lecture at MSU each spring and to engage in lively discussions and methodological debates; 3) the thaw in the Cold War, which led to cultural exchange agreements such as the 1986 pact between Moscow State University and the University of Missouri that established this publication. Vital to originating these multifaceted exchanges were Richard McKinzie at UMKC and Eugene Yazkov at MSU.

To sustain a joint intellectual venture, McKinzie and Yazkov sought to create a dialogue among scholars in the Soviet Union and the United States who shared interest in the study of America's heritage and its relevance to contemporary Russia. The goal of this international cooperative was the production of four volumes, each focusing on a major topic of Russian scholarship in the field of American history. Soviet interest in the field was then peaking in what proved to be the later stages of the Cold War. Each volume would be composed of: 1) Russian journal articles, selected by a Russian editorial board as representative of the interpretations of the era and translated into English; 2) scholarly commentary from appropriate American specialists; 3) opportunity for the Russian essayists to reflect on their original thoughts as well as respond to the critiques.

In 1989 the initial volume of this series, as edited by Otis L. Graham, Jr., appeared. It included eleven essays on the New Deal, a topic Russians recognized as highly pertinent in the history of the U.S.A. and the U.S.S.R. In the period 1989–1993 events large and small stymied the Dialogues project. A period of stagnation affected all areas of scholarship in Russia, while in America Professor McKinzie died. Nonetheless, obstacles were surmounted and, in 1995, a second volume, edited by Gordon and Louise Wood, was published. As these editors noted, "Both the United States and the Soviet Union were born in Revolutions that had universalist aspirations, each claimed to be in the vanguard of history, leading toward its particular kind of future." Two years later came a volume on Russian-American cultural relations prior to 1914. Volume editor Norman Saul, although noting constraints imposed on Soviet/Russian historians, emphasized, "These were pioneer efforts, undertaken with considerable professional risk, that kept study of the West, and of the United States in particular, alive in the former Soviet Union through the ups and downs of the Cold War."

The present volume, edited by Joel Silbey, completes the design of the Dialogues project. As his introduction notes, since the 1960s through the 1980s Russian scholars, especially those under the direction of Nikolai Sivachev at MSU, contributed to "an impressive variety of interesting and important results as well as contentious scholarly disagreements." In turn, American scholars have paused to consider both the nature of the historical evidence they use as well as their interpretative emphases as they ponder the Russian perspective on the distinguishing features of the American political system.

We are pleased to acknowledge the cooperation and fortitude of all scholars noted herein as making contributions to this project. Of particular importance was the late Igor P. Dement'ev of Moscow State University, the tireless mentor to generations of Americanists in Russia. Critical financial support at UMKC was provided by Executive Dean Marvin Querry and James Durig, Dean of the College of Arts and Sciences.

We trust that this volume, and this series, further establish scholarly dialogue among Americanists in both lands. We again renew the pledge of our initial volume that our efforts "may facilitate a new kind of political thinking that is so necessary for both scholars and politicians and, more generally, for all people in these complicated and crucial times."

Eugene F. Yazkov
Louis W. Potts

Editor's Preface

Joel H. Silbey

It is not surprising that a number of Russian historians of the United States have focused their scholarly efforts on examining the fortunes of America's political parties. As the late Professor N. V. Sivachev, Director of the Laboratory of Problems in U.S. History at Moscow State University, correctly wrote in 1980, "the political parties on which the two-party system rests have always been at the very center of political life in the United States."[1] This conviction, which has also always been at the center of the efforts undertaken by generations of American scholars of the nation's political past, stimulated a great deal of activity among Russian scholars interested in American history, particularly those resident in Moscow. There, under Professor Sivachev's direction, graduate students and members of the faculty have spent much of their time over the past thirty years examining the nature, components, and structure of America's two-party system across two centuries.

Sivachev and his colleagues had much to draw on in their endeavors. American historians had always been interested in their nation's political parties and had compiled a massive amount of research on the way that parties operated within the American context since the Federalists and Republicans first appeared in the 1790s. Their studies involved many levels of political activity and allowed many opportunities to detail and analyze specific events, great campaigns for office and elite manipulation of the electorate, as well as incidents of genuine popular expression and influence, even control, of the political world. The books and articles produced had effectively structured the way partisan development had occurred over time, cogently described the settling in of an apparently permanent two-party system, and had looked with much insight at many individual aspects of party operations, from their organizational developments and campaign and election activity to their role in legislative and administrative affairs.[2]

The founders of the United States warned against the danger of internal faction-alism and believed that parties were divisive and too readily promoted debilitating conflict, thereby threatening the existence of the new Republic. But their fears gave way before the needs engendered by a rapidly expanding, pluralistic, and ever more complex country, filled with conflict, great, petty, and otherwise, a society in which

1. N. V. Sivachev, "The Study of U.S. History at Moscow University," *Soviet Studies in History* 19 (summer 1980): 14.

2. The best recent introduction to much of this work is in L. Sandy Maisel ed., *Political Parties and Elections in the United States: An Encyclopedia* (New York, 1991), 2 vols.

more and more citizens were ultimately, if incompletely, drawn into the formal political realm of campaigns and elections. Rising in response to the need to organize political conflict over a broad geographic sweep, to mobilize a large number of voters, legislators, and others, to confront an opposing array of citizens with different policy perspectives, America's two-party system, after a number of fits and starts, hardened into permanence in the fifty years after the Constitution was ratified.[3]

Since then, American political parties have been ubiquitous—organizing, advocating, reflecting, and ultimately managing political warfare in the United States. Their fortunes have varied widely over two centuries, moving from the widespread early suspicion about them, through their extraordinary heyday in the nineteenth century when they dominated politics with a strength and intensity previously unknown, through the assaults on them by reformers and others from the 1880s on, distressed by their power, activities, and alleged corruption, culminating in the parties' significantly waning fortunes in the political world as the United States completed its second century.[4]

Studies of this party experience have produced an impressive variety of interesting and important results as well as contentious scholarly disagreements, while leaving a number of unresolved questions awaiting further research. American political parties have been about pluralist conflict, the inclusion and exclusion of different groups, fighting elections, developing policies. They have unflinchingly presented a divided front to the political world. Their leaders always claimed that they reflected the realities of American political life, its power distribution, its conflict, its divisions. While the various parties took similar organizational shape and behaved similarly to each other, their advocates argued that they represented different groups in the national contest for power, different programs, and different ways of thinking about the present political landscape as well as the nature of its future shape.

American scholars of the party system have emphasized these differences—disentangling the various social groupings that make up each party's supporters, deconstructing why each of them joined the Whigs, Democrats, Republicans, or the others who have come and gone over time, and spelling out what each of the parties stood for as a result. They have explored what have been the results of partisan efforts at the polls and when in office. They have also examined party history from a macrocosmic perspective, detailing the rise and fall of different "party systems," each containing different congeries of players and emphasizing different issues in their different time periods, and the rare, sharp, electoral realignments that abruptly transformed the landscape, changing party directions, agendas, fortunes, and levels of power.[5]

3. Richard Hofstadter, *The Idea of a Party System: The Rise of Legitimate Opposition in the United States, 1790–1840* (Berkeley, Calif., 1969).

4. Joel R. Silbey, "The Rise and Fall of American Political Parties, 1790–2000," in L. Sandy Maisel, *The Parties Respond: Changes in American Parties and Campaigns* (Boulder, Colo., 3d ed., 1998), 3–18; Vadim Kolenko, "American History Abroad: North American History in the USSR before Perestroika and Today," *Organization of American Historians Newsletter* 19 (August 1991): 4.

5. William N. Chambers and Walter Dean Burnham, *The American Party Systems: Stages of Political Development* (New York, 1967, 2d ed., 1975), and Byron Shafer et al., *The*

At the same time, there has been little that has been static in this scholarship. At one time, party leadership was the preferred focus of analysis, an approach emphasizing the toing and froing of the people at the top of the party pyramids, the decisions they made and the actions they took to further their partisan goals; more recently, there has been heavy emphasis on the behavior of party supporters at the polls on election day, and in examining the socioeconomic, ideological, and cultural impulses undergirding the choices that the voters made. Studies of party organizational structures at both the local and larger political levels have waxed and waned over the scholarly generations. Examining party behavior in office has also varied over time, again largely moving from examination of a few critical legislative episodes to much more inclusive studies of legislatures and the extent and reach of public policy commitments over time.

Identification of the primary motive impulses for party activity has varied as well in American scholarship, moving from the regnant economically determined progressive paradigm of the first half of the twentieth century, in which, to oversimplify for the sake of cogency, one party represented agrarian interests, the other, the developing commercial and manufacturing groups spawned by the market revolution underway early in the new nation's history. In this scholarship, one party was reformist, the other reactionary; one reflected the popular will, the other sought to circumvent or short-circuit the people's wishes in favor of continued elite control of the political system.[6]

In more recent times, analyses of party makeup stress a wider variety and number of divisions in American society, including ethnic and religious splits, and variations in the cultural impulses present in the political realm, as the underlying motivators of party choice and activity. One party represents, in this view, a constellation of Protestant and Anglo-Saxon groups, the "host," or dominant, national culture, arrayed against a lineup of Catholic and various sectarian religious persuasions, nested among Irish, Scots, and other "outsider" groups in American culture, deeply conscious of their subordinate status before the dominant Anglo-Saxon host. Other analyses suggest different cultural approaches, such as group attitudes toward change and modernization, for example, as leading one party to be the agent of development, the other the more hesitant lagger behind such transformative socioeconomic change.[7]

Finally, American scholars' understanding of what might be called the moral imperative represented by all of this party activity has changed over the years. Political parties have had a mixed reputation in the scholarly as well as the outside world. Despite their intense and prolonged confrontation with each other, some students of

---

End of Realignment? (Madison, Wisc., 1991), are good introductions to party systems and realignments.

6. See Charles Grier Sellers, Jr., *The Market Revolution, 1800–1846* (New York, 1991), for a sophisticated rendering of a modern version of the old Beardian, i.e., "Progressive paradigm."

7. A good introduction is Robert Kelley, *The Cultural Pattern in American Politics: The First Century* (New York, 1979); Lee Benson, *The Concept of Jacksonian Democracy: New York as a Test Case* (Princeton, N.J., 1961); and Paul Kleppner, *The Third Electoral System, 1853–1892: Parties, Voters and Political Cultures* (Chapel Hill, N.C., 1979). For an especially illuminating application of these notions, see William Gienapp, *The Origins of the Republican Party, 1854–1856* (New York, 1987).

American politics have been much more concerned to sneer at their loud challenges to one another, to emphasize the limits of party warfare instead, the social and group similarities between them most of the time whatever the campaign racket they made, the basic sameness of their policy positions in most eras, and the lack of any real political conflict on American soil as a result. (With, of course, the exception of the Civil War, an era in which, it is often suggested, parties lost their footing and role for a critical period, and then confronted, in much different ways, serious societal divisions for a time.)[8]

But most scholars in recent years have taken the parties much more seriously than that—as organizers and articulators of real political divisions in America—and have seen them less as narrowly focused electoral machines, intent only on getting their people into office with no other purpose than to enjoy the fruits of the power that they accumulate as a result. Parties have been more than electoral machines, in this view, and meant more to everyone involved than whether they held office or not. As that lesson has been emphasized among scholars, more and more of them have been less dismissive of, or as cynical about, the parties, their claims, and their arguments, than some of their earlier counterparts once were.[9]

Russian scholars have clearly digested all of this scholarship about America's political parties and used it as guides in their own work. Their essays suggest that they are well read in what American scholars have been up to in this area of political history, and that they have learned, and readily follow, the main directions the latter have sketched out. Since the 1960s and 1970s, Russian historians have undertaken examination of the evolution, operation, and importance of the two-party system, of the electoral coalitions undergirding the various parties at different moments, of what each party articulated, stood for, and was determined to accomplish in each distinct era, and the two-party system's fortunes over long time periods. The table of contents of any one of their publications, or the list of panels at a scholarly conference in St. Petersburg, Minsk, or Moscow, look quite similar to ones that would be produced and presented by American scholars working in the same field.

The essays included in this volume are a fair representation of the Russian efforts in this area of scholarship. In them, the authors largely focus on the mid–nineteenth century, the era of the so-called second American party system, on the run-up to the Civil War, on the late nineteenth century, and on the most recent era of party activity, as well as some examination of the macrocosmic rise and fall of parties over long periods.

From this output the Russian editors have chosen essays that they believe demonstrate the level and quality of Russian scholarship about American political parties. Most of the essays are products of research undertaken in the 1970s and 1980s and have previously appeared in Russian historical journals. (One of them was presented in the United States at the annual meeting of the Organization of American Historians).

Unsurprisingly, given their financial and travel restraints and the lack of archival

8. Edward Pessen, "We Are All Jeffersonians, We Are All Jacksonians: Or A Pox on Stultifying Periodizations," *Journal of the Early Republic* 1 (spring 1981): 1–26.

9. Joel H. Silbey, *The American Political Nation, 1838–1893* (Stanford, Calif., 1991).

and other library resources to sustain systematic, in-depth research, the Russian scholars break very little new factual ground in their essays. There is much that we still do not know or understand well enough about this area of scholarship. The Russian scholars have not filled in many of the blanks present. But that is less the point than their value in bringing a quite different perspective to the American partisan experience than is usually essayed by their professional colleagues in the United States.[10]

By now, the political environment in which the Russian scholars wrote these papers, and their resulting interpretative framework, is well known. Studies of the United States by generations of Russian scholars have been, in the eyes of their American colleagues, often problematic. Most of the ones included here were written toward the end of what is labeled in Russia as the "period of stagnation," when specific anti-American sentiment played a significant interpretative role in the scholarly world. The writers often reflect, in their presentations, not only the style of research in the Soviet Union twenty years ago, but a set of attitudes about the nature of American history as defined and explained by the then hegemonic Marxist-Leninist model of capitalist development, control, and crisis. These scholars found little to debate when they considered the basic impulses shaping American party development, or the meaning of two-party conflict itself.[11]

Much has changed in Moscow and elsewhere since these essays were originally drafted. Recently, Russian historians have begun to discard what many of them saw as the particular ideological strait jacket in which they for so long found themselves, in favor of more pluralist lines of understanding that are more open to debate. They have come a long way in this intellectual transformation. In fact, one American observer of these matters found himself arguing that it was the American scholars at a Russian-American conference in Moscow held after Mikhail Gorbachev's revolutionary years in office who were arguing for the relevance of class consciousness and other Marxist categories of explanation, while Russian scholars now seemed content to emphasize other, less class-driven, ideological underpinnings for the activities they described, underpinnings that had been present in American scholarship but previously had been largely ignored.[12]

Little of that major shift in emphasis is reflected in this volume, however. Most of the essays included here were written too early for that. And, perhaps as crucial, although several of them have since been revised to some degree, as the Russian historian, Vadim Kolenko, has written, even as times and intellectual currents change,

10. See, for example, Joel H. Silbey, "The State and Practice of American Political History at the Millenium: The Nineteenth Century as a Test Case," *Journal of Policy History,* forthcoming.

11. As Kolenko puts it, "in Soviet historiography in the period of stagnation, the quasi-total study of the USA led to a twisted view, as if the USA were a unitary police state." "North American History in the USSR," 4. See also N. N. Bolkhovitinov, "New Thinking and the Study of the History of the United States in the Soviet Union," *Reviews in American History* 19 (June 1991): 155–65.

12. The American historian was Jesse Lemisch, as reported in Marcus Rediker, "The Old Guard, the New Guard, and the People at the Gates: New Approaches to the Study of American History in the USSR," *William and Mary Quarterly* 3d ser., 48 (October 1991): 580–97.

even powerfully so, "it is difficult for people immediately to reject dogmas and definitions convenient to the past."[13]

But beyond such limitations, if they are that, the Russian scholars have approached their tasks with a great deal of diligence, intelligence, and commitment to say something of value about their subject. Their reading, their scholarly interchanges, and the visits to American archives by some of them, all have enriched their understanding. As noted earlier, most of them are fully aware of what has been going on in American political history studies, some of them have even been attracted to the quantitative analysis pioneered by the American "new political historians" of the 1960s and 1970s. Other of their studies follow more traditional methodological approaches, as does the work produced by a majority of their American colleagues. All of it certainly provokes a great deal of curiosity and interest among the American scholars who deal with party history. I firmly agree with the proposition offered by Gordon and Louise Wood, in their introduction to an earlier volume in this series, that "there is an inherent fascination in finding out what foreign scholars think of one's own national history, and this fascination is increased when the foreign scholars happen to be Russian, and Russians writing when they were citizens of the Soviet Union."[14]

But in the end, there can also be more than fascination. In his editor's introduction to the first volume in this series, *Soviet American Dialogues on the New Deal*, Otis Graham quoted two distinguished Russian scholars discussing their American counterparts, to the effect that "we have a great deal to learn from each other." Graham agreed. "This project is conceived in that spirit," he wrote. "This series of four volumes of Soviet-American dialogues should give concrete experience in the benefits—for how could it be otherwise?—of broadening intellectual exchange."[15] It is a sentiment that has persisted in subsequent volumes and effectively underscores the purpose in this final collection in the series as well. We believe that these essays follow the lead taken in a recent issue of the *Journal of American History,* highlighting studies of American historical problems by foreign scholars. Such studies, the editors of the *JAH* suggested, "illustrate some benefits of approaching themes in American history from transnational perspectives," because they provide "alternatives" that are capable of improving and enlarging our understanding.[16]

In their discussions, the seven American commentators, all of whom are leading historians of the nation's politics and its political parties, seek to review what the Russians have written for its freshness, usefulness, and contribution to the more general understanding that the two scholarly communities seek. Four of the commentaries deal with a single Russian essay, three others take on two essays in a single review because they are closely related to one another and raise a range of

13. Kolenko, "North American History in the USSR," 4.

14. Gordon S. Wood and Louise G. Wood, eds., *Russian-American Dialogue on the American Revolution* (Columbia, Mo., 1995), 2.

15. Otis L. Graham, Jr., ed., *Soviet-American Dialogue on the New Deal* (Columbia, Mo., 1989), 11–12.

16. Willi Paul Adams and David Thelen, eds., "Interpreting The Declaration of Independence by Translation: A Round Table," *Journal of American History* 85 (March 1999): 1279, 1281.

similar matters for discussion. In turn, the original Russian authors have been given an opportunity to respond and to put forward any last thoughts of their own in the dialogue underway. The commentary, and the responses to it, are offered in the style and spirit of the exchanges at any professional meeting, direct, cogent, and sharp, diplomatic in tone at some points, but also often with gloves off. All together, it is hoped that some contribution to additional and mutual understanding of an important topic has been achieved in this volume, a first, important, step toward more to come.

Acknowledgments

Howard T. Solomon of the University of Kansas translated the bulk of the Russian essays with care and efficiency. One essay each was translated by Vladimir Bespalov and Youlia Stepanenko, who both studied in the program developed by Moscow State University and the University of Missouri–Kansas City. I am grateful for their good work. Rosalie Donovan of UMKC provided systematic word processing of this complex set of materials. The general editors of this series, Eugene Yazkov and Louis Potts, were unflaggingly courteous and helpful as we moved through the process of creating this volume together. I thank them for their support, patience, tolerance, and understanding.

I first met the late N. V. Sivachev when he visited Cornell many years ago, and then again in Moscow during my attendance at a number of conferences there in the 1980s. I was always impressed by his dedication to these scholarly interchanges, his deep interest in American history, and the strength of his ideological commitments. Since his death in 1983, he is very much missed by those of us interested in these cross-national exchanges, particularly political historians. Theodore Rabb, of Princeton University, was my close colleague in our visits to Russia. Always thoughtful, clear-eyed, and helpful, he proved to be a good friend and an ideal companion on these international travels and in furthering the efforts underway. I hope that my dedication of this volume to these two fine scholars to some degree repays my debts to them.

Russian–American Dialogue
on the History of U.S. Political Parties

The U.S. Two-Party System: Past and Present (Several Methodological Problems for Research)

by A. S. Manykin and N. V. Sivachev

The history of the United States is difficult to imagine without a component like the two-party system, which has exerted a huge influence on all aspects of the U.S. political process. The flexibility of this institution, supported by the most powerful economic potential of the capitalist world, up to now has allowed the ruling circles in the United States to withstand numerous sociopolitical crises, and to adapt to conditions of intensifying class struggle and the general deepening crisis of capitalism. Vladimir Ilyich Lenin called the two-party system "one of the most powerful means of impeding the rising independent working class, that is in actuality the Socialist party."[1]

The two-party system, being an important attribute of bourgeois democracy, is of a clearly marked class character. All the links in its mechanism are subordinate to the main task at hand—perpetuating the hegemony of the ruling circles in the United States. In obtaining this, the bourgeois parties, regardless of concrete historical conditions, can dress themselves in liberal clothes, but at any moment are prepared to throw out "democratic" phraseology and embark on a path of open suppression of the working and democratic movement. Lately the two-party system has been suffering certain difficulties. But during visible interruptions in the work of its mechanism, the system continued to fulfill its primary mission—to preserve the class interests of American monopolies. The question arises, what allows for the trickery of the political parties united in the two-party system, which for already two hundred years has supported the political hegemony of the American bourgeoisie?

Resilient national parties are the natural result and product of the internal development of capitalism. Liquidation of feudalism has led to a situation in which juridical inequality was formally ended and several hierarchical class barriers were eliminated. Political freedoms were declared and simultaneously certain opportunities

---

1. Vladimir Ilyich Lenin, *Complete Collected Works* [Polnoe sobranie sochinenii], vol. 22, 193. This article by Alexander S. Manykin and Nikolai V. Sivachev was originally published in *Novaia i noveishaia istoria* (Modern and Contemporary History) 3 (1978): 18–38.

for broad participation in political life were created in principle. Compared to the feudal period the social structure was significantly simplified, and many smaller subclasses disappeared completely. Capitalism revealed, however, inherent internal contradictions and a sharply intensified class struggle. As a result, it was necessary to create a political instrument for regulating this struggle. Thus, the foundation and development of the parties should be sought out in the class conflicts born of capitalism.

The founders of Marxism-Leninism distinguished the fundamental methodology necessary to undertake a class analysis of the reasons for the emergence of parties and for their character. "In order to comprehend the true significance of parties, you need to look not at the mask, but at their class character and at the historical conditions for each country," wrote Lenin.[2] These two interrelated conditions are key for the methodology used to study any historical partisan issue. "In order to comprehend thoroughly a party struggle," emphasized Lenin, "you don't have to believe what they say, but rather study the real history of parties, and study not only what a party says about itself, but also what they actually do, how they proceed in making various political decisions, how they behave in their affairs that concern the vital interests of various classes of society, landowners, capitalists, peasants, workers, etc."[3] In other words he insisted that any analysis connected with the study of parties should be concretely historical, and not abstractly political, and should express contemporary language. In addition, the character of the party should be organically integrated into the political history of the country being studied.

The history of U.S. political parties and especially of the two-party system as a whole has not yet been adequately studied in Soviet historiography. These problems have been examined in a number of general works,[4] but the two-party system as such emerges as an object of study on its own merit only in several articles devoted to the study of the activities of the institution in question over the last decade.[5]

American historiography of the two-party system begins with the published political debates following the War for Independence. Then the questions on the role and place of political parties in the life of the new government and their compatibility with the ideals of the Revolution, which had just died down, were actively discussed. It is not surprising that the authors of these first publications were leaders of the American Revolution, who had placed the question about the very wisdom of the

2. Lenin, *Complete Collected Works,* vol. 23, 290.
3. Ibid., vol. 21, 276.
4. V. I. Lan, *Classes and Parties in the U.S.* [Klassy I partii v SSHA] (Moscow, 1937); V. Gantman and S. Mikoian, *The U.S.: Government, Politics, and Elections* [SShA: gosudarstvo, politika, vybory] (Moscow, 1969); A. V. Dmitrev, *Political Sociology of the U.S.: Essays* [Politicheskaia soisiologiia SShA. Ocherki] (Leningrad, 1971); *The U.S. State System* [Gosudarstvennyil stroi SShA], ed. A. S. Nikiforov (Moscow, 1976); A. A. Mishin, *U.S. Public Law* [Gosudarstvennoe pravo SShA] (Moscow, 1976); V. A. Savel'ev, *The U.S.: The Senate and Politics* [SShA.-sednat I polilika] (Moscow, 1976).
5. K. Boiko and V. Shamberg, "The U.S.: The Two-Party System and the Government Policy" [SShA: dvukhpartiinaia sistema I politicheskii kurs], *Mirovaia eknomika i mezhdunarodnye oinosheniia* (1975), no. 2; K. Boiko and V. Shamberg, "Election Results in the U.S." [Itogi vyborov v SShA], *Mirovaia ekonomika i mezhdunarodnye otnosheniia* (1973), no. 1.

existence of parties at the forefront. Subsequently, this theme has been repeatedly put to analysis, primarily in a series of works in political science. Recent studies of the two-party system in the United States have been reflected in publications of a multivolume work on the history of political parties and presidential elections, edited by Arthur Schlesinger, Jr.,[6] and also the three-volume anthology on the place of political parties in U.S. history, edited by Morton Borden.[7] Schlesinger's books, filled with large and valuable appendices of documents, and Borden's collection offer a general interpretation of the evolution of the two-party system from the end of the eighteenth century to the beginning of the 1970s. The authors of the articles, regardless of all their differences in views and the way particular problems are dealt with, have created an idealistic picture of the development of the two-party mechanism, and have not brought to light the bourgeois class character of the primary political parties, thus in essence ignoring the class struggle in the history of the United States.

In the present article attention is focused on this two-party system in the United States; in addition, the components of this mechanism are analyzed. In distinguishing the subject of study it is necessary first of all to reveal the dialectics of the relationship between the two-party system and the general socioeconomic and political history of the United States. In the whole complex of methodological problems that arise in connection with the study of the given institution, this is without a doubt the most important task at hand. Without some account of the primacy of the socioeconomic and common political history over the history of the two-party system, without an account of the fact that the latter is an organic component of the former, it is impossible to determine correctly the place and the role of the studied phenomena in the overall context of the historical development of the United States. At the same time it is necessary to note that the two-party system, as a component of the general socioeconomic and political process, emerges as a relatively independent element of objective historical reality.

What sort of questions should be addressed in order to understand the place of the two-party system and individual parties in the political life of the United States? Of the utmost significance is an explanation of the main operative rules of the two-party system and the interrelationship between the development of this institution and the course of class struggle. To address these problems, a complex analysis of whole series of topics is needed. First, there is the issue of the organizational structure of the parties: their internal structure, development, role in individual links in the work of the whole party mechanism; in brief, the distinctive autonomy of the parties. A group of questions of a different character are to be addressed to explain the role and place of the parties as an institution in the political process, their interrelationship with organs of governmental authority, and the effectiveness of the two-party system. An essential element of analysis here is the illumination of the social base of the parties,

6. *History of American Presidential Elections,* ed. Arthur Schlesinger, Jr., vols. 1–4 (New York, 1971); *History of the U.S. Political Parties 1789–1972,* ed. Arthur Schlesinger, Jr., vols. 1–4 (New York, 1973).

7. *Political Parties in American History,* ed. Morton Borden, vols. 1–3 (New York, 1973– 1974).

the dynamics of their development, and the role of class struggle in this process. The ideology of the parties, its makeup and distinctiveness, is a most important problem that must be addressed in a study of political parties. Finally, an analysis of the two-party system requires for its form and content, at least in principle, consideration of the influence of third parties and movements, which will explain the functioning of the basic party tandem in the concrete historical context.

It is impossible to conduct a study of parties by looking at them individually, isolating them from one another. It is important to emphasize that from the beginning up until today they have existed not as isolated organizations, but rather their functions were closely interconnected and mutually dependent on one another, that is to say that the parties have acted within the framework of a party system. This is exactly what Lenin noted in his own time, stating that parties in America function as "a system of two parties."[8] Creating a scientific methodology for this system is impossible without distinguishing the object of the study. The two-party system is a historical concept. It is firmly institutionalized and at the same time it is a constantly changing mechanism, bent on preserving and achieving the optimal functioning of the whole structure of capitalist society in the United States. The U.S. two-party system can be determined as a combination of bourgeois parties, which function in close interaction and interdependence. The parties have essentially common historical tasks before them, which could be achieved, however, depending on those classes and social groups whose interests these parties represent and express, and on those who interpret them.

In such a manner the institution of the two-party system functions in direct dependence on the state and on the course of class struggle. The process of the development of the two-party system determined by means of class struggle is very complex. As an element of the superstructure, the two-party system in some instances has a certain autonomy, and develops by its own internal rules. For example, in the 1950s, despite a period of relative decline of the class struggle, the two-party system experienced significant changes (the system of nonprofessional groups became widely developed; several times both parties embarked on attempts of long-term planning in their political course; certain changes in the structure of the ruling bodies of the party occurred in the balance of power between them, and the influence of the urban "party machines" was significantly weakened). On the other hand, in the 1960s, a period of sharp rise of the class struggle, almost no significant external restructuring occurred in the two-party system.

But in the long run it was exactly the class struggle that exerted a distinct influence on the transformation of the two-party system. All partisan activities were predicated upon the influence of the multifaceted manifestations of the class struggle, and were influenced by the positions of those classes whose interests the parties defended. The decisive factor in the process of the distinct restructuring of the two-party system was the working and democratic movement. Striving to preserve their leading role, the bourgeois parties were forced to make serious concessions. It is precisely the level of maturity of the antimonopolistic forces that determine the proclivity of

8. Lenin, *Complete Collected Works*, vol. 22, 193.

political leaders of the bourgeoisie to embark upon some sort of changes, which upon realization actually do not change the two-party system in its class essence.

It was noted above that the most important question of this study is elucidating the principles of how the two-party system functions. The optimal state of the two-party system from the point of view of the ruling circles is created only when it takes on an elastic balance, reminiscent of the well-calibrated mechanism, which is attained by a historically developed unique division of labor between parties. The configuration of this balance, especially from 1929–1933, looks like the following: the Democrats occupied the whole centrist position and were somewhat left of center in the mechanism of the two-party system, playing the role of a counterbalance against formation of a third party on the left, and the Republicans occupied a position in the center and somewhat to the right, fulfilling a similar function in regard to a third party on the right. Such a state of the party system allowed it to maintain the majority of voters under its influence, despite the appearance of significant differences in their milieu. Any disturbance of this balance was fraught with serious consequences for the two-party system.

The centrist segments of both parties act as stabilizers for the system, creating something of a two-party center. In the mechanism of the two-party system the center plays a dual role. First, it is a base for forming a two-party political course and stimulating the development of an interparty consensus, one of the cornerstones in the functioning of the two-party system. Second, the presence of a strong representative two-party center to a significant extent provides party leaders the opportunity to ignore representatives of the left and the extreme right wings during the development and implementation of a concrete political course.

This does not mean that the factions that stand on the extreme flanks of the political spectrum do not play a significant role in the mechanism of the two-party system. The left contingent of this spectrum sometimes has a significant influence. For a long time, from the 1890s up until the second half of the 1930s, rivalry for superiority in this environment provided the impetus for radical Republicans (Robert La Follette, George Norris, Jonathan Bourne, Coe I. Crawford, and others) and left Democrats (William J. Bryan, Louis Brandeis) alike. The shift during the period in question basically was on the part of the former. Only during the years of the New Deal, due to a number of reasons, did the radical Republicans lose their position, and the hegemony solidly went to the left wing of the Democratic party (Robert Wagner, Paul Douglas, Rex Tugwell, and Harold Ickes and Henry Wallace, who had come over from the Republican party). These groups, somewhat similar to a strong Social-Democratic party as found in the countries of Western Europe, brought the U.S. trade unions aboard the wagon of the two-party system, which to a significant extent helped make Gomperism the dominant ideology for the union movement. The left Democrats assimilated fresh ideas and transported them to the platitude of political slogans and tasks more easily than other groups.[9] But on account of its weakness they could do no more than this. The mechanism of the two-party system ground up these

---

9. From 1947 the role of the left wing in the Democratic party had been played by the organization, "Americans for Democratic Action," whose influence in the party was not great.

ideas, extracting from them their radical spirit. At times the facade remained, but the contents were to a large extent different.

The history of the United States provides many similar examples. In 1896 the Democrats put at the forefront a popular slogan of the antimonopolistic movement about unlimited minting of silver, and thus placed the Populist party in an extremely difficult situation. If the Populists in their platform of 1892 put forward in addition many radical economic demands for the time (nationalization of the railroads and means of communication, introduction of a progressive income tax, limitations on the influence of monopolies in political life, etc.), if all their program was saturated with antimonopolistic sentiments (monopolies were called the main enemy of society), in the Democratic platform of 1896 the slogan for unlimited minting of silver overshadowed everything. From the antimonopolism of the Populists there remained only the simple desire for the federal government to place stricter controls on violations of antitrust laws. The antimonopolistic content in the platform of the Populist party dissolved into sophisms of moderate bourgeois reformism.

A complex domestic political situation unfolded as a result of the Depression of 1929–1933. Both parties turned out to be unprepared for it. This led to a situation in which the movement for the creation of a third party began quickly to gain momentum. The Communist party attained new influence.[10] In left circles of American society notions about the corruption of the existing system as a whole became more and more widespread. But, thanks to the flexible policy of Franklin Roosevelt, the ruling circles in the United States managed to stabilize the situation. The election campaign of 1936 played a major role in this process when the Democrats managed to appropriate a series of popular slogans and thereby absorb into their ranks a significant contingent from the left radical groups. Speaking about the results of this campaign, Roosevelt without any exaggeration declared: "We have in all certainty eliminated LaFollette and the farmers-workers groups in the Northwest as a real threat of establishing a third party."[11]

In 1972 the left wing of the Democratic party, whose many activists were intimately connected with moderate groups of the antimonopolistic movement, managed for a time to strengthen their position within the party and gain the nomination of George McGovern as presidential candidate. For the first time in the platform of the leading bourgeois party there was sharp criticism of the existing structure. But, having rejected independent political activity, the antimonopolistic forces had once again, like in a number of previous times, tied their fate to the Democratic party, and the huge energy potential of the antimonopolistic movement turned out to be wasted. McGovern supporters did not turn out in force to overcome the resistance of the Democratic party machine. In the Democratic platform of 1976 most of the radical demands of

---

Now George McGovern, Eugene McCarthy, and others are more visible representatives of the Democratic left wing.

10. See A. A. Grechukhin, *Struggle of the Communist Party in the U.S. for Unity within Their Ranks* [Bor'ba Kommunisticheskoi partii SShA za edinstvo svoikh riadov (1927–1972)] (Moscow, 1975), 68–69.

11. *F. D. R. His Personal Letters,* ed. Elliott Roosevelt (New York, 1950), vol. 2, 827.

1972 disappeared. Although individual echoes of this struggle could be traced to 1976, leaders of the Democratic party were forced to call their platform "Contract with the people," including in it many socioeconomic promises.[12] The 1976 elections strengthened the ideological-political spectrum in the Democratic party, which in 1974 had shifted to the center and the right. Thus, the left wing of the Democratic party in the end helped the whole two-party system maintain its mechanism in the capacity of an elastic balance.

Other tasks stood before the right wing of the two-party structure. On the one hand it was called upon to play the role of a counterweight against the formation of an independent party, building its activity on ultra-right concepts. On the other hand, the right wing, as if propping up the two-party center, played the role of a unique protector against the system's excessive shift to the left. In the hands of the leaders of the center, groups on the right play the role of a bugaboo, thus scaring members of the left and forcing them to be more amenable to compromise.

It is true that in some instances extreme right groups threw the two-party system out of balance. The experience of history convincingly shows that as soon as control falls into the hands of extremist forces of one or the other of the leading parties, serious unpleasantries arise both for the party itself and for the two-party system as a whole. Thus, at the end of the 1790s the group of arch-Federalists (Oliver Wolcott, Timothy Pickering, Roger Griswold, and others) rendered the Federalists a great disservice. The extremist group of Jefferson Davis, whose members put much effort toward the secession of the Southern states, played a fateful role in the Democratic party during the 1850s. At the end of the 1920s and beginning of the 1930s Herbert Hoover and his supporters such as Reed Smoot, David Reed, Simeon Fess, and D. Wadsworth rendered the Republican party a great disservice. Because of their sad attempts to keep off the party platform those ideas that did not fit the canon of strict individualism on which all the ideology of "true Republicanism" was based, the GOP was on the verge of bankruptcy during the 1930s. The seizure of control in 1964 by the ultra right, headed by Barry Goldwater, had equally dramatic consequences for the party.

The proposed scheme in reality is not so simple. The complexity lies in the fact that the mechanism of the two-party system cannot remain in a static position. The system should function; that is to say, it should be constantly in a dynamic state. An attained elastic balance cannot long be preserved; at any given moment changes occur in the two-party system.

Then what leads it into action and maintains this state? The antagonism of class interests. One can consider as its unique manifestation contradictions in two fundamental bases on which the two-party system is based—alternatives and consensus. The essence of the first is that the party, if it wants to preserve its mass base, should offer the voters a certain opportunity for choice, that is, an alternative. On the other hand, the interests of preserving the existing structure are pushed forward by the party leaders toward well-known agreements between themselves on cardinal problems, that is to say, toward interparty consensus. In principle one can draw the following

12. *The National Democratic Party Platform,* 1976.

diagram: the ruling circles, which control the two-party system, strive to carry out policy that would suit their interests to a maximum extent. But this policy unavoidably leads to dissatisfaction on the part of the masses, who begin to wage a struggle so that the parties will take their interests into consideration. They attempt to search out an alternative to the policy of the leading parties, which will lead to a growth in the movement for a third party. A conflict arises. Integration by the basic parties of the alternative ideas, which are breaking the consensus, takes the edge off the crisis and pours fresh blood into the arteries of the two-party system. But as soon as the crisis is dealt with, the ruling circles begin once again to strive for interparty consensus on a new basis. Each time a conflict is solved depending on the concrete relationship of class powers.

The capability of integrating alternative ideas is one of the most prominent features of the U.S. political parties. This characteristic is based on several components. First is the exceptionally large economic resources of the United States, which give the monopolistic bourgeoisie wide possibilities for maneuvering. This allows the ruling circles to make serious concessions at times, while not losing a commanding position in political and economic life. It is exactly this process that is the foundation of the structure of bourgeois reformism with which the monopolistic bourgeoisie counter all radical currents, fostering the goal of "saving Capitalism by means of . . . bourgeois reforms."[13]

Second, the noted peculiarity of the two-party system is based on a distinct characteristic of the social structure in American society, which consists of a relatively high (in comparison with Western Europe) social mobility. This leads to a situation in which reformist views of various sorts find suitable ground, and the illusion is created among the masses that thanks to the constant compromises all problems can be solved.

Third, the makeup of the organizational structure of bourgeois parties in the United States plays a large role in this process. They are distinguished by a high degree of decentralization and autonomy of state party organizations. Thanks to such a structure the masses have the opportunity to influence the lower links of the party mechanism. And this in turn binds them to the two-party system, and increases the illusion that there can be a party above classes. The main thing is that in such a structure it is easier to grasp fresh ideas and include them in the party's program, changing the political course of the party not radically, but gradually, so that the leadership manages to adapt to the changing situation and adjust new ideas to the needs of the ruling circles, having emasculated them of their radical content.

It is clearly impossible to go into further detail describing peculiarities of the functioning of the two-party system without an analysis of the organizational structure of the bourgeois parties. This task is at the same time simple and complex.[14] The national political convention, convened once every four years, is the formal highest body of the party, which selects candidates for the post of president and adopts a party

13. Lenin, *Complete Collected Works,* vol. 22, 193.
14. For more detail on the organizational structure of the party see James MacGregor Burns, *Government by the People: National, State, and Local Edition* (Englewood Cliffs, N.J., 1975).

platform.[15] In the interim period between conventions the National Committee (N.C.) is the highest body of the party. It convenes regularly in a plenum, but its executive committee, headed by the chairperson, carries out ongoing work.

The National Committee was first formed by the Democrats in 1848. Later, in 1856, the Republicans followed the example. For a hundred or more years this institution, like other elements of the two-party system, has undergone a noticeable evolution. But even under the strongest chairmen of the N.C. (Edwin Morgan, Mark Hannah, John D. Hamilton for the Republicans, and K. Hell, James A. Farley, F. Harris for the Democrats) its competence was rather limited to conducting election campaigns and providing some coordination of the activities of state organizations. Besides, the N.C. chairman together with the president and other leading party activists curries the system of patronage.[16]

The significant role played by the state party organizations is a peculiarity of the American parties. They enjoy a great deal of autonomy. On this basis several American authors have even put forth the argument that there are no truly national parties per se, but instead there supposedly exists something of a federation of state organizations. This argument is clearly not justified. One can speak of the makeup of the structure of American parties, but not the absence of national parties. By virtue of tasks the activity of state organizations is cemented and steered in one direction, and this helps to overcome narrow local interests. State party organizations in turn have a diffused structure including dozens of committees for counties, numerous neighborhoods, towns, and suburban communities.

An essential component of the two-party structure are the party platforms, which appear as a result of the struggle of the masses for democratization of political life. Platforms appeared after a significant step forward was taken during the years of the Jacksonian Democrats, 1828–1836, which increased political activism of the workers, especially through unions. For the first time the workers manifested themselves energetically in the arena of party political struggles.

Formulated for the election campaign, platforms should show the party in its most appealing light before voters. In trying to achieve this, their authors rather often do

15. At the end of the eighteenth and the first quarter of the nineteenth centuries nomination of presidential candidates took place in a closed session (caucus) of a party faction in Congress. But this was not very democratic even for the procedures of the time, which concentrated the decision of such an important question in the hands of a very narrow circle of the party elite. The struggle with the "King caucus" was an important move in the direction of democratization of political life. As a result the caucus was forced to concede the right to nominate presidential candidates to the national convention. For more detail see Hugh Bone, *Party Committees and National Politics* (Seattle, 1958); idem, *American Politics and the Party System* (New York, 1971); Cornelius Cotter and Bernard Hennessy, *Politics without Power, the National Party Committees* (New York, 1964); James S. Chase, *Emergence of the Presidential Nominating Convention, 1789–1932* (Urbana, Ill., 1973).

16. This system was born at the turn of the eighteenth century, but took its final shape in the years of the Jacksonian Democrats. At its essence lay the fact that the president and his aides appoint to federal service those who have in some way been of service to the party or the powerful people who can bring it some benefit in the future. Having received such a position in this manner, these appointees serve the will of party leaders, they carry out policies for the party.

not avoid rude demagogy. What becomes fixed in the platform will not absolutely be fulfilled. Thus, in the Republican party platform of 1880 there was mention of "faithfully fulfilling all promises, which the government had made to its citizens" (this referred to civil rights for blacks).[17] This point was demagogy in the purest sense because Republicans had already several years earlier rejected the principle of Radical Reconstruction. But, because it was advantageous for the party to preserve for itself the halo of defender of justice, the Republican bosses without any hesitation promised voters to struggle for equal rights for all American citizens.

In 1948 the Republican platform proclaimed the improvement of medical services, development of a system of insurance for the elderly, etc.[18] In practice it was the very Republican senators and congressmen who were in the lead of those forces who rejected even the comparatively limited concrete proposals by Harry Truman aimed at finding a partial solution to these problems. In the mid-1960s, during the period of a sharp rise in the black movement, even the Republicans on the right were forced to mask carefully their true attitude toward the black civil rights movement. In their platform of 1964 there was the triumphant declaration that they would attain a "justified widening of the civil rights amendment of 1964."[19] But it was no secret to anyone that the Republican presidential candidate, Barry Goldwater, had voted in the Senate against the very same law he was promising to broaden in the future.

In U.S. history there have been many instances when, having come to power, the president conducts policies on a number of issues completely contrary to what he and his party promised during the election campaign. For example, in 1932 the Democrats declared in their platform: "We support the immediate and sharp reduction in government expenditures for the disbandment of unneeded committees and institutions."[20] But after 1932, thanks to the Democrats, these expenditures began to grow with fantastic speed. In 1964 in the platform of the very same Democratic party it was declared that the future administration would come out against the "aggression and use of force or the threat of use of force in foreign relations."[21] But it was the administration of Lyndon Johnson that led the country into the most notorious foreign policy adventure in its history—the war of aggression against the Vietnamese people.

It would be a mistake to underestimate the significance of the party platforms adopted, even though they are in the most general form and without any guarantees of fulfillment, because they are nevertheless binding promises by the parties before the voters. The platform is a document that allows voters, to a certain degree, to judge the political character of the party. In actuality, for example, Democratic platforms in 1852, 1856, and 1860 had a clear pro–slave owner character, and Republican platforms of the 1920s-1930s allow one to say that this party zealously defended a foreign policy

17. *National Party Platforms, 1840–1972,* compiled by Donald Johnson (Urbana, Ill., 1973), 62.

18. Ibid., 450.

19. Ibid., 683.

20. Ibid., 331.

21. Ibid., 643.

based on the principles of imperialist isolationism. The Republican platforms of 1968, 1972, and 1976 show the party to have firmly assimilated neoconservative ideology on which the whole internal political program of "The Grand Old Party" of the 1970s was built.

The main criterion in evaluating any platform of course should be the concrete practical activity of the party. Platforms are very sensitive reactions to the political situation, and the level of the class struggle and the degree of acuteness in the competition between parties at the moment platforms are composed undoubtedly affects their degree of openness in proclaiming party goals.

In U.S. political life, party conventions play an extremely important role.[22] Contemporary rules for conducting these assemblies evolved over a long time. At first (up until the 1840s) they only fixed the appointment of already well-known presidential candidates from one or the other party, giving his nomination much weight, uniting around him all the state party organizations. Intense internal party struggle during the 1840s, arising primarily from the emergence of slavery as a central partisan issue, led to the situation in which the problem of candidacy for president was to be resolved only in the course of bitter struggle at the convention itself. In addition, platforms began to be affirmed at conventions.

Moving to the question about the role of ideology in the functioning of the two-party system, it should be noted that in the United States for almost two hundred years there have been heated debates on both theoretical and practical levels about the extent to which there should be ideological differences between the parties that make up this system. A prominent American historian, Henry S. Commager, wrote in this regard: "The merit of the American party system is the fact that it does not force the people to struggle for principles."[23] This comment, however, does not correspond to reality. In the history of the two-party system there has never been a time when there were no ideological differences between the parties. Another matter is the degree of these differences, which fluctuates to a significant extent. If, for example, the Jeffersonian Republicans and the Federalists tried in practice to adhere strictly to their fundamental principles, in the 1920s it would not be so simple to find differences in the Democratic and Republican platforms.

The lack of an alternative undoubtedly lowers the effectiveness of the two-party system and its particular elements. Not coincidentally, Barry Goldwater, frustrated by the failures of his party, advised his colleagues: "The Republican candidate should not be sickly 'Mr. Echo' of the Democrats' ideology inasmuch as this denies the American people a clear choice."[24] Even earlier Robert Taft, during a debate with supporters

---

22. The first National Convention was held in 1831 by the Anti-Masonic party. There had been attempts to convene a convention prior to this in 1808, 1812, and 1814, but they cannot be considered national. Only after 1832 did the Democrats and the National Republicans hold their respective conventions, which since then have become a regular occurrence. For more information on the inception and establishment of these institutions see Chase, *Emergence of the Presidential Nominating Convention.*

23. *Annals of America* (Chicago, 1968), vol. 17, 11.

24. *Republican Politics: The 1964 Campaign and Its Aftermath for the Party,* ed. Bernard Cosman (New York, 1968), 6.

of Wendell Willkie and Thomas Dewey, in every possible way emphasized that "the Republican party is a party of principles." "The only parties that have disappeared are those which have abandoned or consigned to oblivion those principles on which they were founded," wrote Taft.[25] It is well known what these "strong principles," put forward first by Hoover, then by Taft, and finally by Goldwater, led to. As a matter of fact, principles of Republican "strict individualism" were in complete disharmony with reality in the period of state-monopolistic capitalism.

The analysis of the two-party system will not be complete if we don't devote at least a few words to such an important and integral element of the system as third parties. Commager gave the following description, widespread in the political literature of the United States, of the role of third parties in the two-party system: "The task of the primary parties is to seize the governmental apparatus and secure its functioning, which is always complex, demanding compromises and concessions; the task of smaller parties is to make so much noise that one of the main parties is forced to adapt their programs or make political concessions to them. A third party is not only useful as a safety valve in the American political system: in its essence it is the conscience of the main parties. It cannot count on victory, but can cause the defeat of one of the main parties, and this makes the main parties look at the rights of minorities more sensitively."[26] This description of the role and place of third parties, reflecting certain aspects of their activity, substantially distorts, narrows, and disparages the significance of third parties in the history of the United States, reducing their role to appendages, albeit important ones, to the two-party system. There are not any signs here of the significance of the third parties per se.

It should be added that history knows many cases when third parties played an extremely important role in the fate of the two-party system when they not only hung on to the tail, but actively influenced the subsequent development of this institution. Perhaps the first significant third party in the history of the United States was the Liberty Party, which emerged in 1839. It was created on the basis of the abolitionist movement, which in the 1830s resembled a religious movement more than an established political force.

But as soon as the issue of annexing Texas emerged at the forefront of U.S. political life, the status quo in the relations between planters and the bourgeoisie, which had taken shape since the 1820s, was ruined, and a complex regrouping of forces began. This immediately led to the politicization of abolitionism and to the formation of a political party that built its activity on abolitionist principles. In this context the following saying of Lenin should be recalled, when, summing up the experience of Russian parties, he noted that "it would be a mistake to reckon with only formally established parties, omitting political trends that are in full swing. With only the slightest change in the political atmosphere, these trends in several weeks will take on the form of parties."[27] Thus, more than twenty years before the Civil War began, a political organization appeared that openly declared antipathy to

25. *Annals of America,* vol. 16, 564–66.
26. *Annals of America,* vol. 17, 10.
27. Lenin, *Complete Collected Works,* vol. 14, 22.

the interests of slave and free states. Raising acute problems of the day objectively before the American public, this organization, though perhaps tempered in character, exerted a huge influence on the overall development of the two-party system. By all means this system endured complete bankruptcy, trying to find an alternative to the proposals put forward by the Liberty Party.

One can distinguish a host of third parties standing further to the left in the two-party system: Populists, the La Follette movement of 1924, the Progressive party of 1948. But there were instances when third parties occupied a position further right in the political spectrum: the party of the Know Nothings during the 1850s, the party of States' Rights in 1948, the American Independent Party of 1968. It is very complex to assign a one-dimensional mark on the host of third parties (Progressives of 1912, the Union party of 1936). In the history of the United States there were parties whose territorial influence was limited only to one or several states, but their ideological influence was felt across the whole country (the farmers-workers party of Minnesota, the Progressive party of Wisconsin).

All of the organizations listed, despite the fact that they differed significantly from the leading bourgeois parties, agreed that the existing structure in the United States should remain stable at its basis; it was necessary only to protect it from harmful phenomena. All of these parties supported reform (differing in content and depth), and not cardinal restructuring of the political system. Only the U.S. Communist party, created in 1919, in contrast to traditional third parties, put forth as its goal a revolutionary transformation of society on a socialist basis.

A study of third parties should focus primarily on the reasons for the constant failures of these parties. Obviously, these reasons depend on several factors. First of all, the socioeconomic situation in the United States gives the ruling classes enough resources to weaken the social base of third parties through partial concessions. The more chances these parties have for success, the more the ruling classes are forced to take into account their demands and integrate them into the platforms of the leading parties. In addition, third parties were often distinguished by hypertrophy of one or several problems and underestimation of others. This led to regionalism and cut their social base. Third, the weak organizational structure of these parties prevented them from overcoming the gradationalism of voters. And, finally, they lacked financial resources.

The U.S. two-party system went through several important periods in the process of its development. They differ significantly from one another by changes in the combinations of parties involved, and by the tasks pursued.

The problem of dividing the history of the two-party system into time periods can be approached by using certain scientific criteria. First, the socioeconomic development of the United States should be taken into account. In principle, time periods for the two-party system can be derivative of the general periodization of U.S. history. Various stages of the development of capitalism in the United States, pre-monopolistic, monopolistic, and state-monopolistic, should be considered. Each of them exerted its own influence on the transformation of the two-party system, first by breeding instability and fluctuation in the partisan-political structure, then by unifying ideologies and policies of both parties on the basis of serving monopolies under the slogan of individualism, and finally by creating a ramified mechanism of political hegemony for the bourgeoisie based on the statist principles.

Extremely important in the process of choosing criteria for periodization is the factor of class struggle. Its impact is most obvious within the two-party system. It is precisely the change of correlation of class forces that lies at the basis of all party regroupings. At the same time it should not be forgotten that this institution as an element of the superstructure has a certain autonomy. Therefore, the periodization of the two-party system, while being intimately connected with socioeconomic development in American society, nevertheless sometimes differs from it. Thus the chronological framework of one or another period is determined by complex interwoven trends of the basic development of socioeconomic relations and internal laws of evolution of the two-party system itself.

The origins of the two-party system, the establishment of the first political parties, occurred in the last quarter of the eighteenth century and at the beginning of the nineteenth century. During these years the partisan element of the superstructure became a reality of political life in the United States. The class struggle was the cornerstone for the process leading to the birth of parties. It seems that this idea was clear to many contemporaries. Thus James Madison in the tenth paper of the *Federalist* wrote: "Differences in the forms and unequal distribution of property were constant and the most common source of factions. . . . Regulation of these differences and contradictory interests is the main task of contemporary legislation and brings in the spirit of partisanship and factionalism into daily activities of the government."[28]

Indeed, it is on the periphery of the class struggle in those stormy years that the roots of the emergence of parties should be sought. The specifics of this struggle provide an answer to another extremely important question: why did a two-party system and not a multiparty one emerge in the United States? This feature of U.S. political life is explained by the fact that during this period there was simply not sufficient social basis to create a third party. The defeat of the mutinous farmers in 1786–1787, headed by Daniel Shays, undermined the ground for forming a left-radical egalitarian party. The Loyalists, who would have become the main aristocratic party of a Constitutional-Monarchist type, were defeated in the course of the War for Independence. Thus there was only a place left for purely bourgeois parties, which more or less radically supported the development of capitalist relations.

From the time of the bitter political struggle over ratification of the Constitution until 1816, the base of the two-party system was made up of Federalists and Jeffersonian Republicans. They faced a set of important tasks. First, an institution was needed for the bloc of bourgeoisie and planters who had come to power in the aftermath of the Revolution, to preserve their hegemony from encroachment by the other strata of society. The governmental apparatus by itself with its rich arsenal of means of suppressing dissatisfaction of the situation that emerged after the revolution was inadequate. The U.S. Constitution, despite its limitations, proclaimed relatively broad democratic freedoms for its time. The revolution had attracted wide strata of the population into the orbit of political life. The spirit and ideals of the War

28. *The Federalist* (New York, 1947), 64–65.

for Independence, one of "the greatest, truly liberating, truly revolutionary wars," continued to live in American society of the 1790s.[29] The farmers' movement in Pennsylvania in 1791–1794 clearly showed that Americans had not forgotten that the people have the right to rebel. It was already clear to many in the ruling classes that it was necessary to have an institution which would give an outlet to the activity of the masses and simultaneously allow for the preservation of the sociopolitical structure of society without any kind of radical change.

Second, the creation of parties dictated the need for immediately creating a state mechanism, overcoming sectional differences, and consolidating former colonies under the supremacy of one government. The U.S. Constitution and the state constitutions provided for a number of electoral responsibilities, but they said nothing about the techniques of conducting elections. In the first years of the existence of the United States, while a historical tradition had not yet been set, there were many unanswered questions like this one, creating difficulties in the process of the normal functioning of government, and in principle concealing a well-known threat to the existing institutions. A mechanism was needed that would allow for reliable control over the so-called democratic process.

Political parties of the era were characterized by a relatively low level of internal organizational and structural development. At the same time the extent to which ideological differences between the Federalists and the Jeffersonian Republicans evolved was greater than ever. The process of party building from the top down to the rank-and-file reflected another feature of that period. It came to a close in 1816 when the Federalist party left the national arena.

In the next period of the two-party system, a mechanism for redistribution of power was formed and centrist trends were overcome to a great extent. But in the quarter of a century after George Washington assumed the post of president, significant socioeconomic changes occurred. The Industrial Revolution began leading to the emergence of the industrial bourgeoisie, which actively demanded governmental protection of its interests, particularly safeguarding American industry against competition with English goods.

In the South a cotton boom was in full swing. Prospects for becoming rich quick, rooted in this boom, turned the institution of slavery on which the whole plantation system rested into "a positive and fruitful institution," as described by one of the Southern ideologues, John C. Calhoun.[30] Protecting and strengthening this institution by all means became the most important task for Southern politicians. The extensive character of slave ownership and the drive to broaden and strengthen their political position in the government forced Southern politicians to support any territorial expansion. But broadening the area for the spread of slavery and the formation of new slave states threatened to disrupt the balance of political powers that had taken shape in the United States.

Finally, a new large region, the West, was being drawn actively into the political

29. Lenin, *Complete Collected Works,* vol. 37, 48.
30. Richard Hofstadter, *American Political Tradition and the Men Who Made It* (New York, 1948), 101.

and economic life of the country. Representatives of western states introduced a whole set of acute issues to the political arena: free access to land, domestic improvements, prospects for further colonization of the West.[31] All this proved that the ideological-political platforms of old parties had turned out to be to a large extent ill-adapted both to the unfolding circumstances and to new problems of the day. This became the reason for the crisis and gradual failing out of these structures.

The following period, up until the famous arrangement between the Democrats and Republicans in 1877, was one of the more complex eras in the history of the two-party system. It bears the imprint of uncertainty and instability. Never again would the very existence of the two-party system be put under question. Sometimes there was only one party, though divided into many factions, left in the political arena. In the 1850s the situation was quite the opposite—the parties were similar as never before or afterwards; the Democrats, divided practically into two factions, the remnants of the Whigs, the young Republican party, and the party of the Know-Nothings all waged a bitter struggle for survival.[32] The Civil War, when eleven states withdrew from the influence of the two-party system, occupies a special place within this period.

Instability characterized the whole period. Karl Marx stressed this, pointing out that in the United States, "classes already existing, but not yet built up, are in unceasing motion, constantly renewing their constituent parts, and transferring them to one another."[33] The economic diversity, the parallel development of the three socioeconomic processes mentioned above (conditioning one another and at the same time, to a large extent, autonomous), the huge territory (causing certain isolation of major regions of the country), and significant state autonomy within the general federal structure did not, of course, guarantee political stability.

Political life evolved during these years around a unified pole: the struggle between the parties for survival and adaptation to socioeconomic conditions. The prime condition was development of bourgeois relations under the auspices of the fundamental principles of capitalism in the epoch of free trade. This served as the basis for defining these sixty years as a specific period in the two-party system. The completion of Reconstruction, having removed all obstacles to the development of capitalism and simplified the dispersion of class powers, removed the question of the viability of the two-party system from the agenda of the day. The stormy development of monopolies that had been initiated by the Civil War and Reconstruction put new tasks before the two-party system and led to the system's next era.

Naturally, it is impossible to make such a broad generalization about a complicated era. This period culminating in the Reconstruction era began as "the era of good feelings," when the party structure was essentially made up of the hostile factions of the former Jeffersonian Republicans (1816–1828). Next came the stage of gradual development of new parties that made the foundation of the second two-party system,

31. For more detail on these processes see A. V. Efimov, *U.S.: Ways of Capitalism Development* [SShA: puti razvitiia kapitalizma] (Moscow, 1969).

32. In the state of Connecticut, for example, in the 1854 and 1855 elections, twenty-three parties came forward. Wilfred Binkley, *American Political Parties, Their Natural History* (New York, 1968), 193.

33. K. Marx and F. Engels, *Collected Works,* vol. 8, 127.

active from the mid-1830s to the mid-1850s. This process had some peculiarities not found in the formation of the first political parties. If the party organization of the Federalists and Jeffersonian Republicans generally went from the top to the bottom, the development of the new parties, the Democrats and the Whigs, started at the state level, reflecting regional traits of the party mechanism from the very beginning. Both parties, with few exceptions, had almost equal influence in all regions of the country, although the Whigs held a firmer position in New England while the Democrats centered in the South.

The situation was about the same in regard to the social base of both the parties. The Democrats mainly relied on the support of western farmers and planters—that is, support from slave states. But they relied on a rather solid support in the northern states on the side of the petty bourgeoisie and groups of workers. In addition, financial and trading bourgeoisie, whose interests were intimately tied to the English economy, generally supported the Democrats.

The social base of the Whig party was even more varied. Its mainstay was the industrial bourgeoisie of the northern states. The influence of the Whigs was rather significant among the petty bourgeoisie of major industrial cities in New England. In some western states the Whigs successfully competed with the Democrats for influence over the farmers. During the 1830s-1840s the two-party system developed in the South to an extent unheard of before. Democrats controlled rural regions, while the Whigs dominated the cities of the South.

Certain primary tasks faced by the parties can be delineated in these years. First, they struggled to broaden the social base of the two-party system, to include farmers and the growing industrial proletariat in the political process, to democratize political life up to a certain extent, preserving at the same time the hegemony of the bourgeois-planter bloc. At this stage the goal of the two-party system was to support the status quo in the interrelationship of forces between the Northern bourgeoisie and Southern planters, which had been complicated due to the fact that amidst the bourgeoisie, the faction of industrialists had moved further to the center stage. This could be achieved only if the question of slavery was not brought to the forefront. The Whigs and the Democrats managed to carry out this policy for a while. Finally, both parties tried to modify the party mechanism and the rules of the political game, adjusting them to the new situation.

The final years before the Civil War became a unique moment in the history of the two-party system. As a rule, the alignments tried either to alleviate antagonisms, to integrate new, original ideas and movements, or to avoid highly contentious situations. In the 1850s, as Robert W. Johnson, the Democratic congressman from Arkansas, noted, Congress was like a powder keg. "The concept of 'Democrats' and 'Whigs' in Congress disappears instantly," said Johnson, "as soon as the discussion moves to questions of territorial expansion or the fate of slavery."[34]

Passions were exacerbated to the point where Southerners began to doubt the value of the two-party system. The *U.S. Democratic Review,* published by the Democratic

---

34. J. King, "The Concept of Two-Party System in American Political Thought, 1789–1888," Ph.D. diss., Bryn Mawr College, 1950, 111.

party, announced: "The U.S. is obliged for its progress and its might to the fact that there exists and rules only one party, to be more precise, the Democratic party."[35] Slave owners obtained guarantees that the South for time immemorial would dominate in the political life of the United States. But in reality, the course of history irrevocably "turned away" from the South.

Another feature of these years was the emergence of the Republican party from the framework of the old two-party system. The Republicans would soon become the main force in establishing a new variant of the two-party system in the course of the second American Revolution.

The years of the Civil War and Reconstruction became a unique transition stage in the history of the two-party system. At its essence was the liquidation of the remnants in the area of socioeconomic relations, to clear a path for the unencumbered development of capitalism. The parties' adjustment to the new circumstances proceeded in spurts for a long time. Especially slow was the evolution of the Democratic party, which could not be easily reconstructed from a party dominated by slave owners, who had unleashed a bloody civil war, into a party that reflected the interests of the winners in this war. The Republicans faced a significant task of reconstruction as well, as the interests of monopolistic capital, having digested the fruits of the second revolution, demanded the decisive overcoming of radicalism, which had a strong position in the party in the 1860s.

The formation and the spread of monopolies became a distinguishing factor and a common denominator in the further development of the two-party system. It leveled both parties, overcoming radical extremism of Republican and Democratic anachronists, in the form of adherence to the principles of slavery. The end of Reconstruction and the political deal of 1876–1877 between the Republican and Democratic leaders firmly cemented for the time being the antagonistic parties into a new partisan combination and heralded a new period in the history of the U.S. two-party system. Monopolies very quickly seized key positions in the sphere of economics, which helped them to place both political parties under their influence.

This situation gave rise to certain features of the new party system. The primary task of both the Republicans and the Democrats was to create favorable conditions for the development of monopolies and to eliminate all obstacles in their way. The significance of such problems as tariffs and other financial issues connected with economic development grew immensely. But it soon became clear that the uncontrolled development of monopolies hid within it a threat to social stability. Therefore, since the end of the nineteenth century, a new, larger problem has arisen before the bourgeois political parties: the search for ways acceptable to monopolies for regulating their activities. Discussion became more focused on the need for broadening the functions of government.

At the dawn of imperialism, in 1885, the platform of the American Economic Association declared: "We view government as an ethical-educational mechanism, positive cooperation which is the necessary condition for human progress. Recognizing the necessity for individual initiative in industrial life, we believe that the *laissez*

35. Ibid., 119.

faire doctrine is dangerous from a political point of view and unfounded from a moral point of view, that it does not give adequate explanation of the interrelationship between government and citizens. . . . We see that the conflict between labor and capital pushed forward to the center stage a huge number of social problems, which cannot be solved without uniting the forces of the Church, state, and science."[36]

The search for these new practical ways and means to regulate socioeconomic processes should have been realized first by the political parties. The expediency of government intervention in the socioeconomic processes was definitively recognized only in the 1930s. In the party platforms individual elements of such a policy appear in the 1880s and after that practically disappear, with rare exceptions, from the documents of both parties.

With the emergence of the working class in the political arena and with the development of the antimonopoly movement, the importance of such tasks as the preservation of the existing political structure for the party system grew even more. The American proletariat immediately showed its strength. The prospect for creating a mass political party that had as its goal the destruction of the existing structure frightened the American ruling classes greatly. They did everything they could to prevent such a development. The bourgeois parties played a significant role in the struggle against the spread of socialist ideas. To an extent that the development of these trends increasingly revealed, the party system that had taken shape in the last third of the nineteenth century (Republicans and Democrats) could by no means solve the socioeconomic problems of the epoch of the general crisis of capitalism. This led to a deep crisis of the system, culminating in the beginning of the 1930s in a significant restructuring of the traditional combination. The symptoms of the crisis first became glaringly apparent in 1912, when in the presidential elections the candidate from the Socialist party, Eugene Debs, received around one million votes. Not coincidentally, at this time Lenin wrote about the "grave crisis of the bourgeois parties.[37]

The crisis of the two-party system deepened even more due to the Great October Socialist Revolution. As a direct result of the Great October Revolution, a sharp intensification of class struggle and a strengthening of the position of the left in the working movement occurred, culminating in the formation of the U.S. Communist party, the fighting avant-garde of the American workers. An organization had emerged that presented a direct challenge to the hegemony of the two-party system and proposed a constructive program for social restructuring to the masses.

Bourgeois reformism was called upon to play the main role in the establishment of an alternative to the ideas of the Great October Revolution. It was an ideology that called for increased attention to social problems in the platforms and practical activities of the leading parties as well as for flexible government regulation of economic processes. William Jennings Bryan, Theodore Roosevelt, and Woodrow Wilson did much to incorporate these ideas into practice. But the new ideology was in serious contradiction to the principles on which the two-party system was built. It gave rise to a conflict between the individualistic ideology that had outlived itself, but continued

36. *Annals of America,* vol. 11, 82.
37. Lenin, *Complete Collected Works,* vol. 22, 192.

to reign, and the praxis and objective need for the ideology of bourgeois reformism for the ruling classes at the time of the onset of the general crisis of capitalism.

The two-party system could maintain such a state of elastic equilibrium only until the world economic crisis of 1929–1933, which clearly demonstrated the vices inherent in capitalism, and exacerbated all the contradictions to the extreme. The problem of regulating the socioeconomic relations came to the forefront. A suitable solution to this problem could be found only in extreme circumstances. Neither Democrats nor Republicans were able to settle socioeconomic relations. Their political philosophy did not adequately reflect the complexity of the problems facing the country. A significant reorientation of fundamental ideological principles on which the parties were based was necessary as well as change in their social base so that they could function further without interruption. These cardinal changes in essence signified that the two-party system had entered a new period in its development.

Due to the crisis of 1929–1933, the reformist circles in the Democratic party started to play the most significant role in the process of transformation of the two-party system. From the beginning they took upon themselves full responsibility and all the hardships connected with the move from the state-monopolistic pattern. This allowed the Republicans to proceed with the reorientation process for another two decades.

The introduction of the two-party system into a new, contemporary period of its development was accompanied by noticeable changes in the social base of leading political parties in the United States. At that time the social makeup of the Republicans and the Democrats was characterized by diversity. It could be explained to a great extent by the fact that the dividing lines between the Democrats and the Republicans at times were blurred. Of course, there were differences between them and these differences should not be underestimated. They primarily related to the problem of the role of government in the country's socioeconomic life. An American political scientist, James MacGregor Burns, in 1955 wrote in this respect: "It became fashionable to say that these terms [Democrats and Republicans] were devoid of any significance. But this is not so. Party platforms and presidential speeches show that the majority of Democrats stood for the active use of government. They show that the majority of Republicans would like to limit the activity of government [not in general, but compared with the Democrats] to give more room for private initiatives and private investments."[38] This same idea was widely used in the platform of the Republicans in 1976, when they declared: "The Democratic platform repeats the same thing on every page: more government interference, more expenditures, more inflation. In contrast the Republican platform states directly the opposite: less government interference, less expenditures, and less inflation."[39] But these differences, despite their significance, did not create insurmountable dividing lines between the Democrats and the Republicans.

Both parties had supporters across the various social strata. Sharp differences in the approach to the problem of the role of government in the life of society resulted in general support for the Republicans by a large part of the monopolistic bourgeoisie

38. *Annals of America,* vol. 17, 312.
39. *1976 National Republican Convention Platform,* adopted August 18, 1976, in Kansas City. *Congressional Record,* September 2, 1976, 2.

(such as the Rockefellers, DuPonts, Mellons, and Fords) and new multimillionaires such as Hunt. Republicans enjoyed solid backing by well-to-do farmers. Often the petty bourgeoisie of the northeastern states, dissatisfied with the activities of the federal government, supported the Republicans. Recently, the position of this party has noticeably strengthened in the South (in South Carolina and Texas), where it attempted to play on racial prejudices of a significant part of the white population. Finally, in some industrial states in the Great Lakes region, the Republicans have the definite support of workers dissatisfied with inflation, the growth in taxes, and the lack of domestic stability.

At the same time, large financiers and gigantic industrial and trading monopolies actively help Democrats. Generally, the influential Zionist lobby supports the Democrats. Beginning in the 1930s, a contingent of farmers began to sympathize with the Democrats. As earlier, the party reliably controls the South. Thus, they are able to maintain in their ranks both racists (such as John Stennis, James Eastland, Richard Russell) and the majority of the black population. The petty bourgeoisie of the mid-Atlantic states, the well-educated population (especially in New England), and the youth are generally reliable to the Democrats. Finally, the largest trade union organizations, such as the AFL-CIO, as a rule support the Democratic party.

The question arises: how can these different social groups survive in the party; what is the class makeup of these parties? The Democrats are definitely the party that defended the interests of the large monopolistic bourgeoisie. But, subsequently abandoning these interests, Democrats since the time of Franklin Roosevelt have stated that liberal reforms which somehow take into account the interests of the workers are absolutely essential. As Roosevelt himself wrote in this respect, "when this is done, the nation is saved from revolution."[40]

There are two trends characterizing the contemporary state of the two-party system: attempts aimed at ideological-organizational strengthening of the leading bourgeois parties and the struggle by the left-radical groups to turn the Democratic party into a populist party. This struggle, evolving over the last period in the history of the development of the two-party system, undoubtedly requires special study and description. The end of the 1960s and first half of the 1970s, when a deep sociopolitical crisis, exacerbated by economic instability, led to a sharp increase in the activity of liberal and radical reformers, can be considered the apex.

Under the influence of these forces Democratic party bosses in 1968 were forced to agree to create the McGovern-Fraiser commission for working out new rules to elect delegates to conventions.[41] In 1971 the O'Hara commission was created to prepare draft rules for the Democratic party. As a result of the bitter internal party struggle

---

40. See *U.S.: Political Thought and History* [SShA: politicheskaia mysl' i istoriia], ed. N. N. Iakovlev (Moscow, 1976), 350.

41. In 1971 on the suggestion of this commission a series of organizational reforms were carried out. Among a number of the most important were those related to the introduction of a system of quotas during elections of delegates to conventions and to the National Convention of the party. According to this system the makeup of leading organs of the party were to be balanced in such a manner that all categories of the population were represented proportionally to the percentage of these categories in the total U.S. population.

the left-radical wing of the Democratic party in 1972 was closer than ever to gaining control of the party. Not coincidentally did the Republican platform in 1972 sound a feigned alarm for the fate of the two-party system: "This year the choice is between moderate goals, which traditionally have been put forward by the leading parties, and the far-reaching goals of the extreme left. In 1972 the Democratic party turned out to be gripped by radical factions, which consider the past of the nation with malice and which threaten to destroy its future."[42] But the conservative forces managed to beat off the onslaught of the left-radical groups.[43]

But these developments were only one of the rounds, and not the end of the fight for the next restructuring of the two-party system. The fact that this restructuring was not possible without strengthening to a certain extent the organizational framework of the two-party system reflected the specific nature of this fight in a deteriorating crisis situation. But transformation of such scale unavoidably led to conflict with the traditional decentralized structure of the American bourgeois parties.

The two-hundred-year history of the two-party system shows that this institution has played a very noticeable role in U.S. history, actively influencing all aspects of socioeconomic and political development of the country. It would be incorrect to look at the two-party system as some sort of self-containing force. The two-party system can perform its functions only in conjunction with other institutions, which make up the structure of the U.S. political system. Despite the fact that with the help of the two-party system, the ruling classes in the United States have managed to solve many different problems, its potential is far from unlimited. At present the two-party system is experiencing very serious problems. One of the most visible manifestations of its crisis is the growth of absenteeism and the strengthening of the movement toward independent political activity. The pitiful state of affairs for the leading parties is proved by the fact that during the 1960s-1970s both of them (and not any of the third parties) were forced to break the elastic balance of the two-party system, departing in one case far to the right (Republicans in 1964), and in another case, significantly to the left (the Democrats in 1972) from the center of the political spectrum.

At the present time, leaders of the Democratic and Republican parties in the United States and political scientists are trying to assess the detrimental influence of the shocks of the last ten years on the future two-party system, in order to design a program of renovation. In general, one can assume that even at this time the two-

42. *National Party Platforms, 1840–1972*, 848.

43. From the rules approved at the Democratic convention in December of 1974 in Kansas City, the suggestions of the O'Hara commission for introducing membership cards and dues and on creating a special fund for helping delegates who were not well off, and on the mandatory interim party conferences were rejected. It seems apparent that in the text of the rules there were for all practical purposes no serious new items. The main result of the convention in Kansas City is that it can be considered the first time that the already existing organizational structure of the party was fixed in an official document and the already existing set of tasks of the leading party bodies were drawn out again (the text of the rules can be seen in the *New York Times,* December 9, 1974). In 1973 the commission headed by Barbara McCulsky reexamined the fundamental suggestions of the McGovern-Fraiser Commission; as a result the article on the mandatory system of quotas during election of delegates to the convention was rescinded because of a simple desire for a more equitable representation.

party system has changed in form insignificantly, despite the rise of a powerful wave of popular dissatisfaction. "The two-party system," as pointed out in the new program of the U.S. Communist party, "is like a vise for the monopolies to contain class and social conflicts, thus ensuring the preservation of their own personal power. During the periods of increased popular outpourings, these vises are relaxed so as to give way to popular demands. But they remain the same vises, as before limiting the sweep of activity to pattern which, in the long run, is determined by capitalist corporations."[44]

Being a real political embodiment of the idea of bourgeois pluralism, the modern two-party system will not withstand historical competition with socialism in the socioeconomic or the ideological-political spheres. It cannot ensure the full harmonic development of the individual, despite the demagogic concern expressed by bourgeois ideologues and U.S. politicians for human rights around the world. A multiparty system should not necessarily be considered an indicator of the degree of democratism of one or another governmental system. In evaluating democratism it is necessary to analyze first of all the character of industrial relations, the class nature of government power, the acting parties in the given society, and the class makeup of their policies.

Today's bourgeois parties in the United States, just like their predecessors, are forced to mask carefully their exploitative essence, to hide their true goals behind a screen of social demagogy. The fact that despite the constant changes in the U.S. Constitution, adopted in 1787, there is no place for determining the role of parties in the life of American society, is far from accidental.

This question is resolved in a fundamentally different way in a socialist system. In Article I of the new Constitution of the U.S.S.R. characterizing the political system of a developed Socialist society, it is indicated that the CPSU is the "leading and directing force in Soviet society, the nucleus of its political system, of governmental and societal organizations," and the main functions of the party, all the organizations of which act within the constitutional framework, are clearly rooted in scientific Communism. A comparison of the two constitutions convincingly demonstrates the superiority of the political system of socialism in all spheres of social life: in economics, politics, and ideology.

The two-party system, historically developing in the United States, despite all its definitions, has been and still is one of the main instruments of the bourgeoisie aimed at preserving the exploiter class. The political nature and essence of this institution prevents revolutionary, democratic, and progressive forces in the United States from relying on its use in the struggle for radical reforms in American society, and urges one to consider the overcoming of barriers created by the two-party system as a necessary condition for real social progress. "Therefore," as emphasized in the program of the American Communists, "the historical task standing before the workers is to affirm their political independence, and break away from the two-party system controlled by monopolies. It is to become a leading force of a mass, popular anti-monopoly party."[45]

44. *U.S.: Economics, Politics, Ideology* [SShA: ekonomika, politika, ideologiia] 1971, no. 1, 87.
45. *U.S.: Economics, Politics, Ideology* [SShA: ekonomika, politika, ideologiia] 1970, no. 12, 75.

Comment

by Allan G. Bogue

In this paper Professors Manykin and Sivachev set themselves the formidable task of tracing, explaining, and evaluating the history and current operation of the two-party system in the United States. That system's main task, they argue, is to perpetuate the hegemony of the ruling circles and, otherwise stated, to fulfill "its primary mission— to preserve the class interests of American monopolies." The two bourgeois parties have achieved this purpose by dressing in "liberal clothes" and adopting "democratic phraseology" while standing ready, when required, to embark "on a path of open suppression of the working and democratic movement." What about the American system, the authors ask, has allowed such trickery to be successful during the course of the last two hundred years?

Manykin and Sivachev propose to explain the place of the two-party system in America by describing the "main operative rules of the two-party system and the interrelationship between the development of this institution and the course of the class struggle." In order to do this they have analyzed the organizational structure of the parties, their role and place in American politics, their relation to "organs of governmental authority," and the effectiveness of the system. This discussion leads the authors into consideration of the social base of the parties, the dynamics of their development, the role of class struggle in the process, party ideology, and the role of third parties. They then describe various stages of economic development that the United States has passed through and relate these to the successive eras of the two-party system. Throughout the discussion, the authors argue that "resilient national parties are the natural result and product of the internal development of capitalism" and that the major causal element in American politics generally and in the two-party system specifically has been class conflict.

As the capitalistic system of resource management and social ordering developed during the nineteenth century, it "revealed inherent internal contradiction and a sharply intensified class struggle"; the two-party system was the instrument created to regulate the latter conflict. American voters, in the authors' view, are arrayed along a continuum between the poles of the extreme ideological right wing and the radical left. The two major parties, each a bourgeois organization, occupy the center of the spectrum, where their forces overlap. Today's Republicans extend outward toward the right pole and the Democrats project toward the left. "The working and democratic movement" on the left wing has provided the impetus for change in the system. In order to maintain their strengths, the major parties have made concessions to the "antimonopolistic forces" but without changing the basic class essence of the system.

The bourgeois parties have had "essentially common historical tasks" and ulti-mately preeminent among these "was the creation of favorable conditions for the development of monopolies and the elimination of all obstacles in their way." The liberal individualistic ideology espoused by the bourgeois parties has been a mere cloak, a sham, obscuring the major function of the system. Demands for change are implemented by the creation of third parties, espousing radical proposals, on the flanks of the two-party system. The major parties meet such challengers by incorporating emasculated versions of their demands in the bourgeois legislative agenda. But the radical flankers serve as counterweights in the two-party system; increased activity at one end of the continuum renders the radicals at the other end more willing to compromise with the adjacent centrist party.

In terms of political economy, Manykin and Sivachev identify three stages of devel-opment in the United States: premonopolistic, monopolistic, and state-monopolistic. They discern four eras in the development of the party system, covering the periods 1789–1816, 1816–1877, 1877–1933, and 1933 to the present. Although it was clear at the time that America lacked the social base for a multiparty system, events during the first period also showed that "an institution was necessary that would give an outlet to the activity of the masses and simultaneously allow for the preservation of the sociopolitical structure of society without any kind of radical change." The focal point of the next political era was "the struggle between the parties for survival and adaptation to conditions for purposeful development of bourgeois relations in breadth and depth by a complex and conflict-ridden process of unification under the auspices of the fundamental principles of capitalism in the epoch of free trade." During this period, a well-developed two-party system emerged and the premonopolistic stage of American economic development gave way to the monopolistic era that characterized the years between 1877 and 1933. Now, "the primary task of both the Republicans and the Democrats was the creation of favorable conditions for the development of monopolies and the elimination of all obstacles in their way."

The rise of American socialist and Communist parties and the Great October Revolution emphasized the emergence in the United States of a working class and antimonopoly movement and greatly frightened the ruling classes with the possibility that a "mass political party" might destroy the existing political structure. The world economic crisis of 1929–1933 forced a "fundamental ideological reorientation" that justified state regulation and management of the economy and the development of a social safety net. Elements in the Democratic party initiated the reforms, but eventually major segments of the Republican party gave qualified approval to the regulatory state. Now in the two-party system's fourth era of development, bourgeois party differences have centered upon the issue of activism versus less activism.

In conclusion, Manykin and Sivachev suggest that the American parties currently face serious problems. They contrast their disarray in the 1970s with the order to be found in a socialist regime and argue that it is only in the latter setting that individuals can achieve "full harmonic development." They predict that the American system in which bourgeois parties "mask carefully their exploitative essence . . . to hide their true goals behind a screen of social demagogy" cannot indefinitely survive in competition with socialism, a system superior "in all spheres of social life: in economics, politics, and ideology." The American two-party system, they maintain, has been a major instrument in efforts to preserve "the exploiter class." American workers should abandon it and become the leading force in creating "a mass, popular antimonopoly party."

This interesting paper has many virtues. American scholars have been much too parochial in the perspectives that they bring to the study of the political history of their country. Having developed their view within another country and political system, Manykin and Sivachev challenge us to view American political development from a different theoretical perspective and to evaluate the varied insights that appear in their work. Such an exercise seldom fails to be rewarding. Manykin and Sivachev cite Lenin's admonition that investigators should look below the mask that parties assume to see the realities beneath, and American scholars cannot be too often reminded that rhetoric and reality often fail to coincide.

Moreover, these authors understand and accurately describe major elements in the story of American political development. The chronological periodization of American political history that they offer is a defensible one. The picture that they draw of an "elastic balance" at work over time in our national politics does in a general way depict the interaction between American political parties over extended periods of time. They have not fallen into the trap of dealing with the American two-party system in isolation from the activity of other elements in the American polity. They realize that the American political system and its relations to the broader society are complex.

Generations of scholars have been intrigued by the fact that socialist parties have never attracted a significant following in the United States. They have advanced a number of theories in explanation of this characteristic of the American polity. The greatest of modern American historians, Frederick Jackson Turner, believed that the frontier served as a safety valve, draining off discontented workers from industrial areas, and in a broader sense attributed the unique characteristics of American development to the abundant natural resources that the frontier symbolized. Other historians or social scientists have suggested that the "land of opportunity" myth, or the early abolition of feudal distinctions or barriers, or the successive broadening of the suffrage at relatively early stages of national development account for the failure of Americans to espouse political radicalism. In the opinion of some analysts, regional diversity, or ethnic consciousness, or racial antipathies, have appeared to impede efforts to organize the lower classes of society into radical political cohorts. It is also suggested that the key to this phenomenon is found in the inability of radical theorists to develop an ideology that fits the American social and political environment. Some analysts, on the other hand, take a different perspective and argue that the strength of radicalism's opponents in the United States explains its failures. In the mid-1970s a Sombart specialist suggested that the two-party system was responsible for the inability of radical political parties to attain any lasting degree of success within the American polity. Manykin and Sivachev develop this line of argument in considerable detail but also implicitly combine it with the argument that the strength and duplicity of radicalism's opponents has contributed to the failure of parties with radical agendas as well.[1]

We cannot expect scholars to deal with so broad a subject as the American two-party system without resort to generalization. This paper is, however, reductionist to the extreme. Although Manykin and Sivachev present some factual evidence, the class struggle serves as a kind of black box at the center of their argument. The links that run between the class struggle and the two-party system are, for the most part, asserted rather than demonstrated. Nor do this paper's authors explain how such demonstration should be effected.

Both in their treatment of the years prior to the breaking point of 1877 and of American political development thereafter, Manykin and Sivachev's text apparently implies understood objectives and specific planning designed to meet those objectives on the part of those class elements that opposed radical ideas. They write that "even in the first phase of party history it became clear that an institution was necessary which would give an outlet to the activity of the masses and simultaneously allow for the preservation of the sociopolitical structure of society without any kind of radical change." The founding fathers were remarkably sophisticated political economists, but there does not seem to have been any general agreement during the early national period that supplementary institutions were needed to manage the governmental mechanism that they had created. During the years which Manykin and Sivachev designate as the first political party era the "old politics of personal factionalism of the magnates and notables"—the phrase is Richard Hofstadter's—continued to prevail at the state level while leading figures or their supporters strove to weld broader party alliances in an effort to name presidents, implement policy preferences, and benefit from the distribution of the available patronage, while working within the framework of principles and institutional structures enunciated and created by the founding fathers.[2] That some political leaders of the early national period feared the development of urban masses is certainly true. That such fears were so widespread in the political arena of the time that their suppression was a widespread, or implicitly agreed, objective is most unlikely.

Although a new type of political operative, professional or semiprofessional in approach, emerged during the Jacksonian years and political parties assumed characteristics still identifiable in the activities of our present parties, it is something of a stretch to call the system a two-party system until the Reconstruction era. John Quincy Adams was by no means the last prominent American to inveigh against party strife, and the labels and composition of even the major parties underwent major changes. Thus we did not have a true two-party system in the United States until one third and a bit more of our national existence had passed, let alone consensus on the objectives

1. For a summary of the various explanations and a fuller development of the "strength of the opposition" position see Reeve Vanneman and Lynn Weber Cannon, *The American Perception of Class* (Philadelphia, 1987).

2. Richard Hofstadter, *The Idea of a Party System: The Rise of Legitimate Opposition in the United States, 1780–1840* (Berkeley, Calif., 1969), 219.

of the political system, and certainly not a situation where parties implicitly agreed that their basic purpose was to clear the way for monopoly. But perhaps Manykin and Sivachev are speaking figuratively. For them perhaps a reified capitalism, a reified class struggle, and a reified two-party system were at work unbeknownst to the individual politicians, inexorably synergizing to hold the underclass in its place.

Since the Reconstruction era, Manykin and Sivachev suggest, consensual agreement has prevailed within "circles of power" to the effect that the needs of monopolistic aggregations of power, usually economic in nature, should be furthered. American political historians and political scientists have described and interpreted the development and role of American political parties at considerable length. But, as Joseph Cooper and Rick K. Wilson have pointed out, they are in considerable disagreement about the basic dynamics of the American parties, even to the point in some cases of challenging the view that they are an important factor in American governance.[3] But others understand the development of the American party system to be the product of many incremental decisions made in the face of crises or their developments in the socioeconomic life of the country and agreed upon within the framework provided by the constitutions of the federal and state governments and a growing body of judicial and regulatory precedent. Although James Madison might be puzzled by the complexity of government in today's United States, there is much to commend in his explanation of the governing process in the *Federalist,* No. 10: "A landed interest, a manufacturing interest, a mercantile interest, a moneyed interest, with many lesser interests, grow up of necessity in civilized nations, and divide them into different classes, actuated by different sentiments and views. The regulation of these various and interfering interests forms the principal task of modern legislation, and involves the spirit of party and faction in the necessary and ordinary operations of the government." Rather than subscribing to the belief that a concealed but dominating intent to wipe out impediments to the unhampered development of capitalist enterprise has guided our national development, many of us find a law of unanticipated results, or even Murphy's Law, at work as we evaluate the results of legislation and policy. Madison the theorist deplored political parties; Madison the pragmatic politician organized the first great party of opposition in the history of the United States.[4]

In their description of the American party system Manykin and Sivachev do not mention an element that traces back to the beginning of the Republic and beyond that was of great importance in the development of modern American parties. That is the degree to which elections were to be decided on the basis of a simple majority and winner-take-all. The authors suggest that a national third party did not develop during the early national period because the expulsion of the Loyalists and the suppression

---

3. Joseph Cooper and Rick J. Wilson, "The Role of Congressional Parties" in Joel H. Silbey et al., eds., *Encyclopedia of the American Legislative System: Studies of the Principal Structures, Processes, and Policies of Congress and the State Legislatures since the Colonial Era* (New York, 1994), 2, 899–930. The authors include an annotated bibliography. See also Donald C. Bacon, Roger H. Davidson, and Morton Keller, *The Encyclopedia of the United States Congress* (New York, 1995), 4 vols.

4. Jacob E. Cooke, ed., *The Federalist* (Cleveland, 1961), 59. Murphy's Law, a modern American cynicism, postulates that anything that could go wrong, will go wrong.

of the popular uprisings of the 1780s and 1790s had removed the expanded social base necessary for such a development. Later the major parties adeptly stole the proposals of radical parties and incorporated emasculated versions of them in their own agendas. Although there is some truth in these explanations, American analysts also place great weight on the fact that the winner-take-all electoral system deprives American third parties of the patronage needed to sustain a continuing presence in the political arena. This characteristic of American popular politics has had a path dependency effect, just as the decision of U.S. senators to discard the previous question motion in their deliberations in the early national period has worked over the long run to make their chamber a much different deliberative body than the federal House of Representatives.[5]

Manykin and Sivachev have briefly described the major institutional features of the American party system. They note its complexity and its relations to the broader whole. Even so, they fail somewhat in conveying the details and implications of that complexity. The formation and execution of particular policies can be extremely convoluted. A particular element or thread in the various public policies endorsed by a unit of American government may involve the development and passage of many laws and extend across a long period of time; others may be of very short duration. The germinal ideas of policy may be domestic or foreign in origin, find support or promotional activity within many different sectors of the national economy and electorate, be profoundly modified by the political parties that incorporate them in their agendas and pass them into the laws that are the product of complex interaction between legislators, grassroots and industrial spokespeople, and the appropriate executive branches of government. Once passed, the intent of laws may be altered by the courts that interpret their meaning and the bureaucrats that administer them. Political bargaining and feedback characterize the stages through which law and policy evolve at almost every step of the process. The influence of the American party system runs throughout the elaborate system of formal and informal checks and balances that characterize the institutional structure of American government, and that structure involves three interacting levels of activity—local, state, and national.

Granted that it has taken two centuries for the current levels of complexity to evolve in American government, the Manykin and Sivachev model of party interaction is oversimplified. The continuum of political attitudes that stands central to their analysis is a useful heuristic device that catches a major aspect of the party system. But in emphasizing the overlapping nature of the parties at the center of the political spectrum these authors ignore the fact that the central area is composed not of party members but of self-styled independents. Although many of the independents implicitly cherish one major party to a greater degree than the other, their proclaimed lack of affiliation allows for a greater degree of instability in the system than Manykin and Sivachev's

---

5. For the details of the history of American political parties and electoral activity see L. Sandy Maisel, *Political Parties and Elections in the United States: An Encyclopedia* (New York, 1991). Sarah A. Binder, *Minority Rights, Majority Rule: Partisanship and the Development of Congress* (New York, 1997) provides an extended examination of an important dependency effect in congressional history.

model suggests. A more troublesome aspect of their argument lies in the fact that it provides a unidimensional ordering of the American electorate.

We know from our legislative studies that the actions of our representatives usually suggest not one but several underlying attitudinal or behavioral dimensions.[6] We find that legislators support the agendas of their party but their obligations to follow the party line may also be crosscut by other determinants including commitments to region, race, ethnicity, and religious affiliation. Although Manykin and Sivachev allude briefly to the first three of these behavioral factors, their paper is devoid of any reference to religion. But we know that religious convictions and activity powerfully influenced antebellum politics, and the new political historians of the 1950s and 1960s made a strong case for the pervading influence of religion in determining political affiliation in other periods of American history as well. This paper was of course prepared before the current religious right fully demonstrated its political muscle, but recent years have surely exploded any thought that religious commitment has ceased to be an important force in American political life. Here religion has been a political determinant rather than an intellectual opiate. In discussing the phenomenon of multidimensionalism I have focused on the legislator, but we can also be sure that the individual voter views issues in much the same way as his representatives.

In Manykin and Sivachev's model of change in the American political system, economic stresses stimulate radical and third-party activity. The bourgeois parties respond by implementing proposals for diluted versions of radical proposals. Although this scenario has played out at times in the past, examination of the various electoral realignments and the four great surges of federal reform legislation in our national history suggest that the Manykin and Sivachev model greatly undervalues the cultural and ideological determinants of political behavior.[7]

The authors also somewhat ignore the complexities involved in the development of American capitalism.[8] Industries do have incentive to increase their market share on the one hand and ensure plentiful supplies of raw materials for their manufacturing processes on the other; entrepreneurs and companies bring their general needs and specific political initiatives before legislatures and are prepared to use their resources to influence the law makers. It was no accident that lobbying became a recognized factor in American politics at the very time when the growing size and activity of large aggregations of capital caused major concern in the United States during the late nineteenth century. The fear of monopoly has been recurrent in our history, and with some justification, although a current school of scholarly thought believes the concern to have been exaggerated. It is in this respect, perhaps, that the Manykin and

6. Aage R. Clausen, *How Congressmen Decide: A Policy Focus* (New York, 1973).

7. For an introduction to the literature of electoral realignment and a discussion of the four major surges of legislative reform in the U.S. Congress see: Jerome M. Clubb, William H. Flanigan, and Nancy H. Zingale, *Partisan Realignment: Voters, Parties, and Government in American History* (Beverly Hills, Calif., 1980) and David R. Mayhew, "Parties, Elections, Moods, and Lawmaking Surges," in Silbey, *Encyclopedia of the American Legislative System,* 885–97.

8. Thomas K. McCraw, ed., *Creating Modern Capitalism: How Entrepreneurs, Companies, and Countries Triumphed in Three Industrial Revolutions* (Cambridge, Mass., 1997).

Sivachev argument is most persuasive. The old-line parties did steal the clothes of the radicals during the Progressive period and went even further in the New Deal era. But it is wrong to view big business or "the ruling circles" in America as a monolithic force. Intra-industry and cross-industry competition, as well as the phenomenon of organized consumer interests, have ensured that law makers will hear many voices as they perform Madison's task of regulating "various and interfering interests." Successive waves of technological innovation have repeatedly added new voices to the chorus of interests to which the American legislator listens, and voices once thought discordant in the extreme have faded into the background. Who today views the railroads as great predators stalking the capitalist jungle? Rather they are objects of pity, or identified as an endangered species worthy of preservation.

Madison believed that the size of the American republic would serve to pit enough interests against each other that none could exploit the others. The subsequent two centuries of national history has perhaps justified his faith, although they contain bloody civil strife, wrenching depressions, and continuing social inequities. For some two-thirds of that span the two-party system has helped the United States to survive, develop, and adapt. In the face of sweeping changes in the character of the American population, communication technology, and the science of politics, the parties have also adapted. The recent research of Jackson Turner Main shows that the recruitment of leadership in the American polity was remarkably open to the newcomer of lower-class origins during the years of colonial beginnings and the first seventy-five years of self-government. We suspect that this characteristic of American life continued to be the case and, if so, should be numbered among the reasons why Americans have found radical parties less attractive than has been the case elsewhere.[9]

Political analysts of the last generation in the United States, however, have also pointed to disintegrative tendencies in the American polity, although somewhat different in nature than those cited by Manykin and Sivachev. Election turnouts in the United States lag behind those in other major western democracies. The strength of individual party identification has diminished among American voters. As a result, some scholars have diagnosed a civil malaise that they fear will lead to unfortunate consequences. The increasing importance of television in political campaigning has allowed candidates to wage political contests on the basis of their individual personalities, diminishing their dependence on the party and, therefore, their obligations to hew to the party line. Even more disconcerting has been the growing cost of electoral campaigns, placing ever greater pressure upon politicians to accede to the wishes of those who can provide them with the funds necessary to win election. The ever-growing resources of the international corporations are a source of concern within democratic polities. In the broader American society, inequality in the distribution of wealth is increasing and many members of the middle class are hard-pressed to maintain their socioeconomic positioning. But the American party system has survived great crises in the past by a process of electoral readjustment and institutional adaptation. A culture that values innovation and "fixit know-how,"

9. Jackson Turner Main, *Inherited or Achieved: The Social Origins of the Worlds' Leaders, 2000 B.C. to A.D. 1850* (St. James, N.Y., 1998).

a bountiful base of natural resources, a head start in the race to benefit from the information revolution—these provide a foundation for change. So too does the fact that American political ideology, first brought to focus by the founding fathers and centering on the individual rights of men and women, has never frozen into rigidity. These considerations encourage the historical minded to believe that the life of the American two-party system will survive into a distant future.

We conclude our reading of this paper by asking whether we now know the authors' answer to their question, "what allows for the trickery of the political parties united in the two-party system, which for already two hundred years has supported political hegemony of the American bourgeoisie?" This reader did not find a clear answer to this intriguing query in these pages. There has indeed been trickery, bad faith, and deception, as well as downright corruption, in the practice of American politics, but in general we give the American legislative representative credit for representing his constituents, or at least a majority of them, faithfully. Perhaps Manykin and Sivachev's references to the abundant resources and relative openness of the social system indicate their belief that these fostered myopia or lulled constituents into easy acceptance of deception. Or do they place the blame on the two-party system itself? At least implicitly, they suggest periodically that answers lie within the black box of the class struggle. Presenting his presidential address to the American Historical Association some sixty years ago, a radical American historian proclaimed that writing history was an act of faith.[10] In the work of the authors and the response of this commentator we perhaps find opposing acts of faith, in which case only the future will identify the one containing the greater element of truth.

10. Charles A. Beard, "Written History as an Act of Faith," *American Historical Review* 39 (January 1934): 219–31.

Response

by A. S. Manykin

I was curious to read Professor Bogue's comments on the article the late Professor N. V. Sivachev and I wrote in the late 1970s. Our article discussed the methodology of studying the two-party system in the United States. At that time there was a growing interest in the history of this institution. The history department at the Moscow State University was then in the process of establishing a special group to research and analyze the two-party system, its mechanism and its functioning principles.

Preparing to deal with such overwhelming fundamental tasks, we were only trying, let me repeat, trying, to outline approaches to the most important, in our view, problems in American political history. Naturally, we grounded our ideas and suppositions in those commonly used at the time from Marxist theory. We attempted to apply Marxist general postulates to particular themes in American history and see whether the theory would work or would need correction. In essence, it was specific, large-scaled, and a long-term agenda for our collective to work on in the 1980s. In short, that was our original plan.

Reality had demonstrated that some of those ideas were successfully realized, see for instance other publications in this volume. Others had never been brought to life, mostly because the so-called "reforms" in Russia devastated our scholarship in the interval from then to now. Undoubtedly, twenty years after the first publication of this article, I would have tailored some of the deliberations and evaluations, and added other important themes, if I had a chance.

It is noteworthy that such an experienced and accurate critic as Professor Bogue immediately noticed often factually ungrounded generalizations inevitable under these circumstances. To our defense, I should say that an article format does not provide enough space for elaborate factual support of each postulate. Surely, the tone of some of the ideas was greatly affected by flaws of the then dominant approach in history.

So, what exactly is incorrect in our article?

First and foremost, there is certain exaggeration of how class struggle influenced the functioning of the American two-party system. By no means will I discharge this factor. And Professor Bogue does not call for it either. Class struggle was particularly effective at the time of partisan reconstruction, when principal parameters were being formed for the next party system model. It is obvious to me, and research proves it, that class and social struggle significantly affected the fate of the two-party system, and the path of its future development.

Nonetheless, such influence was oversimplified in Soviet scholarship and in our article too. The power of ethnocultural factors, institutional specifics of American parties, the role played by mass media, and electorate mentality were all underestimated.

Secondly, after having read our article I cannot but agree with Professor Bogue that there is a noticeable element of "class determinism" present in our research methodology.

As of today, in my opinion, the major task for historians is to determine priorities when studying this subject. We must analyze interaction of all factors in the framework of American political history to see what place such themes as "class struggle" occupy in modern historiography.

I am sure that dialogue between scholars of our two countries will help better understand the phenomenon of the American two-party system, and will open new horizons for research.

2

The Origins of the American Political Parties in the United States

by Vladimir V. Sogrin

September 1787. The delegates to the Constitutional Convention in Philadelphia, which adjourned with the adoption of the draft of the Principal Law of the United States of America, are leaving for home deeply satisfied. In the twelfth year of Independence and but four years after the completion of the Revolutionary War against England, the foundation, as it seems to them, to overcome the antagonism among states, social contradictions, and political rivalries is at last worked out. The draft proclaims the foundation of a strong executive branch in the person of president; establishes the highest legislative branch of power—the Congress of the United States; declares the supremacy of federal law over the states' rights. The delegates to the convention were sure that their creation would establish civil peace in the country. But the hopes of the framers of the Constitution were not to last for long.

Shortly after the Constitution had been approved, it became clear that the document did not eliminate the ground either for class, partisan, or political cleavages. Moreover, the adoption of the Constitution and the first steps of the government in 1789 laid the foundations for political parties to emerge. Henceforth the interstate contradictions would occur at a national level, in Congress and government, and emerging political parties would act as their proponents.

The first national election in the United States was held on a nonpartisan basis. Only one person, George Washington, aspired to take the office of the president. And it was he who was elected unanimously, carrying the votes of all the electors (the first and the only such precedent in American history). The first government of the United States was also formed on a nonpartisan basis. However, in a short time after Washington had taken the oath of office and the House of Representatives and the Senate had been opened, the formation of political parties began. The irony is that Washington, while being a vehement opponent of factional cleavages, appointed the founders of the future rival political parties, Alexander Hamilton (thirty-four years old) and Thomas Jefferson (forty-six) to the two key offices in the government (secretary of the treasury and secretary of state respectively).

The first political parties emerged in the teeth of acute rejection of any kind of factional and partisan cleavages by their leaders. The attitude toward the partisan opposition of Federalists, who held the power from 1789 through 1801, was invariably negative. Most often they defined the Jeffersonian Republicans as a "faction," the word that bore a negative sense in Anglo-American political tradition. Hamilton regarded factional activities of Republicans tantamount to dissenting activities, directed to undermine the federal union. Washington in his "Farewell Address" to the nation in September 1796 proclaimed the "spirit of parties" to be the bitter enemy of American unity.[1] Having imposed the Alien and Sedition Acts during the presidency of John Adams (1797–1801), Federalists tried at last to put an end to the opposition. Republicans were alleged to be the "foreign agents," a "French faction" (Republicans in contrast to Federalists preferred in foreign policy not Britain but France), and the creatures engendered by external influence.

On their side, Republicans treated their political rivals no less tolerably. One of their prominent ideological and political leaders, John Taylor, argued that the existence of rival political parties contradicted the nature of national government and proposed, if needed, to amend the federal Constitution to suppress dangerous partisan cleavages. Phillip Freneau, the leading Republican editor, as late as 1799 presumed that eradication of ignorance and delusions, as well as persistent enlightenment, would exclude partisan cleavages.[2]

Jefferson added philosophical grounds to the negative attitude toward the political parties. Like other U.S. enlighteners, including Benjamin Franklin, he dreamed of the establishment of a "Kingdom of Reason" based on class peace and political unity right after Independence was acquired and the victory of Republican order celebrated. His theoretical deliberations proceeded from the assumption that different temperaments as well as physical and moral peculiarities of people might be grounds for factional and partisan cleavages. But he was sure that the contradictions between rich and poor, contrasts in property status and class differences, were not found in the United States but were within European societies. That was why there was no socioeconomic ground in the North American Republic for real partisan hostilities and rivalries. Jefferson preferred to have no partisan division in the U.S.A. at all; "If I could not go to heaven but with a party, I would not go to heaven at all."[3] Inaugurated in 1801, Jefferson said a "conciliatory" phrase, which became famous: "We are all Republicans, we are all Federalists." However, in the context of his speech and outlook it implied nothing but the desire to absorb the Federalist party, to dissolve it in the Republican one.

Given such an attitude from the leaders of the North American Republic toward partisan opposition, it seems that very narrow opportunities would have been left for its development. But in fact the process of forming political parties and the ripening of certain principles of bipartisanship became apparent enough in the late eighteenth century. Factional cleavages that gave rise to the origins of political parties appeared distinctly in the U.S. Congress in 1789–1790. In 1792 the division of the U.S. politicians into two rival parties was firmly imbedded in mass consciousness. In

1. Harold C. Syrett and Jacob Cooke, eds., *The Papers of Alexander Hamilton* (26 vols., New York, 1961–1979), vol. 11, 429; Saul K. Padover, ed., *The Washington Papers* (New York, 1955), 317–18. This essay by Vladimir V. Sogrin was originally published in *Voprosy istorii* (Problems of History) 8 (August 1988): 36–48.

2. Noble E. Cunningham, *The Jeffersonian Republicans* (Chapel Hill, N.C., 1957), 134.

3. As quoted in Adrienne Koch, *The Philosophy of Thomas Jefferson* (Gloucester, Mass., 1957), 122.

May 1792 Secretary of Treasury Hamilton pointed out angrily that James Madison and Jefferson had headed a faction "subversive of the principles of good government and dangerous to the union, peace and happiness of the country."[4] In June, Jefferson wrote Madison with undisguised irritation that Hamilton was "daring to call the Republican party *a Faction.*"[5]

The same year Madison came out with an article "The present state of political parties," in which he distinguished three stages of the evolution of partisan cleavages in the United States. The division of the Americans into the adherents and opponents of independence in the revolutionary period he attributed to the first stage, the struggle over the draft of the Constitution of 1787 between Federalists and anti-Federalists to the second one, and partisan cleavages in Congress in the early 1790s to the third.[6] Henceforth the articles and the pamphlets on partisan cleavage became a usual phenomenon in the U.S.A. In 1794 Taylor issued a treatise "A definition of Parties," where he pointed out that "the existence of two parties in Congress, is apparent," and that "Whether the subject be foreign or domestic . . . the magnetism of opposite views draws them wide."[7]

The first conflict of the two political parties occurred while the issues of economic policy were debated. These issues became the focus of the U.S. government attention in the late 1780s-early 1790s. The principles of its policy were stated by Hamilton in the Reports "On the Public Credit" (January 14, 1790), "On the National Bank" (December 13, 1790), "On the Mint" (January 28, 1791), "On Manufactures" (December 5, 1791).[8] The young and vigorous minister openly aspired to become a prime minister (Washington didn't oppose that idea).[9] Hamilton turned out, as historians would conclude later, to be the real creator of a "federalist system" that embodied primarily the interests of financial, trade, and manufactory bourgeoisie.

In the first Report, delivered by Hamilton to the Congress, the need for credit was proclaimed to be one of the paramount needs of the country. To acquire it, the secretary argued, it was necessary for the government to pay its debts properly, and first of all to fund at their nominal value all foreign and domestic debts of the Continental Congress and the states for the period of the War of Independence. Many deputies shuddered at Hamilton's remedy, for the country owed $80 million. That was a huge sum for that time.

Democrats found the proposals of the secretary to be the intrigues of northeastern financial circles: a great bulk of internal debt consisted of the "soldiers' " certificates (bonds given to soldiers by the government during the war), which had switched from the initial owners into the hands of speculators. Given the fact that speculators had

4. Syrett and Cooke, eds., *Papers of Hamilton,* vol. 11, 429.

5. Paul L. Ford, ed., *The Writings of Thomas Jefferson* (New York, 1892–1899), vol. 6, 95.

6. Gaillard Hunt, ed., *The Writings of James Madison* (New York, 1900–1910), vol. 6, 104–23.

7. John Taylor, *A Definition of Parties, or the Political Effects of the Paper System Considered* (Philadelphia, 1794), 2.

8. Syrett and Cooke, eds., *Papers of Hamilton,* vol. 6, 65–168; vol. 7, 305–42; vol. 10, 230–340.

9. N. N. Jakovlev, *Washington* [Vashington] (Moscow, 1973), 324.

been buying these certificates from soldiers for as little as 10–12 percent of their face value, it was easy to calculate: if Hamilton's plan was fulfilled their interest would have been 1,000 percent. That would be an unabashed cheating of the government and taxpayers, and the representatives of the agrarian states pointed that out.

A counterproposal of Hamilton's opponents was as simple as follows: to pay at nominal value only the certificates that were owned by their initial holders, and the rest of bonds to pay according to actual value or cancel. The secretary of the treasury explained to the opponents that the idea was not to cancel the debt but to pay it back to the people, who would then grant new credits to the government again. But it was more likely that the speculators who robbed the soldiers, and not the soldiers themselves, were the people interested in granting new credits. Hamilton's explanation put his opponents on alert even more.

Jefferson and Congressman Madison had headed the opposition to Hamilton. They knew and were in correspondence with each other for many years. But their political alliance looked strange in many respects. They had substantial differences in outlook. Jefferson dreamed of turning the Republic into a republic of farmers and stressed the paramount role of village gatherings and town meetings, and of democratic self-government for small owners. As for Madison, he insisted that the grassroots must be kept away from power, which was to be entrusted to the supreme national body, composed of people mostly interested in the preservation of the foundations of bourgeois and planter society. Then what did unite these two in 1790?

The political partnership of the Virginian politicians was promoted by resolute though differently motivated opposition to the Hamilton plan for the United States' development, which would have paved the way to financial and commercial and manufactory capital at the expense of the agrarian interests of the country. It turned out to be possible to mitigate the divergence of opinions since both politicians, as it proved to be, were to a great extent able to compromise for the sake of a single purpose. Both were political pragmatists. (That was manifested pretty well in their attitude toward slavery. Condemning it theoretically from the point of view of the natural rights' theory of the Enlightenment Age, they paid respect to the planters' interests in their practical activities.)

Hamilton's opponents firmly blocked his proposals in the House of Representatives. Then he decided to undertake a bold maneuver: direct backstage negotiations with Jefferson. One July morning of 1790 Jefferson was ascending a stairway, being in a hurry to have an audience with Washington. Suddenly, Hamilton came across his way. The secretary of the treasury was anxious, he could hardly find words. Jefferson understood; Hamilton was seeking a rendezvous with him and Madison to discuss an extremely important public issue. The meeting was scheduled for the next morning.

During the meeting Hamilton's speech was well thought out and convincing. A rejection to pay off the debts to rich creditors, he argued, would bring the whole fiscal policy to the verge of catastrophe. He would have no other choice but to declare the government bankrupt, close the Department of Treasury, and retire himself. Hamilton prayed the two most influential southern politicians would concede and persuade the congressmen in favor of full funding of public debt. In his turn, Hamilton promised to move the national capital from New York, under control of bankers, to somewhere within the southern states. This idea had been debated in Congress. The southerners were seeking the transfer of the capital to the Potomac River; northerners agreed only to move it to the borders of Philadelphia, that is, to place it in a city where commercial and financial interests dominated.

Hamilton's proposal was alluring to Jefferson. It looked possible to rip the capital out of the hands of the financiers. As for Madison, he considered that the transfer of the capital to the Potomac would reinforce the political positions of the southern states, give rise to development of commerce and industry there, and put an end to their financial dependence on northeastern banks. In two years' time Jefferson would bitterly regret this bargain in his autobiographical notes.

The concession inspired Hamilton. After congressional approval of the Report on Public Credit he secured the other of his important economic measures to be passed through the Congress. The real Hamilton victory was the creation of the National Bank in 1791. Having briefly debated whether such a bank was constitutional, Congress conceded to the secretary of the treasury on this issue. He was indeed very eloquent in persuading that the financial giant promised the United States huge profits. Hamilton's promises were based on the examination of the experience of the English bank. A national bank would issue credit for public and private needs and carry out the emission of money. It was thought of as the source of increasing capital and the nation's wealth. Hamilton declared that the bank would not only grant credits out of the available funds, but also issue extra bills over the reserves of its precious metals available. Thus created, artificial capital would serve as a strong additional leverage to influence industry and commerce.

Hamilton preached especially insistently on the creation of big manufactures. The critics argued the groundlessness of the idea to create big enterprises, for there were shortages in the labor force and big capital was unavailable. Hamilton responded to their objections with reasonable arguments. He pointed out that manual labor would be substituted by machines and given the vigorous introduction of new technical inventions, the deficit of manual force could be easily overcome. Furthermore, in his opinion, the experience of enlisting women and children in manufactures was absolutely ignored in the United States. As for the big individual capital, unavailable in the country and necessary for the development of big enterprises, this problem, explained Hamilton, could be easily solved by the creation of the National Bank, which would grant loans of any size to any number of entrepreneurs.

The activities of Hamilton and the Federalist party, then being formed around him, were directed to stimulate industry and included the whole range of protectionist measures. They suited most of all the interests of the upper strata of the bourgeoisie. As for the middle and small owners, including the owners of scattered manufactures, they were left without government protection.[10]

The energy and successes of the secretary of the treasury made it imperative for Jefferson to broaden the anti-Hamiltonian opposition, make more perfect and varied the methods of political struggle. Step by step the idea to create a political party, able

10. Vladimir A. Ushakov, *America in Washington's Time* [Amerika pri Vashingtone] (Leningrad, 1983), 193–96.

to unite all anti-Hamiltonian groups from different regions and states of the country, occurred to him. The party needed a platform and organizing ideological center. In 1791 a newspaper for Republicans was founded (Hamilton had issued a newspaper, which advocated the interests of his party, as far back as in 1789). Jefferson enlisted the services of Freneau, a brilliant bard of the American Revolution, who was then destitute. Simultaneously he was proposed to work as a translator in the Department of State. The *National Gazette* began to be issued in Philadelphia, where the capital had been moved for the time being (Washington, at the falls of the Potomac River, would soon become the capital, as it was agreed).

By means of newspapers as well as negotiations and active correspondence with like-minded persons, Jefferson and Madison consolidated the anti-Hamiltonian opposition around themselves. Three states—Pennsylvania, New York, and Virginia—became the stronghold of the party. The Pennsylvanian forces made up the nucleus of Jeffersonian Republicans. In 1793 the Republican-Democratic clubs began to emerge in the United States under the influence of the ideas of the French Revolution and Jacobinic reforms. So the biggest and the most influential of them was founded in Pennsylvania—the Democratic Society of Pennsylvania. This organization brought to the Republican party prominent leaders; Albert Gallatin, the future secretary of the treasury, was one of them.

The New York faction with George Clinton at its head took the middle stand in the party. Traditionally, Clinton was regarded in American historiography as a "radical," a "leveler" and without doubt a Democrat, as it becomes a "one hundred percent" anti-Hamiltonian. Only quite recently Alfred Young proved that this leader of Republicans, as well as his adherents, belonged to American "nouveau riches," to those representatives of the lower and middle strata of white colonists who made their fortunes on the hardships of the Revolution and challenged the prevailing family clans of Schuylers, Livingstons, Pendletons, and others.[11]

The conservative wing dominated in Virginia. Taylor, a planter and a senator whose hobby was writing books on agriculture and political economy, was its acknowledged spiritual leader. In his writings he denounced the monied aristocracy of the Northeast and preached the rule "of farmers, by farmers, and for farmers." So were disguised the planters' ambitions, which greatly increased in the 1790s, influenced by a cotton boom. The existence of the planters-slaveowners faction in the party of Jeffersonian Republicans was a kind of a "delayed-action bomb." Did Jefferson realize the danger of putting together in his agrarian party such different social principles?

In forecasting the fate of plantation slavery, Jefferson, like other Democrats, hoped it would die peacefully and in the very near future. In doing that he relied on the economic showings of 1770–1780. Plantation slavery then was mostly involved in the production of tobacco, which had endured a prolonged crisis. Jefferson assumed that the above factor along with the ban on importing slaves projected for 1808 (as the Constitution provided) would result in the natural death of this disgraceful phenomenon. Jefferson could not foresee the unexpected, exceptionally favorable upswing for plantation slavery in its future development.

11. Alfred F. Young, *The Democratic Republicans of New York* (Chapel Hill, N.C., 1967).

The invention of the cotton gin by Eli Whitney in 1793 brought about the "second edition" of slaveowning in the United States. Slaveowners-planters quickly adjusted to the demands of the cotton boom and switched to cotton-growing. The Industrial Revolution played the role of a "midwife" for plantation slavery. Jefferson foresaw many social calamities that would follow the development of industrial capitalism, but such a "surprise" as the cotton boom was expected neither by him, nor anybody else within his party. The economic upsurge of plantation slavery, once begun, had the growing political ambitions of slaveowners as one of its consequences. It was them, not the farmers, who were predestined to become the leaders of the agrarian coalition created by Jefferson.

The Republican party's championing of the agrarian development of the United States was gradually evolving along with attempts to win over the contrasting strata of urban population. The party's rhetoric denounced not the craftsmen and traders, nor even merchants and owners of manufactures, but usurers, bankers, the owners of the public debt, in general all those who managed to create dishonest wealth. While Hamilton's projects were debated the representatives of the opposition faction, William Giles and James Jackson, criticized the conception of public debt and the National Bank as one. These would perpetuate the preponderance of "big money interests," undermine the foundations of republicanism, and create the economic basis for regeneration of the United States into monarchy.[12] Later on the Republicans emphasized more and more the egalitarian, democratic aspects of their criticism: public debt and a National Bank increased the inequality in the distribution of property, created the dangerous caste of money speculators, and engendered political corruption. As for the development of trades, manufacturers, and commerce, their growth was necessary for the nation in most Republicans' eyes.[13]

The Hamiltonian Federalists' opportunities for maneuvering were more limited. The agrarian population dominated in the country in the late eighteenth to early nineteenth century and Hamilton's economic program didn't evoke a response among these strata. In this respect the position of the Jeffersonian Republicans, who stood firmly for the agrarian development of the United States, looked much more acceptable. If Hamiltonian Federalists wanted to be a truly national party, they should have reflected the agrarian interests of the nation in their agenda. They tried to prove that development of industry and commerce implied the best natural solution of all the problems of agriculture.

Hamilton harped on this argument in his "Report on Manufactures." He accepted the point of view of the physiocrats and Jefferson, the Secretary of State, who proclaimed "the tillers of the soil" to be the most useful citizens of the country and the real creators of national wealth. Moreover, Hamilton emphasized that this point of view was most applicable to the United States, where the major part of the

12. *[Annals of Congress], The Debates and Proceedings in the Congress of the United States, 1789–1824* (42 vols., 1834–1856), 1st Cong., 2d sess., 546–48; 1180–82.

13. Lance Banning, *The Jeffersonian Persuasion: Evolution of a Party Ideology* (Ithaca, N.Y., 1978), 181–87, 204–5; John Zvesper, *Political Philosophy and Rhetoric: A Study of the Origins of American Party Politics* (New York, 1977), 123–35.

population was involved in agriculture.[14] At the same time the report of the leader of the Federalists, though abundant in programs of public protection of industrial interests, contained not a single practical proposal to meet the needs of agriculture. It was the southern faction of Federalists that was preoccupied with such a task. But being subordinate to the northeastern leadership of the party, it could not neutralize the Jeffersonians' influence among the agrarian sections of population.

The discussion between Republicans and Federalists broadened. Jeffersonians called themselves not only the Republican party, but also the Democratic one (both names stuck to them in everyday use and literature). Flying the banner of Democracy and Republicanism, they launched an outrageous attack against the Federalists. To the Democrats' way of thinking, the United States abounded with evidence of aristocratic and even monarchical vice being imbedded. There was, for example, the demeanor of the president. In Washington's first address to the Congress, delivered before the deputies of both houses, his inclination for the English tradition was keenly noted, and the legislature immediately replied with an address to the "address from the throne." Republicans found it to be a bad sign (after becoming president in 1801 Jefferson put an end to the imitation of English traditions by refusing to appear before the Congress for an oral address). Washington also proved to be inclined for exuberant and lengthy celebration of his birthday. He clearly wanted to stand out from his surroundings and to emphasize his superiority. His luxurious presidential coach was harnessed to six excellent trotters. "What a kind of monarchical manners!" Democrats exclaimed in a temper at that procession.

The mind and demeanor of the first U.S. vice president, John Adams, contradicted the Republican ideals even more. A vainglorious and boastful man who excessively overstated his services to the Revolution and ignored those of others, Adams even challenged Jefferson and Franklin, claiming to be regarded the most prominent American Enlightener. As the years had passed by, Adams more and more vigorously propounded principles that directly denied the ideals of Enlightenment. Having become the second statesman in the country, he proclaimed the idea of a "natural and ceaseless aristocracy" (namely it was to provide the political leaders for the Republic). Adams asserted that it should distinguish itself by means of respective titles. He persuaded the other politicians that the grassroots could never treat the head of the Republic with respect if he was addressed only as "George Washington, the President of the United States." Many congressmen also took up seriously the issue of giving an aristocratic title to Washington. They argued that at least he should be addressed by words such as "Your Highness" or "Your Elective Highness."

The Republicans didn't dare criticize openly either the president or the vice president. Choosing the target for their assaults, they focused the fervor of their criticism on Hamilton. He was imputed to be the main and the only person to spread the monarchical influence in the United States. Jeffersonians tried to fight Hamiltonians with the same weapons their political opponents wanted to deny them. They declared the secretary of the treasury and his entourage to be the sworn enemies of the Republic, who were plotting a coup d'etat to overthrow it. While Hamiltonians

14. Syrett and Cooke, eds., *Papers of Hamilton,* vol. 10, 233–35.

labeled Jeffersonians as anti-Federalists and anarchists, Jeffersonians decried their opponents as monarchists.

Jefferson's newspaper from time to time accused the secretary of the treasury of having monarchical sympathies and aspiring to reshape the U.S. public order in British style (he was imputed as an author of the reactionary treatise "The Simple Truth," published in 1776 and targeted on the discreditation of the idea of American independence). Newspapers asserted that Hamilton repeatedly proposed that Washington accept a scepter and a crown and tried to implant the customs and manners of the English Parliament in the U.S. government. But these were nothing but the exaggerations of propaganda. On the eve of the War of Independence Hamilton was a left-wing patriot, and in the beginning of the Revolution he came out with ideas that resembled those of Jefferson and Thomas Paine. His evolution to the right began later, but he did not become a monarchist even then.

Examination of the papers of Hamilton provides reason to assert that he spoke positively of the constitutional monarchy and British form of government only once. It happened during the Constitutional Convention sitting on July 18, 1787. Hamilton declared that the British form of government, that is, the constitutional monarchy, was the best the world ever knew.[15] But proving his political wisdom, he said later that this form of government could not be established in the United States unmodified, that only some of its principles might be accepted.

He dismissed the charges of Republicans as nothing but insinuations by Jefferson and his entourage. Hamilton resolutely denied that he nourished any sympathy for the British constitution whatsoever, and called a blockhead anyone who seriously believed the possibility of monarchical rule in the United States. Jeffersonians often charged Hamilton with violating the federal Constitution. For example, it was pointed out that none of its articles provided for the creation of such an institution as the National Bank. Hamilton responded that the Constitution granted the federal government broad authority and the practical exercise of governance implied the possibility of creating such a bank.

Jeffersonians didn't constrict their efforts to the propaganda war against Hamilton. They were eager to discredit him as a person. Jeffersonians started an investigation of his financial affairs and even unscrupulously rummaged in his "dirty laundry." Hamilton and his adherents responded like for like. They denigrated Republicans as Jacobinic spies and spreaders of faithlessness and anarchy, the "French contagion" of the worst sort. How far this squabble was from the "Kingdom of Reason" that Jefferson the Enlightener dreamed of! The political experience of the young Republic proved that stretches and extremes of propaganda were indispensable means of struggle for power. Even the Democrats could not help resorting to dubious means of political struggle.

Nevertheless, the controversy between Jeffersonians and Hamiltonians, despite its sharpness, implied a certain peculiarity that acquires a character of regularity in historical hindsight. To begin with, Jefferson's *National Gazette* did not contradict Hamilton's newspaper in its essence. Rather, it confirmed the idea implicit in Hamilton's *Gazette of the United States*. The first issue of Jefferson's newspaper asserted

15. *Ibid.,* vol. 4, 184, 189, 192.

resolutely the loyalty of his party to the basic party institutions and establishments of the United States. In this respect there was no difference between the *National Gazette* and the Federalists' newspaper. Even the consonance of the editors' last names Fenno (Hamilton's editor) and Freneau (Jefferson's) seemed to symbolize the unanimity in the attitude toward the foundations of the United States. Jefferson unequivocally announced his intention to oppose Hamilton within the framework of the established national political system. Such a kind of political opposition laid the cornerstone of the U.S. bipartisan system: consensus (consent) in maintaining and strengthening the bourgeois world order. The consensus was based on the loyalty of both parties to the federal system of the country, to the Constitution of 1787, and in general to the social and economic principles that triumphed during the last stages of the American Revolution. This became apparent in ideology as well as in political activities of the parties.

Jefferson's conscious and articulate desire to declare loyalty to the federal union and Constitution also implied another meaning. Hamilton and his newspaper all the time tried to discover Jeffersonians' contacts with anti-Federalists, that is, with the people who in 1787–1788 opposed the draft of the federal Constitution and demanded the Articles of Confederation (a fragile agreement of the thirteen states concluded in the War of Independence) remain valid. The Republican party vigorously dismissed all attempts to charge it with antifederalism. Moreover, by comparing the attitudes of the two parties toward the principles of the Constitution, the Republicans asserted that it was Hamilton and his adherents who were the true anti-Federalists. The Federalists in their turn dismissed charges of antirepublicanism. Some of them even proposed to add "Republican" to the name of the party and thus to neutralize the opponents' claims for monopoly in defending the Republican principles of the United States.

But there were political distinctions between Hamilton's and Jefferson's parties, which became especially apparent in the understanding of the ways to strengthen the bourgeois and republican foundations of the federal Union. The political activities of Hamilton and his adherents were directed to cement the institutions and laws that suited the upper bourgeoisie's and planters' narrow class interests, and to conserve the bourgeois democratic reforms of the American Revolution. Besides that, the Federalist party, which held the helm of power throughout 1790s, became notorious as a party of order.

On the contrary, Jeffersonian Republicans proved to adhere to the development and multiplication of the bourgeois democratic innovations of the American Revolution and to extension of democratic rights and liberties to new sections of the population. The political strategy of the Republicans was much more in line with the objective demands of capitalist progress, for the Revolution of 1775–1783 gave rise to the era of the U.S. bourgeois revolutions, which ended in the aftermath of the Civil War and Reconstruction of 1861–1877. Jeffersonian political strategy provided the Republicans with a broader mass support and proved to be important in pushing Federalists from the leading positions in the national political system in the early nineteenth century.

The majority of Federalists demanded to draw a clear line between the notions of "republicanism" and "democracy." They argued that it is democracy that is the real enemy of republican order and contained the sources of despotism of any kind, including a monarchy. This assumption was aimed to affirm that Federalists were real zealots of republican principles, and Democrats were in bitter hostility to them. Federalists referred to examples from ancient history, when one or another political demagogue used his popularity among the people to overthrow the republican freedoms. But most often the leaders of the Republican party appealed to the experience of the French Revolution. Its unexpected metamorphoses and sudden transition from participation of broad masses of population in political activities to the establishment of the rule of the Directory, consuls, and Bonaparte's regime were supposed to serve an obvious demonstration of the thesis that dictatorship stemmed from democracy and was its dark side.

Federalists regarded the coup d'etat of Brumaire 18, 1799, and the proclamation of Bonaparte as the First Consul (actually a dictator) as the completion of the natural degeneration of a democratic republic into tyranny (the beginning of this process was attributed to the Jacobin party's and Robespierre's takeover of power). Federalists' claims to abridge any of the liberties acquired by the people in the War of Independence proceeded from the idea that political democracy was incompatible with the preservation of the foundations of republicanism. Such claims were aired more often after 1793, when mass democratic upheavals, influenced by the French Bourgeois Revolution and farmers' actions, including the rebellion of 1794 in Pennsylvania, occurred.

Hamilton was really omnipresent. Though formally his department dealt with the issues of domestic economic policy, the secretary of the treasury contended to have the final say in the determination of U.S. international relations. In doing so he referred to the impossibility of solving economic problems unless the relations with leading European countries, and first of all England and France, were settled. Just after taking office as secretary of the treasury, he set up tight contacts with Englishman Major George Beckwith. Beckwith was sent to the United States to negotiate the possibility of transporting British troops through the territory of the United States to Louisiana, which was contested by London and Spain for a long time. Hamilton showed much kindness to Beckwith. Sure, Hamilton told him, Louisiana should belong to us. Thus Hamilton hinted at the U.S. aspirations to acquire a part of Louisiana and the right to have a free outlet to the sea through the Mississippi River for the services rendered to England. But that was not all he meant.

Beckwith was astonished by the conversations with Hamilton. He could hardly believe that he was speaking to the leading minister of the country, which only seven years ago had wrung peace from England. Englishmen and Americans, Hamilton said, remained consanguineous. Having the same origins, common language, religion, habits, and culture, he reasoned, Great Britain and the United States should live in peace and friendship, and certainly conclude a treaty on trade in a short time. Hamilton explained to Beckwith that there were two parties in the United States, pro-French in the Jeffersonians and pro-English in the Federalists. He advised the Englishman to refrain from contacts with the secretary of state, a hidebound person and a Francophile in addition. Thus the secretary of the treasury had grasped the relations with the leading western European country into his hands.

Hamilton rather freely interpreted the contents of his talks with Beckwith to Washington and Jefferson. He concealed the negative aspects of England's relations toward the United States and harped on the goodwill of London and the coincidence of interests between the two nations. Historian Julian Boyd, who later discovered the materials on contacts of Hamilton with Beckwith, actually classified Hamilton as a British agent, that is, Boyd affirmed the charges put forward against Hamilton by his political opponents in the 1790s.[16]

To what extent are the thesis of Boyd and the charges of Hamilton's political opponents well-grounded? To my mind they simplify and distort the motives of his actions. It looks at least naive to measure a political figure of such a scale as Hamilton with the labels of a political agent of a foreign country. Indeed, Hamilton is designated in Beckwith's reports to his government as "#7," but this didn't mean that the secretary of the treasury was agent #7. Beckwith had contacts with many Federalists and kept files on many U.S. statesmen, and in his reports to London authorities designated them simply with Arabic numbers. Secretary of War Henry Knox was #4, Chief Justice of the Supreme Court John Jay #12, etc. Besides that, it would be misleading to assert that Beckwith used Hamilton to promote his objectives. There are no less, not to say more, grounds to assume that the secretary of the treasury wanted to make the Englishman carry out his socioeconomic and political projects. It is clear that both Hamilton and Beckwith were playing a subtle diplomatic game; both wanted rapprochement between England and the United States, but tried to play each other up in the issue of terms and aims of the rapprochement.

Hamilton hoped that his foreign policy would create a favorable attitude of the broad masses toward the aims of his party. The persistent idea of his internal policy doctrine consisted in the assumption that the expansion of economic and political relations with Great Britain was a tactical measure. It was the most reliable of all means to provide a lasting, firm political independence and economic self-dependence of the country. The Federalists argued that the United States could not become a mighty state unless a durable peace held. And to keep the peace would require certain concessions, and sometimes even palpable ones, to England. Federalists most often resorted to this argument during elaboration and ratification of Jay's Treaty [1795]. It granted England extremely favorable conditions relative to other countries to penetrate the American market and confirmed the prewar debts of the colonies to the mother country.

The Federalists' economic motivation was based on the one hand on the assumption that the U.S. exports to Britain and its possessions made up the main income of the American merchants, and on the other hand that the money from the dues on the British imports was dozens of times more than from the French, and made up the main source of the National Treasury revenue. Their political arguments against France run as follows. In determining its strategic course the U.S. government had to proceed from the fact that its former ally could not be regarded as a stable, and therefore strong and reliable, political system, owing to the French Revolution. An alliance with a country in disarray was fraught with serious consequences. It was pointed out

16. Julian P. Boyd, *Number 7: Alexander Hamilton's Secret Attempts to Control American Foreign Policy* (Princeton, N.J., 1964).

that after 1792 the preservation of the alliance with France, which declared war on all European monarchies, would result in conflict between the United States and the mighty states of the Old World.

Republicans considered that the anti-English course was the most reliable way to complement the acquisition of U.S. political independence with economic independence and to cement American patriotism and unity. Besides the anti-English views, their attitude toward France was also determined by ideological sympathies to the principles of the Revolution of 1789. The fact that France gave the keys from the Bastille to Washington in 1789 was not a mere gesture in the eyes of the secretary of state, but rather the beginning of a new stage in the political alliance between France and the United States. Henceforth it would develop into an alliance of two nations based on the consent of their people, in contrast to the other states of the world.

But despite the ideological sympathies to the French Revolution, the Republicans' attitude toward their obligations to France were rather complex. Republicans spurned Hamilton's reasoning that the execution of Louis XIV in 1793 had rendered the French-American Treaties of 1778 invalid. In Jefferson's opinion these treaties were concluded by two nations and two peoples and not by their governments. So the change of government in either country could not repeal them. The secretary of state also insisted on recognizing the National Convention as a legitimate government of France and accepting the envoy it appointed to substitute for the previous one.[17]

Jefferson and those around him considered that the U.S. government should act prudently in dealing with military obligations. Americans possessed neither navy nor regular land forces that could give substantial help to France. That is why they could refrain from taking an active part in military hostilities and remain neutral. Hamilton's proposal to Washington to proclaim neutrality met several objections from Jefferson. First, he put himself against the usage of the term "neutrality," which would evoke doubts about the French-American Treaties of 1778. Second, he assumed that the declaration should not be issued by the president, but by the Congress after every one of its words was carefully reasoned out. The compromise attained in this issue was a good example of a foreign policy decision taken on a bipartisan basis. The declaration was issued by the president, but it didn't mention the word "neutrality."

Although the foreign policy strategies of the Federalists and Republicans seemed incompatible, they appeared to bear a principal resemblance. The "super task" of the foreign policy of either of the parties shared a common essence: to provide for the survival of the North American Republic, to strengthen its sovereignty, to keep the United States neutral and unentangled in the conflicts of the European states, and to complement the acquisition of the political independence with economic independence. Simultaneously, both parties saw different ways to achieve these aims, as was evinced in the pro-English orientation of the Federalists and the pro-French orientation of the Republicans.

Conservative and custodian features of the Federalist party became most apparent in the period of John Adams's presidency (1797–1801). In 1798 Congress adopted the Alien and Sedition Acts, which counteracted the democratic provisions of the Bill of

17. John C. Miller, *The Federalist Era, 1789–1801* (New York, 1960), 126–39.

Rights. Several editors of Republican newspapers were accused of casting aspersions on the government, brought to trial, and convicted. The Federalists unleashed an anti-French hysteria in the country. The Congress abrogated all the treaties with France and took a decision to conscript ten thousand volunteers for a three-year term. The Department of the Navy was created. It was decided to build twenty-five frigates and armed merchant ships and sanction the capture of French ships in the open sea. Adams's policy resulted in the exacerbation of relations between the Federalists and the Republicans. In 1798–1799 the Republicans began to prepare themselves for the 1800 election, which from the point of view of their leaders should determine the future of the country. The Kentucky and Virginia Resolutions, prepared by Madison and Jefferson respectively, made up the Republican platform for the forthcoming political fight. Republican propaganda pointed out in lapidary and expressive ways the unpopularity among the masses of the Federalists' rule. Its results were British influence, the Regular Army, direct taxes, the public debt, the expensive navy, and the spirit of aristocracy. Jefferson Republicans promised to turn it all over.

The Republicans equated their impressive victory over the Federalists in 1800 as tantamount to the Revolution of 1776.[18] The Republicans firmly established themselves in power. Three of their acknowledged leaders, Thomas Jefferson, James Madison, and James Monroe, successively held the presidency between 1801 and 1825. They seemed to have all the opportunities to destroy the "Federalist system." However, the foundations built by the Federalists remained intact in the period of the "Virginian dynasty" rule (the three Presidents were Virginians). The National Bank, the public debt, public protection of manufactures and external trade, strengthening of the sovereignty, and territorial expansion—all these creations and aims of the Federalists were bequeathed by the Republicans.

The American partisan system had taken a shape of bipartisanship. In the late eighteenth and early nineteenth centuries the basic features of the system were still in embryo. The strong rivalry between the Federalists and the Republicans and the issues they were divided upon indeed were matters of principle. The wide range of ideological differences between the Federalists and the Republicans enabled them to encompass almost all the voters. This left only very narrow opportunities for any third political party to emerge.

At the same time, despite all the differences between the two parties, the principles of consensus and continuity, which provided the strengthening of the American bourgeois state and proprietary interests even in case one party was substituted by the other, became apparent in their mutual relations. Both parties piously believed in the inviolability of private ownership, bourgeois-republican order, and the Constitution of 1787.

18. Ford, ed., *The Works of Jefferson*, vol. 12, 136.

3

Democrats and Whigs

An Exercise in Quantitative Analysis

by M. A. Vlasova

The Democratic and Whig parties did not last long. They made up the two-party system that had developed fully by the early 1840s and then fell apart in a decade. Nevertheless, in the country's political history its legacy is far from ordinary.

The emergence of the Democratic and Whig parties between the 1820s and 1830s was mainly related to important changes in the American sociopolitical system. The Industrial Revolution in the Northeast, the farmers' expansion and colonization of the West, and the development of the plantation system in the South accelerated such demographic processes as population growth, migration, and immigration.

Those changes also stimulated shifts in the society's structure. There was a deeper social differentiation taking place. Gradually, new social groups were being consolidated. Those included the industrial bourgeoisie, the proletariat, and capitalist farmers. It turned out that class, social, ethno-religious, and regional contradictions, which underlay these groups' interactions, could not be solved with the old partisan, political, and governmental structures still in place. Democratization of the current political system became a pressing necessity.

To a certain degree, the transformations of the 1820s and 1830s had their effect on all governmental and public institutions. But the parties were to play a pivotal role in facilitating those transformations. Democrats and Whigs were called to bring new social forces into the process of political power execution. Smoothing and neutralizing the internal conflicts within the ruling bourgeoisie-planters bloc in order to develop a consensual political agenda was another task the parties were to perform.

The parties sought to establish a constant two-way communication line between elected political leadership on federal and local levels on the one hand and the mass of the electorate on the other. In this particular case the parties functioned to ensure regular elections in the country where almost universal white manhood suffrage existed, and the tendency toward widening administrative powers prevailed. Unlike their predecessors, Democrats and Whigs acted as "enlighteners." They introduced wider masses of the population to the political process, and as a result of this promoted more open access to political decision-making. The parties' impact on the establishment of ideological and organizational components of the two-party system is noteworthy. They must be given well-deserved credit for the formulation and justification of the parties' positive role in the society, and also for creating the organizational structure that, despite certain changes, exists today.

It is necessary to mention that both Democrats and Whigs depended on the support of each of the nation's regions. Since their predecessors—Jeffersonian Republicans and Federalists—were deprived of such a wide-based electorate, Whigs and Democrats can be rightfully reckoned as the first nationwide parties in American history.[1]

The scholarly interest in the history of the parties corresponds to the significance of the roles they played in the development of American society between the end of the 1820s and the beginning of the 1850s.[2] However, a wide range of questions deserve more focused consideration. For instance, exactly when did the Democrats-Whigs system arise?

When it comes to methodology, periodization is among the most difficult problems. This article focuses on a narrowly defined goal. It examines and analyzes changes in several dimensions that describe two spheres of the parties' activity: elections and the U.S. Congress. Analysis of the dynamics of the parties' development will allow for clarification and revision of the periodization criterion for that period.

A party's participation in the election process constitutes one of its most essential characteristics.[3] Thus the election results could provide an insight, though not free from simplification, into the mechanism of a party's activity. The hypothesis is that the conspicuous changes in the election results correspond to some changes within the party itself.

The electoral process in the United States at the time included numerous elections in legislative, executive, and judicial bodies on the federal, state, and local levels, including counties and townships. Thus, the research task would be to choose the level on which to work with such data most effectively. As we consider Democrats and Whigs the all-national parties, presidential elections' results appear to be a preferable choice for analysis. In our case, the analysis was based on the aggregated data from the state-level electoral campaigns. Mostly, these are the presidential election returns, and other variables.[4] In particular, such a simplistic variable as the difference between votes cast for the leading parties' candidates (in percent), or margin, was analyzed. The informativeness of this variable is noticeably enhanced if data are scaled to show its negative and positive measures (see Tables 1–4).

1. E. F. Yazkov, ed., *The Principles of the American Two-Party System: History and Modern Tendencies, from the End of the Eighteenth Century to 1917,* vol. 1 (Moscow: 1988), 8–22. This essay by Vlasova was originally published in *Amerikanskii Ezhegodnik [Annual of American Studies]* 1989 (Moscow, 1990).

2. The American historiography of the Democrats and the Whigs is immense. As far as Soviet scholars are concerned, there is a reviving interest in the establishment of a two-party system in the first half of the nineteenth century. See, for instance, G. A. Dubovizki, "The Two-Party System of the Democrats and Whigs: Peculiarities and Role in the Political Development of the United States in the 1830s-1850s," *On the History of Political Struggle and Public Thought in the U.S.* (Kuibyshev: KGU Press, 1981), 26–44.

3. M. P. Marchenko and M. H. Pharukshin, *Bourgeois-Political Parties* (Moscow, 1987), 45–68.

4. Data on presidential election returns was borrowed from computer-based sources of the InterUniversity Consortium for Political and Social Research. See *State-Level Presidential Election Returns, 1824–1827* (ICPSR 0019).

Table 1
Presidential Election, 1828 (average difference ratio: 36.4 percent)

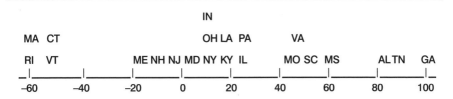

Table 2
Presidential Election, 1832 (average difference ratio: 34.1 percent)

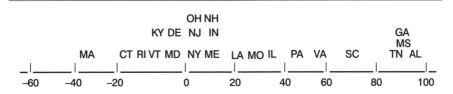

Table 3
Presidential Election, 1836 (average difference ratio: 11.1 percent)

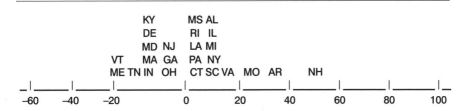

It seemed expedient to use the margin, that is, the break in the number of votes cast for each candidate, because the latter enables a researcher to compare the "competition" of the oppositional groups. In fact, we draw the conclusion that if almost equally powerful political groups participate in the same campaign, this break would be minimal. Likewise, the more unequal they are, the higher the margin would be.

Data in Table 1 represent the 1828 campaign, in which the National Republican presidential candidate John Quincy Adams lost to Democrat Andrew Jackson by a wide margin. The distribution of the margin indicates the generally low level of competition between Jacksonians and National Republicans. In fourteen out of twenty-two states the winning group received more than two-thirds of the votes. The

Table 4
Presidential Election, 1840 (average difference ratio: 10.9 percent)

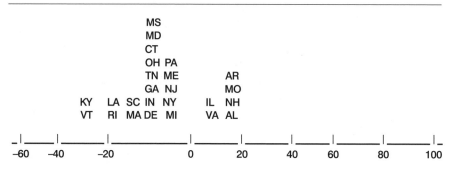

states with the lowest average difference ratio, closest to the zero point on the scale, are mostly in the mid-Atlantic region. Apparently the states that experienced higher rates of socioeconomic and political development also witnessed a more dynamic process of party formation.

The computed results clearly demonstrate also the sectionalism of electoral behavior, as well as a balance of powers on the federal level. The southern and southwestern states are clustered in the positive pole of the scale. Six New England states and the state of New Jersey—all from the mid-Atlantic region—favored Adams. Considering the general low level of "competition" (the average difference ratio is 36.4 percent), it is no exaggeration to say that in regard to their sectional composition and political power, Jacksonians and National Republicans in 1828 were poles apart.

How different was the 1832 presidential campaign, during which Jackson had to face two oppositional nominees—National Republican Henry Clay and Anti-Mason William Wirt? At first glance, data in Table 1 and Table 2 are alike. As in 1828, the maximum margin is represented by southern and southwestern states, and the minimum difference ratio remains the same in New England. The only exceptions were Kentucky and Maryland, where opposition to the incumbent political group grew considerably.

As in 1828, the "competition" in most states remained low with the average difference ratio at the 34.1 percent level. The decreasing gap in the numbers of the administration's supporters and its opposition was evident in eleven states. Only in Missouri and Indiana did this gap change due to the declining advantage of Jacksonians. The growing power of the incumbent group proved to be the general trend.

Comparison of the presidential campaigns results do not suggest serious differences in the composition of the electoral behavior of major political forces. They stayed unbalanced and sectional.

If the mass electorate was to become a new battlefield of the developing political groups and factions, then the U.S. Congress remained the traditional arena for their competition. American political parties were "genetically" connected to the "competition" level in the Congress. The first political parties—Jeffersonian Republicans and Federalists—arose directly from the basis of the Congressional factions.[5] Subsequently, the problem of interaction between the new bourgeoisies' political parties and the legislative branch must be addressed. It would be interesting to see how closely in time the Whig and the Democratic parties both in Congress and on the electoral level coincided. The ability to extend its influence over the country's main legislative body may serve as an indication of a party's political maturation. In this regard, it is necessary to analyze the partisan divisions in the Congress and to measure their boundaries and steadiness.

The methodology of quantitative analysis as applied to roll-call voting in representative bodies for the purpose of studying partisan struggle is deep-rooted. V. I. Lenin in his work "One Step Forward, Two Steps Backward" (1904) wrote that division on various questions that are subject to roll-call voting "provides a unique, irreplaceable in its precision picture of an internal struggle within the party, and of its fractions and groups." To make it more illustrative, he used the diagram method otherwise known as unidimensional scaling. If one regarded all the votes, he noted, the "exact and most objective exposure of political struggle could be obtained."[6]

This article uses such methodology in a computer analysis of the roll-call voting in the U.S. Congress. The U.S. Senate was chosen primarily due to the fact that in it were the most important representatives of Jacksonians and of the opposition: Martin Van Buren, John Caldwell Calhoun, Daniel Webster, Henry Clay, and others. The bulk of data includes seventy-five thousand individual senatorial votes in the Nineteenth through Twenty-sixth Congressional sessions (1825–1841).[7] The major statistical methods used were cluster analysis, unidimensional scaling of Guttman-MacRae, and index method.[8]

Even during the years of John Quincy Adams's presidency (1825–1829), articles about the two parties' rivalry in the Congress began to appear in the national press.[9] Since contemporaries usually linked the emergence of political parties to the divisions in the Congress, it is clear that the analysis of this process, at least in the Senate, was fully informative.

The study of the senatorial voting in the first session of the Nineteenth Congress (1825–1827) lets us single out a structure consisting of four blocs (Table 5).[10]

5. M. P. Ryan, "Party Formation in the United States Congress, 1789–1796: A Quantitative Analysis," *William and Mary Quarterly* 3d ser., 28, no. 4 (October 1971): 523–42; John F. Hoadley, "The Emergence of Political Parties in Congress, 1789–1803," *American Political Science Review* 74, no. 3 (September 1980): 757–79.

6. V. I. Lenin, *The Complete Collected Works,* vol. 8, 321–22.

7. Data on roll-call voting was partially collected by the author, and partially borrowed from computer-based sources of the Inter University Consortium for Political and Social Research. See *United States Congressional Voting Returns* (ICPSR 0004).

8. E. I. Popova and C. B. Stankevich, "Mathematical Methods in American Historiography of the Congressional Political Struggle," *Amerikanskii Ezhegodnick* [Annual of American Studies] 1981 (Moscow, 1981), 118–42.

9. *National Intelligencer,* March 10, 1827.

10. During the above-mentioned period congressional sessions differed in duration. Also, the congressional composition underwent a considerable change—that is why the primary

Interpretation of such a structure was preceded by clarifying the senators' party loyalty to either the Adams administration or to its opposition. The first two blocs count exclusively Jacksonians, the third one, the most coherent of all, included fifteen Adams supporters and two oppositionists. The fourth bloc was composed of seven National Republicans and five Jacksonians. In general, the U.S. Senate structure corresponded to the perception of the two existing parties in the Congress, because the voting patterns of the senators justified the partisan labels that were given to them a priori and thus united them into party blocs.

This raises a question, however, about the contentious character of the divisions. In order to answer such a question, it is necessary to use the procedure, offered by V. I. Lenin, to choose the major types of divisions, hence to point out the major thematic groups. In the Nineteenth Congress these groups were: foreign policy, internal improvements, governmental service, and procedural questions. Voting in each group was subject to cluster analysis. The results show that the universal structure is copied only in one group, which included voting on the foreign policy questions.

Table 5
Cluster analysis of roll-calls in the U.S. Senate during the first session of the Nineteenth Congress (44 senators, 79 roll-calls).

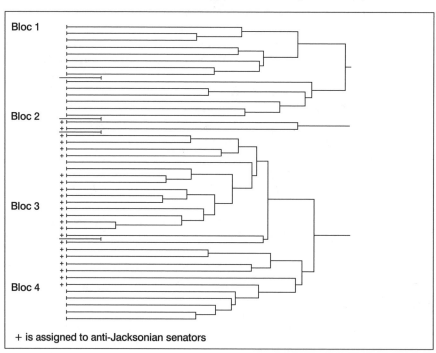

+ is assigned to anti-Jacksonian senators

---

attention was focused on the materials of the first sessions. Nevertheless, the comparisons between all roll-call voting were constantly drawn.

Foreign policy accounted for approximately one-third of all the roll-calls. In other groups the division could not be described as "partisan," and the blocs included in equal proportions both Jacksonians and Adams's supporters. This qualifies these senatorial groups as weak and unstable.

The same result has been attained in the process of index analysis, the method used to compare the groups derived on the basis of cluster analysis. Index analysis selects solid and measurable indicators, in this case, those that describe behavior of senators, and constructs a formula, hence index. Since the analysis interprets the visible groups in the Senate as partisan factions, the following indexes are used: a measurement of the "cohesiveness within the party" and another that assesses the senators in regard to their party's overall positions.[11] Both indexes are characterized by a certain degree of haphazardness, which undoubtedly hampers the interpretation of the results. To avoid mistakes, several alternative methods should be applied simultaneously. In our case, index method was accompanied by cluster analysis and Guttman-MacRae scaling. Table 6 and Table 7 present the average ratio of "cohesiveness index" and the "likeness index," computed on voting results in the Senate of the Nineteenth to Twenty-sixth Congresses.

The "parties" weakness in the Nineteenth Congress is confirmed by the indexing results. The average ratio of the "party cohesiveness" index is 60 for the Adams's supporters, and 47 for their opposition. That means that on average only 60 percent of all National Republican Senators and 47 percent of Jacksonians cast similar

Table 6

The change of an average ratio of the "cohesiveness index" (the first sessions of the Nineteenth through Twenty-sixth Congresses, U.S. Senate)

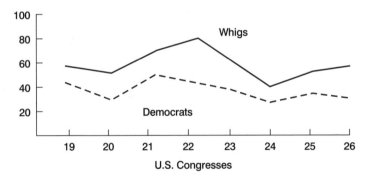

U.S. Congresses

11. The index of "voting cohesiveness" presents the absolute difference between the percentages of positive and negative votes, cast by each member of the party. It can deviate from 0 to 100. Maximum is achieved when all the members vote unanimously. The index of "partisan relativity" is derived from the absolute difference between the positive votes cast by both parties. It can deviate from 0 to 100. The maximum demonstrates the utter relativity of both parties' positions in each voting. The computer program to create the indexes was developed according to its description in L. F. Anderson, M. W. Watts, Jr., and A. R. Wilcox, *Legislative Roll-Call Analysis* (Evanston, Ill., 1966), 184–85.

Table 7

The change of an average ratio of the "likeness index" (the first sessions of the Nineteenth through Twenty-sixth Congresses, U.S. Senate)

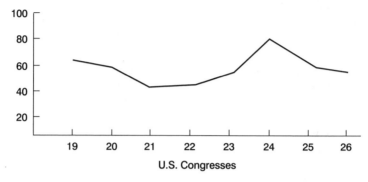

U.S. Congresses

votes. Only in 8 percent of roll-call votes of Jacksonians did the index exceed 90. "Cohesiveness" among Adams's supporters was slightly higher, which was also demonstrated by the cluster analysis. Consequently, the "party likeness" index in the Nineteenth Congress is high—61.

The comparison of the voting results in the Nineteenth and Twentieth Congresses is employed to find the dynamics in the partisan factions formation in the U.S. Senate.

Cluster analysis, applied to the individual senatorial votes in the first session of the Twenty-second Congress, indicated four cluster blocs. Each of them was homogeneous in its partisan composition (Table 8).

As a result, almost all the National Republicans joined in one bloc (1), characterized by the highest level of cohesiveness in comparison to other groups. The Jacksonian Democrats' group was divided into three principal blocs. The majority of Democrats, representatives from the southern and southwestern states, were united in cluster 3. The speculation that the oppositional group appeared to hold more homogeneity is confirmed by the indexing results, for the average ratio of the "cohesiveness index" among National Republicans is 78 and only 50 for Jacksonians (see Table 6).

The explanation of the peculiarities in the senatorial behavioral mode leads one to break all the groups by a thematical principle.[12] Then a different picture from the one of the Nineteenth Congress emerges. With few exceptions, voting on major problems fits into the scheme of the partisan split, which in turn indicates clear-cut partisan blocs present in the U.S. Senate. A partisan split is manifested in almost each of 192 individual votes cast at the session.

Though the quantitative data prove an ongoing "partisan" split in the Senate, there is no need to overestimate its scope. The mean ratio of the "cohesiveness index" remained relatively low. Ninety percent of National Republicans cast similar answers only in 50 percent of all the roll-calls. Jacksonians demonstrated solidarity only in

---

12. The following roll-call groups were formed: "federal bank," "public lands," "internal improvements," "finances," "procedural questions," and "federal service."

Table 8
**Cluster analysis of roll-calls in the U.S. Senate of the first session
of the Twenty-second Congress (48 senators, 192 roll-calls)**

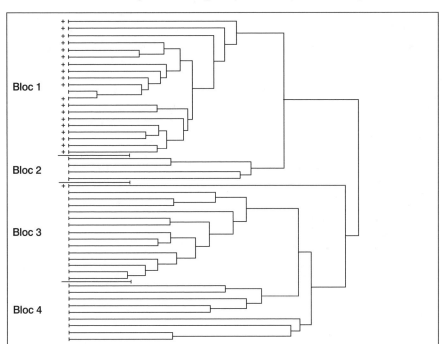

7 percent of all the cases. During the two sessions of the Twenty-second Congress there was no vote recorded in which 90 percent of National Republicans opposed 90 percent of Jacksonians, which, in our opinion, means that the so-called "parties" in the Senate were weak. Furthermore, they lacked any kind of a formal organization.

Data used in this study pertain to 1824–1832. To draw some conclusions, it is necessary to highlight the most significant stepping-stones in the parties' formation and to compare them to the results of quantitative analysis.[13] The era 1824–1828 could be characterized as a preparatory period. At that time, wide although organizationally amorphous electoral coalitions of Jacksonian Democrats and National Republicans were formed. A long-term disruption of the former Jeffersonian Republicans and Federalists came to an end, and the trend toward political groups' unity prevailed. The Jacksonians' attempt to unite various groups nationwide succeeded and propelled Jackson to a victory in 1828.

13. My understanding of the parties' development was reflected in an unpublished candidate dissertation, "Emergence of the Whig Party in the U.S.A. (1828–1840)" (M.S.U., 1986) and some other publications; e.g., "The Quality of the National Parties: Democrats and Whigs in 1830s," in *Principles of Functioning of the American Two-Party System: History and Modern Tendencies* (Moscow, 1988), 1, 97–120.

Andrew Jackson's domestic policy fueled centrifugal as much as centripetal tendencies in the process of a party's formation. President Jackson and his supporters rested the success of their party on a numerically sound yet socially and politically diversified coalition that drew together planters and farmers on the one hand and members of financial, commercial, and industrial bourgeoisie and the proletariat on the other. Explicitly, Jackson's first term contained many contradictory elements. He advocated, for instance, lower protectionist tariffs to meet the demand from planters and farmers. Yet at the same time, he called for military actions against South Carolinians who declared the federal tariff of 1828 unconstitutional.[14] In the same fashion, he imposed the so-called Maysville Veto on a bill providing federal aid for building the National Road system, which evoked a great political resonance. And simultaneously he approved some other similar bills.[15]

The absence of explicit ideological differences between the administration's supporters and the opposition was the result of the lack of integrity in the Jacksonian coalition itself and the fact that the course of domestic policy was still in the process of formation. The opposition itself was divided into several groups: the National Republicans, Anti-Masons, and southern states-righters.[16]

Despite its amorphousness, the Jacksonian preelectoral coalition was a new political phenomenon, considerable in the magnitude of its structure and goals. Jacksonians adapted to a newly democratized political situation and appealed to a wider range of ordinary Americans. The party championed popular demands for "equality of opportunity for all" and for cheaper public land, and fought against "financial aristocracy."[17] For the first time in American history, Jacksonians attracted professional politicians and set up local partisan organizations. They also attempted to exercise control over national organizations.

Before 1832 the first national conventions were held to nominate partisan presidential and vice-presidential candidates. Prior to that year the nominations were made at the elitist caucuses. Of the three conventions held (by the Anti-Masons, National Republicans, and Jacksonians), only the Jacksonian convention represented numerous local organizations and could be considered truly national.[18]

Generally speaking, the period of 1824–1832 witnessed several contradictory tendencies developing within the parties. On the one hand the new political groups

14. William W. Freehling, *Prelude to Civil War: The Nullification Controversy in South Carolina, 1816–1836* (New York, 1968).

15. *History of the United States*, 4 vols. (Moscow, 1983–1987), vol. 1, 314.

16. The Anti-Masonic party was founded in the end of the 1820s in the majority of the northeastern states. The party accented a strong egalitarian motive, and pushed forward for some political reforms. Most important, it sought to deprive the "old" Masonic elite of its power through democratic elections and to ensure more access for ordinary people to the political process. Anti-Masons took a stand against Mason Jackson and endorsed their own presidential candidate. William P. Vaughn, *The Antimasonic Party in the United States, 1826–1843* (Lexington, Ky., 1983).

17. Robert V. Remini, *The Election of Andrew Jackson* (Philadelphia, Pa., 1973).

18. James. S. Chase, *Emergence of the Presidential Nominating Convention, 1789–1832* (Urbana, Ill., 1973).

emerged. One of them, the Jacksonians, acquired a diversified and centrally controlled organization strong enough to ensure Jackson's two presidential victories. But on the other hand, it would be too early to say that a new two-party system was already in place, mainly because there was no viable oppositional party present. The results of the quantitative analysis also bear proof to that: the 1832 electoral votes, for instance, demonstrated a low level of competition between oppositional groups. Even Jacksonian electoral support, regardless of the Democrats' superior organizational structure, varied significantly among geographic regions.

The results of Congressional votes appear to be vitally important in comprehending the internal partisan processes. The development of political groups in the U.S. Senate showed some positive dynamics. At the same time such important characteristics of a two-party system as Congressional partisan factions and a party's control of the legislative branch were not yet developed. That is why the final stage of the Democratic party's foundation should be attributed to 1832–1833 rather than to 1828.[19]

The second conglomerate of analyzed data refers to the period of Jackson's second administration (1833–1837). Here the attention is centered on the results of the 1836 presidential election.

At their second national convention the Democrats nominated Martin Van Buren, the vice president under Jackson, as their new presidential candidate. The opposition, having called itself "Whigs," chose three candidates: Daniel Webster, Hugh Lawson White, and William Henry Harrison. Each of them was regarded the strongest in various sections of the country. The comparison of Table 2 and Table 3 reveal the change in distribution of states on the scale. The cloudlike configuration in Table 1 and Table 2 has a higher level of stress, that is, loose fit. At the same time Table 3 has good fit: only in four states did the difference ratio exceed the 20 percent level, with the majority of states clustered around 0.

Increasing difference ratio by more than three times affected the number of states on the negative pole of the scale: they sprang from seven in 1828 to eleven in 1836. Apparently, Anti-Democrats improved their positions. These scores are best demonstrated in the changes of negative and positive clusters of sectional support. According to the voting results, Van Buren failed to retain as many votes as Jackson had in the southern and southwestern states. Georgia and Tennessee repudiated Van Buren, and moved from the radical positive positions in Table 1 and Table 2 to the negative pole of the scale.

Supposedly, a complete electoral turn-about took place: in 1832 voters endorsed Jackson, but in 1836 they cast their votes for a candidate of the opposition. These shifts were connected with the transformation of the sectional electoral structure into the national one. If previously Jacksonians dominated the South and Southwest, and the opposition held New England, in a new political order both groups gained relatively equal electoral support.

19. Such a time frame is set in some works. See *History of the United States,* vol. 1, 312–13; A. S. Manykin, *History of America is Two-Party System, 1789–1980* (Moscow, 1981), 39; I. C. Romanova, *Andrew Jackson's Reforms, 1829–1837* (Moscow, 1988), 27, 33–36.

When interpreting the parties' electoral policies, one particular factor should be considered. The Democrats' grip on the states was weakened by the growing opposition, and also by the simple fact that Van Buren represented a non-slave state. The following discussion of the senatorial voting behavior reveals an impact of the slavery controversy on the composition of political forces.

Cluster analysis of roll calls in the Twenty-fourth Congress (1835–1837) gives evidence of two consistent blocs, unequal in their unanimity. Furthermore, a large group of senators does not fit into any of these blocs (Table 9).

The first bloc was exclusively composed of Democrats. Eleven out of twenty-one Whig senators and one Democrat formed the second bloc. Outside of these polarized blocs were predominately Whigs (ten and eighteen), who formed the so-called "swale," mostly unaligned with principal groups. These senators in most cases—from 40 percent to 70 percent of the time—didn't vote.

At the core of the Twenty-fourth Congress's debates was the antislavery agitation, and especially a "gag" rule that automatically laid all antislavery petitions in Congress on the table. Such a maneuver was initiated by the southern Democrats. The discussion of abolitionist pamphlets and antislavery petitions was steadily increasing in the North and reflected different views both groups held on slavery. Before that period the

Table 9
Cluster analysis voting results in the U.S. Senate of the first session of the Twenty-fourth Congress (48 senators, 198 roll-calls)

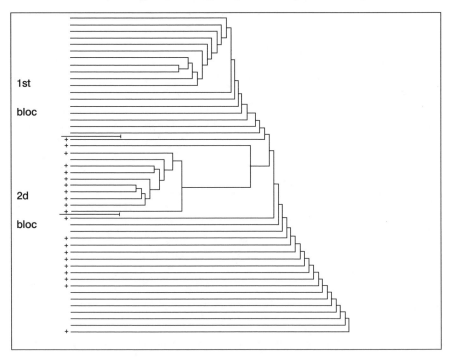

incumbent political groups avoided discussing the problem, and were driven by the idea of maintaining unity within their organizations. But the slavery question then came to the fore. It turned out that Democrats unanimously supported the practice of keeping off the agenda any possible discussion of slavery. Whigs, on the contrary, were divided on this problem into southern and northern groups. This last fact explains the structure of the Twenty-fourth Congress: on the basis of roll-calls, Democrats constituted a unified bloc, while half of the Whig senators avoided voting and finally found themselves isolated from the Whig political bloc.

The destabilizing effects of these discussions may explain the Senate's voting pattern in general. In Table 6 a decrease of an average ratio of "cohesiveness index" occurred during the first session of the Twenty-fourth Congress. Such a decrease was more important for Whigs than for Democrats. Consequently, there was an increase of an average ratio of "likeness index" (Table 7).

It is then necessary to place the analysis of congressional and electoral variables in a broader historical context. In 1833–1837 sharp polarization of the country's political and social forces was in progress. This process was escalated by the fast-growing discontent between supporters and opponents of the Bank of the United States, the American central financial institution, which exercised monopoly over note issues, domestic exchange, and credit operations. The Bank was widely disliked by farmers, planters, workingmen, and entrepreneurs. With their support, the presidential faction in the Democratic party was determined "to kill" the Bank and to transfer its capital to the state banks.

However, the Bank had many supporters too.[20] It was no accident that in 1833 the Bank controversy was labeled by Democrats "the struggle of the majority against the financial aristocracy," and that it served as a catalyst to the development of the party system.

For Democrats it was a period of intense political strife. As a result, the party emerged more ideologically and organizationally unified. During 1832–1836 the opposition gained a chance to "gather the forces" and unite various groups under the banner of the Whigs preelectoral coalition. The study of the Democrats' and their opponents' behavior leads to several conclusions. First, during this period the growth of partisan competition was most noticeable. Second, the partisan electoral split occurred in almost every state. Third, the parties retained their solidarity in Congress despite the interference of antislavery discussions. All this points to 1832–1836 as a new stage in the two-party system's formation. Nonetheless, this process was far from complete, for there is a complex of such factors that are difficult to formalize, and that prove the immaturity of the partisan structure in 1836. In particular, the Whigs had not yet reached the stature of a national party. The powerful preelectoral Whig coalition lacked a national center. In a number of southern states Whig organizations were too weak; their organizational amorphousness went hand in hand with their passive partisan rhetoric and insufficient ideological agitation.

---

20. For the interpretation of the Bank War by the Russian historian see I. C. Romanov, "Reasons for Andrew Jackson's Fight Against the Bank of the United States (1829–1831)," *Amerikanskii Ezhegodnick* [Annual of American Studies] 1977 (Moscow, 1977): 86–108.

The dynamics of the studied variables can clarify the nature of changes among Democrats and Whigs in 1836–1840. The 1840 presidential campaign was demonstrative of how both groups worked within the electorate. Two candidates—Democrat Van Buren and Whig William H. Harrison—competed that year. In Table 4 states's symbols are configurated on the scale in accordance with the percentage of votes cast for each presidential candidate. Unlike in Table 1 and Table 2, the cloud-shaped configuration is stretched vertically, which is due to the relatively low difference in margins. They vary from +10 to -10. The fact that the majority of the states moved to the negative wing of the scale indicates the Whigs' success. Noticeably, the comparison of the above-mentioned tables is not very informative, as was the case in the previous presidential campaigns. To see more clearly changes in partisan electoral behavior, additional data needs to be applied.

Scholars often use the index that shows turnout—the level of participation, that is, the proportion of all the voters to the total number of population, or to the population eligible to vote.[21] Table 10 shows the percentages of voters as compared to the number of potential eligible voters in 1828–1840. In 1828–1830 deviations from the mean level of turnout were slight. But 1840 saw a sharp rise in their numbers. Since there was no considerable extension of suffrage between 1836 and 1840, the growth of voters' participation was mainly due to the success of a party's propaganda. Only well-organized parties, capable of initiating ideas that would have a widespread appeal among the masses, could manage to organize 80 percent of the voting population to render their support to the party's course. Probably in 1836 the parties with these capabilities did not yet exist (Table 10).

Before we move to the last example of the Senate's roll-call analysis, the historical situation in which the Whig-Democrat political contest was taking place merits a

Table 10
Participation in the 1828–1840 presidential elections

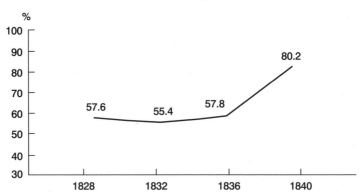

21. G. J. M. Clubb, W. H. Flanigan, and N. H. Zingale, eds., *Analyzing Electoral History: A Guide to the Study of American Voter Behavior* (Beverly Hills, Calif., 1981), 137–50.

short discussion. This period was marked by a severe economic crisis that shook the country in 1837 and aggravated social and political tensions. In this situation the Whig opposition capitalized on the economic and social plight, accusing Democrats of inability to prevent it.[22]

The severity of the crisis helped the preelectoral coalition develop rapidly into a nationwide oppositional party. At the time when social conflicts (unemployment, rising prices, and pauperism) were extremely poignant, each party's leaders had to improve the most important "instrument" of their power—the party's mechanism. In 1840, for the first time in the American political history, a party platform was adopted.[23] The political propaganda and agitation rose to unprecedented highs; the first cheap, mass publications appeared; thousands of Whig and Democrat supporters gathered at the public rallies, previously unknown in the American political practice. The parties' actions lost their parochialism, and presidential contests became full-blown nationwide campaigns.

Under these circumstances, the behavior of legislators underwent a number of changes. During the special session of the Twenty-fifth Congress, held in the spring of 1837—at the early stage of the crisis—for the first time each congressman was referred to in accordance with his partisan loyalty and affiliation. The two main criteria then were "renegade" and "partisan." Moreover, because of the widely used system of lobbyism on the part of the constituencies and the state legislatures, congressmen openly expressed the point of view of those local "parties" that elected them.[24]

As a result of all analyzed data from this special session, the following structure was formed. It included two homogeneous blocs, which were nevertheless different in size and in level of cohesiveness (Table 11).

The Whig bloc (1) is different from the Democrat bloc in two ways: there were four Democrats among its members, and the senators who constituted the Whig bloc showed less cohesiveness, evident from the comparison of the levels on which the clusters were composed.

Guttman-MacRae scaling was added to cluster analysis and indexing to analyze the available data.[25] Scaling will provide a better opportunity to expose the ideological underpinnings of the partisan split. Since the two-party system was known to be coming of age, even more important appear to be the divisions within the Senate, which might have contained possible political platforms.

All the votes during the special session of the Twenty-fifth Congress were computed. They gave the scale of ten roll-calls (with forty senators participating), in most of which financial problems dominated the agenda.

22. *Congressional Globe. United States Congress,* 46 vols. (Washington: Blair and Rives, 1834–1873). 25th Cong., 1st sess., vol. 5, 167–74, 179–84.

23. The Democrats were first to do it in May 1840.

24. Charles F. Adams, ed., *Memoirs of John Quincy Adams, Comprising Portions of His Diaries: From 1795 to 1848,* 12 vols. (Freeport, N.Y., 1969), vol. 9, 389–99.

25. Charles M. Dollar and Richard J. Jensen, *Historian's Guide to Statistics; Quantitative Analysis and Historical Research* (New York, 1971), 116–21, 198–205; *A Sociological Working Book* (Moscow, 1983), 245–48.

Scores	9	8	7	6	5	4	3	2	1
Whigs				1		1	1	3	6
Democrats	1	9	7	7	1			2	

Coefficient of reproducibility = 0.90

The distribution of senators on the scale is subordinated to the content of bills and resolutions of the ten roll-calls. The president's legislative proposals, compromising in nature, were aimed at dealing with the financial consequences of the economic crisis, and were incorporated into the senatorial bills.[26]

Even though a large number of senators are clustered in the central part of the scale, a partisan split is easily detectible. The majority of Whigs—ten out of thirteen—received the minimum number of scores—from 0 to 2. On the other hand, seventeen out of twenty-three Democrats received the highest scores: 9-8-7. The fact of the matter is that approval of the majority of the included bills corresponded to the

Table 11
Cluster analysis voting results in the U.S. Senate during the special session of the Twenty-fifth Congress (49 senators, 30 roll-calls)

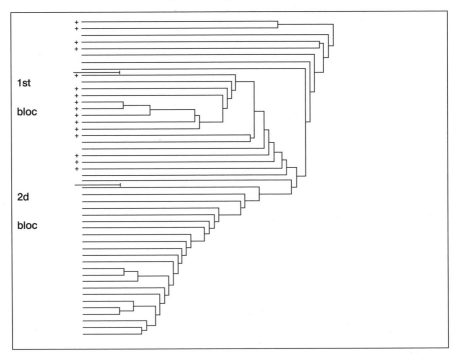

26. Thomas Brown, *Politics and Statesmanship: Essays on the American Whig Party* (New York, 1985), 37–39, 163–64, 172.

position held by the Democratic party. Meanwhile the Whigs' interests were better served if the bills were killed.

The main conclusion to be drawn from the described scale is that senatorial reaction to Van Buren's program bore signs of partisanship. Whigs demonstrated a more consistent cohesiveness in their opposition to the program than Democrats did in supporting it.

Despite their significance, the debates over the financial problems did not exhaust the congressional agenda during that period. Another major problem was the procedure of the sale of public lands. In fact, Democrats were in favor of easier access to free western land.

Out of nineteen roll-calls of the Twenty-fifth Congress (second session), eleven fitted the requirements of Guttman-MacRae scale (with thirty-five senators participating). The bills were presented by Whigs to discuss the preemption rights of settlers and their rights. If enacted the bills could impose limitations to the size of the groups of settlers granted those rights.

Scores	11	10	9	8	7	6	5	4	3	2	1	0
Whigs	5	3		1				1				
Democrats			2		1	1			4		8	9

Coefficient of reproducibility = 0.96

The distribution of senators on the scale yields the conclusion that the split over agrarian bills coincides with the Whig-Democrat dichotomy. The majority of the factions' members are gathered on the opposite wings of the scale. There are no sectional groups formed. Our suggestion that the partisan affiliation correlates to the attitude toward "preemption rights" bills is reinforced by the fact that there were pro-bill Democrats from all the states who received the lowest scores—0 and 1.

These agrarian and financial legislative measures as analyzed prove that the partisan split was connected to the parties' different ideological positions. It seems that senatorial factions defended definite partisan economic agendas. To bring together all the results of roll-calls and to compare them to the electoral data is possible through the interpretation of the "cohesiveness index" deviations throughout the entire period. At least two conclusions come to mind. First, the partisan senatorial factions were characterized by a relative weakness during all three periods of the new two-party system's development. The average ratios of the "cohesiveness index" are less in comparison to the next decades.[27]

When this particular index is applied, all roll-calls are counted, and the index then can indicate the level of a partisan discipline. More "tight" would be a faction in which members vote as a bloc on a majority of issues. So, a second conclusion is that neither Whigs nor Democrats showed such a pattern. And above all, the faction, defined in modern terms as the one to have a fixed organizational structure, did not exist.

27. During the Twenty-second Congress there were no roll-calls where 90 percent of one party's members would have opposed 90 percent of the members of another. In the Twenty-ninth Congress (1845–1847) the party's "cohesiveness" reached the 15 percent level.

Unlike their predecessors—Federalists and National Republicans—Democrats and Whigs consolidated their forces on the local level rather than on the basis of the congressional factions. The growth of their support there was triggered by the fight over political control. It was no accident, then, that in the 1790s U.S. congressional factions exhibited a higher level of cohesiveness.

By 1840 the nationwide Democratic and Whig parties were ideologically and organizationally capable of competing for the support of the mass electorate. In fact, this moment marked the very beginning of the new two-party system. The congressional factions undoubtedly felt common pressure coming from the party's formation and from the two-party split on all levels. This pressure was analyzed and finally exposed in the study of roll-calls.

Deviations of the indexes used in this analysis prove the reliability of three periods in the process of party formation. In 1828–1832 the future Democrats and Whigs were "preparing the grounds." By the end of this period the Democratic party emerged as an independent entity. After that, the struggle for political control took on new forms.

Changes in the presidential and congressional elections are the major landmarks that enable us to designate 1832–1836 as a special period. The two-party system was yet to come. There were two highly visible general trends in the process of party formation: the Democrats' consolidation, and centripetal tendencies transparent in the actions of their opposition. Finally, the level of competition between political alignments grew so substantially that it forced the majority of states into more active participation.

In 1836–1840 the Whig party was finally formed, with the process accompanied by the emergence of the new two-party system. Since that time the bipartisan form of political competition has continued on all levels and in all possible spheres of power.

Comment

by William G. Shade

These essays by Vladimir V. Sogrin and Marina A. Vlasova, first published in Russian slightly less than a decade ago, deal with two crucial stages of early American party development that focused the interest of the so-called "new political historians" who emerged in this country during the 1960s and 1970s.[1] Thus it seems only fair to compare them to the state of the art in this country as it had developed by the early 1980s and only briefly at the end of the essay relate them to any subsequent trends. While these two essays use similar language and cover some of the same subjects, they are distinctively different in both their substantive claims and the methods which they employ—Sogrin's essay resembles the traditional understanding of party origins embodying elements of both the Progressive historians of the first half of the century and the Consensus historians of the postwar era, while Vlasova reflects perspectives associated with the "new" political and social historians who consciously borrowed both models and methods of the social sciences.

The elastic concept of party employed by Sogrin is something like that of Arthur Schlesinger, Jr.[2] The term has a fixed meaning in that Jefferson and Madison used it to refer to the same sort of institutions twentieth-century scholars call parties. Consequently, those institutions that appeared in the 1790s were the first modern parties as both the Progressives and their critics argued. These parties emerged early in our history and established a two-party template that has remained relatively constant. Of course Schlesinger (and I assume Sogrin) accepted change particularly in party structures and acknowledged some reshuffling of names and various kinds of mechanical innovations. But the American "party battle" has exhibited a relatively consistent set of characteristics since its inception.

Also for Sogrin and Schlesinger, traditional two-party politics represented a difference in principle between conservative and democratic forces over economic questions. This was most clearly characterized by the conflict between their leaders Alexander Hamilton and Thomas Jefferson. The standard view appeared in Beard's *The Rise of American Civilization* and widely used texts such as the classic written by Samuel Eliot Morison and Henry Steele Commager that continues to dominate the popular history embraced by most Americans, who are not scholars, for these

1. Allan G. Bogue, "The New Political Historians of the 1970s," in Michael Kammen, ed., *The Past Before Us* (Ithaca, N.Y., 1980).
2. Arthur M. Schlesinger, Jr., ed., *History of U.S. Political Parties,* 4 vols. (New York, 1973) and Arthur M. Schlesinger, Jr., *The Age of Jackson* (Boston, 1945).

years. Their Republicans and Federalists structure electoral and legislative behavior—organize the patterns of both popular response and governance—at the federal, state, and local levels. They are the marvelous machines that integrate conflicting groups and create legitimacy for the regime.

For Vlasova, the Jacksonian Democrats and Whigs were the first modern parties. She acknowledges that they were short-lived institutions whose electoral aspect carried over into legislative activity, existing in something like party systems, which were differentiated not so much by their contrasting principles but by their relative strength and coherence. The parties with which Vlasova deals, like those of Richard P. McCormick, were primarily the electoral machines whose behavior is seen in voting returns and the roll-call votes cast in Congress. While she does not use the language of party systems or realignment, Vlasova's essay is certainly compatible with the work of those who do.[3]

This surprised me, since the position has been rejected by many American Marxists and neo-Progressives. I had assumed the Russian historians would possess a keen sense of the difficulties inherent in establishing the legitimacy of a government in a postrevolutionary world, be interested in and attuned to ideological subtleties, and be well-versed in the basics of American economic history. On each of these matters the essays of both Sogrin and Vlasova are relatively silent or superficial. Their lack of understanding of American economic history makes policy analysis nearly impossible.

Sogrin begins his narrative with reference to the seeming incongruity that intrigued Richard Hofstadter and others in the early 1960s—a political elite that rejected parties and partisanship that managed to invent the first modern parties amidst a frenzy of party passions.[4] But he goes little beyond a brief reference to "Anglo-American political tradition" to explicate the political culture in which anti-party sentiments were embedded. Although Sogrin does footnote in another context the books of both Lance Banning and John Zvesper, he does not engage the debate over Republicanism. It is almost impossible to exaggerate the role this controversy has played in writings on not only the 1790s but also the entire period of the early Republic.[5]

But Sogrin proceeds in a relatively traditional fashion that accepts a story composed of undiluted Progressive elements. The most obvious is the early date at which he argues "national parties" appeared, although he follows Madison, denying a connection between the "parties" that fought over the Constitution from 1787 to 1789 and those that emerged in the First Congress. The first modern parties—of course he takes none of the national pride of American textbook writers, but interestingly assumes our shared origin as peripheral peoples, that is those on the periphery of the

3. Richard P. McCormick, "New Perspectives on Jacksonian Politics," *American Historical Review* 65 (January 1960): 288–301; and McCormick, *The Second American Party System* (Chapel Hill, N.C., 1966). McCormick was influenced by not only his mentor Roy F. Nichols but also the French political scientist Maurice Duverger.

4. Richard Hofstadter, *The Idea of a Party System: The Rise of Legitimate Opposition in the United States, 1780–1840* (Berkeley, Calif., 1969).

5. See for example the widely used text by Harry L. Watson, *Liberty and Power: The Politics of the Jacksonian America* (New York, 1990).

European metropole—emerged quickly and primarily in response to the Hamiltonian economic program in 1789–1790 and had entered the "mass consciousness" by 1792. His evidence is selective quotation from letters of Madison and Jefferson and an elastic use of John Taylor.

Sogrin locates most of the action in the early 1790s. Newspapers appear from the start (1791) as partisan organs; party labels, while mentioned later in the essay, are attached from the beginning (1789) and presumed to be well understood. He accepts the one-to-one relationship organizationally between the Republicans and the Democratic Republican societies, as did various Progressive and Old Left historians. Although it takes him a while to get to them, Sogrin adds in the Whiskey Rebels (and while he fails to mention them, the followers of Jacob Fries might be included) into the rising tide that lifted the Jeffersonian boat in 1800.

There is also a Progressive sense that the fundamental differences are rooted in economic conflicts that were expressed sectionally—although what he is talking about is really localism. In an environment in which the National Book Award is now given to a beautifully written, but critical, biography of Jefferson and the Thomas Jefferson Professor at the University of Virginia plugs a new study that essentially gives substance to the often dismissed "Black Sally" rumors, Sogrin's veneration of the third president seems quaint.[6]

The cult of Jefferson that we have often seen in the Third World was clearly alive and well in the Russia of the 1980s. Sogrin's apologetics for Jefferson and the Republicans on slavery—he does not acknowledge that Jefferson was a slaveholder— would dismay most American historians of any ideological stripe. However, his sharp separation of Jefferson and Madison on democracy would fit the singular views of radical political theorist Richard K. Matthews.[7] With this goes a hostility to John Adams that can be seen in Sogrin's discussion of the Alien and Sedition laws.

These are portrayed as the point of a Federalist attack on a growing Republican majority that took the form of a prejudicial indictment against the innocent French. Although he does not make reference to John C. Miller's *Crisis in Freedom* (1952), Sogrin portrays a similar sort of McCarthyism at work.[8] As with his discussion of the Jay Treaty, however, Sogrin's rendition of this legislation is not connected to any action from the external superpowers. Neither the XYZ affair that preceded the

6. Joseph J. Ellis, *American Sphinx: The Character of Thomas Jefferson* (New York, 1996); Peter S. Onuf quoted on the dust jacket of Annette Gordon-Reed, *Thomas Jefferson and Sally Hemings: An American Controversy* (Charlottesville, Va., 1997). The most bitter attack on Jefferson is the work of the Irish historian Conor Cruise O'Brien, *The Long Affair: Thomas Jefferson and the French Revolution, 1785–1800* (Chicago, 1996). Actually, Jefferson received his lumps in Peter S. Onuf, ed., *Jeffersonian Legacies* (Charlottesville, Va., 1993), and is denied the place he wished in the writing of the Declaration of Independence by Pauline Maier in *American Scripture: Making the Declaration of Independence* (New York, 1997).

7. Richard K. Matthews, *The Radical Politics of Thomas Jefferson: A Revisionist View* (Lawrence, Kans., 1984); Matthews, *If Men Were Angels: James Madison and the Heartless Empire of Reason* (Lawrence, Kans., 1995). Matthews was a student at the University of Toronto of C. B. Macpherson, one of Lee Benson's favorite Marxist theorists.

8. He does cite John C. Miller, *The Federalist Era, 1789–1801* (New York, 1960).

Federalist military buildup of which the Alien and Sedition Acts were a part nor the quasi-war which accompanied the enforcement of this legislation are even mentioned.

He believes that by at least 1792 the "Democrats" were the party of the American masses who embraced the French Revolution and only by a set of undefined tricks, played in undefined ways, could the Federalists—who Sogrin suggests, correctly but a bit oddly, were never really a national party—somehow maintain control. (In a way it is too bad he never had Richard N. Rosenfeld's *American Aurora* [New York: St. Martins, 1997] to work with.) It has always been terribly difficult, however, for those imbibing the mother's milk of Jeffersonianism to square the unusually hostile response to the Virginia and Kentucky Resolutions from the legislatures of all nine of those states that responded and to the Federalist success in the congressional elections, which were at the time the only national indicator of popular response of such beliefs.

One might go on in many directions. In the wake of the various public displays of patriotism connected with the bicentennial of the Revolution and then the Constitution, we have undergone a "Jeffersonian Surge," which has involved a good deal of popular interest in, and veneration of, the era. In any case it is clear that the narrative put forth by Sogrin is one that no professional American historian interested in this period now fully entertains. He does face a language problem in an area where the usage of words has become crucial, but more important, he does not treat party development as just that, a process.

American historians for some time, at least since Joseph Charles, have tried to sort the problem out by introducing some behavioral criteria, acknowledging the obvious point that the word "party" can mean so many different things.[9] Part of this problem relates to political culture and Sogrin, as I mentioned, fails to acknowledge what sometimes seems the dominant debate in this area. The other side of the problem involves examination of political structure, at which the "new" historians excelled. They studied electoral behavior, legislative behavior, and organization. In every case they adopted quantification to enhance their arguments. From these studies one could project development as institutionalization related to what was termed by some "stages of party development" and others the theory of "critical elections" or "partisan realignment." It is not too hard to make the lions and the lambs in this debate lie down together—at least in intellectual terms. One can shed the seeming commitment to progress by creating indicators that might reflect Samuel Huntington's idea of decay.

---

9. Joseph Charles, *The Origins of the American Party System* (Williamsburg, Va., 1956); William Nesbit Chambers, *Political Parties in a New Nation* (New York, 1963); and John F. Hoadley, *Origins of American Political Parties, 1789–1803* (Lexington, Ky., 1986). The problem has been specifically addressed in two essays by Ronald P. Formisano: "Deferential-Participant Politics: The Early Republic's Political Culture, 1789–1840," *American Political Science Review* 58 (June 1974): 473–87; and "Federalists and Republicans: Parties, Yes—System, No," in Paul Kleppner et al., *The Evolution of American Electoral Systems* (Westport, Conn., 1981), 33–76. Formisano and the other "new" political historians were influenced by not only Americans such as Gabriel A. Almond and Sidney Verba but also English scholars such as Edward Shils and T. H. Marshall, and Europeans such as the Norwegian, Stein Rokkan, and the German, Ralf Dahrendorf.

The short version here is that the gulf between what Sogrin's essay and what the academic historians in the United States and England were writing at the time he wrote is immense.[10] They addressed the related concepts of "party" and "party development," and, ultimately, "party systems," imported from political science. They tried to relate this to "political culture," including party "ideology" or "persuasion," which involved a terrain that was fraught with its own controversies. Most obvious is the debate among intellectual historians and political theorists over Republicanism and its place vis-a-vis Liberalism and other modes of discourse.

The most recent work in the United States, responding to the internal dynamics of European Marxism rather than the fossilized Soviet version, involves studies of "Public Culture." There has been a somewhat precipitous announcement of a "new new" political history based upon the study of crowds, parades, and public celebrations extending the concept of the political more deeply into the society and focusing upon the marginalized.[11]

These recent trends, however, do not take into account a generation of scholarship and the primary set of conceptual and methodological tools that both journalists and political scientists continue to use and hone to an increasingly sophisticated edge. Thus, returning to the basis of the "new" political historians in social science allows us to examine the current dispute over realignment and its meanings and the alternatives. Some scholars have emphasized the need to place greater emphasis on policy— the ways in which successful policy is made and the relationship between popular behavior and policy outputs.[12] This had been an interest of the Progressive historians and of their critics, whose simple economic determinism reflected in Sogrin's essay served to explain such policy initiatives as the Hamiltonian program. Others such as Lee Benson and Joel Silbey would replace the "party systems" model, which is primarily structural, with one based on the idea of "political eras," which integrates political culture more fully.

In terms of her concept of party, methodological commitments, and feel for the subject, Vlasova participates in the discourse of the "new" political historians. It is delightfully ironic that Vlasova, for obvious political reasons, defends her modest embrace of the quantitative methods of American social science with the assurance that these can be derived from V. I. Lenin himself—I have to admit loving her brief argument, which is totally at odds with criticism of some American Marxists who insist that social science and quantification are inherently reactionary.

But Lenin aside, Vlasova approaches the question of party analysis in a way that better reflects the "new" political historians' work than does Sogrin. She sees parties functioning in the different branches of government and uniting the electorate and the elite—that is, she considers them instrumentally or pragmatically. Vlasova is

---

10. M. J. Heale, *The Making of American Politics* (London, 1977) may serve as an example of the quality of not only Heale, but also English Americanists generally.

11. David Waldstreicher, *In the Midst of Perpetual Fetes* (Chapel Hill, N.C., 1997); and Simon P. Newman, *Parades and Politics of the Street: Festive Culture in the Early American Republic* (Philadelphia, Pa., 1997).

12. Richard L. McCormick, *The Party Period and Public Policy* (New York, 1986).

also aware of the federated nature of American parties, which when well developed penetrate down into the system to effect state and local politics. Many of the "new" political historians—the most obvious being Lee Benson, whose book *The Concept of Jacksonian Democracy* is certainly one of the most important studies of American political history written since World War II—did study partisan behavior in a single state.

Finally, Vlasova makes generally fruitful use of quantitative methods that were associated with the "new" political historians of the 1960s and 1970s from the start. (She even cites the work of a very young Mary Ryan and John Hoadley, whose findings would have been useful to Sogrin as well.) In the United States, all too often critics dismissed the "new" political historians as simply "quantifiers," and there are some signs of mindless quantification in Vlasova's essay. But the main problem is that her essay attempts to prove some of the things that Richard P. McCormick had impressed upon American historians in the 1950s and early 1960s. In a slightly different way (but using the same data) Vlasova repeats McCormick's tongue-in-cheek hypothesis of "Harrisonian Democracy" without using the same terminology or even being aware of it.

Vlasova should be praised for seeing that parties as coherent institutional structures have a short shelf-life; the Whigs with whom she deals did disappear within a decade of her story and the "Democrats" of the 1830s—not Sogrin's prepubescent "Democrats" of 1789—were only in a very limited way the "Democrats" who chose the role of defenders of "the white South" in the 1870s. She takes a cool behavioral perspective, although she does not fully spell out her model and does not go far enough with it. Vlasova attempts to chart the shift from local to national organization. And she does show party in the legislature—in this case, oddly, the Senate—by examining the very sort of behavior that Sogrin might also have found useful. In order to enter the current debate, however, she has to be more attuned to the changing relationship between levels of the system.

One must look at the electoral aspect of party development, and Vlasova's methods reflect all the strength and weakness of those of McCormick. Essentially, they both focus upon presidential returns and are limited to a relatively small number of elections.[13] Vlasova can be congratulated that she took this beyond what McCormick examined in his 1960 article, presenting an analysis of voting blocs in the Senate. But somewhat oddly, she carries neither exercise forward in a systematic fashion over an adequate time period. (Why she chose to use a single-week special session *before* the Panic of 1837 actually began rather than the special session Van Buren called to deal with the problems is something of a mystery.) The data are available and were available to her and it is quite clear from the studies of legislative roll-call behavior that were done somewhat earlier, particularly those by Thomas P. Alexander and Joel Silbey, that she is turning well-spaded turf. I had surveyed most of what had been

13. There are many data problems, but the current First Democracy Project headed up by Andrew Robertson and Philip J. Lampi intends to make available for students of the earlier period, 1789 to 1836, the same sort of electoral material that W. Dean Burnham collected and which is now available from the InterUniversity Consortium for Political and Social Research.

done on presidential elections and congressional behavior in a chapter of a book that appeared in 1981.[14]

Nonetheless, Vlasova adds to our understanding by her study of the Senate in the 1830s. She is quite right in arguing that this was the arena in which the major figures of the day strutted on the stage. Sogrin's paper could have been greatly improved by Vlasova's sense of process and the application of Vlasova's approach to congressional voting. Both authors, however, should have shown more awareness of the relationship between the layers of the political system. Vlasova does allude to this problem, but she seems to assume that organization proceeded at the same pace on all levels. The existence and strength of these links are a measure of the development of the national parties. Clearly, the first party system was characterized by far less correlation between behavior at the federal and state levels than the second party system.[15]

Most surprising is that both Russian scholars comment on the economic basis of the parties and connect them to certain economic groups, but neither explicitly does an analysis of voting behavior or its socioeconomic roots—one of the hallmarks of the "new" political historians in the United States. Admittedly, this would be hard for Sogrin, given the nature of presidential elections in the 1790s, but it is certainly something that generations of American historians have tried to examine. Just who supported which party requires much more analysis than either of these historians attempt.

Sogrin sometimes sounds like a Progressive in his economic determinism, although he also tries, like Hofstadter and other Consensus historians, to make distinctions within the bourgeois supporters of the parties. Yet he really never analyzes this. Similarly, while Vlasova indicates that she intends to test the hypothesis that the "emergence of the Democratic and Whig parties between the 1820s and 1830s was mainly related to important changes in the American sociopolitical system" such as westward expansion, the Industrial Revolution, and the rise of the plantation system, she fails to show how these economic changes were related to party development. Both of these Marxists are unable to relate changes in the substructure to changes in the suprastructure. They affirm the basic elements of Consensus history.

Vlasova has nothing to say about the way in which economic development has determined the changes in political culture that permitted an embrace, however limited, of partisanship in the mature phase of the second party system. While she briefly deals with the turnout, which was the primary focus of McCormick's work (although Vlasova uses Burnham's figures), she is interested in neither the social analysis of voting behavior, nor legislative behavior or any kind of conflict over policy, that might reflect partisan persuasion. All of these are matters that have occupied American historians.

---

14. "Political Pluralism and Party Development: The Creation of a Modern Party System, 1815–1852," Kleppner et al., *The Evolution of American Electoral Systems*, 77–111.

15. See Ronald P. Formisano, *The Transformation of Political Culture* (New York, 1982); Formisano, *The Birth of Mass Political Parties* (Princeton, N.J., 1971); and William G. Shade, *Democratizing the Old Dominion: Virginia and the Second Party System, 1824–1861* (Charlottesville, Va., 1997).

In sum, it appears that Vlasova reflects a sophistication of those doing American studies in Russia that equals that of the Europeans, who have contributed an invaluable outside perspective. Sogrin, whose work presents reasonable arguments shared by many Americans, illustrates that European Americanists can be seduced by the romance of their subject.

Response

by Vladimir V. Sogrin

Comments by Professor Shade come across as typical of the American national-messianic approach to foreign scholars and foreign culture. From this point of view, everything accomplished outside of the United States is a priori inferior to American products. And everything should be leveled to an American standard that corresponds with the taste of one particular American commentator, Professor Shade in this case. Blinded by his own messianic ideology, Professor Shade manages to ignore the obvious themes of my article, and yet ascribes to it something that I did not talk about at all. For instance, he states that I am avoiding the subject of Republicanism in discussions in the 1790s wherever I interpret this theme in the article as a major reason of disagreement between Federalists and Republicans. Should the truth be spoken, my interpretation does not go along with Shade's blueprint.

Other comments by Professor Shade are naive and remind me of attitudes often assumed by first-year college students. He would like to see me cover the entire political history of the United States in one short article. Since I have not done that, he accuses me of downplaying the impact of political culture and economic factors and of further "ignorance." His inspirations for scientism go hand in hand with "presentism" and antihistoricism. This is most clearly manifested in his evaluation of Thomas Jefferson. According to his logic, the fact that I consider Jefferson a Democrat stems from my inability to admit that Jefferson belonged to the class of slave-owners. Elaborating on this logic, we should then demolish all Jefferson and Washington monuments in America. Thus American scientism reverses into barbarism.

Response

by M. A. Vlasova

If many years ago I had the most feeble idea that William G. Shade one day would comment on my article, I would definitely have changed the topic or at least prepare more comprehensive footnotes to the text. Professor Shade, whose early works stimulated my interest in the study of voting behavior, had to deal with the text that was written for Russian readers of the late 1980s.[1] What makes the situation even worse is that my article had a very modest and pragmatic message—to show my colleagues, majoring in American history, the possibility (despite limited access to primary sources) of using methods of historical research which were at that time widespread among American historians and also among our specialists in Russian history. Unfortunately, Professor Shade for some reason didn't pay proper attention to the goal of my article, how it was "narrowly defined" in the text. This is, in my mind, the main source of his criticism and the impression of unsatisfied expectations one can easily trace in the comment.

What is true is that this commentator and most of his American colleagues know almost nothing about Russian studies of American political parties. The publication of this volume of *Dialogues* might help to fill the gap. So it is not strange that he tries to operate with familiar terms: because I'm using some quantitative methods, my work should be analyzed in the context of "new political history," its relationships with American Marxists and neo-Progressives. The desire to operate with convenient definitions is understandable, but ineffective when you face something new. This inefficiency is especially obvious when Professor Shade writes about my own and Vladimir Sogrin's silence, superficiality, and "incredible" naïveté on the point of "ideological subtleties" and "basics of American economic history." It is needless to remind that these very important questions were beyond the themes of both articles. What is more, the preoccupation with ideological conflicts and economic and social aspects of party development was widespread in Soviet studies of the United States almost from the very emergence of this field.[2]

---

1. The first work of W. G Shade I read was the article "Consensus or Conflict? Political Behavior in State Legislatures during the Jacksonian Era," which he and Herbert Ershkowitz published in the *Journal of American History* in 1971, vol. 58 (December).

2. There are some English-language texts on the Russian historiography of American History. The best are still in Russian. See N. N. Bolkhovotinov, "SShA: Problemy istorii i sovremennaya istoriorgaphia" [USA: Historical Problems and Contemporary Historiography] (Moscow, 1980), 339–79.

My own interest in those dimensions of political parties that were connected with their electoral and legislative activities was to some extent connected with an attempt to step beyond dogmatic, exclusively "class" or "ideological" interpretations of the "bourgeois" political parties, which were often treated in Soviet works as merely instruments of class dominance.

This attempt to escape dogmatism was in my instance associated with application of "new," interdisciplinary methods of analysis to the traditional field of an ideologically biased topic, the history of American political parties. It reveals the logic that differs radically from what happened in American historiography: as Professor Shade points out, "in the interpretation of American Marxists social science and quantification are inherently reactionary." It is not strange that such terms in Shade's comments as "reactionary" or "political reasons" might have quite different meanings in the American and Russian contexts. At the time of "perestroika" (or Gorbachev's era) when my article was published, all the political definitions had strange, unusual meanings: the anti-Marxists and economic liberals were on the radical left side of the political spectrum, while Marxists and Communists were labeled as "right" and "conservatives." In Shade's understanding the citation from V. Lenin's work could be justified only by "political reasons." Meanwhile, Lenin was famous not only for leading the proletariat revolution but also for statistical research. In mentioning Lenin, I tried to show that quantitative analysis of legislative votes had a long history in Russia and was used even by a highly politicized author. It was a real surprise for me to read about "scaling" of roll-calls in Lenin's works. In one of the American periodicals I met another example of what might happen with a "political" term: the author wrote about "a unique Marxist tradition forged in American studies . . . a synthesis derived from three distinct schools of Marxism: the school of Karl Marx, Leo Marx, and Groucho Marx."[3] I'm sure the Marxism mentioned by Professor Shade is of the more traditional or academic sort.

The main lesson that one may derive from the comments of Professor Shade is that to establish an effective dialogue between American and Russian historians we must try to step beyond our national contexts and try to learn more about each other. I'm glad to stress that former Soviet historians are in this respect a bit better equipped than Professor Shade and some of his colleagues: our ability to read in English lets us not only "to return well-spaded turf" but to learn about the works of American historians of political parties.[4]

3. Elaine Tyler May, "The Radical Roots of American Studies: Presidential Address to the American Studies Association, November 9, 1995," *American Quarterly* 48 (June 1996): 181.

4. *Annual of American Studies* for 1996 published a review on American historiography of the Whig party by G. Dubovitskii. This is only one, the closest to the topic of my article, example of the rather vast literature on this theme: *Amerikanskii ezhegodnik, 1995* [Annual of American Studies] (Moscow, 1996), 162–81.

4

Parties and Political Debates in the Secession Crisis (1860–1861)

by S. A. Porshakov

American capitalism's entry into the final stage of the Industrial Revolution led to a severe intensification of the conflict between two systems—free labor and slavery. It also brought the contradictions in the ruling bourgeois-planter bloc to a head. The two-party system, consisting of the Democrats and the Whigs, which directed all of the elements of its political mechanism toward the task of strengthening the alliance of the bourgeoisie from the North and the planters from the South through mutual compromises, proved to be incapable of constructively solving the complex of problems standing before the country. The system became a hindrance to the development of capitalist relations within the United States. In addition, in the 1850s the political system endured a crushing ideological blow as its organizational structure disintegrated. The Whig party disappeared from the country's political arena. The National Democratic Convention in 1860 culminated in a deep ideological-political crisis in the party and a schism within its ranks between the Northern-conservative wing and the Southerners, supporters of the uninhibited expansion of slavery. The whole political system in the United States was knocked off-balance. The slavery issue affected practically all branches of government—the executive, legislative, and judicial.

With the shake-up of the old two-party combination, the political forces of slavery's supporters and the opponents of slavery expansion, earlier constrained by the system, became more prominent. The clash and open struggle between them in all spheres of public life characterized the main ingredient of the political process during the second half of the 1850s. The Republican party, formed in 1854, became the focal point of all antislavery forces. Having emphasized the problem of territorial limits on the institution of slavery, the Republicans proposed a whole complex of reforms, meant to transform substantially the socioeconomic structure that had taken shape in the country. In the long run the agenda of the Republican leadership was directed at preventing slavery's expansion and clearing the way for rapid and unhindered consolidation of capitalist relations within the United States.

The key question of the 1860 presidential election revolving around political power within the federal Union was decided in favor of the industrial bourgeoisie from the Northern states, who relied upon the support of broad segments of the population in their struggle against slavery. Republican party candidate Abraham Lincoln became the head of the executive branch. With his inauguration the principle of territorial limitations on slavery was elevated to the level of official government policy. The assumption of power by the Republican administration marked the overthrow of the slaveocracy's political domination in the Union through peaceful constitutional means. The extremist circles of planters, understanding clearly that a decisive blow had been dealt to their political prowess in the country, entreated the population of the Southern states to secede from the federation and form an independent slave state and government. "The most reactionary class usually resorts first to violence and civil war, making bayonets the order of the day," pointed out Vladimir Lenin.[1]

From the very first days after Lincoln's election as president of the country, "fire-eaters"—representatives of the extremist movement in the Southern wing of the Democratic party—had united around the inveterate separatists. Men such as Edmund Ruffin (Virginia), former Senator Robert Rhett (South Carolina), William Yancey (Alabama), and former Governor John Quitman (Mississippi) held the initiative firmly in their hands. Established planters who produced cotton for export and also midlevel slave-owners with an insatiable appetite for obtaining and assimilating additional property (which meant for them the opportunity to strengthen their economic position and move up in their society) provided the primary fodder for this political extremism. The most zealous defenders of slavery strove to establish complete political hegemony for the slave-owners in the federal Union and supported the most extreme methods in the struggle up until secession. In all truth, their expansion knew no bounds: they would extend slavery not only in the western lands of the United States, but also in the territory of a series of some Central American countries.

Supporters of a break with the government attempted to convince Southerners that only by means of secession could the institutions of slave society be protected from the threat of aggression from the monolithic front of free states. Their political line was built upon the basis of the doctrine of states' rights. In accordance with the Constitution, thought the separatists, the Union was established as a voluntary union of the states, which carried on their shoulders all the burdens of the American Revolutionary War and reserved for themselves the right to terminate the bonds holding the Union together at any time after reflection. "I have not a shadow of a doubt that leaving the ranks of the United States is a sacred right and duty," asserted the former congressman and Secretary of the Treasury Howell Cobb. His remarks to the residents of Georgia on December 6, 1860, would become an example of the extremists' political rhetoric: "Prepare to declare and preserve your independence from the Union in as much as you will never obtain within it equality and justice."[2] Using the Declaration of Independence, the separatists asserted that as long as the people remain the main source of political power in the country, the people have the irrevocable right to change the form of government if it ceases to act in accordance to

1. V. I. Lenin, *The Complete Collected Works* [Polnoe sobranie sochinenii], vol. 11, 123. This essay by S. A. Porshakov was originally published in *Problemy amerikanistiki* [U.S. Studies] 3 (1985): 53–75.
2. "The Correspondence of R. Toombs, A. Stephens and H. Cobb," in *Annual Report of the American Historical Association for the Year 1911* (continued in Annual Report . . . 1911) (Washington, 1913), vol. 2, 516.

the goals for which it was established, and this is what supposedly had occurred with respect to the slave states. Secession, the epilogue for the extremists, was crowned by decades-long struggle by the "fire-eaters" for the political independence of the South. The election of a Republican as president of the United States, they considered, was none other than a fortuitous pretext for dividing the Union. In the separatist camp there was not, however, unanimity on the question of how to secede; one faction supported the idea of individual respective states declaring their independence while another agreed to breaking up the federation only with a joint action by a significant majority of slave states.

In the border states of the South, the bastion of conservative forces in the country, the situation at first unfolded in favor of the moderate supporters of secession. They were prepared to refrain from leaving the United States until the last attempt for resolving the conflict on a constitutional basis by means of a new compromise by the sides was exhausted. They felt that the simple fact of the Republican candidate's election as head of the executive branch in and of itself did not present a threat to the institution of slavery, and as long as the ruling party planned on supporting the existing status quo on the question of slavery, they were prepared to remain faithful to the federal government. Moderates drew up plans counting on the support of conservative forces from the Northern states, which provided for guarantees of the rights and privileges of the planters. They pushed for holding a forum of slave-owners that would identify the conditions under which the Southern states would remain in the Union. Foremost, these demands would have provided for strict guarantees by the administration to safeguard slavery in the U.S. territories, for the rigorous enforcement of the fugitive slave act, and for noninterference in the process of the slave trade among states. In the event of a rejection of the ultimatum, the moderate supporters of slavery were prepared to resort to secession. In addition, in many respects they purposely played up to the extremists in the hope of frightening the Northerners with the prospect of splitting the federation and thus forcing them to compromise. In their opinion, prematurely resorting to a double-edged weapon such as secession could deny the slave-owners the support of a significant number of conservatives in the free states and force them to resort to measures of compulsion for putting down the rebellion and preserving the unity of the country. The poor whites in the South, a milieu in which the idea of creating a separate government at first did not meet with a particular flood of enthusiasm, presented a potential threat to the planters. While taking this into account, moderate circles of slave-owners tried not to inflame hysteria in the Southern states to the extreme.

A less influential force in the South at the height of the dispute over secession was the group of Unionists, supporters for preserving the Union at any cost and under any circumstances. They viewed secession as a scandalous infraction of all constitutional norms, but they showed visible inconsistencies in thinking that the federal government did not have the authority to retain states in the federation by means of force. The Unionists made a real impact on the political process only in the border states of the South.

The areas of the Deep South and the Southwest became the epicenter of the movement for secession. It is significant that the first wave of political extremism swept over seven slave states of this region, where from the middle of the 1850s the Democratic party enjoyed an absolute hegemony and where the framework of the two-party system was upset. This in turn created favorable conditions for the growth of radicalism among the planters. One feature of the social structure of these states was that a sizable part of the white population was directly connected with slavery and completely dependent upon it materially.

The initiation of secession arose from the efforts of the planters from South Carolina, who twice before, during the political crises of 1832 and 1849–1850, had attempted to assume control of the movement of the most fierce advocates of slavery. But both times they did not receive the necessary support from the majority in the remaining Southern states and were thus forced to back down. In his address on November 5, 1860, to a gathering of the state legislature, Governor William Gist sounded a call to action in which he proposed convening a state convention to determine a policy if the Republican candidate should win the U.S. presidential election. The election of the delegates brought an impressive victory to the separatists, and as a result, the character of the upcoming forum was determined. The convention in South Carolina took place from December 17–26, 1860, initially in Columbia and later in Charleston. It culminated in the unanimous adoption on December 20 of an ordinance on separating from the Union.[3]

The Unionists in Mississippi retreated with practically no serious fight. On November 26, 1860, a special session of the state legislature approved a bill calling for a convention to decide the question of relations with the federal government. The assemblage began work in Jackson on January 7, 1861, after supporters for the immediate withdrawal from the Union received a solid majority of votes during the election of delegates. The extremist majority at the convention rejected a proposal to resolve the differences between slave and free states, and also a bill on enacting an ordinance on the separation of Mississippi only in the event that the majority of states from the Deep South withdrew from the Union. In the final tally, the bill on terminating the state's relationship with the federal government was passed 84 votes to 15, and it was officially signed on January 15, 1861.[4]

The situation was different in states where moderate supporters of the expansion of slavery continued to hold real political power and influence. There was an exceptionally tense debate around the question of secession in Alabama, where the election of delegates to the convention gave the separatists a rather precarious majority. The debate during the first days of the convention, which opened on January 7, 1861, turned into alternating successes for all sides. Under pressure from the Unionists a resolution was shelved that denied the federal government authority to compel by force any of the seceding states to rejoin the Union. The extremists hoped to use this resolution to set the tone for all subsequent discussion at the convention. In their own right, the separatists succeeded in taking revenge and blocking a proposal to allow the residents of the state to ratify the bill on secession. Yancey's ordinance on secession, presented on January 10, caused some heated discussion. In response

3. *New York Herald,* December 25, 1860.
4. *New York Daily Tribune,* January 18, 24, 1861.

to it, the Unionists proposed a "minority report" containing the idea of holding a conference of slave-owners in order to find some basis for a possible compromise and thus eliminate conflict. Representatives of the moderate movement set as conditions for remaining in the Union the strict enforcement of the 1850 law on capture of fugitive slaves and preserving slavery by the federal government in the territory of the United States and also in the District of Columbia. The majority of delegates rejected the Unionist plan and came out in favor of secession.[5]

Under the direct influence of the secession of South Carolina, Mississippi, and Alabama, the state of Florida announced its withdrawal from the federal Union. At the convention in Tallahassee, which began on January 3, 1861, the opposition was easily overcome, and on January 10 an ordinance on secession was ratified.[6]

In Georgia the extremist movement embarked on an energetic campaign against the moderate wing of the Democratic organization, which was headed by former Governor Herschel Johnson and Congressman Alexander Stephens. The moderates had called for a conference of representatives from the South in order to work out a list of demands to secure additional guarantees for the institution of slavery. If upheld, then the federal government could count on the slave states remaining in the Union. The most authoritative figures among the secession supporters were Senator Robert Toombs and Howell Cobb, who had in December 1860 retired from the post of Secretary of the Treasury. They managed to gain control of the convention, which took place from January 16 to January 29, 1861. Attempts to circumvent secession did not meet with success, and on January 19 delegates voted for withdrawing Georgia from the federation.[7] "Results of the convention have shattered my hopes once and for all that Georgia will preserve its place in the Union," wrote Stephens with deep regret. "I consider secession an unwise step, and I did everything in my power to avoid it. But this movement is already out of control, even by those who are its initiators."[8] In the beginning of January 1861 Governor Joe Brown ordered the state militia to seize federal Fort Pulaski.

Among the states of the Deep South, Louisiana was tied to the economy of the North by the most substantial commercial ties. Federal tariffs reliably protected sugar production in the state from foreign competitors. In its politics, Louisiana was visibly influenced by the conservatively inclined well-to-do planters, who gained much from an alliance with the Northern bourgeoisie. The elections of the delegates to the state convention of slave-owners brought a difficult victory to the separatists. This heralded a bitter struggle. At the convention, which opened in Baton Rouge on January 23, 1861, supporters for preserving the Union attempted to block the adoption of a bill for secession, figuring that the U.S. Congress would soon manage to work out a compromise plan. The proposal to hold a consultative Congress with participation by delegates from Southern states over the issue of secession on a referendum did not receive sufficient support. On January 25 the ordinance on secession went into force.[9]

5. Ibid., January 24, 1861.
6. *New York Herald,* January 15, 1861.
7. *The Confederate Record of the State of Georgia* (New York, 1972), vol. 1, 314.
8. *Annual Report . . . 1911,* vol. 2, 527.
9. *New York Herald,* January 30, April 4, 1861.

Secession by Texas from the federal Union was accompanied by heated controversy. The governor of the state, Sam Houston, a former "Jackson" Democrat who was a very popular personality among the voters, decisively condemned secession and planned on announcing elections for delegates to a state convention. At the end of November 1860 he appealed to the governors of the Southern states with a proposal to hold a conference to find "the means to restore good relations between residents of the two regions."[10] In this context the separatists launched a démarche, publishing an appeal in which they called for the population of the state to participate in elections. Houston answered by calling a special session of the legislative assembly of the state and firmly recommending that its deputies turn down the idea of a convention. "In this terrible time we can only hope for the preservation of the Union and the adherence to the principles of the Constitution," he wrote in an address to the members of the legislature. "Having preserved the Union, we can count on everything, and if it turns out different then the result will be anarchy in its most destructive form."[11] Despite the governor's wishes the lawmakers of the state supported the idea of a convention. On January 30, 1861, delegates who had gathered in Austin approved an ordinance which was then ratified in a referendum on February 23 by 44,317 votes to 13,020. On March 5 Texas officially joined the rebel Confederacy. Governor Houston refused to take an oath to the new government and was removed from office.[12]

In the border states of the South during the course of January to March 1861, the conservative forces for a time managed to withstand the separatists' pressure. This region was deeply drawn into the central structure of the economic-trade relations in the country, where many influential agriculturalists and representatives of commercial circles who had supported close business contacts with the bourgeoisie of the Northern states maintained political and ideological loyalty to the Union and demanded curtailment of the extremist movements. In Virginia, Arkansas, North Carolina, and Missouri elections of delegates to state conventions culminated in convincing victories for the moderate supporters of slavery, who had managed to neutralize the attempts by the extremists to introduce secession ordinances. In Kentucky a proposal to hold a forum of planters was voted down in the beginning of February 1861 by the legislative assembly. A similar decision was adopted by

10. *The Writings of S. Houston,* 8 vols. (Austin, Texas, 1939–1943), vol. 8, 198.

11. Ibid., 119.

12. *New York Daily Tribune,* March 7, 19, 1861. According to American researchers, in the states of the Deep South and Southwest, residents of counties located in productive cotton-producing regions supported secession as a rule, with a high enough percentage owning slaves (more than 50 percent) in the general population traditionally leaning toward the Democratic party and supporting the Southern Democratic candidate, John Breckinridge, in the 1860 presidential election. The Unionists found support mainly in those counties where the land was less suited for plantations and slavery did not play a decisive role in the economic life, the number of slaves was relatively small, and there was a large percentage of farmers, tradesmen, representatives of free professions, and a poor white population, which in 1850 leaned toward the political principles of the conservative party of Whigs and the "Know Nothings" and were sympathetic during the course of the 1860 election to the candidate from the Constitutional-Unionist party, John Bell, and to the candidate of the Northern wing of the organization of Democrats, Stephen Douglas (R. Wooster, *The Secession Conventions of the South* [Westport, Conn., 1962], 257–66).

the population of Tennessee as a result of a referendum on February 8, 1861. The governor of Maryland, Thomas Hicks, considered that remaining faithful to the federal government was not up for discussion. Until the beginning of April 1861 he did not embark on any steps to convene a special session of the legislature. The lower house of the legislative assembly of Delaware in the middle of February 1861 rejected a plan to secede and expressed their adherence to the federation of states. "The residents of Delaware consider preservation of the U.S. the primary political problem," it was noted in the resolution approved by the deputies to the state legislature, "and they express their firm confidence in the fact that Delaware . . . under no circumstances will leave the Union."[13]

On February 4 representatives from the secessionist states gathered at a convention in the city of Montgomery, Alabama, proclaiming the creation of the Confederate States of America. They adopted a constitution and elected Senator Jefferson Davis (Mississippi) as president of the Confederacy, and Alexander Stephens (Georgia) as vice president.

The administration of President James Buchanan looked extremely helpless during these months. In December 1860, members of his cabinet who represented Southern states announced their resignations. Under the influence of secession the personal political philosophy of the president, based on conservative principles, went to pieces. In his annual address to Congress on December 3, 1860, he condemned the movement in the South for secession from the Union as being devoid of legal basis, and noted that it "is completely incompatible with the character of the federal Constitution." Along with this Buchanan pointed out that the head of the executive branch was not endowed with the power of force to hold individual states in the federation, which in essence sanctioned its schism: "After serious thought I have come to the conclusion that neither Congress nor organs of the federal government have the power to compel states to remain in the Union through force. The truth is that our Union . . . is impossible to build upon the blood of its citizens, spilled on the fields of a civil war."[14] He also expressed great sympathy to the South.

The withdrawal from the Union by the states of the Deep South and Southwest caught many leaders of the Republican party by surprise. They had not correctly evaluated the nature of separatism among the planters and were convinced of the possibility of solving the conflict by means of compromise. At first they perceived secession as another trick by the Southerners meant to frighten the residents of the Northern states with the prospect of splitting the United States in order to gain additional guarantees and concessions.[15] But to the extent that the floodgates of secession opened all the new slave states to a deluge, illusions about a quick resolution

13. Cited from *A Report of the Debates and Proceedings in the Secret Sessions of the Conference Convention for Proposing Amendments to the Constitution of the United States.* Held at Washington, D.C., in February 1861. L. Chittenden (New York, 1864), 459.

14. *A Compilation of the Messages and Papers of the Presidents, 1789–1897* (Washington, 1897), vol. 5, 626.

15. *The Diary of Edward Bates, 1859–1866,* in *Annual Report of the American Historical Association for the Year 1930* (Washington, 1933), vol. 4, 157.

of the crisis were shattered and replaced by sober reflections and a search for means of stabilizing the political situation in the country.

During the 1860–1861 political crisis, disagreements in the Republican camp stood out more prominently on fundamental problems of party policy. Moderate and radical opponents of expansion of slavery on the one hand and conservative elements on the other stood in opposition. Directly impacted by the events at the end of 1860 and the beginning of 1861, the moderate opponents of expansion of slavery—Senators Lyman Trumbull (Illinois) and Thomas Fessenden (Maine), Congressman Israel Washburn (Maine), *New York Daily Tribune* publisher Horace Greeley—showed quite a bit of vacillation. Not expecting such a serious turn of events, these prominent Republicans had concluded that the conflict between the free and slave states had gone far enough, and in the name of preserving the Union they would not oppose making several concessions to the planters. They departed somewhat from the traditional party line and acknowledged the rights of the Southerners to demand the return of fugitive slaves and to carry on slave trade between states. Leaders of this moderate group tried to convince the planters that they did not intend to impose upon the South their will and principles by force and interfere in questions of slavery in the states where it had long existed. In addition, they maintained faith in the cardinal position of the party, on limiting slavery within the boundaries of the old territory and not allowing it in the land of the American West. It was on this question that they came out as a united front with the radical movement.

In all forms of proposals, directed at curtailing the intersectional conflict, there was not a lack of extremes. Greeley, quite influential in the Republican party leadership, allowed for the possibility of the Southern states separating from the Union, thinking that the bitter conflict in the country over the question of slavery had already torn apart the foundation of governmental authority, and that such an act would become the solution to all problems. "It is difficult to live in a republic where one part is pinning down the other with a bayonet," he wrote in December 1860. "If the slave states become convinced that it is better for them to be outside the Union, then we will insist that they be allowed to leave in peace. . . . If we justify the separation of three million colonists from the British empire in 1776, why shouldn't we understand the secession of five million Southerners in 1861."[16] As a necessary condition for peaceful secession, however, Greeley insisted upon the payment by the planters of all debts to their Northern creditors.

Several representatives of the radical wing in the Republican party wavered in the face of the United States falling apart and the imminent threat of civil war. For the sake of pacifying the rebels the governor of Ohio, Salmon Chase, proposed that the authorities in the free states should pay monetary compensation for fugitive slaves to their owners.[17] Congressman Charles Adams (Massachusetts) did not object in principle to the incorporation of the territory of New Mexico into the Union as

16. *New York Daily Tribune,* December 15, 1860.
17. "The Diary and Correspondence of Salmon Chase," in *Annual Report of the American Historical Association for the Year 1902* (Washington, 1903), vol. 2, 293.

a slave state.[18] But the basic cell of the radical Republicans, headed by Senators Charles Sumner and James Wilson (both from Massachusetts), and Congressmen Joshua Giddings (Ohio) and Thaddeus Stevens (Pennsylvania), maintained their self-control in this exceptionally complex situation and met secession fully armed. The radicals subsequently argued for territorial limits on slavery and decisively rejected any compromise with the Southerners on this question so important for the fate of the country. The complex of measures directed against slavery proposed by them also included annulling the 1850 law on return of fugitive slaves, the prohibition of slave trade among states, and rescinding slavery in the federal District of Columbia. The Republicans from the radical group sharply denounced the initiators of secession for their disregard of the fate of the Union. They determined to achieve restoration of its foundation while this was possible through peaceful means, but in the event of extreme necessity supported using military measures. "Well the crisis is upon us, and it depends upon the attitude of the Republicans to make its result final and decisive," wrote Carl Schurz (Missouri). "If the North now remains firm, the slave-power is done for. Prudence seems to dictate . . . [we] meet treason when and where it is committed, and put it down by all the means which manifest destiny has put into our hands. I deem it of the highest importance that the Republicans should drop their defensive attitude and resume the aggressive with resolution and vigor."[19]

Dressing themselves in the garb of defenders of the Union, representatives of the conservative movement in the Republican party, Congressmen Thomas Corwin (Ohio) and Simon Cameron (Pennsylvania), and the influential political activist from Missouri, Edward Bates, insisted upon the necessity of concluding a new compromise with the slave-owners, and accused the Republican leadership of showing dogmatism and of blindly following the party platform. Consigning to oblivion the cardinal principles of the party, they hatched plans to split the western territories into free and slave areas, agreeing to the incorporation of additional slave states into the United States. They also expressed a readiness to achieve a recision of the laws on granting freedom to fugitive slaves, which were passed in the legislatures of the majority of the Northern states. The leaders of the Republican party "at the present time agree to such conditions of compromise with the South, which just a month ago any Republican would have considered insulting to the dignity of the most slavish of duplicitous politicians in the Northern states," stated a conservative newspaper of the Democratic party, the *New York Herald.*[20]

The shocks of 1860–1861 fundamentally altered the political worldview of one of the acknowledged authorities among Republicans, Senator William H. Seward (New York), who decisively rejected the radical rhetoric characteristic of his speeches during the time the party was establishing its foundations. He now chose a course that brought him closer to the conservative wing. "At this period of time, during the winter session of Congress, Seward became the center of all attempts for compromise," pointed out

18. *Congressional Globe,* 36th Cong., 2d sess., appendix, 125–26.
19. *Speeches, Correspondence and Political Papers of Carl Schurz* (New York, 1969), vol. 1, 165, 175.
20. *New York Herald,* December 4, 1860.

Karl Marx, "Northern advocates of the South . . . unexpectedly began to exalt him as the government figure who personified reconciliation."[21] Seward's speech in the upper house of Congress on January 12, 1861, became the party line of conservative Republicans. For the sake of saving the Union, the senator expressed the intent to carry out the enforcement of the law on the return of fugitive slaves and to reject the idea of prohibiting slave trade in the western territories. In hypothetical terms Seward even permitted that "the federation can be broken, but not by means of secession, with or without resorting to arms, but rather as a result of the voluntary expression of the will of the people of the U.S. in conjunction with the American Constitution." He was far from the thought of using armed force for suppressing the rebellion. "I cannot imagine what will come of the Union if it will be preserved by means of the sword," stated the senator.[22]

Unabashed gestures by the conservatives toward the Southerners proved to be a dispiriting influence on the rank and file supporters of the party. The atmosphere in the Republican camp became heated to the extreme. The elected president of the United States, Lincoln, clearly realized the destructive consequences that a departure from the original principle of territorial limits on the system of slavery would have for the political future of the country and the Republican party itself. He hastened to intervene in intraparty discussions and to define clearly the prospects for the policies of the new administration on the question of slavery. "Prevent, as far as possible, any of our friends from demoralizing themselves and our cause, by entertaining propositions for compromise of any sort on slavery's extension," wrote Lincoln in a letter to Congressman Elihu Washburne on December 13, 1860. "There is no possible compromise upon it, but which puts us under again and leaves all our work to do over again."[23] The steadfastness and decisiveness shown by Lincoln to attain his set goals in the long run helped many Republicans who were vacillating to overcome their short-term weakness and once again join the ranks of the opponents of slavery's expansion.

An important characteristic of the political process during the heated secession debates was a significant growth of conservative forces in free states not only among Republicans, but also among Northern Democrats and Constitutional Unionists. Notwithstanding the significant differences in the social and political doctrines held by these groups, they were united by the drive to quickly overcome the crisis in the country by means of concluding a compromise between the free North and the plantation South. The existing structure of commercial ties between the Northern states and the slave South served as the economic basis of conservatism. As far as social issues the conservatives represented first of all the interests of the trade and financial circles of the Northeast, which supported mutually beneficial business contacts with the planters and provided the latter with solid monetary subsidies along with investing capital in the slave states' economies.

21. K. Marx and F. Engels, *Essays* [Sochineniia], vol. 15, 391.
22. *Congressional Globe,* 36th Cong., 2d sess., 341, 343.
23. *The Collected Works of Abraham Lincoln,* Roy Basler, ed. (New Brunswick, N.J., 1953), vol. 4, 151.

Under the conditions of a worsening political crisis in the country, the prestige of the Northern conservative wing of the Democratic party fell catastrophically. They had launched desperate attempts to persuade the Southerners to reach some sort of agreement. The legal recognition of slavery in the Southern states was the source of the Northern Democrats' political philosophy. Conservatives publicly declared the planters' rights to colonize the new western lands, and insisted on strict guarantees for the Southerners' property. They also condemned in the harshest terms the attacks on the institution of slavery.

The Democratic conservatives tried their best to whitewash the slave-owners on the one hand, and on the other to show the political principles of the Republican party in a poor light. The roots of secession lay, according to them, only in the unwise policy of the Republicans, who pushed the Union to the brink of catastrophe and in the long run forced the Southerners to unravel its ties. Along with this they felt that the simple fact that a Republican candidate won the presidential election should not serve as a sufficient weighty justification for splitting up the federation, and they condemned this step by the slave-owners as extremely unwise, feeling that this would only make matters worse for the country. The conservative Democrats attempted to persuade their Southern colleagues that their fears relating to the election of Lincoln did not have any serious grounds, especially when taking into consideration the fact that the opposition party would be able to bind the hands of the Republican administration by using its control over the lower house in Congress and using the U.S. Supreme Court to prevent any measures directed at undermining the institution of slavery.[24]

As far as the question of the authority of the federal government to use force to compel the slave states, which had broken off, to return to the Union, in the Northern Democratic camp two diametrically opposed points of view became clearly distinguished. Representatives of the first, led by Senator Stephen Douglas (Illinois), maintained that in the event that all peaceful means to control the conflict had led to a dead end, the administration would have all the legal grounds to resort to arms in the struggle against the rebellion. "Without any doubt we are endowed with the authority to use all the power and force at our disposal necessary to return this region of the U.S. [South Carolina], and to compel its residents to follow the Constitution and laws," remarked Douglas in a speech to the Senate on January 3, 1861. "Compulsion is one of the founding principles on which rests the policies of any administration. . . . The goal of all governments consists of forcing each person to fulfill their duty even when they do not wish to do so."[25] The adherents to the line of President Buchanan blindly followed a course in close alliance with the planters and were ready to make any sacrifice for the sake of stabilizing the political situation in the country. Remaining a prisoner of the theory of "narrow" interpretation of the American Constitution, the doctrine of states' rights, they asserted that the fundamental law of government prohibits secession, just as it does not provide for measures to stem it. The federal Union was established solely as a voluntary willful expression of individual states, and it would be illegal to hold them against their will to remain in the Union. Having

24. *The Letters of Stephen Douglas* (Urbana, Ill., 1961), 500–501.
25. *Congressional Globe,* 36th Cong., 2d sess., 40–41.

fallen into this vicious circle, the supporters of alignment with the slave-owners were not able to break out of it until the Democratic term in the White House had come to an end.

The Democrats in the North were convinced that the only way to resurrect the basis of the Union would be the provision of additional guarantees for slavery, but at the same time the supporters of Douglas considered only the annulment by authorities in the free states of the laws on freeing fugitive slaves and on assimilation of western territories as allowable compromises to the Southerners. Those who thought like President Buchanan were ready to address the Southerners' claims.

The idea of the possibility of heading off disagreements between the two regions on the basis of the doctrine of "popular sovereignty," that is, the transmission to the settlers of the right to determine the status of slavery in the territories of the West by means of voting, became the leitmotif of Douglas's speeches and his concrete proposals. "Until the federal government will attempt to get a handle on the solution to the question of slavery in the acquired territories, discord and intersectional confrontations will continue unabated," said Douglas. "Peace, harmony of interests, and good will return to us only under the condition that Congress refrains from similar interference. I am convinced that it is necessary to take the problem of slavery once and for all outside the walls of Congress and from the national political arena by means of a constitutional amendment."[26]

As for the supporters of the administration's policies, in their attempts to please the plantation owners they had gone so far that they were prepared to satisfy the Southerners' petitions for the protection of slavery in the western lands—a principle that was the cornerstone of the U.S. Supreme Court's Dred Scott decision in 1857 and which became the apple of discord during the National Democratic Convention of 1860. "I hold to the opinion that the residents of the Southern states with their slaves have fundamental constitutional rights to settle in the common territories," asserted Senator William Bigler (Pennsylvania). "The territories were obtained with the blood and efforts of all and therefore are a common acquisition . . . and should be open to all. . . . The South needs to offer additional guarantees against the possibility of interference and aggression in the future . . . and in that case peace in the country will be restored. Without concessions and compromises our lot is unavoidable. We will face schism, civil war, and anarchy."[27]

The Constitutional Union party shared the Northern Democrats' position on the question of secession of the slave states. They had continued to hold an insignificant segment of the conservative voters both in the North and in the South. Having endured a catastrophic loss during the presidential election of 1860, the party was on its last legs. The leaders of the Constitutional Unionists, Senators John Crittenden (Kentucky) and John Bell (Tennessee), former Congressman Edward Everett (Massachusetts), and former Secretary of the Navy William Graham (North Carolina), wise with substantial political experience, desperately tried to find an effective antidote to extremism, which could localize the conflict and return life in the country to a peaceful course. They

26. Ibid., appendix, 38.
27. Ibid., 492.

tried to convince the Southerners that the Republican administration did not have as its goal the prohibition of slavery in the states where it had long existed and that the administration was not encroaching on the political privileges and economic position of the planters. The Unionists assured the planters that the best guarantee for the institution of slavery was the preservation of the Union and called upon them to tone down their demands, foremost to reject the principle of legalizing slavery in all the territories of the American West. The Unionists condemned secession in the most severe way, figuring that the election of a Republican to the head of the executive branch of the United States should not serve as a pretext for leaving the federation.[28] They appealed to the patriotism of the residents of the free states and tried to convince them of the necessity of making several concessions to the planters in the name of saving the Union, first of all to annul legislation concerning the freeing of fugitive slaves. The Constitutional Unionists hoped to solve the problem of the western lands by means of erecting a geographical barrier and dividing the territories into free and slave areas. The growing aggressiveness by the separatists of the South took the ground right out from under the feet of the Unionists and sowed doubt regarding the realistic possibility of a new compromise between the two regions.

By 1860–1861 American political parties had accumulated enough rich experience in heading off crisis situations that arose over the sharp differences in the country on the question of slavery. The whole arsenal of means and methods of "crisis management" was put to use in order to prevent a final split of the Union. "Never before in American history has the spirit of cooperation manifested itself so brightly as during the final days of the 36th Congress," wrote Republican Congressman George Julian. "Right up to the last moment the Northerners used the old medicine of compromise, tested by time, having shown with this all the flimsiness of their situation. Only when the thunder of shells rang out over Fort Sumter did they awake from their dream."[29]

The first attempt to work out a plan of political compromise and curtail secession by the slave states was initiated in the halls of the American Congress on December 4, 1860, when Alexander Boteler (Virginia) introduced a resolution to the House of Representatives to create a special "Committee of Thirty-three," made up of one representative from each state, which would study the critical situation taking shape in the country and determine measures to avoid the conflict. The initiative was approved 145–38; a significant majority of members from both party factions expressed their support for this bill. The committee was formed on a nonpartisan basis: in it were included sixteen Republicans, fifteen Democrats, and two representatives from the Constitutional Union party. The proceedings of the extraordinary body were presided over by one of the leaders of the conservative wing of the Republican party, Congressman Thomas Corwin (Ohio).[30]

On December 11 the "Committee of Thirty-three" began to execute its charge. By the next day Congressmen Thomas Nelson (Tennessee) and Joseph Taylor (Alabama) had made their proposals. The draft for the constitutional amendments proposed by

28. *The Papers of William Graham,* J. Hamilton, ed. (Raleigh, N.C., 1961), vol. 5, 223.
29. *Political Recollections of George Julian, 1840 to 1872* (Chicago, 1884), 38.
30. *Congressional Globe,* 36th Cong., 2d sess., 794–95.

Nelson provided for the division of the western territories of the United States along 36°30'N. To the north of this latitude, slavery was outlawed. To the south, for the time that the regions mentioned above held the status of a territory, slavery could flourish and, moreover, would be defended by the federal authorities. Upon entering the Union as states, the residents of these territories would face a referendum to decide for themselves the question of preserving or abolishing the institution of slavery. Congress was forbidden from interfering in the process of slave trade between states, and also in questions of slavery within the District of Columbia. The plantation owners were bestowed with the right to receive compensation for lost property in the form of fugitive slaves. For the sake of support from the varied parties making up the delicate intersectional political balance the bill set the condition that the president and vice president of the United States would by necessity belong to two opposing regions—the free and slave states.[31] On questions concerning carrying out slave trade and compensation for slaves who had run away from plantations, Congressman Taylor's version concurred with Nelson's plan. Unlike the latter, the Taylor version strengthened the privilege of Southerners to keep slaves in all western territories up until the moment of their entering the federation of states.[32] It was quite obvious during the voting that through the efforts of the Republicans the adoption of these proposals was put off for an indefinite time.[33] The sole real measure taken by the committee was the approval of a resolution by Democratic Congressman Henry Davis (Maryland), which called upon the authorities of Northern states to annul laws proclaiming fugitive slaves free.[34]

Upon the initiative of Senator Lazarus Powell (Kentucky) on December 6, 1860, the formation of a special "Committee of Thirteen" was announced in the upper house of Congress; the committee was made up of seven Democrats, five Republicans, and one representative of the Constitutional Union party.[35] On December 18, Senator Crittenden (Kentucky), a member of the committee, put forward a recommendation for a peaceful resolution of the conflict. He proposed introducing a series of amendments to the American Constitution, which would provide for the prohibition of slavery in the western lands north of 36°30' and the sanctioning of it to the south of this marker. Congress was denied the right to abolish slavery in those states where it already existed and in the District of Columbia. Slave trade between states was not liable to prohibition. The U.S. government took upon itself the responsibility for paying owners appropriate compensation for their fugitive slaves. The proslavery character of the Crittenden compromise was obvious. This gave Congressman Julian grounds to call the plan "a complete capitulation before the slave owners."[36] During the Senate vote the Crittenden amendments were rejected by an absolute majority of Republicans and a contingent of Northern Democrats.

31. Ibid., 134.
32. Ibid., 168.
33. Ibid., 224.
34. Ibid., 794–95.
35. Ibid., 114.
36. *Political Recollections of George Julian,* 185.

After it became evident that the higher legislative body of the country was not in a position to produce a peaceful resolution to the conflict, other echelons of power were forced to take the initiative upon themselves: the executive and legislative bodies of the states. On February 4, 1861, in the U.S. capital a conference was convened at the initiative of the Virginia legislature. This body was called upon to work out a plan of reconciliation between the free and slave states, and thus halt the collapse of the federal Union. "Until the disagreements, which at the present time are tearing apart the Union, are dealt with in a satisfactory manner, a final collapse of the federation [The United States] is unavoidable," observed the resolutions of the Virginia legislative session, adopted January 19, 1861. "The state Assembly . . . is trying to use any appropriate means to curtail the terrible tragedy and is intent upon launching a final attempt to restore the foundation for the Union and the Constitution."[37] Conservative elements had pinned high hopes on this endeavor. The favorable results of the peace forum, which attained a consensus between the conflicting regions and its subsequent ratification by Congress and approval by the country's president not unlike the 1850 compromise, gave hope that the discord would be controlled and the rebel slave states would return to the main body of the United States. In laying out future plans the organizers of the conference envisaged two extremely important goals: to try to win time for a mobilization of all conservative forces into a united front, and to deal a blow to the wave of secession. In this the Unionists at first succeeded. The authorities of the border slave states delayed deciding the question of secession until the end of the forum in Washington. From February to the middle of April 1861 a pause had settled into the separatist movement.

There were twenty-one delegations from the Northern states and bordering Southern states present at the conference. The states of the Deep South and Southwest, which had left the federation, refused the invitation. Congressional delegations represented Maine and Iowa at the forum, while the remaining states were represented either by gubernatorial appointees or state assemblies. Former president John Tyler, a slave-owner from the state of Virginia, was chosen as chairman of the conference. The composition of the conference was very representative. Among its delegates were prominent political leaders: Republicans—Senators William Fessenden and Stephen Foster (both from Maine), James Harlan and James Grimes (both from Iowa), Congressman David Wilmot (Pennsylvania), the former governor of Ohio, Salmon P. Chase; Democrats— the just recent Secretary of the Treasury, James Guthrie (Kentucky) and Congressman Thomas Ruffin (North Carolina); members of the administrations of presidents Tyler and Taylor and former Whigs—Franc Granger (New York), Thomas Ewing (Ohio), Reverdy Johnson (Maryland), and Charles Wickliffe (Kentucky). Business interests were also well represented—presidents and members of the Board of Directors of important companies of the time such as Ohio River Salt, Cincinnati and Chicago Railroad, New York Central, Cleveland and Mahone, Atlantic and North Carolina, Mobile and Ohio, and others.

A wide spectrum of social and political forces in the country found a place

37. *A Report of the Debates and Proceedings in the Secret Sessions of the Conference Convention,* 468 (referred to hereafter as *A Report of the Debates . . .*)

at the Washington conference. Among the representatives of the border South the conservatives prevailed. But also prominent was the influence of extremist elements, who rejected any compromise drafts and set up their own plans hoping that a failure at the forum would deny the opponents of secession their final arguments and would open up the path for the slave-owners to form a Confederation of Southern states. The delegations from the Northern states were also not united. Representatives from the states of New England, and also Iowa, among whom the radicals and moderate Republicans dominated, denounced secession, rejected the claims of the planters for additional guarantees for the institution of slavery in the territories of the American West, and decisively rejected any possibility of compromise with the Southerners on this principal question. Delegations from the mid-Atlantic states and a host of states from the Northwest, where there were many conservatives, were not against making well-known concessions to the slave-owners nor rejecting territorial limitations on slavery in the name of preserving the indivisible Union. As regards to upholding a possible compromise, however, their opinion was far from that of the Southerners.

The proceedings of the conference were held in secret, behind closed doors. On February 15, 1861, a concluding document was published, which was handed over to the U.S. Congress for subsequent review. It proposed to add seven new amendments to the Constitution.

An analogous item from Crittenden's plan was taken for the basis of the first amendment. The amendment provided for the prohibition of slavery in all territories of the United States located to the north of 36°30'. In the western lands south of this line slavery maintained its legal status. Congress and legislative assemblies of the territories were forbidden from hindering the relocation of slaves to these regions or "infringing upon the rights arising from the relations between master and slave, which should be under the jurisdiction of the federal courts, in accordance with the common law." Upon attaining the required population in the territories located to the south or north of the indicated border line, they had the right to enter the Union as rightful states with a constitution sanctioning or, vice versa, prohibiting slavery.

The second amendment proposed that the acquisition of new territories by the United States should occur only with the sanction of two-thirds of the senators from free states and two-thirds of the senators from slave states. The third amendment proclaimed that "Congress is not endowed with the authority to regulate within the borders of any state, prohibit or control the established or recognized laws of relations touching upon the status of persons . . . employed in forced labor, or interfere by abolishing slavery in the federal District of Columbia without the consent of the authorities of Maryland and the owners of slaves." Congress did not have the legal rights to prohibit slavery within the borders of areas located in the sole jurisdiction of federal authorities, where "these relations are established and acknowledged," to declare illegal the import or export of slaves from one state or territory to another, and to raise taxes on slaves. The import of slaves designated for sale to the District of Columbia was forbidden.

The fourth amendment to the Constitution proposed by the conference demanded strict adherence to the law on capture of fugitive slaves; the fifth prohibited the import from abroad of additional parties of slaves; the sixth assured that the first, third, and fifth amendments to the Constitution enumerated above could not be annulled or amended without the agreement of all the states. The seventh proposal stipulated that the higher legislative organ of the government pass a law according to which the federal government took upon itself the responsibility of compensating the owner of a fugitive slave for his value, and in the event that this was not possible then to find him and return him to his master.[38]

The most stinging part of the proposals arising from the Washington conference was more an ultimatum than a compromise meant to satisfy conflicting parties. If it should be followed by the federal government, then the slave states would remain in the Union. During the vote on individual sections of the document, delegations from the mid-Atlantic and the majority of the northwestern states expressed their readiness to satisfy the fundamental demands of the Southerners.[39] This highlighted demonstratively the intention by conservatives from the Northern states to placate the slave-owners at any cost. A threatening situation arose for the Republican party. "Everyone shares the opinion . . . that not one state controlled by the Republicans will send a delegation to the conference, but they nevertheless are not planning on abandoning it," wrote a prominent activist of the radical wing of the party, U.S. Senator Zachariah Chandler (Michigan), in a confidential memo to Montgomery Blair. "Ohio, Indiana, and Rhode Island are gradually giving in and there is the danger that Illinois will follow. We are being implored to come to their aid right away and save the Republican party from schism."[40]

The supporters of secession could not wait to wrap up discussion as soon as possible and to put their words into deed. "I consider the mission of this convention fulfilled," declared Thomas Ruffin (North Carolina), "and I hope that there is no sense in focusing attention on new problems, which can only sow discord among us."[41] While closing the conference, its chairman, former president Tyler, expressed the hope that "the results of the forum will facilitate reestablishing the peace and tranquility in our country. . . . And although these proposals are far from what I desired . . . my duty is to express my official support and approval of them. . . . In all likelihood, this result is better than could have been expected under the circumstances."[42]

At the insistence of the Southern and Northern Democrats the final document of the Washington conference in the last days of February 1861 was given to a special Senate committee for review. A majority of its members decided to incorporate the recommendations of the forum into a bill for the upper house of Congress. They placed

38. *A Report of the Debates . . .* , 440–45.

39. All the articles of the conference plans were supported by the delegations from New Jersey, Pennsylvania, Ohio, Rhode Island, Maryland, Tennessee, Kentucky, and Delaware; representatives from Illinois recognized the final document with the exception of the second amendment, and Indiana did so as well except for the first and the third, and Missouri the first and the seventh; delegates from North Carolina, Kentucky, Connecticut, Vermont, New Hampshire, and Kansas only for two; delegates from Massachusetts, Maine, and Iowa rejected the conference draft completely (Ibidem).

40. *A Report of the Debates . . .* , 469.

41. Ibid., 448.

42. Ibid., 451–52.

alongside the resolution a statement, which proposed that the state authorities discuss their recommendations in the capacity of proposed amendments to the American Constitution. For the Republican faction in the Senate the proslavery bias of the conference report was extremely obvious, and as a result when it was put to a vote, opponents of the expansion of slavery rejected it. In the House of Representatives the Republicans, holding a solid majority, easily prevented the "Peace" faction's plan from even being offered for discussion. Not finding a positive response in Congress, the resolutions of the peace conference hung in the air. The forum of conservatives, the character of its debates, and the fate of its resolutions showed that a peaceful resolution of the root disagreements through compromise was impossible; the views of the opposing sides on key issues of domestic politics remained irreconcilable.

On March 4, 1861, in Washington the inauguration ceremony for the U.S. president took place. Lincoln's speech was restrained, with subtle peace overtures. He hastened to assure the Southerners that the Republican administration would be bound strictly to follow the guarantees for the institution of slavery as laid out in the Constitution. Having severely condemned secession, Lincoln declared that his primary task was the preservation of the indivisible Union. He expressed his readiness to refrain from resorting to military force as regards the rebel states in the hope that the latter would recognize the groundlessness of their fears as to the fate of slavery and return to the body of the federation. "I only press upon the public attention . . . that the property, peace and security of no section are to be in anyway endangered by the now incoming administration," pointed out the president. "We must not be enemies. Though passions may have strained, it must not break our bonds of affection."[43]

Lincoln clearly realized that a critical situation had developed in the country, and this forced him to act with extreme caution. The fate of the border states of the South was up for grabs. They had not definitively chosen between the slave confederation and the U.S. government, and the side they would take in the near future depended upon whether the rebellion would receive an additional impulse or be left in isolation and recede. The president could not ignore the existing rifts within the Republican party over the methods of countering secession and also the sentiment in the Northern states where conservative elements continued to exert influence in politics.

The fate of Fort Sumter, blocked from access to Charleston (South Carolina) by sea, became the central problem facing the Republican party during its first days in power. The solution to this problem hinged on the direction the struggle between the administration and Confederates would take. Members of the cabinet could not find consensus over this issue. The conservatives—Secretary of State William Seward, who was negotiating behind the back of the president with the rebels, Secretary of War Simon Cameron, Attorney General Edward Bates, and Secretary of the Interior Caleb Smith—considered that reinforcing the fort would only provoke a military conflict, and thus they insisted on the evacuation of the garrison. Opposed to this line, Secretary of the Treasury Samuel Chase and Postmaster General Montgomery Blair energetically argued that such a step would appear to be a capitulation to the rebels and would only encourage further acts of secession. They proposed to increase the

43. *The Collected Works of Abraham Lincoln,* vol. 4, 263, 271.

number of troops at Fort Sumter and continue to keep it in the hands of the federal government. Shedding his final doubts, President Lincoln, disregarding the desires of the conservative Republicans, gave the order to prepare a relief expedition with an additional military contingent to Charleston.

At the same time the aggressiveness of the separatists increased from day to day. They openly carried out military preparations and increasingly provoked run-ins with troops loyal to the federal government. On April 12, 1861, a military formation of slave-owners launched an attack, and after a short siege forced the garrison at Fort Sumter to capitulate. In response to this act, President Lincoln announced the mobilization of a militia loyal to the government and offered the Confederates twenty days to cease the rebellion.[44]

The failure of the conservatives' attempts to localize the conflict gave the second wave of secession an impulse, this time to the border states of the South. The very shaky coalition of Unionists with moderate proponents of secession fell apart for good. The latter took the side of the separatists and set a course for immediate withdrawal from the Union. The events unfolded with amazing speed. On April 17, delegates of the Virginia state convention who had gathered in Richmond approved the ordinance on secession by a vote of 88 to 55. It was subsequently ratified on May 23 during a referendum.[45] On May 6 Arkansas left the Union. In Tennessee the question of secession was put to the ballot of the state's residents by decision of the legislature. They approved the bill on splitting off from the Union on June 8. Not waiting for the final count of the referendum, Governor Isham Harris, an avowed separatist, entered into negotiations on establishing a military alliance with the rebel government with the blessing of the legislative assembly. On May 20, 1861, an ordinance on secession was approved by a forum of North Carolina slave-owners in Raleigh.[46]

In the remaining Southern states the balance of power was on the side of the Unionists. The head of the executive branch and deputies of the legislative assembly from Kentucky, having broken the resistance of the separatists, in the middle of May decided to maintain their strict neutrality. Similarly, the Delaware legislature rejected a proposal to enter the Confederacy of Southern states. After a fierce struggle between the Unionists, headed by Governor Thomas Hicks, and the supporters of secession, who had a stronghold in the legislative assembly, Maryland also preserved its support for the federal government. Delegates to the state convention in Missouri, who had gathered in St. Louis in the beginning of March 1861, came to the conclusion that separating from the Union would be an unwise step, and expressed their support for dealing with the disputes at a national conference. In the end of July at a new session of the convention at Jefferson City, the Unionists managed to replace Governor Claiborne Jackson, who was aiming for the state's secession.[47]

The political crisis of 1860–1861 culminated in the schism of the United States and

44. Ibid., 332.
45. *Proceedings of the Virginia State Convention of 1861, February 13–May 1*, vols. 1–4 (April 16–May 1), George H. Reese, ed. (Richmond, Va., 1965), 144.
46. *New York Herald*, May 12, 26, 1861.
47. *New York Herald*, April 6, May 26, August 6, 1861.

the onset of the Civil War. The blame for its unraveling lay wholely on the Northern radicals and the extremist slave-owners of the South, who rejected a resolution to the question of slavery by constitutional means and resorted to secession. Not managing to regulate the conflict between the free and slave states and prevent a civil war, American political parties endured a decisive failure. The institution meant to strengthen and stabilize the hegemony of the ruling classes turned out to be inadequate to fulfill its preconceived function. The two-party system showed demonstratively the limitations of its possibilities, and displayed its inability to resolve the key question of slavery for the fate of the country. The bankruptcy of the parties was an indicator of the crisis that had gripped the ruling "elites" of American society. The political course that aimed to achieve compromises between the Northern bourgeoisie and the slave-owners of the Southern states had definitively outlived its time. This crisis was predicated by the pressure of the popular masses, who did not desire to be resigned to the further existence of slavery.

5

Conservatism versus Revolution

The Erosion of the Conservative Political Tradition in the United States of America

by Alexander A. Kormilets

The conservative tradition appeared on the U.S. political scene simultaneous to the formation of the American state system. The Constitution of 1787, which had become the most complete expression of the philosophy and politics of bourgeois liberalism in constitutional rights around the world for its time, contained conservative features itself. While sanctifying the existence of slavery, for many decades it upheld the indivisible supremacy of the bourgeoisie in the North and the plantation owners of the South, who were united in one bloc by common economic and political interests. Up to that time the exceptionally favorable conditions, both extrinsic and intrinsic, for the development of capitalism in the United States ensured the harmonious coexistence of two leading trends in the economic policies of the ruling classes: intensive development, which was connected to safeguarding industrial capitalism in the Northeast with protectionist measures and was directed toward accelerating the Industrial Revolution in the country; and extensive development, which was suited to the agrarian type of capitalist economy of western farmers and Southern plantation owners.

The contradictory nature of these policies, rooted in the contradictions of the American bourgeois government from the very beginning, with its various forms of economies and its national and racial prejudices, was the main topic of the internal political debates within the country. This led to discussion of 1) broad and narrow interpretations of the Constitution, 2) the relationship between the powers of the central federal government versus the rights of states, and 3) the priority of industry over agriculture and vice versa.[1] These discussions in the first quarter of the nineteenth century, however, did not leave any doubt about the value of compromise by different classes, which the founding fathers had achieved on the issue of slavery—the primary basis of economic and political hegemony by the bourgeoisie–plantation owners' bloc.

---

1. See A. V. Valiuzhenich, *American Liberalism: Illusion and Reality* [Amerikanskii liberalism: illiuzii i real'nost'] (Moscow, 1976), 47–58; and N. Kh. Romanova, "On the Question of the Politics of Economic Liberalism in the U.S. (1829–1837)" [K voprosu o politike ekonomicheskogo liberalizma v SShA 1829–1837], *Amerikanskii ezhegodnik* (Moscow, 1986): 68. This essay by Alexander Kormilets was originally published in *U.S. Studies* 8 (1990).

The entry of American capitalism into the initial stage of the Industrial Revolution during the 1830s and 1840s led to a severe intensification of class conflicts, arising from the coexistence of two social systems—one of free labor, and the other of slavery. It was exactly during this period that the conservative tradition finally took shape within the sphere of politics and became an integral feature of the party tandem. When applied to the problems of political party struggles during 1840–1850, a time of unquestionable domination by the conservative tradition in politics, the term "conservatism" itself signified a current in popular thought that envisaged the preservation in the country of traditional structures of socioeconomic relations as stipulated by the articles of the Constitution, and also the stabilization of the foundations of the state political system by means of eliminating disagreements between the bourgeoisie of the North and the plantation owners of the Southern states through compromise on the issue of slavery.[2] During the course of the two decades leading up to the Civil War, compromise was the banner of conservatism in the struggle with the politically organized movements regarding slavery—from liberals to abolitionists, on the one hand, and extremist plantation owners from the South, on the other. Nevertheless, conservative politics proved inadequate for the practical demands of the time.

The necessity of an immediate solution to the problem of slavery, which had become the main obstacle in the path of the development of U.S. capitalism, upset the balance of conservative powers in politics. The revolutionary tendencies in American society ran so deep that they could not be overcome even with the most refined policies of compromise. The two-party system of that period, which had turned into an obstacle to sociopolitical development, by the middle of the 1850s had been wrecked, and had fallen into disorganization. The Whig party had finally disappeared from the political arena. The disintegration of the two-party combination unleashed the forces of supporters and opponents of slavery, earlier suppressed within its devices. The struggle between them became the primary ingredient of U.S. politics right up to the beginning of the Civil War. But the adherents to the conservative tradition did not surrender. Throughout all this time the defenders of the idea of compromise did not lose hope for the possibility of returning politics to the conservative helm. The secession of the Southern states and the Civil War that followed, which had become the logical result of the growth of class antagonisms in American society, created completely new and unfamiliar conditions in which the conservative tradition was forced to operate. Conservatism's fight against the approaching revolution of the Civil War during a critical period of American history constitutes the subject of this study.

The campaigns for the presidential election of 1860 completed the process of demarcation of the country's political forces over the issues of slavery and the attitude toward hegemony of Southerners in the federal Union. It also contributed to the crystallization of ideological positions by various divisions within the parties. The

2. See A. A. Kormilets and S. A. Porshakov, *The Crisis of the U.S. Two Party System of the Eve of the Civil War (the End of the 1840s to 1865)* [Krizis dvukhpartiinoi sistemy SShA nakanune i v gody grazhdanskoi voiny-konets 1840-x-1865 g.] (Moscow, 1987), 160.

spectrum of politics, which preached conservative ideology on the eve of the Civil War, was broad enough to cover to some extent or another all the existing parties.

One of the bastions of conservatism was in the Republican party, which had entered the national political arena in 1856. The conservative Republicans—of whom one-third were in a party faction from the beginning—were quite a strong and influential group in political circles. Their leaders consisted of Abraham Lincoln's ally Orville Browning (Illinois), the well-known Missouri politician Edward Bates, Supreme Court Justice John McLean (Ohio), Senator William Dayton (New Jersey), plus Congressmen Thomas Corwin (Ohio), Edgar Cowan (Pennsylvania), and Albert White (Indiana). The conservative faction consisted of former representatives of parties that had fallen apart: "The Know Nothings" and "Jacksonian" Democrats, opponents of slavery; however, the largest conservative contingent carried under their belts the experience of political struggles under the banner of the Whig party. Proof of the durability of the conservative positions in the party was their dominating influence in the Republican organizations of Indiana, Pennsylvania, and New Jersey, and the visible effect on the course of party organizations from New York, Massachusetts, and Illinois. The conservative Republicans' program on the issue of slavery, completely inherited from the ideological baggage of the Whigs, demanded a resurrection of the conditions of the Missouri Compromise of 1819–1821 on laying the borders of the free and slave territories. It meant virtual acceptance of the distribution of the slave system in the West, which extended to the South from a conditional line of the 1820 compromise, and the entry of new slave states into the Union. Conservatives opposed expansion of slavery, but they did not consider appealing to the federal authorities for help in stopping expansion, declaring this ploy unconstitutional. They reduced the whole specter of contradictions between the North and South to a rivalry in the struggle for political power over the Union, striving to put an end to the Southerners' hegemony in deciding key domestic political issues. The conservatives condemned slavery only from the point of view that it was the foundation of the South's absolute power.[3] At the same time, taking into account the actual scale of the intersectional conflict, they declared their readiness to make new compromises with the Southerners to achieve political stability in the country. "The polemics over the issue of slavery did not bring anything useful to the parties, sections, or classes," wrote Edward Bates.[4]

The conservative Republicans expressed the interests of the American bourgeoisie from heavy industry, who had long concentrated on markets in the free states and relied little on deliveries of goods from the slave South. They continued to follow the Whig conception of socioeconomic development in the country. They were supporters of rapid industrialization, and they held to the theory of an active role for government in stimulating economic growth in the United States. The conservatives also defended the idea of introducing protectionist tariffs and of creating a central banking system. They called for broadening the complex of internal improvements at the expense of the federal treasury.

---

3. *Disunion and Slavery. A Series of Letters to Hon. W. L. Yancey of Alabama by H. Raymond of New York* (New York, 1861), 28–30, 32–33.

4. Howard K. Beale, ed., *The Diary of Edward Bates, 1859–1866* (Washington, 1933), 1.

The conservatives differed rather significantly from their party colleagues—both the radical and moderate Republicans—in their views on the issue of slavery. Both the radicals and the moderates forcefully upheld the principle that had formed the foundation of the Republican party platform during the campaign of 1860, which limited the system of slavery to within its existing boundaries. Both the former and the latter group planned on strictly following this principle in executing national policy in the event that the party should win the election. They would use all the prerogatives of federal power in order to carry through on this. Unlike the radicals who lobbied to rescind the laws of 1850, which called for the return of fugitive slaves and for the prohibition of interstate traffic in slaves, the moderate Republicans, who played a leading role in the governing organs of the party, condemned such demands and tried to keep the party from attacks on the institution of slavery. Nevertheless, representatives of the moderate faction were much closer to the radicals in their views than to the conservatives.

A significant contingent of the Whigs and Nativists from the mid-Atlantic and border states, and from the states of New England, who did not wish to be associated with the Republican party, a party openly opposed to slavery, also held conservative views. They came forward on the eve of the election campaign of 1860 with the idea of forming a new organization—a Constitutional Union party. In a special address to the electorate, the leaders of this conservative movement, Senators John Crittenden and John Bell (Tennessee), and former congressman Edward Everett (Massachusetts), called for "all supporters of preserving the Union of states to unite forces to fend off blows . . . to political institutions and avoid the disastrous results for the country that will ensue from the policies of the Democrats and Republicans."[5] The Constitutional Unionists gathered at a convention in Baltimore in May 1860. Bell and Everett, well-known leaders of the former Whigs, received the party's nominations for president and vice president. In complete congruence with the old Whig conception of "platforms are nothing" while the party's candidates themselves "should embody the platform,"[6] the Constitutional Unionists proposed one political slogan: "The Constitution and the Union." They did not bother to decipher this nor comment on it, and at the same time attempted to get around the issue of slavery with silence.

This development did not go unnoticed by the Republican leadership. While on the whole giving positive marks to the emergence of a new political force in the national arena that was ready to support a compromise solution for the conflict between the North and South, the Republicans nevertheless pointed to the nonconstructiveness of the Unionists' course. One newspaper, the *Springfield Republican,* directed attention to their clear incapability to adopt "a realistic program."[7] The famous publisher Horace Greeley said that the candidates from the Unionist party did not correspond to "the present geological age."[8]

The conservative faction of the Democratic party, which had nominated Stephen

---

5. *New York Herald,* February 18, 1860.
6. George H. Mayer, *The Republican Party 1854–1966* (London, 1967), 66.
7. *Springfield Republican,* May 11, 1860.
8. *New York Tribune,* May 11, 1860.

Douglas (Illinois) as its own candidate for president, was quite numerous. Besides Douglas, the acknowledged leaders of this group were Senator Lewis Cass (Michigan) and the well-known political activist Samuel Tilden. The conservative Democrats drew support mainly from those states in the Northeast and the territories where there was a concentrated established bourgeoisie of trade and finance who had prospered from commercial enterprises with the plantation South. These conservatives were intimately connected politically to the slave-owners from the Southern states. Conservative Democrats were extremely neutral about slavery in general, but they defended its existence in the South as guaranteed by the Constitution, and affirmed the rights of plantation owners to assimilate new western territories. They called for the strict guarantee of Southerners' rights to property and condemned any attacks on the institution of slavery. Along with this, the conservative activists attempted to stem the extraordinary strengthening of the position of the reactionary Southern wing of the party, and they saw its indivisible hegemony as a dangerous development for the Democrats. It was exactly these thoughts that spurred them in 1860 to split formally from the Southern wing.

Conservative Democrats, brought up in the spirit of Northern political traditions, saw a destabilizing influence in the conflagration of the slavery problem that threatened the foundations of the political system in the country. They followed the widening conflict between the North and the South with alarm, and attempted to stifle the dangerous topic of slavery with all their power, and to neutralize the growth of the political influence of both its open opponents and extremists from the Southern camp. The representatives of the conservative wing of the Democrats were impressed, as before, by the political tradition for compromises to solve the intersecessionist conflict. They put forward the doctrine of "popular sovereignty" as its primary basis, according to which the status of slavery should be decided by the vote of the settlers themselves. At first, putting this doctrine into action was supposed to muffle the conflict between the North and South and in the long run lead to the development of a system of free labor, but it was to be based on the unconditional respect for the rights of the slave-owners to expand beyond the boundaries of the old territory. Adherence to the doctrine of "popular sovereignty" reflected the conservative Democrats' antipathy toward strong governmental powers and their inclination to a so-called "narrow" interpretation of the Constitution, which called for the limitation of the power of the federal government, and as a result an increase in the power of the states.

Despite all the differences in the views of the conservative groups from various parties on the issue of slavery and the ways to deal with it, they were undoubtedly united by one thing—an obvious attempt to prevent the conflict between the North and the South from becoming worse, a conflict fraught with the most unpredictable fate for the federal Union. They also shared a guarded attitude toward the secessionist attempts by the Southern extremists. The conservatives considered the activities of the radical Republicans as secessionist by their very nature and equivalent to those of the unceasing warriors against slavery, the abolitionists, who had called for the immediate end of the institution of slavery by any means.[9] The pivotal belief held

---

9. *The Papers of Andrew Johnson*, LeRoy P. Graf and Ralph W. Haskins, eds. (Knoxville, 1976), vol. 4, 136.

by all the conservatives, regardless of their political persuasion, was that the Union could only be saved through a compromise that did not go outside the framework of constitutional prescriptions.

Abraham Lincoln's victory in the 1860 presidential election marked the end of the slave-owners' political hold on national power and served as a signal to the Southern extremists to secede and form an independent slave government (the Confederacy). From the beginning of secession the conservative Republicans, similar to their radical and moderate party colleagues, refused to recognize states' rights to secede. In the words of one of the leaders of the faction, Henry J. Raymond, the Southerners' aspirations for "a peaceful secession" were based "either on a serious overestimation of our disinterestedness and goodwill or on just as serious underestimation of our reason and common sense."[10] The demand to halt secession, however, did not lead the conservatives to conclude that military means were necessary to solve the conflict. Out of the sheer inertia of past political thinking, they counterposed the idea of compromise to the inevitability of war. In the name of preserving the Union the conservatives appealed to both the North and the South to accept the practical realization of the policy of "setting aside any minor differences in order to cool off passions, and open up the broad path toward mutual understanding of the needs and demands of each side and . . . to show a real movement toward compromise."[11]

The conservative Republican appeals met with a warm response among the conservative Democrats. They also appealed to their party comrades to treat the Southern demands with more patience. "Nothing comes as difficult as gaining the ability to see simultaneously two sides of a coin," lectured Samuel Tilden. "We, educated under the influence of the idea of the North, and tempered by inter-party dissension, should become more than simple mortals in order to evaluate the positions of our rivals impartially and without prejudice. It is necessary to do something more—to put ourselves in their place so that we can work out an adequate policy for their situation."[12]

The political crisis of 1860–1861, which preceded the onset of the Civil War, witnessed every kind of attempt to spur the conservatives into action. The leaders of the conservative wing of the Republican party attacked their own party leadership with accusations of dogmatism and an unwillingness to submit to the political principles of the party in the situation that had been created. The leadership of the Republican party machine from New York, led by Thaddeus Weed, proposed to satisfy the Southern demands for rescinding the laws on "personal liberty" and on guarantees to safeguard slave-owners' property in the western territories in order to halt the secession of the state of Georgia.[13] Edward Bates, Thomas Corwin, Simon Cameron, and William Seward also agreed to the incorporation into the Union of new states with the right to preserve within them the property of slave-owners, and to please the secessionists they stood up for the strict enforcement of the federal slave law.[14]

10. *Disunion and Slavery,* 18–19.
11. Ibid., 27.
12. John Bigelow, ed., *The Letters and Literary Memorials of Samuel Tilden* (New York, 1908), vol. 1, 148.
13. David Potter, *Lincoln and His Party in the Secession Crisis* (New Haven, 1971), 71.
14. *Congressional Globe,* 36th Cong., 2d sess., 341.

The political crisis of 1860–1861 became the primary test for the conservative Democrats from the Northern states, the supporters of the Union Constitutional party, and the durability of their political philosophy of compromise. They insisted on the strict guarantee of property rights for Southerners. In addition, they tried to convince the latter that the Republicans, having come to power, did not intend to prohibit slavery where it already existed, and that they were not encroaching on the economic position of the plantation owners. The controversy over permitting slavery in the western territories could be resolved by various methods, according to the Democrats and the Unionists, on the basis of the doctrine of popular sovereignty only by means of a geographic division into free and slave territories. Nevertheless, both the Democrats and Unionists appealed to the Southerners to refrain from their attempts to legalize slavery in all the western territories on the basis of the 1857 Supreme Court decision in the case of Dred Scott. They also demanded in the interest of the normalization of life in the country and the prevention of secession that the population of the North back down and completely annul state laws on "personal freedom," which held that fugitive slaves who reached the North were considered free.[15]

The conservatives in the U.S. Congress launched initiatives to create special organs, the Senate "Committee of Thirteen" and "Committee of Thirty-Three" in the House of Representatives, which were entrusted to study various possible compromises. All the hopes of the conservatives were pinned on these committees. But it was not meant to be.

The conciliatory resolution by Eli Thayer, John Sherman, William Kellogg, and Thomas Corwin, which addressed the concerns of all the conservative groups represented in the committees of the lower House, ran into the stubborn resistance of Southern extremists unwilling to give in to the North.[16] The counterresolution by the Southerners Thomas Nelson (Tennessee) and Miles Taylor (Louisiana) demanded constitutional recognition of slavery in the western territories to the south of the 36°30' line and the safeguarding there of the institution of slavery by the federal authorities until these regions would enter the Union as states. The attempts by Southerners to deny the U.S. Congress the power to resolve questions of interstate slave trade and of the existence of slavery in the federal District of Columbia also appeared outrageous to the North. The Southerners demanded the restoration of their former political power, putting forward the condition that one of the two positions in the executive branch, either the president or the vice president, would without fail represent the interests of the slave South in the government.[17] To top it all off, the Southerners added to the Nelson-Taylor draft the right to maintain slaves in all western territories without exception up until their incorporation into the Union as states enjoying full rights.[18]

The demands of the plantation owners (more an ultimatum) and their political ambitiousness alienated not only moderate Republicans but also conservative Democrats. Thanks to the efforts of the Republican faction in the "Committee of

15. Ibid., 492; Appendix, 38.
16. Ibid., 76–77.
17. Ibid., 134.
18. Ibid., 168.

Thirty-Three," the Southerners' proposals were rejected.[19] The failure to achieve compromise in the House of Representatives forced the conservatives to switch their focus of finding some agreement to the Senate "Committee of Thirteen," where by the end of December 1860, Crittenden's compromise plan was sent. In essence, it was a repeat of the already mentioned resolution by the Southerners in the committee of the lower House, only it was devoid of what the North and the victorious Republicans considered as several of the most offensive and insulting proposals.[20] In this version also, however, the compromise plan had no hope of approval by the Northern representatives, and most of all by the Republicans. Their leadership, which had followed the activation of the conservatives within the Republican ranks with alarm, interfered with the conciliatory process in the Senate just in time. Lincoln, clearly recognizing the harm that excessive adherence to a course of compromise would bring, advised the Republican leaders in Congress not to compromise on the question of the nonproliferation of slavery on the frontier. In addition, bowing to pressure from the conservatives, led by Thaddeus Weed, the president was forced to indicate to the Republican lawmakers those places where compromise with Southerners was allowed during the course of discussions over proposals such as the agreement to confirm the law on fugitive slaves by a special act of Congress and to rescind all state laws on "personal freedom."[21] Lincoln's intervention in many ways determined the future course of the Republicans' attempts at conciliatory measures in Congress, having limited their options for compromise within strict parameters. The refusal by Republicans in the Senate committee to support any of the points of the Crittenden plan soon led the conciliatory efforts up a dead end.[22]

The futility of the conservative attempts to stop secession became very obvious during the course of work on the "Peace Conference" in Washington. The conference, which came at the beginning of February 1861 at the initiative of the Virginia legislature and was directed to work out a universal plan of agreement between the free and slave states, was conceived by the supporters of the idea of compromise as "unconditionally conservative" in character. According to the plan of the conservative Democrats from the Constitutional party of the Union, the conference was to discuss different variants of constitutional amendments, all based on modifications of the Crittenden compromise.[23] The first amendment proposed to preserve the status of slavery in the western territories south of the 36°30' line. In the event of a new state entering the Union, regardless of whether it was north or south of the dividing line, its population had the right to determine whether it would sanction or prohibit slavery in its constitution. The second proposal established new procedures for acquiring new territory by the United States, according to which this act would receive the sanction of no less than two-thirds of the Senators from the free states and two-thirds of the

19. Ibid., 224.

20. Ibid., 114.

21. Roy Basler, ed., *The Collected Works of Abraham Lincoln* (New Brunswick, 1953), vol. 5, 156–57.

22. Clinton Everett Knox, "The Possibilities of Compromise in the Senate Committee of Thirteen and the Responsibility for Failure," *Journal of Negro History* 17 (1932): 465.

23. *The Letters and Literary Memorials of Samuel Tilden,* vol. 1, 151.

Senators from the slave states. The third proposal essentially limited the power of Congress to regulate the institution of slavery, refusing the higher legislative body the right to prohibit the slave trade or to eliminate slavery in the District of Columbia. The fourth amendment to the constitution would perpetuate the law on capture and return of fugitive slaves. The fifth prohibited the import from abroad of additional slaves. The sixth guaranteed the impossibility of rescinding the first, the third, and the fifth without the agreement of all the states of the Union. The seventh proposal obliged Congress to pass a law on compensation from the federal government to slave-owners for fugitive and withheld slaves.[24]

The Soviet scholar Sergei A. Porshakov rightly points out that "the fact that it was more reminiscent of an ultimatum than a compromise meant to satisfy conflicting parties, which if agreed to by the federal government, the slave states would remain in the Union, became the point most vulnerable to criticism in the Washington conference draft."[25] In comparison to the proposals introduced by the Southerners for discussion in the congressional committees, the Washington draft was perhaps to a large degree unacceptable to the North. Despite the endorsement of the constitutional amendments by the majority of conservatives from the mid-Atlantic and northwestern states, who sacrificed many of their principal ideological positions, the draft was rejected by the U.S. Congress.

The failure of the Washington conference hastened the process of secession, which had for a time been stalled. Toward the end of May 1861 eleven Southern states withdrew from the Union. The shelling of the federal Fort Sumter (South Carolina) became the logical outcome of the increased aggressiveness by the Southern separatists. Thus began the bloodshed and the prolonged Civil War. This marked the bankruptcy of the former political system, which had been called to strengthen and stabilize the hegemony of the ruling bourgeoisie–plantation owner bloc. Conservatism lost the weighty part of its ideological baggage, having taken pride in its political philosophy of compromise over the course of so many decades. Without doubt, the conservatives still hoped for the possibility of forming a political consensus between the North and South. But under the conditions of war, accomplishing this task was put off for the time being. A new series of complicated problems connected with attaining the primary goal of the immediate restoration of the Union to its entirety became foremost on the agenda.

"A deep, all-encompassing feeling of patriotism," which was widespread around the North from the beginning of the Civil War, was to a large degree characteristic of the conservatives too.[26] From the first days of armed conflict, representatives of this movement declared their complete support for the idea of fighting until victory. The Republican conservatives, who only recently were ready to sacrifice their party

24. *A Report of the Debates and Proceedings in the Secret Sessions of the Conference Convention for Proposing Amendments to the Constitution of the United States. Held at Washington, D. C. in February 1861,* L. Crittenden, ed. (New York, 1964), 440–45.

25. S. A. Porshakov, "The Parties and Political Struggles during the period of Secession of the Slave States of the South (1860–1861)" [Partii i politicheskaia bor'ba v period setsessii rabovladel'cheskikh shtatov Iuga], *Problemy amerikanistiki Z. M.* (1985): 72.

26. *New York Times,* April 15, 1861.

principles to please the Southerners, characterized the Southerners as none other than criminals and traitors who deserved the harshest punishment.[27] The champions of conservative ideology in the Democratic party matched the Republicans in their accusations against the rebels, calling for the annihilation of Charleston as "the nest where treachery was hatched."[28]

As far as working out a concrete and constructive program of action in conditions of war, here the adherents to the conservative doctrine clearly were indecisive. The irony of the situation was that they were not at all planning on renovating the essentials of their ideological baggage and political tools, although the principles of the conservative tradition, which were from the beginning oriented toward the evolutionary development of social institutions and relations, struck a discordant note in the face of the objective goals of the Civil War. The conservatives perceived the war as none other than something unnatural to the idea of American government, and to the spirit and letter of the Constitution. The narrow-mindedness of class interests prevented them from seeing the revolutionary nature of the Civil War, and the inevitability of those deep socioeconomic changes that it brought to society. The conservatives tended to see the rebellion by the Southern states as only an uprising against the Constitution and the Union. Because of this in particular, the struggle with the rebels—for the Constitution and Union—was thought to be possible only with the unconditional adherence to the Constitution.[29] The path, which the conservatives had proposed, for the quickest resolution of the armed conflict was clearly a dead end. The Civil War was objectively aimed at destroying the institution of slavery and it could not avoid going outside the bounds of the Constitution, inasmuch as slavery was defended by the Constitution. The main weakness in the conservatives' position, which, however, had still not become evident in the beginning stage of the war, was the absence of political realism.

The failure of the politics of compromise during the period of the 1860–1861 crisis in no way humiliated the conservatives in their own estimation. Moreover, the campaign against secession gave them confidence in their power, having presented them with the opportunity to recognize in their dealings with colleagues, other supporters of conservative ideas in various parties. The common ground in the ideological views of all the conservatives gave rise to a rather solid coalition. During the elections of 1860 the conservatives were divided into various parties, and so in the struggle for power, they did not in any way follow identical political goals, but rather each built different and sometimes hardly reconcilable plans for regulating the secessionist conflict on the basis of compromise. Secession, which had proven the impossibility of compromise with the Southerners as such, had completely destroyed the ideological position of the conservatives. Most importantly, it had eased the disagreements between conservative Democrats, headed by Stephen Douglas, and supporters of the Constitutional Union Party, led by John Bell.

27. M. G. Baxter, *Orville H. Browning, Conservative in American Politics,* unpublished Ph.D. diss. (University of Illinois, 1948), 131.

28. M. Lichterman, *John Adams Dix, 1789–1879,* unpublished Ph.D. diss. (Columbia University, 1952), 476.

29. *Congressional Globe,* 37th Cong., 2d sess., 1679.

The New York Unionists, who to a large degree leaned toward the Democrats, continued to assure their voters during the period of secession that there were none of the principal disagreements between their party and Douglas's group as existed between the Republicans and the Southern extremists. They also asserted that in their platforms could be observed "if not entirely identical stands, then at least more affinities to the principles," which gave rise to "a mutual sympathy" by these alignments. Their representatives, pointed out the Unionists, were "bound to the idea of the Union, faithful to the Constitution, law-abiding, and were against sectionalism in any manifestation, and against intervention in the slavery conflict." The fact that both organizations were in the center of the political spectrum, "between two extremes," only brought them closer together, providing them with the opportunity to unite forces in the struggle against the "abolitionists, nullificators, supporters of splitting the Union, and secessionist demagogues who had flooded the country."[30]

The conservative Democrats of the North also understood the advantages of forming an alliance with the Unionists. In the estimation of one of the leaders of the conservative wing of the Democrats, M. Marble, in the border states the Unionist party enjoyed the support of "huge masses of people who were conservatively inclined." This party, he pointed out, could "sweep everyone away if we join forces with it."[31] The leaders of the Democrats felt that traditional conservatism held much promise for the issue of reunification of the Union. Huge masses of Americans were "conservative in spirit," wrote Samuel Tilden. "We only need time to set them on the right path."[32] Resolving the question on uniting with the Unionists gradually went beyond the stage of mere declarations. According to the senator from Virginia, Robert M. F. Hunter, the activities of the secessionists there ran into the resistance of the supporters of Douglas and Bell, who were joined together by mutual "attempts to create a new party."[33] A similar process was taking place rather actively in other states as well. The party covenant of the Democrats from the state of New York, which invited all conservatives regardless of their former party affiliations to unite in their efforts, gave evidence of this. "We have gathered together the conservative delegates who differ from each other in their views on the methods of governmental politics, but are ready to sacrifice these ideological differences," declared one of the organizers of the convention. "You cannot be considered a true patriot if you are not ready to set aside your prejudices and step aside from any theory and even reject your own party platform if this will serve the business of saving a country from imminent destruction."[34]

Stephen A. Douglas devoted a speech in the Illinois legislature, two weeks after the beginning of the war, to the new efforts at uniting all conservative forces in the northern United States. Douglas, having decisively come out in favor of the

30. *Union and Republican Parties. Address of the Union Electoral Committee to the Union Men of Utica, New York* (New York, 1960), 2–3.

31. M. Marble to S. G. Arnold, April 7, 1861, *M. Marble Papers,* Cont. 2, LC, MD.

32. *The Letters and Literary Memorials of Samuel Tilden,* vol. 1, 151.

33. Robert W. Johannsen, "The Douglas Democracy and the Crisis of Disunion," *Civil War History* 9 (1963): 239.

34. *Proceedings of the Democratic State Central Convention held in Albany, January 31 and February 1, 1861* (Albany, N.Y., 1861), 5, 10.

war, announced the intention of his supporters to support all the necessary measures by the government for its successful prosecution. Expressing the will of the "War" Democrats, who had recognized the need to cooperate with the administration in carrying out the military plans of the North, Douglas appealed to all parties who supported the idea of reunification of the Union to refrain temporarily from including the war in their factional disagreements.[35]

The attempt to create a conservative interparty bloc reflected the intention of the "War" Democrats and Unionists to discover a way of more effectively hammering out a government course regarding the war. The conservatives, attempting to make reunification of the Union their primary and only goal, viewed with trepidation the supporters of those political movements that had gone outside the framework of the conservative tradition on the issue of slavery during the preceding period.

The radical Republicans represented a threat from the left to the conservatives' war plan. Their hope that slavery would be abolished during the course of the armed struggle with the rebels significantly increased in the initial period of the war. "Right now slavery itself proved to be more vulnerable to our attack," considered C. Shwartz, one of the more visible radicals, "than at any other period of our century."[36] Inasmuch as the radicals considered the liquidation of slavery as the primary condition for restoration of relations between the North and South, they categorically rejected any other way of victory over the Confederacy. "Confirm that we struggled for a political abstraction called the Union, but not for the destruction of slavery, which would mean a contradiction against common sense, as far as nothing different than slavery led the Union to the point of catastrophe, and one could wage war to its successful conclusion only having eliminated its reason,"[37] wrote subsequently another well-known radical activist, George Julian.

The threat to the conservative line from the right stemmed from those representatives of the Democratic party from the border states, who during the election of 1860 had put forward the nomination of John Breckinridge (Kentucky) as presidential candidate, and had proclaimed their solidarity with the expansionist South. Zealous defenders of the institution of slavery, these Democrats supported the Southern extremists to the utmost during the period of secession in their separatist intentions and tried to persuade the legislative bodies of their states to secede from the Union and join the slave Confederacy. Not able to attain this goal, they set aside their personal participation in secession, but continued to sympathize with its initiators. From the beginning of the war, for which they blamed only the abolitionists and Republican radicals in their threats to free immediately the slaves, and in their unwillingness to back down on the question of compromise with the South, the supporters of the reactionary proslavery wing of the Democrats lobbied to conclude immediately a peace agreement with the rebels. Their leader Breckinridge publicly declared that he

35. Johannsen, "The Douglas Democracy," 245; *The Letters of Stephen Douglas,* R. Johannsen, ed. (Urbana, 1961), 511–13.

36. T. Dennett, *Lincoln and the Civil War in the Diaries and Letters of John Hay* (New York, 1939), 22.

37. George Julian, *Political Recollections, 1840 to 1872* (Chicago, 1884), 222.

preferred "to see a peaceful secession of the Southern states rather than to witness endless, pointless, and devastating war."[38] In the name of ending the war as soon as possible, the "Peace" Democrats put forth a provocative slogan: "Millions for defense: not one dollar for waging a war of aggression."[39]

The conservative Democrats were not alone in their fears regarding the character and possible development of the war that had begun. The conservative Republicans exhibited just as much concern in this regard. No less than "War" Democrats and Unionists, they were worried about the influence of radical Republicans and "Peace" Democrats on the government's course. In their search for allies, they appealed to conservatives from the camp of the political opposition, just as they did during the period of secession, proclaiming their intention to reject the more odious, from the Democrats' point of view, positions of their party program. "The argument being waged now between the government and the states which have seceded went beyond the framework of interparty polemics," thought conservative Republicans. "The issue of slavery ceased to be a basic discord."[40] In order to neutralize the powerful radical wing in their own party and simultaneously resolve the pressing problem for the Republican leadership of permissible boundaries of the political opposition's activities in conditions of war, the conservatives proposed to "throw out the old and adopt a new name, the Union party," where they would unite under one roof all the patriots of the Union.[41] To realize this goal, William Seward strongly advised President Lincoln to refrain from antislavery rhetoric and to "deflect public attention away from the issue of slavery and direct it to the issue of the Union."[42] The plans to establish a Union party envisaged limiting the activity of the opposition within the boundaries of loyalty to the military course of the administration, that "true loyalty, which stands higher than all suspicions of sympathies for rebellion and the rebels."[43] The conservatives were convinced that a well-thought-out political line by the administration on global questions of prosecuting the war would become the indisputable basis for politics of all parties because "during the time of war the administration's party . . . in actuality is turning into a party of the nation."[44]

To gain the loyalty of the representatives of the opposition who were invited to join the Union party, the conservatives demanded from the Republican leadership strict guarantees that its war plans would not be concerned with the existence of slavery. One of the leaders of the right, Henry Raymond, warned that "any attempt to make this war into a means to emancipate the slaves will lead to a rebellion by the border states, divide the North and West, and will hasten the victory of the opposition party and in such a manner, discredit itself."[45] Even the new name of the party proposed

38. *Congressional Globe,* 37th Cong., 1st sess., 378–79.
39. *Speeches, Arguments, Addresses and Letters of Clement L. Vallandigham* (New York, 1864), 305.
40. *New York Times,* April 1, 1861.
41. *The Letters and Literary Memorials of Samuel Tilden,* vol. 1, 156.
42. *The Collected Works of A. Lincoln,* vol. 4, 317.
43. *Springfield Republican,* May 17, 1862.
44. "W. Claffin to J. Holt, October 20, 1862," *J. Holt Papers,* Cont. 35, LC. MD.
45. *The Collected Works of A. Lincoln,* vol. 4, 545.

by the conservatives had a practical purpose—it was to dispel doubts of the loyal opposition as regards the Republicans' intentions. The fact of the matter is that the term "Union" in party lexicon of the prewar period was intimately bound with the line of conservative compromise in politics. As is well known, in 1851 the proslavery-inclined Unionists of the South defeated the supporters of secession, relying on the principles of the Union party platform. But having defended slavery, the Unionists of the North attacked the Whigs of Seward and the supporters of Wilmot from the Democratic camp with the help of a Unionist coalition during the elections.

The conservative Republicans' initiative turned out to be quite attractive to many political activists from the North. The creation of a conservative coalition under the aegis of the Republicans entirely suited President Lincoln, leader of the ruling party, who was interested in finding support for the government's military efforts: after all, even after winning in the 1860 elections, the Republicans remained a minority party in the North.[46] Lincoln, not wanting to drive away representatives of the loyal opposition from his party, but at the same time submitting to the conservative Republicans' demands to refrain from a programmatic party stand on the issue of slavery, presented the essence of the administration's political line in the very streamlined formula: "My first goal in the struggle is to save the Union, and not destroy or save slavery."[47] The new patronage policy, which opened up the doors of federal institutions wide to representatives of the opposition who had declared their loyalty, aimed to prevent turning "this war into a partisan war," according to the justifiable estimation of the Secretary of War, the conservative Simon Cameron.[48] As expected, the position taken by the Republican leadership significantly hastened the process of creating a Union coalition. The "War" Democrats and Unionists, having left aside their reservations as to the intentions of the ruling party, overwhelmingly agreed to join the new political organization. Their leaders declared that "the Unionist movement is a grass-roots one, and nonpartisan," and therefore they felt that "all loyal people should join it with all their heart and all their soul."[49]

The goal, which led the conservatives to create the Union party, stimulated resistance from both reactionary elements in the Democratic party and radicals who safeguarded the purity of Republican party principles. The Peace Democrats saw a threat to their own political plans in the consolidation of conservative forces interested in the Confederacy's military defeat. Their leaders, trying to prevent this process, declared that the Democratic party leadership was betraying the interests of its followers by agreeing to accept "any proposal to unite with former political adversaries."[50] The radical Republicans, on the other hand, saw in the creation of a politically amorphous

46. Voters from the states that remained in the Union during the course of secession in 1860 cast 1,864,523 for Lincoln and 1,960,842 in favor of other presidential candidates (Potter, *Lincoln and His Party,* 189).

47. *The Collected Works of A. Lincoln,* vol. 4, 388–89.

48. Benjamin Butler, *Butler's Book. A Review of His Legal, Political and Military Career* (Boston, 1892), 239.

49. *Speeches, Correspondence Etc. of the Late Daniel S. Dickinson of New York,* J. Dickinson, ed. (New York, 1867), vol. 1, 200, 215.

50. *New York Tribune,* August 9, 1861.

and deideologized Union party an attempt by the conservatives to limit the emergency military powers of the government and weaken the ruling party, having taken away its antislavery potential. Leaders of the radical wing pointed out that the Union coalition, as envisaged by its creators, should have "excluded abolitionist elements from the Republican party," and they considered that its manifestation was a "a clear political mistake" and a voluntary shedding of the "prestige arising from the political success" in the 1860 election by the Republican party.[51]

The conservative Union coalition firmly announced its existence during the first session of the Thirty-seventh Congress. In the House of Representatives the united bloc of supporters for the successful prosecution of the war consisted of 158 Congressmen (102 were Republicans, 27 War Democrats, and the remaining represented the Union Constitutional party). They were opposed by only 20 Peace Democrats. In the Senate a shift of power in favor of supporters of the administration's policy was also evident, although not as much as in the lower House: 32 Republicans, 2 Unionists, and 5 War Democrats stood against 10 Peace Democrats. The initial disposition of political forces in many ways characterized the ongoing struggle heating up in Congress. On July 10, 1861, the Senate introduced a joint resolution that approved all military measures taken by the president during the period preceding the Congressional session. The Peace Democrats harshly criticized the government's actions mentioned in the resolution, raising doubts as to their constitutionality. The president's repeal of the law on personal immunity during the period of war especially infuriated the reactionaries. The unified bloc of representatives from the Union coalition did not allow the Peace Democrats to change the character of the resolution through amendments, having unanimously voted for its approval.[52] An attempt by one of them, the Democrat Willard Saulsbury (Delaware), to decrease the number of soldiers requested in the bill on recruiting volunteers, also ended in failure: 34 voted for the bill and 4 against it.[53]

On that very day a struggle between the Union coalition and the Peace Democrats began in the House of Representatives. One of the acknowledged leaders of the Peace faction, Clement Vallandigham (Ohio), declared that the bill on legal sanctions for increasing federal income during war was unconstitutional. He demagogically accused the Republican party of hatching a "vile plot with the goal of encouraging and aiding secession."[54] The next day Vallandigham and Henry Burnett (Kentucky) came out against the bill on appropriations for the army. In response the War Democrats, headed by John McClernand (Illinois), accused them of attempting to "sit idly twiddling their thumbs right at the time when rebel batteries were headed for the capital."[55] When Vallandigham stressed the need in the House to create special commissions within the standing "activated" armies, which would examine all enemy proposals for peace, the conservatives attacked him. The War Democrat Horatio

51. Cited from Hans Trefousse, *The Radical Republicans* (Baton Rouge, La., 1968), 137; *Springfield Republican,* September 10, 1864.

52. *Congressional Globe,* 37th Cong., 1st sess., 41.

53. Ibid., 53–54.

54. Ibid., 57–60.

55. Ibid., 73.

Wright (Pennsylvania) declared in the name of the supporters of the Union coalition that a peace with the Confederates was only possible if "they lay down their weapons and give up their leaders." Vallandigham's proposal was unanimously rejected by the conservative Congressmen.[56] The supporters of the Union coalition came out just as decisively and unanimously in support of the bill on conspiracies that mandated a prison sentence for attempts at overthrowing the government (the bill passed with 123 votes for and 7 against), and also of McClernand's resolution that envisaged the necessity of approving any request by the government for appropriations and additional volunteers in order to defeat the Confederacy as soon as possible (the resolution passed 121 votes to 5).[57]

The conservatives' highest achievement in Congress was the approval on July 22, 1861, in the lower house of John Crittenden's resolution that called for the immediate rout of the Confederacy and at the same time promised to preserve slavery in the South. The resolution was a blow to the Peace Democrats for two reasons. First, according to them, it was proposed by the author of an outstanding compromise with the South during the period of secession. Second, the promise to preserve slavery in the South contradicted the Peace Democrats' conviction that the Republicans were planning on waging war under the banner of antislavery slogans. Voting on various parts of the resolution confirmed the movement by the various groups that made up the Union coalition toward consolidation. The first part of the resolution was approved 121 votes to 2 (with fifteen abstentions during the voting by Peace Democrats). The second proslavery part passed in the House 117 votes to 2 (with 38 abstentions by Republicans). As expected, out of 26 representatives of the radical wing of the Republican party in the House, only John Potter (Wisconsin) and Albert Riddle (Ohio) voted against the resolution, but Thaddeus Stevens (Pennsylvania) and Owen Lovejoy (Illinois) abstained.[58]

A similar resolution introduced for discussion by the War Democrat Andrew Johnson (Tennessee) in the Senate was approved 30 votes to 5. Out of 12 Senators representing the interests of radical groups in the upper house of Congress, 10 voted with the majority. Only Charles Sumner (Massachusetts) abstained during the voting, and Lyman Trumbull (Illinois) voted against the resolution, having joined the minority, the Peace Democrats.[59]

The undoubted success achieved by the supporters of the conservative military-political course gave new life to their efforts during the 1861 election campaign. The atmosphere in the country was not favorable for the Republican party. Of sixteen states from the North, which it had controlled up to the beginning of the war, representatives of the ruling party felt confident only in Vermont and Massachusetts. In the remaining states the Democrats had strong organizations that were, as a rule, under the control of leaders from the reactionary Peace faction and were capable of competing with the Republicans in the elections. The Confederacy showed itself to be much stronger in

56. Ibid., 97, 98.
57. Ibid., 130, 131.
58. Ibid., 223.
59. Ibid.

the military sense than had been presumed earlier. This led to a loss of hope in a quick victory by the North in the war. Psychological problems were not the only issues that the main opponents of the administration in the election, the Peace Democrats, could use for political capital. The Republicans were concerned about the old Northwest region (the states of Ohio, Indiana, Illinois, Wisconsin, and Michigan), which had experienced serious economic difficulties after the Mississippi River was closed to commercial navigation. The farmers from the region expressed their dissatisfaction with the federal government's policy because they were forced to use more expensive railroad transportation for carrying their agricultural products. The bankruptcy of many of the banks in Wisconsin and Illinois also had very serious consequences for the farmers.[60]

Despite all the hopes of the Peace Democrats, the election turned out to be a catastrophe for them. In the vast majority of instances their defeat was predicated upon alliances of the interparty Union coalition of states, supporters of continuing the war. In Ohio, Wisconsin, and Pennsylvania, candidates from these coalitions had the reputation of being extreme conservatives on the issues of slavery and the methods of waging war. This convincingly showed the strength and influence there of War Democrats and Unionists. Slavery was barely mentioned in the campaign platforms of the Union coalition in the states mentioned above and was barely visible in the form of terminology from the well-known Crittenden resolution. The desire by the conservative Democrats and the Unionists to avoid discrediting themselves by cooperating with the radical Republicans led them to campaign as independents against the Peace Democrats and Republicans in elections in the states of Maine, Maryland, and California. In a whole series of incidents, however, candidates nominated during the Union conventions by the War Democrats in Iowa, Minnesota, and New York, for example, refused to run in the elections. This benefited the conservative Republican candidates who had called for maintaining the principle of noninterference in the issue of slavery. The Peace Democratic candidates only partially competed with the representatives of the Union coalitions in the elections in Illinois and Pennsylvania, and they won in New Jersey. In this traditionally Democratic state, on the eve of the elections, the War Democrats in large number united with the Peace faction. Careful attempts by the Republicans to break up this alliance and form a Union coalition on a particularly proslavery platform were fundamentally criticized by the radical wing. "They attempted to defeat proslavery democracy by means of proslavery republicanism—a policy, which will never succeed because it should not succeed," commented the publisher of the *New York Tribune,* Horace Greeley, on the actions of his conservative colleagues.[61]

However productive the alliance with the conservative opposition forces may have seemed to the leaders of the ruling party, the radical Republicans were more realistic in their evaluations of the results of the 1861 elections. They saw that support for continuing the war with the Confederacy held sway over the electorate despite the

60. Frank Klement, "Economic Aspects of Middle Western Copperheadism," *Historian* 14 (1950): 27–44.
61. Cited from C. Dell, *Lincoln and the War Democrats* (Rutherford, N.J., 1975), 121.

temporary disappointments arising from the North's military failures and the serious economic situation in the country. Moreover, they correctly felt that the main reason for the electorate's dissatisfaction was the indecisiveness of the North's military efforts. The barometer of the election campaign of 1861, from the point of view of the radical Republicans, did not in any way show that the majority in the North were in favor of conservative plans for a struggle with the Confederacy as envisaged by the creators of the Union coalition. Its arrow, thought the radicals, more likely pointed to a shift in the Northerners' sentiment toward an escalation in the government's war plan. The radicalization of popular opinion in this region was observed by several conservatives as well. Joshua Speed, an activist in the right wing of the ruling party, already by the end of 1861 had discerned with alarm the formation of "a numerous and powerful party of representatives of the ultra-left movement," which was prepared "to declare war on the president and his conservative policies."[62] The *New York Times* wrote about the manifestation in the North of "tens of thousands of people who demand that the government immediately raise the banner for emancipation of the slaves."[63]

Numerous slave uprisings in the South, and also "the underground railroad" of fugitive slaves to the North, especially from the border states, confirmed the radicals' premise that escalation of the government's war policy and a frontal assault on the institution of slavery were necessary.[64] The military occupation of plantation owners' property during the advance by Union forces into the South forced several officers to make practical attempts to free slaves. General Ben Butler in July 1861 declared fugitive slaves as "military contraband," which meant their freedom. General John Fremont, the commander of the Western army in the state of Missouri, was even more decisive in carrying out the policy of emancipation. In August 1861 he announced the confiscation of property, including slaves from the rebels in the region under his control.[65] Although his antislavery activities cost Fremont his military career— the conservatives managed to rescind his orders and removed him from his post as commander—his actions nevertheless met with resounding approval in the North. Even the conservatives themselves could not but recognize the enormous popularity of Fremont's measures regarding slavery. "The people applaud General Fremont's actions," wrote the *New York Times,* "They have delivered a blow to deepest roots of evil, and mortally wounded the hydra of rebellion."[66] All of this showed what Karl Marx wrote in December 1861, that "in the United States a crucial moment over the fundamental issue of the whole Civil War has arrived, that is over the issue of slavery."[67]

The rise in the mass antislavery movement in the North contributed to the rallying of the radical Republicans and spurred them into action. With the appearance of wide support for escalation of the war by the North, the radicals were presented

62. "J. Speed to J. Holt, Dec. 8, 1861," *J. Holt Papers,* Cont. 31, LC, MD.
63. *New York Times,* August 6, 1861.
64. G. P. Kuropiatnik, *The Second American Revolution* [Vtoraia amerikanskaia revoliut-siia] (Moscow, 1961), 109.
65. *Tribune Almanac 1862* (New York, 1862), 45.
66. *New York Times,* November 9, 1862.
67. K. Marx and F. Engels, *Essays* [Sochineniia], vol. 15, 429.

with the opportunity to begin an attack on all fronts on the positions of the conservative Union coalition. The first blow was delivered by the radicals who occupied key posts in the new entity of Congress, the joint Committee on War, created in December 1861. Thanks to their efforts Generals Robert Potter, Charles Stone, and also the commander-in-chief of the North's armies, General George McClellan, all of whom were Democrats famous for their defeatist attitudes, were removed from their commands. The activities of McClellan had long been a source of displeasure among the widest circles in society. Even many conservatives who sympathized with McClellan condemned his criminal sluggishness and indecisiveness.[68] The radicals managed to convince society that the military failures of the North were in large part due to the proslavery sentiments of the head commander and his sympathies with the Confederates. McClellan's harsh admonition of the president for the inexpedient contemplation by governmental bodies of "confiscation of property, political executions of persons . . . or forcible abolition of slavery" served as a warning that "a declaration of radical views, especially upon slavery, will rapidly disintegrate our present army."[69] Bowing to pressure from the radicals, Congress took this admonition as a show of disloyalty to the government. The application of the criteria "loyalty to the government" in the context of adherence to the political principles of the Republican party became the first evidence of the Republicans' retreat from the declared principle of a nonpartisan Union coalition.

The active and popular political course of the radicals, which began to tear apart the Union coalition, manifested itself in full color in the House of Representatives during the recurring discussion of the ideological credo of the conservatives—the Crittenden resolution—in the second session of the Thirty-seventh Congress. The conservative Democrat W. Holman (Indiana), once again putting the resolution to a vote, expressed the intention of the conservatives from the opposition camp to reaffirm the main condition for support of the administration's military efforts—noninterference in the existence of the institution of slavery. In the new conditions, however, not only the radicals and moderates but also the majority of conservative Republicans already did not wish to bend to the proslavery dictates of the opposition. The Crittenden resolution was rejected 71 votes to 65.[70]

All the growing pressure on the president from the radical Republicans and the mobilization of the popular masses in the North could not but lead to a definite shift in the policy of the administration. Up to that point, the only measure of an antislavery character supported by Lincoln was the law on confiscation of rebel property dated August 6, 1861, which freed slaves used in rebel military operations. The radicals, who headed the Joint Committee of Congress on War, explained during the course of investigations that this law was being ignored in practice by the conservative-leaning Democratic officers.[71] Direct sabotage of the government's military measures

68. "G. Welles to M. J. W., August 18, 1861," *G. Welles Papers,* Cont. 47, LC, MD.
69. *General McClellan's Letter to President Lincoln, July 17, 1862* (New York, 1862), 1–2.
70. *Congressional Globe,* 37th Cong., 2d sess., 15.
71. Ralph Korngold, *Thaddeus Stevens, A Being Darkly Wise and Ruddy Great* (New York, 1955), 171.

by conservative activists from the Union coalition affected the president's policy and his surroundings in the party leadership in the most serious way. Having set aside all previous fears of destabilizing the antislavery course in the interparty coalition, moderates in Congress introduced a bill on compensated emancipation of slaves in the federal District of Columbia. In the process of its prolonged deliberations the conservative bloc in Congress was split.[72] The conservative Republicans, who considered the bill too radical, were satisfied only after an amendment was added regarding the necessity of colonizing freed blacks abroad.[73] Leaders of the conservative opposition, led by Joseph Wright (Indiana), on the contrary disagreed completely with the bill, considering any appearance of emancipation as an unconstitutional act.[74] The War Democrat John Creswell (Maryland) incited the January and February 1862 meetings of his state legislature, where special appeals to the U.S. Congress were adopted warning about the unacceptability of infringing on the personal property of slave-owners.[75] In the final tally the bill was approved 32 votes to 10, having received the support of only one conservative representative from the opposition.[76]

As a result of this, the radicals managed to mobilize relatively easily the forces of the Republican party to support a bill on the emancipation of the slaves without compensation in the western territories and in the territories located under the direct jurisdiction of the federal government (forts, docks, arsenals, etc.). In the House of Representatives, 85 votes were cast in support of the bill (besides all the Republicans, 2 Unionists voted for it as well), with 50 against it. In the Senate it was approved 28 to 10, during which not one Republican Senator voted against it, and only one War Democrat voted for the bill.[77]

The radicalization of partisan and governmental politics included working out measures to provide the Union armies with all the necessary legal authority for the immediate emancipation of the slaves in territory liberated from the enemy. The passage of a special law that prohibited Union officers from returning fugitive slaves to slave-owning Confederates under threat of removal from command became the embodiment of this political line. Long and enormously difficult deliberations on this law at first brought to light significant opposition to it by conservatives—both Republican and Democrat—who were aiming to weaken it with an enormous number of amendments. Only the stubborn efforts of the radicals led to positive results. Although many conservative Republicans abstained during the final vote, not one of them came out against the bill in the Senate or the House of Representatives. The conservatives, War Democrats, and Unionists formed the opposition to the law during voting, during which two representatives of the opposition supported the bill in the Senate.[78]

The struggle to adopt a law on the mobilization of freed blacks in the Northern army was the next stage in the radicals' antislavery efforts. Attempts to legalize drafting

72. *New York Times,* April 1, 1862.
73. *Congressional Globe,* 37th Cong., 2d sess., 12, 16, 36, 89–90.
74. Ibid., 1468, 1479.
75. C. Clark, *Politics in Maryland during the Civil War* (Chesterton, Md., 1952), 164.
76. *Congressional Globe,* 37th Cong., 2d sess., 1179, 1192.
77. Ibid., 2041–54, 2066–69, 2618.
78. Ibid., 955–59, 1142–43.

freed slaves into the service in divisions of the militia, which had already taken place, did not succeed for a long time due to the fierce resistance by the opposition joined by the conservative Republicans: Senators Orville Browning, Edgar Cowan, James Doolittle, and Timothy Howe (both from Wisconsin) and a contingent of the moderates.[79] Only after a concession to the opposition that provided for freeing only slaves of rebels and drafting them for military service was the bill unanimously approved by the Republicans in Congress. During this, two War Democrats joined forces with the majority.[80]

The most important component of the antislavery attack by the radicals on the position of the conservative Union coalition was their struggle to pass a second law on the confiscation of rebel property. The bill, proposed by Zachariah Chandler and Lyman Trumbull, allowed for the confiscation of all possessions (including slaves) and property of both the rebels themselves and their accomplices. By this, the geography of confiscation widened. In accordance to the conditions of the bill, besides the slaves confiscated from the rebels, all fugitive Confederate slaves received freedom. Freed blacks were permitted to serve in the Northern army and navy, as was mobilization into special black divisions.[81]

The new initiative by radical Republicans was especially dangerous from the conservatives' point of view. It not only reflected the progress in public opinion on the question of emancipation but also put under doubt the hallowed constitutional principle of the inviolability of private property both in rebel and loyal states. The appearance of this law, thought the representatives of the opposition, was necessary for the Republicans not so much for the struggle with the Confederacy as for suppressing political opposition in the North. Having united with the Democrats, conservative Republicans Edgar Cowan, Jacob Collamer (Vermont), James Doolittle, and Orville Browning organized a broad front of resistance to the law on confiscation. Their efforts were successful: in the Senate, by the beginning of May only four radical Senators supported the bill.[82] In order to tone down the bill, the conservatives managed to have it transferred to a select committee in the Senate in which only three of nine members belonged to the radical wing of the Republicans.[83] A similar action was undertaken by the conservatives in the lower House, where a select committee of seven congressmen was created for examining legislation on confiscation.[84] The activity of the select committees, which accepted for examination dozens of amendments that at their root changed the initial substance of the proposed law, could not but differ in their final overall draft. A conciliatory committee of the lower House, which was convened to balance the drafts of the bill coming from the Senate and the House of Representatives, also introduced their own corrections to the legislation. As a result, its basic component, which earlier had allowed for confiscation of all rebel

79. Ibid., 3197–3207, 3227–36, 3249–54.
80. Ibid., 3337–52, 3397–98.
81. Ibid., appendix, 412–13.
82. *Congressional Globe,* 37th Cong., 2d sess., 1040, 1049–54, 1074–77, 1136–41, 1157–62, 1557–62.
83. Ibid., 1954–65.
84. Ibid., 1815–20.

property and that of their accomplices unburdened by long judicial procedures, was significantly weakened by the conservatives; appended conditions for the legislation that freed confiscated slaves and sanctioned drafting them into the military services underwent slight changes.[85] The report of the conciliatory committee was approved in the House 82 votes to 42; four Unionists from the border states joined with the Republican majority, but the conservative Republicans Bradley Granger (Michigan) and Benjamin Thomas (Massachusetts) joined the minority.[86] In the final vote in the Senate the bill was supported 27 to 12. Only one War Democrat, John V. Wright, supported the bill, while two conservative Republicans, Browning and Cowan, joined forces with the opposition.[87]

At its very core, the antislavery attack by the radicals contradicted the goals and the very idea of creating a nonpartisan Union coalition. It also helped to intensify the spirit of partisan rivalry between the Republicans and Democrats. Like a powerful catalyst, the radicals' legislative initiatives polarized the whole scepter of political forces in the North. The Union coalition, which had become the main embodiment of the former conservative tradition in politics at the beginning stage of the war, fell apart right before their very eyes with each of their new actions. Radical politics convincingly proved that the transference of the modus of relations between the Democrats and Whigs, which had rested upon the basis of conservative ideological compromise, to a new party tandem of Republicans-Democrats was entirely artificial and in the long run impossible. The Republican party, formed in a wave of resistance to the government's policy of compromise, could not be fitted into the framework of the conservative political tradition.

Separate attempts by the conservatives from both parties to resurrect the spirit of a Union coalition during the course of legislative action and at the same time halt the strengthening of the radicals did not bring the desired results. On May 10, 1862, conservative Unionists from the border states held a conference of conservative senators and congressmen on a nonpartisan basis, with the goal of organizing an "opposition to ultra-abolitionist measures" by radical Republicans. Of forty-three congressmen who gathered under the chairmanship of John Crittenden at the first session, only two were conservative Republicans—William Sheffield (Rhode Island) and William Kellogg (Illinois). The rest represented various movements within the opposition bloc.[88] Declaring their disagreement with the radicals' antislavery course, the "conservative caucus" nevertheless supported as before the government's military efforts and objected to any attempts to create a new opposition conservative party. The only real achievement of the caucus was the formation of a special committee of conservative congressmen for working on the recommendations to stem the radicals' attack.[89] The extreme volatility of the conservatives' proposals during the course

85. Ibid., 3266–67.
86. Ibid., 3266–68.
87. Ibid., 3275–76.
88. William D. Mallam, "Lincoln and the Conservatives," *Journal of Southern History* 28 (January 1962): 35.
89. Leonard P. Curry, *Blueprint for Modern America: Nonmilitary Legislation of the First Civil War Congress* (Nashville, Tenn., 1968), 87.

of the caucus reflected their feeling of being lost in the face of the Republican party's consolidation over antislavery principles. This mood among the conservative representatives of the opposition caused the second session of the caucus to fall apart later during the last six weeks. Having gained the attendance at the conference of only thirty-five conservative lawmakers, not one of whom represented the Republican party, the caucus finally closed powerless.[90]

The polarization of political forces, brought on by the radicals' antislavery efforts, marked the departure of the conservative Republicans from support of the course of the Union coalition. The centrifugal tendency also spread to the conservative Democrats. One contingent of them, having supported radical legislative measures, at the same time for all practical purposes identified themselves with the Republican party, while another contingent, numerically surpassing the first group of War Democrats, turned their sights on their former party colleagues, the Peace Democrats. Although the group of War Democrats, led by the well-known New York activist Horatio Seymour, did not deny their intentions to help the government in its war efforts as before, it put forward an ultimatum of federal nonintervention in the issue of slavery as a condition for their support.[91] Several general positions in the views of Peace and conservative Democrats who had left the Union coalition, especially their mutual interest in not allowing the Civil War to be turned into an antislavery contest, gave rise for the first time during the war years to the possibility of a strong opposition bloc. Already in May of 1862, on the suggestion of the leader of the Peace Democrats, Clement Vallandigham, a representative group of Democratic congressmen met to work out a concrete course for the party during wartime conditions. Those present, both the Peace and War Democrats, unanimously approved a programmatic declaration of the opposition, "An appeal by the Democratic congressmen to the representatives of the United States Democratic party." In its preamble they stated outright that there "should be and will be an opposition" in the country in the interest of "public safety." The Democratic party, as set out in the appeal, "is a party of the Union inasmuch as it preserved the Union by means of wisdom, peace and compromise in the course of more than half a century." A clearly proslavery call to "support the Constitution as it is, and the resurrection of the Union as it was," became the slogan of the opposition. The principles of the opposition were set out in the following manner: "Democrats recognize that it is their duty as patriots to support the government and at the same time oppose the war against any state . . . with the goal of subjugating or enslaving it, or for the purpose of interfering in the activities of the institutions established therein."[92]

President Lincoln delivered the final blow to the conservative political tradition. In a letter to the chairman of the National Committee of the Democratic Party, August Belmont, written in July 1862, he set aside any sort of diplomacy and declared: "This government cannot much longer play a game in which it stakes all, while its enemies stake nothing. Those enemies must understand that they cannot experiment

90. Mallam, "Lincoln and the Conservatives," 35.

91. S. Alexander De Alva, *A Political History of the State of New York* (New York, 1906), vol. 3, 27–29; *New York World,* February 24, 1863.

92. *Speeches, Arguments, Addresses and Letters of Clement L. Vallandigham,* 362–69.

for ten years trying to destroy the government, hoping that in the event of failure they can return to the bosom of the Union untouched."[93] Having ascertained the ineffectiveness of his own plan for the gradual emancipation on the basis of payments to slave-owners and colonization of blacks abroad—a plan approved by Congress, but rejected by every legislature from the frontier states,[94] Lincoln bowed to the inexorable logic of the development of the revolutionary events taking place in the country and appealed to the people in September 1862 with the famous Emancipation Proclamation. Effective January 1, 1863, it gave amnesty to those rebels who laid down their arms during a three-month period, and guaranteed freedom to the slaves of those participants in the rebellion who refused to capitulate. The blacks did not receive land or equal political and civil rights on par with the whites upon their emancipation. The Proclamation did not extend to that territory already won from the enemy.[95] With all its limitations, the president's proclamation was in fact a great document of a revolutionary epoch that witnessed significant changes in partisan and governmental politics on the basic question of the Civil War. Thanks to the efforts of the radical faction of the ruling Republican party and the leadership's position in tune with the times, headed by Lincoln, the war definitively and irrevocably entered a new and revolutionary phase. The transition to a "revolutionary war," in the words of Karl Marx, left the conservatives with no hope for forming a Union coalition in its previous form and with the previous set of ideological-political values. The old conservative tradition faded into the past for good.

The elections of 1862 served as proof of the irrevocable changes initiated in the political specter of the Union coalition. Unlike the campaign of 1861, the Democrats managed to win certain political successes. The Republicans lost thirty-five places in both houses of Congress and ended up in the minority in the legislatures of Ohio, Pennsylvania, Illinois, Indiana, and New Jersey. They also lost in the gubernatorial elections in New York and New Jersey. On the whole, however, out of twenty-one states where election campaigns were held, the Republicans were victorious in fifteen. The Democrats' successes in the polls were explainable not only by the fact that they managed to use the population's weariness of a prolonged war and economic difficulties, which prompted their dissatisfaction with the administration's policies, but also the very significant and in some places negative reaction by the Northerners to the publication of the president's Emancipation Proclamation. The main reason for the comparatively quick spread of a broad base for the opposition party in the elections of 1862 was that a significant contingent of War Democrats had withdrawn their support for the Union coalition and had united with the Peace Democrats, traditionally standing up for the interests of the opposition.

The Democratic party conventions stressed the need to unite all opposition forces and strengthen in any way the spirit of party loyalty in the ranks of the opposition. The New Jersey Democratic committee called on "conservatives from everywhere to fight

93. *The Collected Works of A. Lincoln,* vol. 5, 350.

94. *Congressional Globe,* 37th Cong., 2d sess., 1172, 1192; Dell, *Lincoln and the War Democrats,* 144.

95. *The Collected Works of A. Lincoln,* vol. 5, 433–36.

the abolitionists by means of the ballot."[96] Democratic leaders in Wisconsin appealed to the electorate with the request "to support experienced candidates, true Democrats, who adhere solely to party principles."[97] A call to toughen criticism of the Republican administration became the dominant note in all party documents of the Democratic party of this period. In a resolution approved by the party convention of Pennsylvania, the Republicans were evaluated as "not deserving to be invested with power," in connection with the demands from the voters for a "change of administrations."[98] The delegates to the Indiana convention decisively declared that "the Democratic party and its patriotic allies in the border states . . . were and always will be opposed to the most important endeavors of the Republican administration."[99]

The states of New Jersey and New York gave more convincing examples of the growth of the opposition's power during the election campaign as a result of the alliance between the War and Peace Democrats. In New York an absolute majority of thirty-five lawmakers, elected in 1861 to the state legislature as candidates from the Union coalition, were reelected in 1862 as representatives of the opposition Democratic party. In the states of Ohio, Pennsylvania, and Indiana the opposition camp of Peace Democrats also grew on account of those conservative Democrats who had left the Union coalition, of which the latter were so numerous that they completely took over the process of nominating candidates for elections and putting together a campaign platform.[100]

The disintegration of the Union coalition in the elections of 1862 was even more evident in the planned exit from it by the radical Republicans. Assessing the election campaign overall, one could ascertain with a good deal of certainty that the split of the interparty bloc ran mainly along the lines of "radicals-conservatives." In addition, in several states the schism was evident in Republican organizations themselves. The increasing certainty of the radical Republicans in their power, and the conservatives' hostility toward several outcomes of the antislavery attack in Congress, facilitated the radical Republicans' break with the conservatives. Thus, for example, in New York the conservative Republicans nominated a Democrat, General John Dix, for the gubernatorial post to offset the radicals' candidate, General J. Wadsworth, but when the latter received the overwhelming majority of votes at the convention, they refused to support him in the elections. In the state of Wisconsin the conservative Republicans attempted to upset the reelection of the radical Congressman John Potter, putting an independent candidate against him in the elections. In Illinois the conservative Republicans formed an alliance with the Democrats in order to prevent the reelection of the radical Owen Lovejoy. Radical Republicans occupied the more solid position in

96. *Address of the New Jersey Democratic State Central Committee to the Voters of the State* (Trenton, N.J., 1862), 14–15.
97. *Address to the People by the Democracy of Wisconsin, Adopted in State Convention at Milwaukee,* September 9, 1862, 8.
98. *Proceedings of the Democratic State Convention Held in Harrisburg, July 4, 1862* (Philadelphia, 1862), 4.
99. *Address of the Democratic State Central Committee to the People of Indiana, on the Crisis of the Country* (Indianapolis, 1862), 32.
100. Dell, *Lincoln and the War Democrats,* 172–73, 179.

the party organizations of Kansas, Michigan, and Massachusetts. Therefore the break by the Republican organizations with the Union coalitions proceeded at the quickest pace. It is worthy of note that a contingent of conservative Republicans remained in the ranks of the Union coalition in Michigan and Massachusetts, attempting by joint efforts with conservative Democrats to seize control over state legislatures and hinder the reelection of well-known leaders of the radical wing, Zachariah Chandler and Charles Sumner. The results of the election campaigns, however, proved the fallibility of the conservatives' plans.[101]

Outside the mainstream, the radicalization of the ruling party's course on the issue of slavery, which had been carried out by the representatives of its left wing, did not turn voters away from the Republicans. The departure of many Republican organizations controlled by the radicals from alliances with the conservative Union coalitions was not reflected in any sort of negative way on the Republicans in the polls. On the contrary, losses by the radical faction during elections were less than overall losses by Republicans. The main losses in the polls were suffered by the conservative wing of the party. Soon after approval of the second bill on confiscation in the House committee, Horace Greeley declared in his paper: "A dozen congressmen from the Republican or Union party from free states who had voted against the legislation, without doubt, already understood that they would not be supported by their voters in the elections."[102] His prediction turned out to be prophetic. Of all the conservative congressmen mentioned by Greeley, only John Hale (Pennsylvania) was reelected in 1862. In the whole House of Representatives of the Thirty-eighth Congress only four congressmen returned who had a reputation as conservative. The losses incurred during the elections mostly by the conservative Republicans showed the scale of popular support for the new antislavery course of the Republican party in the North.

The conservative political tradition did not withstand the onslaught of the bourgeois-democratic revolution. For a short period (1860–1862), from the beginning of secession and up to the end of the first stage of the Civil War, the ideology and politics of conservatism twice endured failures. If the secession of the Southern slave states sealed the conservatives' fate in not being able to preserve the "Union as is," then the Civil War's revolutionary phase definitively destroyed all their hopes of creating a "Union as it was." The abolition of slavery by the revolutionary act of Lincoln's government, which opened a new epoch in the history of American capitalism, marked a break with previous philosophical conceptions about the development of society. With the abolition of slavery the conservative political tradition was denied the basis of the existence of its ideological values and it thus lost all sense.

The inevitable crisis of conservatism in the politics of the prewar period was predicated primarily upon inherent contradictions within the American socioeconomic system, between slavery and free labor. At its utmost peak, the crisis revealed class interests surrounding the resolution of the problem of slavery and became heated to the point of antagonism. The crisis determined the whole course of political development

101. Ibid., 176, 189.
102. *New York Tribune,* June 19, 1862.

in the United States and ran counter to the intentions of the creators of the conservative tradition. The failure of this political tradition, based on the idea of compromise on the issue of slavery, did not mark the disappearance of conservatism per se. Conservatism continued to exist in sharp contrast to other ideological currents. Now, however, it could not take account of those cardinal changes in the socioeconomic structure and the political makeup of American society, which were shaped by the bourgeois-democratic revolution.

Comment

by Phyllis F. Field

During the American Civil War the attitude of European powers toward the conflict concerned many Americans both in the North and South, for European actions as mediators, participants, or interventionists could directly affect the war's resolution. When the Russian fleet steamed into New York harbor in 1863, Northern newspapers, on no particular authority, assumed it represented the best wishes of the Tsar for Union success. Only much later did different motivations emerge.[1] Today's U.S. historians of the Civil War perhaps share some of the insularity of the Northern journalists of 1863. They read primarily American views of the conflict and make assumptions about the views of others. Yet now, with an ever-shrinking world, it is more important than ever to communicate across the boundaries of ideology, culture, and national history. These essays on the Civil War published in the Soviet Union in 1985 and 1990 and now available to U.S. readers present important steps in this direction.

Sergi Porshakov and Alexander Kormilets view the Civil War as an important transition in American history and reach very similar conclusions about the meaning of the period's politics. Indeed, according to Kormilets' footnotes, the two men have coauthored a book on American politics from the late 1840s to 1865. To them the war marks the inevitable failure of a political system trying to accommodate both the demands of expansionist planters committed to slave labor and Northern industrial capitalists dependent on free labor. Given rival and incompatible sectional economic interests, compromises between sections, while attempted out of respect for property rights, were destined to fail. Porshakov demonstrates this failure in the secession crisis of 1860–1861 while Kormilets notes conservative attempts to defend slavery that continued through the war's early stages but declined with the inevitable shift to emancipation in the context of warfare against a slaveholding regime. With slavery's demise, U.S. politics could finally center entirely on the needs of industrial capital.

One may compare these historians' understandings of this political era with that of their U.S. counterparts. The emphasis on sectional economic differences is obviously familiar territory beginning with the work of Charles and Mary Beard on the "Second American Revolution" during the 1920s. Over time historians in this tradition have broadened their economic analyses to see rival labor systems as the basis

1. E. A. Adamaov, "Russia and the United States at the Time of the Civil War," *Journal of Modern History* 2 (1930): 586–602.

for not only opposing sectional economies but also social systems and ideologies.[2] While Marx has been an important figure for such historians, he is a starting point only, and interpretative differences, especially over the inevitability of proletarian revolution, have caused some Marxists to label many such U.S. historians "liberal bourgeois."

But American interpretations of the politics of secession and emancipation are not confined to variants of Marxist analysis and indeed are quite broad-ranging, often providing sharp critiques of both Marxists and rival non-Marxists. While arguments among historians may at times recall the passions of the war itself, mutual criticism in a pluralist setting does serve to expose the assumptions that individual historians are making that others do not share. This is especially important when historians' theoretical approaches deny that such assumptions are being made. Marxism, as one example, is a type of structuralist interpretation which assumes that an economic structure based on who controls the means of production underlies (and causes) events as well as social, governmental, and cultural differences. Marxist education enables one to perceive this structure, but the possibility that the structure does not exist or does not operate as posited is seldom pursued. Thus, interpretations stemming from non-Marxist viewpoints may seem of limited use to Marxists, especially if the latter write for an audience who share Marxist assumptions.

The Cold War has obviously denied Porshakov and Kormilets access to not only unpublished primary sources in the United States but also the interpretations of many American historians, for only a handful of the secondary works from this country dealing with secession and emancipation appear in their notes and rarely are these findings even then discussed. For example, Porshakov reports in a note the conclusions of Ralph Wooster's 1962 study of voting for secession conventions but without commenting on variables such as previous party affiliation that do not form part of his own analysis.[3] A more sophisticated statistical analysis of these data done in 1978 is not cited.[4] If challenge and debate strengthen argument and conceptualization, the post–Cold War era may hopefully see Russian historians directly addressing (and disputing) the most recent American interpretations.

The lack of such scholarly interchange is obvious in what Porshakov assumes as requiring no proof, "facts" that American historians have argued over for many years. These include claims that 1) politically successful secession efforts originated with a core of fire-eaters who appealed primarily to cotton planters and aspiring planters; 2) the aim of secession was political power; 3) the differences between cooperationists and immediate secessionists were ones of strategy, not attitudes toward the Union; and 4) "trade ties" primarily explained reluctance to secede. Among American historians, competing ideas on these points have led to searching out new sources (e.g., evidence

2. A nice synthesis of these interpretative trends, which shares many insights with Porshakov and Kormilets, is Bruce Levine, *Half Slave and Half Free: The Roots of Civil War* (New York, 1992).

3. Ralph Wooster, *The Secession Conventions of the South* (Westport, Conn., 1962).

4. Peyton McCrary, Clark Miller, and Dale Baum, "Class and Party in the Secession Crisis: Voting Behavior in the Deep South," *Journal of Interdisciplinary History* 8 (1978): 429–57.

of popular racial fears fueling the secession of South Carolina) or analyzing old sources in new ways (e.g., statistical analyses of secession votes).[5]

Given the decentralized nature of U.S. politics in the nineteenth century, localized studies have further enriched the understanding of secession-era politics. The result has been a more complex (and much less tidy) picture of reality. Instead of the opposite extremes of fire-eaters and antislavery Republican leaders acting within economically incompatible sections to create a war, one sees a variety of forces and issues operating within many different local political contexts to bring about the same result. Michael Holt's study of the prominence of ethnocultural issues in the emergence of the Republican party in Pittsburgh is an example of this.[6]

Assuming, rather than documenting, profound sectional differences based on incompatible labor systems, Porshakov looks to the secession crisis to demonstrate the inability of the party system to generate compromise. The chief significance of the interlude between Lincoln's election and Fort Sumter *is* to demonstrate that political failure. While most U.S. historians likewise see little possibility for a union-saving compromise by 1860–1861, some nonetheless view the crisis as significant in other ways. They portray a political system struggling to define how many slave states would secede, whether there would be war or peace, and who would bear the blame for disunion. These were important outcomes, and the political maneuvering occurring cannot be understood or appreciated, they insist, without their consideration.[7]

Indeed, Porshakov loses the sense of a real crisis, with uncertainty and changing calculations on a daily basis, because he organizes his discussion topically, with separate discussions of Lower South secession, party positions, Buchanan's activities, Congress's efforts to compromise, and the Washington peace convention. Each separate context illustrates for him the failure to attain compromise. Yet these episodes were complex, frequently overlapping, and affecting one another. Lower South secession conventions were being authorized and delegates elected at the same time Congress was asked to create a compromise. Men who supported secession still held their seats in Congress and could easily undermine compromise. Republicans were clearly on the defensive as secession moved from abstraction to reality but were less constrained later on when the Upper South held firm. Party, factional, and individual positions were debated and changed to respond to new conditions over time. Seeing only the ultimate result of failure, Porshakov rarely identifies participants in the congressional and peace conference activities by state, party, factional affiliation, or personal agenda, making these patterns of behavior difficult to understand or evaluate.

With his belief that the political extremes dominated and were responsible for system failure, Porshakov also slights the Constitutional Union party despite its strength in the key area of the Upper South. A party that denied the automatic incompatibility of free and slave labor and insisted on compromise and respect for the

5. Steven A. Channing, *Crisis of Fear: Secession in South Carolina* (New York, 1970).

6. Michael F. Holt, *Forging a Majority: The Formation of the Republican Party in Pittsburgh, 1848–1860* (New Haven, 1969).

7. David M. Potter, *The Impending Crisis, 1848–1861* (New York, 1976), chap. 19 provides an interesting synthesis of the works discussing this maneuvering.

Constitution is clearly an anomaly given Porshakov's view of the South, and some fuller explanation of its behavior is clearly warranted. Daniel Crofts's monograph on the Upper South Unionists was not published until 1989, four years after Porshakov's essay, but four articles outlining his arguments preceded it.[8] They question the idea of a unified South using electoral as well as documentary analysis and echo the suggestion of Michael F. Holt that those Southerners outside the Cotton South saw the political system as a still viable way to pursue goals.[9] So convinced is Kormilets, in his turn, of Southern unity based on demanding protections for slavery that he even attributes the secession of the four Upper South states to the failure of the Washington Conference rather than Fort Sumter and Lincoln's call for volunteers.

Those U.S. historians who have emphasized Southern diversity posit issues other than living in a slave economy affecting political behavior there. Holt, for example, argues that secessionists spoke in the nationally shared language of republicanism, which depicted battles to protect liberty, equal rights, and self-government from threats by power, privilege, and despotism. In the Upper South a two-party system remained that could assure voters they might protect important values through voting for parties rather than fighting; in the Lower South, it did not. Parties stood for something important in this view and were more than just a conglomeration of economic interests. Holt also sees voters as more independent and important actors than does Porshakov. Bourgeois parties, in the latter's view, cannot represent the ideas of the masses who are simply manipulated by leaders. Elections thus cannot reveal popular opinion or shape leaders' strategies, an assumption rarely shared by U.S. political historians. Thus, perceiving a South of different and competing voices, these U.S. historians have come to see more in the secession crisis than just the failure of a political system under siege from extremists.

Some U.S. historians also see the diversity of views within the North somewhat differently than does Porshakov. Emphasizing the extremes, he sees radical and moderate Republicans as the key to the rejection of compromise, noting their unwillingness to compromise on the extension of slavery. In contrast, some U.S. historians have pointed out the peculiar nature of this crisis.[10] The trigger was the secession of seven states in the wake of Lincoln's election, not any issue before Congress. In the North neither antislavery nor "capitalism" made the strongest rallying point but instead the idea that secession was unacceptable because it violated the principle of democratic elections, the cornerstone of the political system. Many Northern Democrats, such as John A. Dix and Edwin Stanton, both serving in Buchanan's cabinet, took this position. Whether guarantees to the slave states could or should be used to restore the Union was a more open question between parties and factions. Would it be submission to Southern blackmail (the radical view) or merely generous reassurances to alleviate groundless fears? In either case secession was unacceptable and therefore the likelihood of war greater; in this view commitment to the political system by a

8. Daniel W. Crofts, *Reluctant Confederates: Upper South Unionists in the Secession Crisis* (Chapel Hill, N.C., 1989), iv.

9. Michael F. Holt, *The Political Crisis of the 1850s* (New York, 1978).

10. Potter, *The Impending Crisis,* chap. 19 again offers the most succinct statement.

broad spectrum of Northerners who didn't necessarily agree on other issues ironically led to the war.

Kormilets extends the argument that extreme positions on slavery could no longer be contained through politics into the early stages of the Civil War. Believing that slavery was the central issue, he divides the political universe into conservatives (Democrats, Constitutional Unionists, and conservative Republicans who favored compromise to protect property in slaves) and radical Republicans and their usually accommodating moderate allies. He traces conservative efforts to sustain a war solely for the purpose of restoring the Union and their inevitable failure. This is illustrated by the decline of the Union movement after the 1861 state elections, the growing partisanship in votes on slavery-related matters, and the discrediting of conservatism through the efforts of the radical Joint Committee on the Conduct of the War, which exposed conservative incompetence and alleged "sabotage" of the war effort. Radicals, encouraged by African American slave escapes and sustained by popular opinion as confirmed in the 1862 elections, compelled Lincoln to issue the Emancipation Proclamation. Although the proclamation was limited in scope, Kormilets sees it as radical in effect. From this point on "conservatives" in U.S. politics would be protecting the interests of industrialists, not slave-owners.

Although some U.S historians have emphasized the limits of the Emancipation Proclamation and the continuance of racism in the Civil War era, Kormilets' conviction that emancipation was a revolutionary act would also find ready supporters in this country.[11] In general, however, U.S. discussions of the war's revolutionary impact seem more broadly based (in the destruction of Southern infrastructure and the dislocations in the economy and society rather than solely in emancipation) and less exclusively intended for the benefit of industrialists.[12]

But Kormilets' intent is less to examine emancipation's consequences than to explain how it came about. As he notes, none of the major parties in 1860 endorsed abolition. His approach, however, is not to show the growing strength of abolition as much as the weakening of conservative defenses. Within a context of military ineffectiveness and slave restiveness, Kormilets sees radicals in Congress introducing legislation turning the war from one to preserve the union to one to free and arm slaves. Noting the appearance of "Union" electoral tickets in many states in 1861, he posits these as an attempt by conservatives to control the radical wing of the Republican party by threatening to withhold support for the administration if the war became too radical. When partisanship increased in 1862 and "Union" tickets disappeared in states like New York, he sees this as proof that conservatism had declined. He also interprets the congressional elections in 1862, despite Republican losses, as a defeat for conservatives since, as Horace Greeley noted, conservative, not radical,

11. These divergent views are reflected in Louis Gerteis, *From Contraband to Freedman: Federal Policy toward Southern Blacks, 1861–1865* (Westport, Conn., 1973) and Herman Belz, *A New Birth of Freedom: The Republican Party and Freedmen's Rights, 1861–1866* (Westport, Conn., 1976).

12. An excellent discussion of how U.S. historians have viewed the war's revolutionary impact is in James M. McPherson, *Abraham Lincoln and the Second American Revolution* (New York, 1991).

Republicans were the most likely to have lost their seats. Lincoln thus was forced to the extreme position of issuing the Emancipation Proclamation by the conservative collapse.

While some U.S. historians have likewise pursued the idea of congressional radicals pushing Lincoln toward emancipation, e.g., Hans L. Trefousse,[13] who is cited frequently by Kormilets, the idea of a conservative coalition that weakened over time is far less popular. From the outset these "conservatives" were in different parties that responded not to just one issue, slavery, but to many. Thus cooperation as a self-understood "conservative" group was always difficult. Kormilets relies on analyzing self-selected congressional votes (usually final) on slavery to establish patterns. He does not comment on or refer to Allan Bogue's 1985 quantitative analysis of Senate voting patterns which suggests that the breach between radicals and moderates was greater than Kormilets acknowledges and that conservative influence showed itself in the amending of Senate slavery legislation. Rather than slavery dominating overall voting patterns, Bogue sees a traditional to modernizing continuum characterizing the Senate.[14] In this case as in others, the opportunity to debate different interpretations has been lost.

U.S. historians have also been less certain than Kormilets that conservatives were cooperating electorally. As Kormilets acknowledges, parties were decentralized in this era. Thus, a "union" movement linking Democrats and Constitutional Unionists to Republicans might not be the same in New York and Kentucky. In the border states, where the Republican party was barely organized, a union movement served as a way for people to support the Lincoln administration without becoming Republicans. Many unionists were former Whigs. Their goals might be to foster recruiting, earn civil or military patronage, or root out local secessionists as well as to protect slavery. Further north, backers of "union" tickets might be Democrats intending, as Joel H. Silbey has noted, "to forgo partisanship at this moment in order to allow the war to be won by a united country."[15] No factional organization united conservative unionists or, given the partisanship of the time, was likely to.

While Kormilets portrays unionism as initiated by conservatives to control radicals, most U.S. historians have understood the reverse. Republicans stood to gain from unionism political support in the strategically important border states as well as Democratic acquiescence in the Lincoln administration's war measures. They promoted "no-partyism" even as Democrats complained that they could never regain power under it.[16] Many Democrats felt that abandoning the union movement made conservative voices stronger, not weaker.

Like his U.S. counterparts, Kormilets is drawn to the analysis of the election of 1862 to see whether there was a conservative backlash against emancipation.

13. Hans L. Trefousse, *The Radical Republicans: Lincoln's Vanguard for Racial Justice* (New York, 1968).

14. Allan G. Bogue, *The Earnest Men: Republicans of the Civil War Senate* (Ithaca, N.Y., 1981).

15. Joel H. Silbey, *A Respectable Minority: The Democratic Party in the Civil War Era, 1860–1868* (New York, 1977), 40.

16. See ibid., 42.

In this country the election has been interpreted in widely different ways—as a rejection of emancipation because of overall Republican losses, as a moral victory since Republicans lost fewer seats than in an average off-year, or as an ambiguous outcome because of the presence of many issues.[17] Disagreement over the meaning of the results has forced U.S. historians to ever-greater precision in defending their stands as indicated in particular by quantitative analyses of election returns at the state level.[18] Kormilets does not participate in this debate, merely quoting Horace Greeley's optimistic analysis of the returns.

U.S. historians have also argued over the role of the Joint Committee on the Conduct of the War. Did it advance public sentiment in favor of emancipation by exposing conservative generals as ineffective and possibly pro-Confederate in their efforts to protect Southerners' property, or was it so clearly partisan that its exposés were discounted by nonradicals?[19] Kormilets assumes that its claims were influential without addressing the contrary argument.

If conservatism (on property rights, on constitutionalism, on race as well as on slavery) remained important in the United States of 1862, as some U.S. historians assert, then Lincoln's role in emancipation becomes more significant than Kormilets admits. Lincoln's genius lay precisely in his ability to maximize support for the essentially radical act of emancipation by reassuring wary voters of emancipation's constitutional validity, military necessity, racial conservatism, and protection of private property in slaves unless of value to the enemy. The fact that his audience was largely nonslaveholding and at war with the South clearly helped.

Overall, Kormilets and Porshakov have approached secession and emancipation with many of the same questions as have U.S. historians. Ideology directs them more toward materialistic factors to understand political behavior than is true of the wide range of U.S. political historians. Competition between historical interpretations has directed U.S. historians to construct ever more elaborate defenses for their viewpoints. With the opening of greater communication with Russian scholars, one may anticipate more challenges as well as fruitful exchanges on both sides.

17. James M. McPherson, *Ordeal by Fire: The Civil War and Reconstruction,* 2d ed. (New York, 1992), 295, provides a convenient summary of the arguments.

18. See, for example, Phyllis F. Field, *The Politics of Race in New York: The Struggle for Black Suffrage in the Civil War Era* (Ithaca, N.Y., 1982).

19. Allan G. Bogue, *The Congressman's Civil War* (New York, 1989), 101–3, provides an interesting summary of the historiography of the committee.

Response

by Alexander A. Kormilets

From the very beginning, in the process of preparing our articles for this publication, we have been very optimistic about the opportunity to test some of our ideas on secession and the Civil War in an open dialogue with our American colleagues. The opening of the post–Cold War decade made the significance of such joint ventures as "The Russian-American Dialogue in History" series even more obvious than ever before. A long era of misunderstanding between American and Russian scholars—if not an era of conscious unwillingness to understand each other—seemed to come to an end. New possibilities to exchange views on a pluralist basis—or, using the terminology of our commentator, Professor Phyllis F. Field, "to communicate across the boundaries of ideology, culture, and national history," mean exactly what they mean: that is, the necessity to wage an open-minded dialogue, sacrificing the previous comfort of neglecting each other to the aim of mutual understanding. To use these possibilities, both sides might at least come to compromise on abstaining from Cold War stereotypes in approaching each other.

To our regret, it looks like interaction with Professor Field on the pages of this publication is far less encouraging than it is disappointing for both sides. It is quite obvious that the major point of Professor Field's disappointment with us was our alleged inability as Marxists to challenge the American historical community with the new interpretations of secession and the Civil War, as well as an inability to answer their new challenges. It looks to her that we have lost almost all chances to dispute with our colleagues from overseas on the principal questions of that crucial period of American history. Even the final passage of Professor Field's comment, surprisingly portraying both Russian authors in compromise terms (with the exception, of course, of their strict ideological commitment), contains as well a great dose of the same disappointment.

Ironically enough, our disappointment with Professor Field's comment concentrates around the like areas of debate and has the same ground. Although she proclaims the necessity "to communicate across the boundaries of ideology," it looks as though she is not ready to pursue that goal.

The inability and unwillingness to see rationale and challenge in almost any scholarly argument based on Marxist theory of understanding history, and the concurrent desire to label that kind of scholarly work as ideologized nonsense, not even worth counterargumentation, is simply another kind of the same ideologization she is against so much, no matter with what mark—"plus" or "minus."

If it was not the case, one can hardly find in the comment a short, but meaningful further guide for readers of the book, explaining to them the "essence" of Marxism in terms so oversimplified, if not vulgar, that finally the whole passage happened to have nothing in common with the said Marxism and scholars, using its methods and instruments in understanding history, economics, culture, and social life. The basic assumption of Professor Field—that Marxism is equal to the primitive economic determinism—will never find understanding in the Russian historians' community.

If that is not the case, what was the reason for the author of the comment on secession and the American Civil War studies merely to mention in her argumentation the term "inevitability of proletarian revolution"—other than to frighten the reader one more time with the remnants of Bolshevism and Cold War?

If that is not the case, was it really necessary to summarize the argumentation of both articles so briefly and with such abridgments that it gives the commentator the chance to subscribe to us conclusions we have never made in our works? For example, Sergei Porshakov has never stated that "bourgeois parties . . . cannot represent the ideas of the masses who are simply manipulated by leaders," and that "elections, thus, cannot reveal popular opinion or shape leaders' strategies." In the same way, I have never come to the conclusion that "Lincoln in issuing the Emancipation Proclamation . . . was forced to this extreme position by the conservative collapse."

O, those Russians! They really do not understand how to satisfy their American colleagues. In order to do that, of course, if they want to be understood at all, they should submit their scholarly works in the format their American counterparts have gotten used to—i.e., free from notorious terminology including "class struggle" and "ruling classes" and with necessary homage to all founding fathers of all new concepts in national American studies in every article submitted to the critic (no matter how many articles, chapters in the books and the books themselves you might have in your research file, which were directly devoted to the full-scale debates with the prominent American scholars). Otherwise, you will be blamed for intention to consciously neglect non-Marxist viewpoints—the intention seemingly so natural for every true old-fashioned Marxist. I think I could afford only one final question addressing Professor Field in this regard: How many Russian historians appeared in the footnotes of your scholarly works? And if, presumably, they are few, if any, why so?

Despite all above-mentioned disappointments with the unsuccessful experience of public debate with our respectful American critic, and with excuses for the sarcasm exposed in the last paragraph of my reply, which I hope will be understood and forgiven by Professor Field, let me conclude on her own optimistic note, which I totally share with her: "With the opening of greater communication with Russian scholars, one may anticipate more challenges as well as fruitful exchanges on both sides."

6

Silver against Gold

On the Genesis of the Reformist Policy in the United States (the First Half of the 1890s)

by Larisa V. Baibakova

The last decade of the nineteenth century, which was characterized by the evolution of capitalism to its highest, monopolist stage of development, witnessed the exacerbation of the conflict between labor and capital in the United States. The workers' struggle had also acquired new features. It became more organized, and conscious political demands were put forward more often. The Socialist party campaigned more actively; in 1892 and 1896 it won 21,164 and 36,456 votes respectively.[1] There was a strong sense of unrest among the petty bourgeoisie. Farmers, urban unincorporated bourgeoisie, and the intelligentsia began to struggle with more vigor against the economic advance of capital. The new conditions of class struggle made it imperative for the ruling elite to discard the old ways of exercising power and find new techniques. Since violence and relentless denial of reforms failed to produce any result, the tactics of maneuvering and compromise were preferred. The first attempt to adopt certain principles of the reform strategy turned out to be fruitful. The ruling circles were able not only to rebuff the upsurge of the antimonopolist movement, unmatched before, but also to channel it in a safe direction. The use of new and up-to-date methods of leadership stabilized the political system and its basic institution, political parties.

The problem of the origins of the reform course in the last decade of the nineteenth century has had pride of place in contemporary American historiography.[2] Political scientists claimed that expanded federal regulation of social relations proved the existence of the democratic form of government in the United States, "the rule by people." However, the real facts of the growing class struggle were substituted for

1. U.S. Bureau of the Census, *Historical Statistics of the United States, Colonial Times to 1970* (Washington, 1975), vol. 2, 1073. This essay by Larisa Baibakova was originally published in *Vestnik Moskovskogo Universiteta* [Moscow University Herald], Series 8, History, 1987, no. 4.

2. Bruce A. Campbell and Richard J. Trilling, eds., *Realignment in American Politics: Toward a Theory* (Austin, Texas, 1980); Jerome M. Clubb, William H. Flanigan, and Nancy H. Zingale, *Partisan Realignment: Voters, Parties and Government in American History* (London: 1980); Robert W. Cherny, *Populism, Progressivism and the Transformation of Nebraska Politics, 1885–1915* (Lincoln, Nebr., 1981); and Richard J. Jensen, *Grass Roots Politics: Parties, Issues and Voters, 1854–1953* (Westport, Conn., 1983).

election returns. It was concluded that the internal contradictions could be resolved within the two-party system by means of class peace, "without violence and without conspiracy."[3]

American authors have considered the reasons for the modification of the political line of the ruling class in different ways because of the diversity of methodological approaches. Some scholars followed Walter Burnham and William Chambers, whose thesis was based on opposing "agrarian" interests to "industrial" interests. They saw the basis for reorganization of the bourgeois parties in the ongoing conflict between the western and southern agrarians and the representatives of corporate capital, "the northeastern industrial elite."[4] Those who adhered to another point of view (Philip Converse and others), related the evolution of the two-party system to the involvement of new groups in the electoral process in the 1890s.[5] The representatives of the "ethnocultural" school, which stressed the primacy of religious and ethnic factors in the political attitudes of the voters, asserted that the reconstruction of the bourgeois parties took the shape of the "religious battles" among the members of different congregations and denominations.[6]

In Soviet historical science, bourgeois reformism as one of the basic trends of political process has been better studied for the twentieth century.[7] However, its genesis and the evolution of the ruling circles' tactics in the earlier period has been studied insufficiently.[8] An examination of the bourgeois parties' activities in the last decade of the nineteenth century provides opportunity to discover the mechanism of modification of the political line by the bourgeoisie through transition from classical liberalism to the adoption of some elements of the reform strategy.

3. Walter D. Burnham, "The Changing Shape of the American Political Universe," *American Political Science Review* 59 (March 1965): 25.

4. William N. Chambers and Walter D. Burnham, eds., *The American Party System: Stages of Political Development* (New York, 1975), 283.

5. Philip E. Converse, "Comment on Burnham's 'Theory and Voting Research,' " *American Political Science Review* 68 (September 1974): 1025.

6. Richard J. Jensen, *The Winning of the Midwest: Social and Political Conflict, 1888–1896* (Chicago and London, 1971), 58–59; and Samuel T. McSeveney, *The Politics of Depression: Political Behavior in the Northeast, 1893–1896* (New York, 1972), x.

7. See Irina A. Beliavskaia, *Burzhuaznyi Reformizm v SShA, 1900–1914* [Bourgeois Reformism in the U.S.A., 1910–1914] (Moscow, 1968); Viktor L. Mal'kov, *Novyi kurs v SShA.: Sotsial'nye Dvizheniia I Sotsial'naia politika* [New Deal in the U.S.A.: Social Movements and Social Policy] (Moscow, 1973); Vladimir O. Pechatnov, *Demokraticheskaia partiia SShA: Izbirateli I Politika* [The U.S. Democratic Party: Voters and Politics] (Moscow, 1980); and Boris D. Kozenko, *"Novaia Demokratiia" I Voina: Vnutrenniaia politika SshA, 1914–1917 gg.* ["New Democracy" and the War. The U.S. Internal Policy, 1914–1917] (Saratov, 1980).

8. See Vladimir V. Sogrin, *Istoki Sovremennoi Burzhuaznoi Ideologii v SShA* [The Origins of the Modern Bourgeois Ideology in the U.S.A.] (Moscow, 1975); A. Bochkarev, "Demokratich-eskaia Partiia na rubezhe XIX–XX vv." [The Democratic Party at the Turn of the 19–20 Centuries], in Nikolai V. Sivachev, Galina A. Golovanova et al., eds., *Politicheskie Partii SShA v novoe vremia* [The U.S. Political Parties in Modern Times] (Moscow, 1981); and A. Salamatin, "Problema 'Serebrianyh Deneg' I Krizis Demokraticheskoi Partii v Seredine 90-h gg. XIX v." [The issue of Silver Money and the Crisis of the Democratic Party in the mid-1890s], in *Problemy Novoi I Noveishei Istorii* [Problems of Modern and Contemporary History] (Moscow, 1982).

The Second American Revolution (1861–1877) ushered in a new stage of evolution of the U.S. two-party system. Basically, it was characterized by the party system becoming totally subordinate to big business and rising monopolist capitalism. All the manifestations of social discontent were bitterly suppressed and the demands of the working people ignored. To justify their unwillingness to resolve the problems produced by the rapid growth of monopolies, the leaders of the bourgeois parties resorted to the ideology of Herbert Spencer's social Darwinism. It proclaimed individual freedom and noninterference with business to be the only laws of social development. Through the pressure of the popular masses Congress was forced to approve antitrust legislation in 1887 and 1890, but most of it remained only on paper. Such measures were regarded by contemporaries "to befool the people."[9] They could not reduce the social tension in the country.

The late 1880s were marked by a growing class struggle and strike movement (130,000 took part in strikes in 1881 and 610,000 in 1886).[10] Simultaneously, the new rise of the antimonopolist movement began. Its mass base consisted of impoverished small farmers, who became dependent in one way or another on bank, commercial, or land capital. The popular demand among the masses for "cheap money," independent and free coinage of silver dollars, whose value would be almost three times less than the gold ones, became the slogan of the day. Farmers, small businessmen, and even some workers considered this to be the basic solution to the internal problems. The explanation of such a phenomena lies in the fact that in the 1890s silver became a concentrated expression of social discontent and a symbol of protest against the growing exploitation caused by the emergence of a qualitatively new form of capital, financial capital, in the course of monopolization. As the transition from the domination of capital in general to the domination of the financial oligarchy was under way, tycoons step by step seized control of the great bulk of the country's revenue and the key branches of the economy, primarily industry and banking. Their contemporaries clearly realized the sociopolitical polarization of the society. They pointed out that "all the issues of monometallism and bimetallism did not bear on the monetary system at all; gold implied the capitalist and his immense social power, and silver implied small fry, seeking the means to overturn this power."[11]

The growing social antagonism became apparent in the process of the restructuring of the electorate, its ebbs and flows, and "pendulum like" fluctuations of large groups of voters within the two-party system as well as their shifts to parties without. The 1890 midterm election ushered in the era of party instability and tore asunder the broad coalition that had voted for the bourgeois parties in the 1880s. The strong unrest among the lower strata of the population resulted in the increase of the number of independent voters and the emergence of the farmers' parties in the West and in the South. These parties took an active part in the 1890 campaign. The emergence of the Populist party on the national political scene in the 1892 election indicated

9. *New York Times,* April 1, 1890.

10. U.S. Bureau of the Census, *Historical Statistics,* vol. 1, 179.

11. Arkhiv Vneshnei Politiki Rossiiskoi imperii [Archive of the Foreign Policy of Russian Empire], f. [record group] 170, op. [inventory] 512/1, d. [folder] 101, l. [sheet] 173.

the instability of the two-party system. The platform it adopted in 1892 set forth planks on the democratization of political life as well as economic demands directed to weaken the strength of big capital. Some ideas related to the reorganization of the financial system (introduction of an income tax, repeal of the tariff, establishment of subtreasuries, which would assume the functions of the national banks, etc.). The resumption of free coinage of silver was proclaimed to be the main measure to relieve the plight of the working people. Having put forward a leftist alternative to the policies of the bourgeois parties, the young Populist party became their serious rival.

Increased social activity of the masses caused the split among the ruling classes and exacerbated the intrastructural conflict between the unincorporated groups of bourgeoisie and the monopolist upper strata. The different groups of the ruling class disagreed upon the best and the most efficient means to reduce the range of the class struggle and upon the extent of the possible concessions to the broad masses of population. In the course of the ideological and political struggle the shrewdest statesmen realized that antidemocratic policy squeezed the opportunity for maneuvering. They came out with an idea of seeking more flexible means to overcome social protest and to elaborate "the methods which will satisfy and appease the present discontent of the great masses of the people."[12]

The creation of the two-party bloc in the Congress, which consisted of the majority of the western and southern Democrats and the western Republicans, reflected the changing alignment of political forces within the ruling class. This left bloc did not have a clear-cut program. It put forward the ideas that originated "from below." Its activity became apparent during the debates on the antitrust legislation in 1887 and 1890. The proposals of the members of the coalition to fine the corporations, to inspect their yearly accounts, to prohibit the practices of stock-watering, and to define clearly the notion of "monopoly," in sum to fight effectively corporate capital, indirectly reflected the antimonopolist demands of the broad masses. In this respect their ideas to prohibit pools, trusts, and other monopolies and to create a national mechanism to regulate the activities of private business seem especially important.

When the proposal of President Benjamin Harrison to stop the coinage of silver dollars and to substitute them for bonds was debated in the Congress in the spring of 1890, the members of the two-party bloc took a special stand. They opposed the aims of both parties, which called for the gold standard, and supported the demand of the masses for free coinage of silver. However, not everyone in the bloc shared this idea. A split occurred in the left wing of the Republican party. The midwestern liberals declared their adherence to "sound money" and focused their efforts on measures to bring about political democratization. The silver cause was upheld only by the representatives of the Far West within the Grand Old Party.

The social structure of the two-party liberal bloc presented a conglomeration of different groups of bourgeoisie. It included farmers, unincorporated entrepreneurs, and a part of the rapidly growing stratum of monopolists. In their eyes free coinage of silver and expansion of the amount of money in circulation would quickly heal all the social "ailments." It would "revive industries and put millions of laboring men now out

12. *Congressional Record,* 53d Cong., 3d sess., January 15, 1895, 970.

of employment to work, giving them bread."[13] Their efforts were aimed at returning to the policy of bimetallism, introduced by law in 1837, which had established the parity between silver and gold at a ratio of 16 to 1. This demand implied that $1.29 would be paid for an ounce of the "white" metal while its market price did not exceed $0.70 in the early 1890s. In other words, the idea focused on the improvement of the plight of broad masses of population at the expense of federal subsidies.

Liberal-minded politicians took up the mass demand about "rehabilitation of silver."[14] They not only urged the party leadership to put it on their agenda but also sought immediate action to be undertaken in the Congress to fulfill this idea. "If adoption of free coinage for silver and for gold is not promptly undertaken by the Democratic Party which is in such overwhelming majority in the House, a *suspicion* will arise in minds. . . . The danger of awakening any such *suspicion* may amount to actual peril and therefore ought by all means to be avoided."[15] In their opinion, if the political course was switched to bourgeois reformism, it would be the very means they needed.

In the spring of 1890 the slogan referring to free coinage of silver was included in the platforms of almost all the Democratic conventions of the western and southern states. It was also upheld by the Republican parties of California, Colorado, Montana, Nevada, Oregon, South Dakota, Indiana, and Kansas. Then in the summer of 1890, the members of the liberal bloc (twenty-seven Democrats and fifteen Republicans) secured the adoption of the bill on free coinage of silver by the Senate. However, it was blocked in the House of Representatives by the conservatives. Only when the adoption of the main Republican program measure, the protectionist tariff, was at stake, did their leadership make some piecemeal concessions. The measures, introduced by the new act on money circulation named after John A. Sherman, its originator, were very limited. The monthly purchase of 4.5 million ounces of silver by the federal government could not remove the popular demand of expanding the amount of money in circulation from the agenda. In January 1891 and July 1892 the two-party bloc managed to pass the bill on free coinage of silver through the Senate again.

As the election of 1892 approached, the greater number of bourgeois politicians came out in favor of using the popular slogan in their campaign tactics. "The subject is too firmly imbedded in politics to be ignored," they pointed out.[16] The shortsightedness of the party leadership, whose platforms emphasized only protectionism, was under fire from critics. The adherents of the silver "panacea" argued that tariffs were no longer as attractive to voters, who were much more concerned about other issues, primarily "contracted money supply and the appreciating standard of gold monometalism."[17]

13. House of Representatives, Report no. 1086, 51st Cong., 1st sess., 1890, 19.
14. R. Lacey to David Hill, December 5, 1891, David B. Hill Papers, New York State Library, Manuscript Division, box 1, folder 17.
15. W. John to David Hill, December 10, 1891, David B. Hill Papers, New York State Library, Manuscript Division, box 1, folder 27.
16. H. White to S. Webster, September 2, 1891, New York State Library, Manuscript Division, box 1, folder 30.
17. S. Nicholson to David Hill, December 24, 1891, David B. Hill Papers, New York State Library, Manuscript Division, box 1, folder 22.

However, the ruling conservative elite was reluctant to discern the great potential contained by the demands of broad masses of population. Championing the interests of the northeastern tycoons, who came out for the preservation of the gold standard, the conservative elite flatly denied the possibility of the "dangerous and reckless experiment."[18] The issue of protectionism was given preference in the 1892 party platforms.

The great potentialities of social maneuvering were demonstrated by David B. Hill, the Democratic governor of New York. This conservative politician was the greatest of the demagogues of his time. For tactical reasons he claimed to be a liberal politician. His criticism of the Sherman [Silver Purchase] bill yielded him electoral support, even though his program contained nothing extraordinary. He enlisted the support of several party organizations throughout the West and the South by taking up the slogan of "parity between the two metals, equality in the intrinsic value of all dollars."[19] Hill's hypocritical aspiration to oppose himself to the traditional establishment coincided with the upsurge of the movement for independent political action. Having declared their political incompatibility with the conservatives, some politicians pursued a course of breaking their relations with party leadership. Henry M. Teller (Colorado) coordinated the new movement among the liberal-minded Republicans and Hill among the Democrats. However, Hill failed to cope with the task to which he was entrusted by the local organizations. Becoming scared by the development of the political situation, he began to propound the necessity of preserving party unity. "Shall we break our party formation and go to pieces," he questioned rhetorically, " . . . or shall we simply vote to repeal the two McKinley Acts and to destroy the bounty and subsidy system root and branch?"[20]

The sharpness of the ideological differences among regional factions became apparent during the national conventions in the summer of 1892. The delegates from the southern and western states initiated the vehement discussion over the issue of money. In their opinion, "the recognition of the doctrine of free bimetallic coinage" and "the coinage of gold and silver dollars of a fixed parity, and each dollar containing metal of intrinsic value"[21] were the most important among all the issues discussed.

The pressure of popular masses compelled the leadership of both parties to include the ideas of bimetallism in their platforms. The Democrats came out for "the use of both gold and silver as the standard money of the country." The Republicans added that there should be "such restrictions and . . . provisions, to be determined by legislation, as will secure the maintenance of the parity of values." Thus the stand of either party was declared vaguely. In fact they denied the idea of free coinage of silver and reflected the interests of northeastern conservatives, who flew the banner of bimetallism.

In the 1892 campaigns the Democrats attained success, not only electing Grover

18. Grover Cleveland to E. Anderson, February 10, 1891, in Allan Nevins, ed., *Letters of Grover Cleveland, 1850–1908* (Boston, 1933), 246.

19. Governor Hill's Great Speeches at the Democratic Ratification Meeting, October 8, 1891, New York State Library, Manuscript Division, box 15, 11.

20. The Issues for 1892, December 4, 1891, New York State Library, Manuscript Division, box 15, page 23.

21. *Official Proceedings of the National Democratic Convention, Held at Chicago (Ill.), June 21, 22, 23, 1892* (Chicago: 1892), 94–95.

Cleveland president but also preserving their majority in the House of Representatives. The previous steady balance that had existed between the bourgeois parties in the 1880s was upset and the new alignment of forces emerged. The monopoly of the two-party system in the electoral process was challenged by the activities of the Populist party, which had won more than one million votes. It swept the core Republican states of Idaho, Kansas, Colorado, and Nevada. The support of the ideas of the third party by southern farmers weakened the base of the Democratic party in the region. Three senators and eleven representatives made up the Populist faction in the new Congress.

The radicalization of the masses made it imperative for the bourgeois parties' leadership to seize the political initiative and find the means to channel the activities of the third party into a safe direction. However, while the left-wing representatives of the bourgeois camp were eager to soothe the sharp social conflict by means of reforms, the ruling elite drifted in the opposite direction. The severest of the nineteenth century's economic depressions, which began in 1893, disclosed the danger of the policy of "stubborn conservatism." The old-type leaders, who had outdated experience in running the country, proved to be insufficiently trained to meet the challenge of more complex socioeconomic problems of the forthcoming age of imperialism. In 1893 the volume of production dropped sharply, the number of bankruptcies was immense, and unemployment reached the level of 11.9 percent, unmatched in the nineteenth century. The capital drained abroad in growing amounts and money deposits were withdrawn from banks all over the country. The budget deficit reached $70 million for the first time in U.S. history. Silver was exchanged for gold at a market ratio of 31 to 1. Contemporaries "can't fail to see that financial question is the all important one and is the one which is fast forging to the front in national politics."[22]

The conservative government of Grover Cleveland reacted by taking measures to preserve reserves of gold and to liberalize the system of protectionism to a certain extent. On August 8, 1893, the president exhorted Congress to repeal the Sherman Act. The pro-monopolist bias of Cleveland's proposal caused disaffection among his supporters. The recommendations of the president "contained not a word in sympathy with bimetallism," Hill pointed out, "and tends to make the fight . . . between bimetallism and monometallism."[23] Indeed, bitter factional struggle within the parties had broken out again. Political passions seethed in the discussion of the issue of money circulation. Contemporaries even noted that the air smelled of a new civil war.[24] The primary results were a sharp weakening of party ties and the disappearance of the traditional division of political organizations into factions: the "conservative" faction that had propounded the interests of northeastern monopolist capital and the corporations of the Middle West within the Republican party and the interests of the southern business circles within the Democratic party; the "moderate" faction within the Democratic party based on southern and western agrarians, and

22. A. Van Hagenen to David Hill, March 22, 1893, David B. Hill Papers, New York State Library, Manuscript Division, box 3, folder 18.
23. As quoted in Jennette Paddock Nichols, "The Politics and Personalities of Silver Repeal in the United States Senate," *American Historical Review* 46 (October 1935): 27–28.
24. D. Barry, *Forty Years in Washington* (New York, 1947), 186.

"moderate" Republicans, based on the farmers of the Middle West and the Far West. The steady balance of power that had existed between these factions within each party since the 1870s gave way to party diffusion. Contemporaries pointed out that "silver is tearing the parties to pieces."[25] The growing bipolarity of the structure of the political organizations brought together conservative politicians on one side and liberals on the other. They made up the right and the left wings respectively. The emergence of interparty coalitions was a deviation from the normal functioning of the two-party system, whose constituents had been highly disciplined after the Civil War (1861–1865).

The new party cleavage was an obvious effect of the deepening crisis of the bourgeois parties. This became apparent in 1893, when the problem of money was debated in the Congress. Two coalitions emerged both in the House of Representatives and in the Senate. One of the blocs was represented by the proponents of "cheap money." It consisted of the liberal-minded Democrats from the southern and western states, the western Republicans, and the Populists. Their agenda provided for: "First. in general terms, more money; and that it should be silver money, as there is not enough gold. . . . Second . . . the coinage of gold and silver without discrimination against either metal."[26] The repeal of the Sherman Act without taking any obligation to remonetize silver was regarded as "unreversible refusal" to coin the "white metal."

The right wing of the Congress included the adherents of the "gold standard" idea. It was dominated by the Republicans from New England and the Middle West, who were supported by the Democrats from the Northeast and the South. The conservatives sought to prevent the issue of money from becoming the strategic point of their agenda. They regarded the repeal of the Sherman Act as the first step in carrying out their main party measure, tariff reform. More than once they tried to reduce the emission of silver dollars and shift the country to monometallism, and to resist the parity between the two metals to be established at a ratio of 16 to 1. They argued that the remonetization of the "white metal" would "at once seriously impair the obligations of all existing contracts, destroy credit, deprive labor of employment, expel capital of the country and cripple all our industrial and commercial enterprises."[27] However, while Democrats fought for the resumption of money circulation of both metals at a "nominal value," the Republicans emphasized the necessity to conclude a treaty with other countries on a single silver standard on a "common basis or a parity." They viewed the establishment of a monetary union as a part of a broader international agreement on protectionism that would embrace primarily the states of Central and South America. Some Republicans even nurtured the ideas of "tough," forced inclusion of the Republics of Latin America in the customs union by means of imposing economic sanctions on them.[28]

25. Henry Adams to Charles Milnes Gaskell, September 27, 1894, in Worthington C. Ford, ed., *Letters of Henry Adams, 1892–1918* (Boston, 1938), 57.

26. *Congressional Record,* 53d Cong., 1st sess., 18, 1479.

27. J. Carlislie to Everett Wheeler, April 27, 1895, in Everett Wheeler, *Sixty Years of American Life: Taylor to Roosevelt, 1850–1910* (New York, 1917), 217.

28. *The Nineteenth Century,* vol. 41, 1897, no. 239, 3.

Cleveland's administration succeeded in achieving its aims through resorting to "arm-twisting" tactics in dealing with the Congress. Under the enormous pressure of party leadership, congressmen were compelled to sanction the repeal of monthly purchases of silver (by a vote of 131 to 108 in the House and 43 to 32 in the Senate).[29] The Republicans made up the majority of the supporters of the government's course. The three-party coalition, consisting of the southern and western Democrats, the Republicans from the Far West, and the Populists, voted against the repeal. The southern Democrats were the nucleus of the opposition. Seventeen out of 28 senators and 52 out of 101 representatives from the region opposed the repeal of the act. In other words, the policy of Cleveland was supported by the majority of the Republicans and the minority of the Democrats. As the country's highest legislative power, the Congress faced an anomalous situation. Short-sighted policy of the conservative government exacerbated the relations within the Democratic party. The president had found himself void of the support of the majority of his party. The rival factions became even less compatible after the bill, introduced in 1894 by Richard Bland (Missouri), was debated. The bill provided for the emission of silver bonds for a total of more than $55 million, accumulated by the treasury while the Sherman Act was in effect. It was a kind of a compromise, aimed at the appeasement of the factions, that would reckon with the demands of the adherents of silver and could hardly affect the interests of the Wall Street financiers. However, the "stubborn conservatives" with Grover Cleveland at their head spurned it, qualifying the introduction of one more bill on the remonetization of silver as a "disgrace," a crime, and an abandonment of national interests. But the alignment of forces in the Congress was not in their favor. In March the Bland bill had passed through the House of Representatives by a vote of 168 to 129. The three-party coalition, consisting of 136 Democrats, 22 Republicans, and 10 Populists, voted for it. The number of those who supported the idea of a silver "panacea" had increased markedly since 1893.

The decision of the House of Representatives predetermined the future of the bill. Silver sentiments were strong enough among the senators, and the bill passed easily through the Senate (44 to 31). However, having qualified the decision of the Congress as "hitting at the stability of currency," the president vetoed it. The members of the three-party coalition failed to override the veto. They were thirteen votes shy of the majority they needed. Nevertheless, the number of those who disagreed with the political course of the government was significant: 144 congressmen voted against the veto, and only 114 endorsed it.[30] The opposition to the conservative leadership increased within the Democratic party.

Given such a situation, the conservative government resorted to violence. It crushed the Pullman strike of 1894, the largest labor movement of the century, and dispersed the unprecedented march of the jobless to Washington the same year. Yet the real balance of class power made it impossible to resolve the sharp social conflicts

29. *Congressional Record,* 53d Cong., 1st sess., August 28, 1893, 1008; October 17, 1893, 2598.
30. *Congressional Record,* 53d Cong., 2d sess., March 1, 1894, 2517, 2524; April 4, 1894, 3460.

by means of suppression. The political unsteadiness of Cleveland's administration increased. The policy of "stubborn conservatism" had nothing to do with the interests of the majority of voters and led the Democratic party into a deadlock.

In May 1894 an article by Bland, one of the leaders of the anti-Cleveland opposition, was published in the *North American Review*. Bland pointed out that the split among the Democrats had loomed large. The clinging of Cleveland's administration to the old methods of governing was assessed as a "great mistake" that would entail the losses of the party's mass support.[31] Bland's forecast came true. The pro-monopolist course of government resulted in the Democrats' utter defeat during the 1894 midterm elections. While the Democratic party had 62 percent of the seats in the House of Representatives in 1893, after the 1894 elections the Republicans won 69 percent of the House's seats.

It was the first substantial Republican success since 1890. As the internal difficulties increased and the economic situation deteriorated, business circles began to associate the stabilization of the economy with the Grand Old Party. "Protectionism" remained the main slogan of the Republicans. However, they increasingly stressed its positive impact on the living standards of the popular masses. The Republican strategists adroitly avoided the controversial issues. They pursued the political line that could be summed up as follows: "remain calm and wait for the development of events within the Democratic Party."[32]

Simultaneously, the inability of the two-party system to exert influence on the masses any more became apparent when the Populist party got 1.5 million votes, almost half a million more than in 1892. The growing alienation of broad masses of the population from the bourgeois parties made their leadership anxious. It had to adjust its strategies and tactics. The southern and western Democrats, urged by the decreasing influence of their party among the voters, proved to be the most active in this sense. During the 1894 midterm elections the party organizations of the regions tried to take advantage of using such popular proposals as free coinage of silver, nationalization of transport, compulsory arbitration in labor disputes, and direct elections of senators. The Republican conventions of the western and southern states included the plank on the "silver panacea" in their platforms. The Republicans in Nebraska, New York, and Wisconsin even demanded "workers' right to organize."[33] The fact that some party organizations adopted these ideas, popular among the masses, indicated the trend for further transition from the principles of classic liberalism to the introduction of the elements of bourgeois reformism. This provided for the expansion of federal regulation.

After the 1894 elections the left-wing Democrats became increasingly insistent in putting forward the reform alternative to the "stubborn conservatism" as a means to overcome crisis. The slogan of the day was taken for granted. Everybody agreed that the money issue became of primary importance for the political life. In the fall

31. *North American Review* 148 (1894): 560.
32. O. Platt to H. Conkling, June 12, 1893, in Richard McCormick, *From Realignment to Reform: Political Change in New York State, 1893–1910* (Ithaca, N.Y., 1981), 57.
33. Anna Rochester, *The Populist Movement in the United States* (New York, 1943), 93.

144 Larisa V. Baibakova

of 1896 it became known that the adherents of silver "are making the plan for 1896, when the silver party shall have swallowed the Populists as the Republican party did the Free-Soilers."[34]

To carry out the policy of making advances to the masses, it was indispensable to break with the conservatives, who blocked the efforts to liberalize the political course. The issues of "taxation, currency and strained relations between capital and labor" became the main criteria of ideological and political cleavages within the bourgeois parties.[35] The Democratic party was torn apart by sharp contradictions. By the beginning of 1895 "the line of battle is drawn between the forces of safe currency and those of silver monometallism" among the Democrats.[36] Further coexistence of rival factions within the same party was impossible. More often the political opponents uttered the slogan "Long live the struggle" at the end of their speeches.

Cleveland's administration sought to discredit the idea of "free, unlimited and independent coinage of silver [by the Government] at a ratio which will add to our circulation," which experts assumed would add "unrestrained millions of so-called dollars."[37] All over the country the conservatives sought to increase gold standard sentiments.[38] Through the mediation of the Republicans they concluded the contracts with the biggest banks on granting loans totaling $273.5 million. Such a financial deal would increase the country's debt to $607 million. In people's eyes it proved that a secret conspiracy between the representatives of the ruling classes and big business existed indeed. William Jennings Bryan (Nebraska) pointed out: "The Democrats of the East and the Republicans of the East lock arms and proceed to carry out their policies regardless of the interests and the wishes of the rest of the country. If they form this union, offensive and defensive, they must expect that the rest of the people of the country will drop party lines, if necessary, and unite to preserve their homes and their welfare."[39] These words, uttered by one of the leaders of the "silver" movement, meant more than a mere threat. The process of consolidation of the "left" opposition was gaining momentum. In February 1895 the conservatives failed to pass through the Congress a bill providing for the issuance of 3 percent interest bonds for a total of $65 million. One hundred sixty-seven congressmen, or 58 percent, condemned the extortionate provisions of the bill that promised fabulous profits to the Wall Street "golden bugs." The analysis of the voting makes clear that both parties were bitterly divided. The conservatives' support was limited to the Northeast, the most industrially developed region. The number of their adherents in the West and the South shrank drastically. As estimated by American historians, two-

34. Francis L. Statson to Grover Cleveland, October 7, 1894, in Nevins, *Letters of Cleveland*, 369.
35. T. Rosser to David Hill, December 5, 1894, David B. Hill Papers, New York State Library, Manuscript Division, box 3, folder 36.
36. Grover Cleveland to W. Baker, G. Smith, J. Roach, T. Harvey, D. Kelly, H. Robins, April 13, 1895, William Gorham Rice, New York State Library, Manuscript Division, box 1, folder 5.
37. Grover Cleveland to John S. Mason, May 20, 1895, in Nevins, *Letters of Cleveland*, 394.
38. Grover Cleveland to Chicago Group, April 13, 1895, in Nevins, *Letters of Cleveland*, 384–85.
39. *Congressional Record*, 53d Cong., 3d sess., Appendix, 287.

thirds of the Democrats and two-fifths of the Republicans did not support the stand of the party leadership.[40]

By the national convention of 1896 the southern and western Democrats had achieved a high level of cohesiveness. The adherents of the circulation of gold money, represented basically by the states of New England, constituted a clear minority. Their number was not higher than 342, while 586 delegates were on the silver side. The resolution condemning the policy of "stubborn conservatism" was adopted by 564 votes to 257. The majority of the convention's participants rejected the efforts of the "Gold" Democrats at reaching a compromise. The latter considered it possible to nominate their candidate for the president provided the plank on free coinage of silver was included in the platform. The leader of the "Silver" Democrats, William J. Bryan, was nominated to run for the White House. In the opinion of contemporaries, the victory of those who adhered to the reform methods of resolving the grave social problems would mean the "birth" of the new party: "It is not the old traditional Democracy . . . but an entirely different opposition force."[41]

The adoption of a platform became the apotheosis of the convention. It marked the abandonment of the principles of classic liberalism in favor of the elements of bourgeois reformism. The inclusion into the platform of such populist demands and ideas as free coinage of silver at a ratio of 16 to 1, the introduction of an income tax, the establishment of arbitration in labor disputes, and governmental control over the implementation of the antitrust legislation made it possible for the Democrats to seize the initiative from below.[42] In July 1896 the conservative leadership of the Populist party managed to nominate William Bryan as a presidential candidate, despite the protests of the party's left wing. Thus the Democratic party accomplished one of the challenges the two-party system had faced. It managed to channel strong and dangerous insurgents in a safe direction. Bryanism had become a classic example of moderate bourgeois reformism.[43]

By the fall of 1896 the positions of each side were clear. The South and the West, reflecting the agrarian interests, came out for silver, the industrial Northeast stood for gold. It was universally recognized that this was "the first national campaign in the U.S.A. when the majority of debtors were on one side and the creditors on the other."[44] The powers were almost equal. Ten northeastern states with a population of 32 million people confronted thirty-eight southern and western states with the population of 30 million. The Middle West was to determine the winners and losers. The election resulted in the defeat of the Democrats. They won 46.7 percent of the popular vote; 51 percent of voters gave their votes to the Republican nominee, William

40. Rochester, *Populist Movement,* 100.

41. *Review of Reviews* 14 (1896): 312–13.

42. On the 1896 electoral campaign see A. Bochkarev, "Demokraticheskaia partiia," 188–97.

43. See Alla A. Porshakova, "Demokraticheskaia Partiia v Oppositsii: Vnutripoliticheskaia Bor'ba I Genezis Burzhuazno-reformistskoi Doktriny (1900–1912)" [The Democratic Party in Opposition, 1900–1912] in *Problemy Amerikanistiki* [Problems of American Studies] 4 (Moscow, 1986): 126.

44. *Atlantic Monthly* 78 (July–December 1896): 450.

McKinley. Assessing the results of the election, it is worth agreeing with the opinion of Soviet historian Vladimir Sogrin that "the hour of bourgeois reformism in the United States had not struck yet."[45] Nevertheless, the bourgeois reformism slowly but steadily sprouted. In the early twentieth century not only Democrats but also Republicans resorted to the strategy of social maneuvering.

45. Grigorii N. Sevost'ianov et al., eds., *Istoriia SShA v chetyrekh tomakh* [History of the U.S.A.], vol. 2 (Moscow, 1985), 39.

7

The Democratic Party in Opposition

Political Debates and the Origins of the Reformist Ideology (1900–1912)

by A. A. Porshakova

The United States' entry into the twentieth century was accompanied by a significant worsening in the socioeconomic problems that faced the country's political parties. In the 1890s, a strong wave of antitrust sentiment forced the ruling circles to search for more effective means in political maneuvering and to attempt to integrate the Democratic opposition forces within the framework of the two-party system. The Democratic party began to reevaluate its traditional laissez-faire doctrine. The party organization had been noted for its deep-rooted conservatism. During the 1896 elections, as clear symptoms of a crisis became vividly evident during the years of the second administration of Grover Cleveland,[1] the party presented itself before the electorate as the party of the "common people."

The specific makeup of the broad electoral base of the party, a significant part of which was composed of farmers from western and southern states, became an important factor in the earlier adjustment by the Democrats to the changing mood of the electorate. Distancing themselves from the conservative party leadership and purposefully stressing the issue of free minting of silver, the reformers managed to integrate the powerful Populist movement into the two-party system—a splash of agrarian radicalism uncharacteristically powerful for the first half of the 1890s—and significantly broadened their influence on the voters.[2] The Democrats then neutralized a strong anti-imperialist movement that had arisen at the turn of the century in reaction to the Spanish-American War of 1898.[3]

1. The Democrat, Grover Cleveland, twice headed the White House, from 1885 to 1889 and from 1893 to 1897. This essay by A. A. Porshakova was first published in *Problemy amerikanistiki* [Problems in American Studies] 4 (1986): 108–31.
2. For more detail on the Democratic party during the 1896 elections see G. P. Kuropiatnik, *The Farmers' Movement in the U.S. from Grangers to a Populist Party, 1867–1896* [Fermerskoe dvizhenie v SShA. Ot greindzherov k Narodnoi partii. 1867–1896] (Moscow, 1971); A. G. Bochkarev, "The Democratic Party during the 1896 Elections" [Demokraticheskaia partiia na vyborakh 1896 g.], in *Problems of Recent and Contemporary History in the Countries of Europe and America* [Problemy novoi i novelshei istorii stran Evropy i Ameriki] (Moscow, 1978).
3. For more detail on the anti-imperialist movement see I. P. Dement'ev, *The Ideological Struggle in the U.S. over Expansion at the Turn of the 19th-20th Centuries* [Ideinaia bor'ba v SShA po voprosam ekspansii na rubezhe XIX-XX vv.] (Moscow, 1973).

In party ideology, the tendency to move from the principle of classic liberalism to reformism, which aimed at strengthening, albeit insignificantly, the regulatory role of government, began to gather strength. The new ideological-political movement, Bryanism, named for its ideologue and avowed leader of the Democratic party, William Jennings Bryan, was a manifestation of this trend. Bryanism was not a clearly defined and comprehensive doctrine. The Democrats' defeat during the 1896 and 1900 elections precluded them from putting it to use in practical policies. But the combination of the essentials of moderate reforms, with hints of antimonopolistic Populist criticism as leveled by a rural population, spurred the Democratic party leadership into action to work out alternatives to the political course of the Republican administration of William McKinley. Moreover, Bryanism, having gone beyond the boundaries of a particular party ideology, turned out to be a significant influence on reformist trends in the two-party mechanism as a whole.

In the beginning of the twentieth century new socioeconomic trends swept over much of the United States. Corporations became firmly established in the leading branches of industry and became a determining factor for the economic development of the country. Just in the period from 1899 to 1902, eighty-two trusts were formed with a combined capital of more than four billion dollars. Among these were United States Steel Corporation, Amalgamated Copper Company, Consolidated Trans-Atlantic Steamship Company, Consolidated Tobacco Company, and a host of others.[4] The trend toward intensive concentration of industry was accompanied by industrial capital being combined with financial capital.

Two of the most influential financial groups, the Morgan group and the Rockefeller group, controlled the largest part of the base capital of all deposits in American banks. Six of the most important banks, including National City Bank, National Bank of Commerce, and Chase National Bank, were among the ranks of the so-called monetary trust, which held major power over the financial and credit system of the country. The connection between corporations and politics became increasingly close. Various trusts attempted to use the governmental apparatus for their own personal interests through large monetary donations to both the Democrats and Republicans and through the direct bribery of political leaders. "A monopoly," emphasized Vladimir I. Lenin, "once formed and managing billions, with absolute inevitability will creep into *every* area of social life."[5]

The first years of the twentieth century were characterized by an increase in a new wave of social protest in the United States. Despite the definite demise of the farmers' movement at the turn of the century, which was to a large extent connected to the split in the Populist party, protesters retained real power as before. But at the forefront, the sociopolitical movement for progressive reforms in the states began to take precedence. The movement gripped primarily the urban segments of society, the working class, liberal circles of the middle class, and the highly educated. The general focus of the movement was the struggle against the power of corporations in the economic and political life of the country.

4. *Congressional Record,* vol. 36, pt. 2, 1788.
5. Vladimir Ilyich Lenin, *Complete Collected Works* [Polnoe sobranie soch.], vol. 27, 355.

The strong fervor of the opposition democratic movement, and ideological impetus provided by Bryanism, confronted the two-party system with the task of working out the principles of sociopolitical maneuvering. The period when the principles of reformism became manifest was extremely complex and painful for American political parties. The bitter clash of the old, but far from outlived, doctrine of laissez-faire with the new, still not clearly defined trends toward social engineering, had a twofold effect. This struggle slowed down to a certain extent the process of political party realignment, but at the same time facilitated the appearance within the parties of new ideological watersheds.

The genesis and delimitation of political factions in the Democratic party intensified after the 1900 campaign, which brought victory to the Republican party coming on an industrial boom and the end of the Spanish-American War. The Republicans gained not only the presidency (McKinley was reelected) but also the majorities of both houses of Congress.[6]

After the 1900 elections the Democratic party was split into two hostile factions. On the left was the group of "Silver" Democrats, headed by Bryan, which represented the interests of small farmers and the primarily unincorporated, agrarian middle class of the western and southern states. The main demand of this faction, which the Democrats had adopted (thereby absorbing the Populist party), remained the free minting and use of silver coins alongside gold coins in the currency exchanges.

Expressing their support for this slogan after 1900 were such politicians as Joseph Blackburn, William Maurer, Frank Walsh, Robert Henry, and others.[7] The discovery of new gold reserves in Alaska led to an improving economy. Passage in March 1900 of the act on the gold standard significantly decreased the popularity of the slogan for free silver minting. Bimetallism had exhausted itself as a national issue and appeared only on the periphery of interparty and internal party debates. That is why the "Silver" Democrats in Congress, headed by Senators Joseph Rawlins (Utah) and James Berry (Arkansas), called for lifting the demand to issue silver currency. A general poll of party supporters on the state level in May 1901 showed a sharp drop in interest in this issue. More than 994,000 of the questioned 1.3 million Democrats declared the inexpediency of further agitation for silver currency. Especially characteristic was the position taken in the states of Colorado, Georgia, Texas, North Carolina, Nebraska, and Kansas, the former strongholds of supporters of silver, where more than 200,000 Democrats called for an end to the debates on this issue.[8] A close ally of Bryan, Senator William Stewart (Nevada), in September 1902 declared in print that the issue of silver currency had ceased to be a pressing concern and should be eliminated from the party platform.[9]

6. *Historical Statistics of the United States. Colonial Times to 1970,* pt. 2 (Washington, 1975), 1083.

7. B. McMillin to W. J. Bryan, September 7, 1901; E. Ballard to W. J. Bryan, September 25, 1901; R. Henry to W. J. Bryan, February 15, 1902, *William J. Bryan Papers,* LC. MD, box 27, folders September 1901, February 1902.

8. F. Randle to D. Hill, May 22, 1901, *David B. Hill Papers,* New York, SL, MD, box 7, folder 29.

9. *Forum,* July–September 1902, 14.

Focusing on foreign policy issues during the 1900 election campaign was in essence only a tactical maneuver for the Democratic party in the pre-election fight. Anti-imperial slogans no longer occupied the Democrats.[10] The sharp increase after the elections of support for a more active foreign policy in the party served as a confirmation of this. A public opinion poll, conducted in November 1900 to May 1901 by the National Democratic Committee, found more than 1.5 million of the 2.3 million supporters of the party were riding the wave of chauvinism and expressed their approval of an expansionist policy.[11]

Under these conditions, Bryan was compelled to reexamine his positions and to bolster his initial formula of "the fight between plutocracy and democracy" with new ingredients. If earlier the issues of silver and foreign policy were at the center of the political structure of the "Great Commoner's" party, now trusts became the regular theme of his articles and public speeches. In essence, the problem of trusts was not new for Bryan's range of concerns. Back in the 1890s, as a young congressman from the state of Nebraska, he had unconditionally supported the proposal directed at strict enforcement of antitrust laws and the strengthening of the authority of the Interstate Commerce Commission.[12]

Elements of antimonopolism in Bryan's worldview as well as his extraordinary ability as an orator allowed him even then to attract farmers' votes. He thus strengthened simultaneously the influence of the Democratic party among a significant segment of the American electorate. The antitrust theme was then concentrated on the fight for a silver currency. Now, when the issue of bimetallism ceased to be practical under the conditions of the political party debate, Bryan was forced to change the emphasis in his political credo.

With growing dissatisfaction in American society with the power of corporations, opposition to trusts became the cornerstone of Bryanism, which was a moderate variable reshaping the reform movement. Bryan emphasized that government should prohibit corporations from controlling production and prices.[13] He viewed trusts as breeding corrupt legislation, more the result of the influence of political and legal factors than economic ones.[14] Bryan had in mind the destruction of trusts as he proceeded to lobby for passage of a series of antitrust bills. This would allow for the rooting out of "illegitimate methods of competition" and restore principles of free enterprise, which he considered incompatible with the activities of monopolies. The government would be allotted an insignificant role: its regulating function limited to restoration of *laissez faire.*[15]

---

10. The anti-imperialism of the Democrats led only to a speech against imperialist foreign expansion, but not imperialism as a whole. For more detail about anti-imperialism in the Democratic party see I. P. Dement'ev, *The Ideological Struggle,* 268–72.

11. F. Randle to D. Hill, May 22, 1901, D. B. Hill Papers, New York, SL, MD, box 7, folder 29.

12. See for example *Congressional Record,* vol. 26, pt. 2, 1655–66.

13. W. J. Bryan, *Under Other Flags, Travels, Lectures, Speeches,* (Lincoln, Nebr., 1905), 260.

14. W. J. Bryan, *Speeches of William Jennings Bryan,* 2 vols. (New York, 1909), 87–88.

15. W. J. Bryan, *Under Other Flags,* 75.

Bryan pursued far-reaching goals through calls for the "disbanding" of trusts, the source of which went back to the radical antimonopoly criticism of the Populists. Having secured the support of a multitude of small farmers and the unincorporated part of the middle class, which as a majority adhered to the belief in the possibility of eliminating the hated power of monopolies and the return to the times of free competition, he considered rehabilitating himself for a twofold strike in the elections and a revival of his political influence within the Democratic party.

Bryan's elevation of the antimonopoly slogans to the forefront significantly hastened the disintegration of the group of "Silver" Democrats, since the group lacked unity on the question of trusts. Some representatives from the faction called for their complete repeal, others recognized the legality of the existence of trusts and called for regulating their activities, while a third group continued to believe in the power of a silver panacea.[16] The inevitable bankruptcy of the group became absolutely clear after the 1902 congressional elections. The "Silver" Democrats, whose ranks were steadily divided, could not distinguish their position on the more pressing domestic policy issue.

The Republicans did not fail to take advantage of this situation. With Theodore Roosevelt's assumption of power in September 1901, after the assassination of McKinley, reforms soon became the official political doctrine of the Republicans. The party was capable, in the view of its leaders, of stifling the antimonopoly movement, and also adjusting the state's role to the long-term demands of American society.[17] Having put forward as the main principle of the administration's domestic policy the idea of "regulating trusts," that is, establishing federal control over the growth and activities of corporations, the new president by 1902 helped bolster the position of the party in Congress and in the local legislatures by significantly pushing the Democrats to the side.[18]

Complex trends were also taking place in the right wing of the Democratic party, in the group of "Gold" Democrats. Its representatives reflected mostly the interests of corporate business from the Northeast and from southern planters, adhering to the doctrine of rugged individualism. The majority of the "Gold" Democrats, among whom David Hill and William Cockran (New York) were the most influential, returned to the Democratic party after the presidential election of 1900.[19] They were intent upon attaining the repeal of all reformist party slogans. "The Democratic party is the main

16. W. Gougar to W. J. Bryan, August 19, 1901; D. Patterson to W. J. Bryan, October 14, 1901; W. Vail to W. J. Bryan, October 15, 1901; *W. J. Bryan Papers,* LC, MD, box 27, folders August 1901, October 1901.

17. In Soviet historiography, the essence and main directions of the politics of reforms were examined in the works of I. A. Beliavskaia, *Bourgeois Reformism in the U.S. (1900–1914)* [Burzhuaznyi reformizm v SShA] (Moscow, 1968); V. V. Sogrin, *Sources of Contemporary Bourgeois Ideology in the U.S.* [Istoki sovremennoi burzhuaznoi ideologii v SShA] (Moscow, 1975); B. D. Kozenko, *The "New Democracy" and War. Domestic Politics in the U.S. (1914–1917)* [Novaia demokratiia i voina. Vnutrenniaia politika SShA] (Saratov, 1980).

18. *Historical Statistics,* pt. 2, 1083.

19. In 1896 the opponents of the Chicago platform of the Democrats abandoned the party convention and formed the National Democratic party. They put out a platform imbued with the philosophy based on the doctrine of laissez faire.

conservative force in the country. . . . Our foremost duty is to strengthen the party organization and create a solid bloc of defense against radicalism," wrote the former governor of New York, David Hill.[20]

The Democratic bosses, Robert Van Wyck of New York and James Smith of New Jersey, Senator Thomas Martin of Virginia, congressmen Joseph Goulden of New York, Joseph Shull of Pennsylvania, Donelson Caffery of Louisiana, and a host of others, held a similar position. They, however, did not abandon the party for the sake of preventing a schism, and in 1900 even supported Bryan. After the elections there remained no trace of their inclinations toward reconciliation. Through cooperation with the "Gold" Democrats who had returned to the party, they counted on undermining Bryanism and reorganizing its scope on the basis of the principles of classic liberalism. Thinking that with the adoption of the gold standard the epithet of the "Gold" Democrats would no longer reflect the political look of the group, they shed this prefix and renamed themselves the "reorganizers."

In all reality these were the same conservative Democrats of the 1890s, once again affirming their support for the ideas of government noninterference and states' rights. But now the conservative group has been enlarged by supporters of the laissez-faire doctrine in the South, who in light of their interest in the issue of silver currency had earlier supported Bryan. Among them were Senators Arthur Gorman (Maryland), reelected in 1903 and Murphy Foster (Louisiana), Congressmen Dudley Wooten (Texas), John Sh. Williams (Mississippi), and others. "The South was completely freed from the trance of the silver panacea . . . and will no longer support the West on this issue," noted the Democrat from North Carolina, Edward Green.[21]

The rallying of conservatives after the defeat suffered in the 1900 elections on the one hand, and the disintegration of the group of "Silver" Democrats who had cemented the Democrats on the other, strengthened the centrifugal tendency within the party. This clearly played into the hands of the "reorganizers." Steeping themselves in calls for unity within the party ranks, they tried to bring the Bryanists under their influence and subsequently attain a change in the party course along the old ideological-political rails. For this they used all sorts of tricks, keeping as their goal undermining the prestige of Bryan in the Democratic camp. Conservatives accused the leader of the party of being a mercenary, and they proclaimed the impracticality of his principles, which, according to them, had led to the defeat of the Democrats in 1896 and 1900. They even announced under their banners the promise to fight political corruption and the system of patronage.[22]

These tactics did not bring the "reorganizers" the desired results. Despite a definite loss of influence by the party in the western states, Democrats from Idaho, Montana, Nebraska, Colorado, and Nevada affirmed their loyalty to Bryan. Moreover, his influence was strengthened in such states as Kansas, Ohio, and Illinois, where the party leader earlier had not enjoyed popularity. The growing pull toward Bryanism

20. D. Hill to R. Hipp, February 21, 1901, *D. B. Hill Papers,* New York, SL, MD, box 7, folder 13.

21. E. Green to D. Hill, January 14, 1901, ibid., box 7, folder 19.

22. *New York Times,* June 17, 1901; July 30, 1902.

by many rank-and-file Democratic supporters was mainly based upon the loss of trust in the conservatives, who, as events had shown, were capable of leading the party to a schism. "It is possible that you are not the most successful candidate. But now we are sure that you will not abandon the party at decisive moments as the supporters of Cleveland are capable of doing, and therefore we are unconditionally on your side," wrote John Barnes, an Ohio lawyer, to Bryan in November 1901.[23]

Bryan's popularity contributed objectively to the creation of favorable conditions for reformist ideas to penetrate society. The beginning of the debates in Congress in 1902–1903 over antitrust legislation undermined the conservatives' plans for good. For the Bryanists they were a clear signal for further delimitation of forces in the left wing of the internal party spectrum, and they set off a search for an independent political program, which would be able to oppose the course of the Republican administration of Theodore Roosevelt.

The Sherman Antitrust Act of 1890, which declared illegal "every contract, combination in the form of trust or otherwise, or conspiracy, in restraint of trade or commerce among the several States, or with foreign nations," in practice was of a very limited nature.[24] Different companies managed to circumvent the statute with little difficulty by changing the organizational form of their activity. But then the law worked without a hitch in the sphere of labor relations. The act's inclusion, right after the bill on interstate trade of 1887, of an article for labor injunctions spurred a vicious fight by the political elite with labor organizations.[25]

The workers, farmers, and urban small businessmen were distressed with the activities of trusts, which with each year took on a wider scope. The middle class with liberal attitudes and even segments of representatives of corporate business, who were just beginning to get drawn into the forced process of monopolization, showed elements of dissatisfaction. These factors compelled the Republican administration of Roosevelt soon after coming to power to focus attention on the issue. The state of affairs in the leadership of the party itself pushed the president toward this.

Within the Republican party, under the influence of the strong antimonopoly wave that had gripped the country in the beginning of the 1900s a group of progressives began to form, representing the interests of the unincorporated middle class and farmers primarily from western states, all of whom showed a heightened interest in the issue of trusts. Roosevelt and his supporters lobbied for moderate reforms to strengthen the social responsibility of government only to the extent that this course could stifle the explosive situation in the country. They thought that by introducing discussion on the antitrust theme in the highest legislative organ they would be able to neutralize the political radicalism of the Republican progressive faction. In this endeavor they were prepared, should the circumstances warrant, even to reach an

23. J. Barnes to W. J. Bryan, November 11, 1901, *W. J. Bryan Papers,* LC, MD, box 27, folder November 1901.

24. *Anti-Trust Laws with Amendments. 1890–1964,* compiled by G. Udell (Washington, 1964), 1.

25. For more detail on the judicial injunctions in the Sherman law see N. B. Sivachev, *Legal Regulation of Labor Relations in the U.S.* [Pravovoe regulirovanie trudovykh otnoshenii v SShA] (Moscow, 1972), 18–19.

agreement with the conservatives, headed by the party boss, Marcus Hanna. The conservatives occupied a solid position in the party and zealously defended laissez-faire doctrine.

The political debate in Congress over the issue of trusts left a lasting imprint on the Democrats. They became active participants in the unfolding discussion. The amendment by Republican progressive Charles Littlefield (Maine) to the Sherman law, introduced for discussion in 1901, provided for prison sentences for action contrary to its articles. This served as a spark to begin the debate.

The Democrats from the ranks of Bryan's supporters then made concrete proposals to expand the law to companies that "had a tendency toward monopolization." The proposals also provided for reports by influential businessmen to government organs with detailed accounts of the work of their firms. In the proposed law trade-union organizations would be removed from the jurisdiction of the bill. The latter had even managed to pass through the House of Representatives, but the attempt to put the amendment up for discussion in the Senate turned out to be in vain as it was rejected by the majority of conservatives from both parties.[26]

The Bryanists once again declared themselves to be at full strength in 1902 when Senator Henry Teller (Colorado), once a leader of the "Silver" Democrats, came out in support of adopting an amendment to the bill on regulating the activities of an entrepreneurial oil company, according to which it was proposed to classify the company as a trust and to levy a 10 percent tax on production. Only twenty-one Democrats and three Republicans spoke in support of the amendment, and the conservatives did not allow its passage.[27]

This failure, however, in no way discouraged the Democrats, who had managed to strengthen the Sherman law. A year later they once again went further than the proposed bill introduced by Littlefield, which obliged previously formed corporations that engaged in trade between several states to provide an annual detailed account of their deposits, employee rosters, organization, and management of business to the Interstate Commerce Commission. This time the Bryanist Democrats put forward a series of amendments in the "minority report," which contained demands to broaden the articles of the bill to include corporations with common capital of more than one million dollars that already existed at the time discussions began. Their decisiveness during this was so great that when through the efforts of the Republicans the report failed, they came out against the Littlefield bill as a whole, although at first they had supported it.[28]

The proposal by the progressive Republicans was easily torpedoed by pillars of both parties. In its place in no time came the very moderate Elkins bill, which called for the necessity of strict compliance by railroad companies in taking and publishing tariffs for transportation of cargo.[29] The new bill gained unconditional support from moderate Republicans, while a wave of growing protest against the

26. *Congressional Record,* vol. 34, pt. 4, 3439; pt. 7, 6495, 6500, 6502.
27. Ibid., vol. 35, pt. 5, 4740.
28. Ibid., vol. 36, pt. 2, 1743–44.
29. Ibid., 1030.

illegalities of railroad entrepreneurs forced many conservatives to reconcile with the bill. Progressive Republicans decided after the defeat of the Littlefield bill to abstain and refused to vote. In this situation only reform-oriented Democrats tried to strengthen the antitrust thrust of the bill, which according to them "did not propose to punish railroad companies for declining established rates for transportation and at the same time legalize their further arbitrariness." "No one can dispute our right to propose amendments, which have as their goal to work out more effective methods to fight the great evil in our country [trusts]," stated James Richardson (Tennessee), expressing the general opinion of the opposition Democratic congressmen.[30] But their attempts to change the contents of the bill turned out to be in vain. In a short time it was passed by the House of Representatives and the Senate, and also approved by the president.[31]

The debates in Congress in 1902–1903 over antitrust legislation revealed important trends in the Democratic party. They showed that the group of "Silver" Democrats right behind the "Gold" Democrats had disintegrated. This did not signify the bankruptcy of Bryanism. On the contrary, among Democrats in the higher legislative body, reform sentiments grew stronger. The struggle for strengthening judicial sanctions against trusts became a pivotal theme, preparing the way for rallying Democratic supporters of various stripes into one unified camp.

One particular landmark in the Democratic party's adoption of the ideas of Bryan was the presidential election of 1904. These results showed the hopelessness of nominating representatives from the conservative group as candidates, since they tried to prevent the ideological and political evolution of the party toward reform. Confirming this was the decisive victory of Roosevelt, who with a flexible domestic policy course gained rather solid support from the voters and left the Democratic candidate, the "reorganizer" Alton B. Parker, far behind.[32] The course of the campaign and the fight at the national convention, concluded with the inclusion in the Democratic platform of demands from the Bryanist wing such as the disbanding of trusts, strengthening the prerogatives of the Interstate Commerce Commission, introducing direct elections of senators, and others.[33] This showed the weakening in the party of supporters of the doctrine of rugged individualism, who had been forced to go from a tactic of attack to one of defense.

This knockout blow to the conservatives made Bryan's claims for further working out of a political strategy for the Democratic party more relevant. The reform program he proposed in December 1904 included demands for the nationalization of the railroads, the abolition of trusts, and the rescinding of protective tariffs.[34] The document was in its own way a response to Roosevelt's address to Congress in which

30. Ibid., pt. 3, 2153–54.
31. Ibid., pt. 2, 1634; pt. 3, 2159.
32. Roosevelt received 7.6 million popular votes and 336 electoral votes. Parker received a little over 5 million popular votes (around 38 percent) and 140 electoral votes. E. Robinson, *The Presidential Vote, 1896–1932* (New York, 1970), 11.
33. *National Party Platforms,* compiled by D. Johnson and K. Porter (Urbana, 1973), 132–33.
34. *Outlook* (December 10, 1904): 920–22.

the president expressed his support for strengthening federal control over monopolies, expanding the authority of the Interstate Commerce Commission, establishing moderate tariffs on railroad cargo, and a series of other measures that showed his previous support for the policy of moderate reforms.[35]

Putting forward a new program of reforms, Bryan counted on once again emerging as the leader of the party. But this turned out to be no easy task. The document provoked a storm of indignation in the Democratic conservative camp. The press of the "reorganizers" charged that the program was rooted in populism and socialism. "The party now is half Democratic and half Socialist," asserted the *New York Times*.[36] But socialism was deeply alien to Bryan, whose political credo was based on the principle of stability of the institution of private property. That is why the accusation of the conservatives sounded like an outrage to Bryan. He hastened to counter it with the reservation that nationalization was necessary only if all the possibilities had exhausted themselves for free competition. The blame was placed completely on the Republicans, who "are not taking any measures at equal count in order to stave off the flood of joint stock capital and consolidation of railroad companies."[37]

Having deepened the division with the conservatives, Bryan's project for reforms also hastened the process of demarcation of Democrats in the reformist camp. The lessons of the last three presidential campaigns showed that internal party discord could only be dampened if the leadership worked out a strategy capable of attracting not only Bryanists but also those former representatives of the conservative group. In an atmosphere of widening the front in the democratic movement in the country, and of a fall in prestige of the Democratic party among a significant segment of American voters, they became very more convinced of the necessity for carrying out a series of moderate reforms.

The demand to nationalize the railroads, which went back to the radical points of the populist program for its source, clearly could not satisfy the supporters of the centrist course from the former "reorganizers." Discussion, which unfolded in 1905 in the Democratic party, regarding the role of the federal government in regulating the activities of the railroad became the testing ground for the vitality of Bryan's program.

The growth in society's disappointment with the increasing power of the railroad enterprises had forced federal authorities back in 1887 to enact a law establishing an Interstate Commerce Commission charged with controlling the transport of cargo by rail. In the course of the next decade, however, through the efforts of the Supreme Court, the functions of the committee were cut to such an extent that it in essence worked only on paper.[38] Roosevelt's attention to this problem, grounded in the president's general attempt to smooth over the sharpness of social contradictions in the country, provoked different responses in the opposition party.

Conservatives from the northeastern and southern states "in conjunction with

35. *The State of the Union Messages of the Presidents* (Washington, 1967), vol. 3, 2145–49.
36. *New York Times,* December 13, 1904.
37. *New York World,* December 17, 1904.
38. Gabriel Kolko, *Railroads and Regulation: 1887–1916* (Princeton, 1965), 16, 33.

Democratic principles" forcefully defended the idea of noninterference by government in the affairs of the railroad business.[39] The more radically inclined supporters of the party, mainly from western states and the Midwest, on the contrary agreed with Bryan's effort to nationalize the railroad and demanded its immediate implementation. In support of this position were influential Democrats such as Senator Henry Teller (Colorado), the progressive mayor of Chicago Edward Dunne, Congressman Henry Rainey (Illinois), the well-known Ohio politician Tom Johnson, and others. "Nationalization of the railroads will lead to suppression of the misuse by private enterprises, reduction in tariffs, destruction of the system of political patronage," asserted Senator Francis Newlands from Nevada.[40] Another senator, Fred Dubois (Idaho), declared in print that this measure was no less important for the country than the legislative initiative and referendum.[41]

But more moderate supporters of reform approached this project of nationalization very hesitantly. As a whole they were inclined more to support the Roosevelt variant for resolving this issue, which provided for expanding somewhat the federal regulation of the transportation of cargo by railroad companies. For example, the resolutions adopted in the summer and fall of 1905 by the Democratic state organizations in Iowa, Ohio, Maryland, Kentucky, West Virginia, and Tennessee, which expressed readiness to "abstain from extreme radicalism and conservatism, and to begin to work out a program of moderate reform," called for exactly this sort of change.[42]

The latter tendency became rather evident during the course of debates in Congress in 1906 over the Republican bill introduced by William Hepburn, which affirmed the right of the Interstate Commerce Commission to control business operations of the railroad companies and fix tariffs for shipping cargo by rail. The composition of the committee was expanded and the salaries of its members were increased. In addition, the bill established a transportation court of five circuit judges, which was essentially the primary means of appeal for the enterprises to check the activities of the committee. This completely depersonalized the court, without which the bill was a rather moderate piece of legislation.[43]

The debates over the Hepburn bill became the original catalyst for the demarcation in the reformist camp of Democrats. During the course of discussion of antitrust legislation in 1902–1903, despite the existing disagreements, the supporters of reform on the whole emerged as a unified bloc, but now the picture began to change. Adherents to the idea of nationalizing the railroad, among whom were Senators Henry Teller (Colorado), Francis Newlands (Nevada), William Stone (Missouri), and William Clark (Montana), rejected the bill, which in their opinion had as its sole goal the achievement of a compromise with conservative Republicans.[44]

Democrats of a more moderate view adhered to a different position. On the whole,

39. *Literary Digest* (May 6, 1905): 647.
40. *The Public Papers of Francis G. Newlands,* vols. 1–2 (Boston, 1932), vol. 1, 345.
41. *New York World,* April 14, 1905.
42. *Literary Digest* (October 28, 1905): 604.
43. *Congressional Record,* vol. 40, pt. 2, 1854.
44. Ibid., pt. 6, 5483; pt. 7, 6620; pt. 8, 7014.

158 A. A. Porshakova

having supported the bill, they also initiated fifteen amendments in the Senate directed at strengthening its reformist contents. They primarily touched on three groups of issues. First, they sought to narrow the authority of the courts in controlling the Interstate Commerce Commission's autonomy in establishing tariffs and rescinding them. Second, they proposed to deny railroad enterprises the right to sanction duty-free transportation of cargo, including freight produced by subsidiary companies. Finally, the third group of amendments, an initiative by more moderate Democrats, touched on the jurisdiction of the Interstate Commerce Commission over telephone and telegraph companies, the establishment of tariffs on the basis of the cost of property of a given railroad enterprise, and the introduction of stricter measures for punishing those not adhering to them.[45]

The demarcation of forces, which was taking shape in the Democratic reformist camp, complicated the task of Bryan in his struggle for party leadership. The situation was aggravated by the fact that the position of the party's head was disputed by one more contender, William Randolph Hearst. The personality of Hearst was rather odious. A pioneer of the yellow press who yearned for national political popularity, he had the ability to grasp astutely the sentiment of the mass of voters. Hearst could see that there were two important pressing political issues: trusts and labor. During 1902–1903 he repeatedly expressed support for establishing federal control over trusts, expanding the prerogative of the Interstate Commerce Commission, and establishing an eight-hour workday in government institutions; in 1904 he sought the Democratic presidential nomination, but all for naught.[46]

The conservatives' guarded attitude toward Hearst, strengthened by his reputation as a "radical and inciter in the Democratic party," was a source of annoyance for the newspaper magnate, who had supported the reforms not from ideological beliefs but for tactical reasons in the pre-election fight. Not attaining recognition in the Democratic camp, he decided to attack the prestige of Bryan in the party from the outside and made a stand as an independent. With this purpose, in December 1904 Hearst established in New York a new political organization, the Municipal League, renamed in February 1906 as the Independent League.[47]

The League's program called for federal limitations on the activities of corporations, the introduction of municipal ownership of public utilities, improvement of work conditions, and an increase in workers' salaries. This program, according to the plan of the newspaper magnate, was to garner around him the urban electorate of the Northeast and Midwest, where Bryan's position had always been, even without this, rather vulnerable.[48]

Hearst's attempt to take a commanding position in the party and his striving to win the support of the antimonopoly movement attracted more and more working-class voters, concentrated primarily in the Northeast. He won over to his cause urban, mainly unincorporated middle-class voters from those states of the Midwest where in

45. Ibid., pt. 7, 6370, 6455, 6571, 6672, 6783, 6797, 6809, 6944–45; pt. 8, 7014, 7088.
46. *Independent* (August 20, 1905): 1950; *American Review of Reviews* (April 1904): 392.
47. *New York American,* October 5, 1905; February 27, 1906.
48. *New York American,* March 17, 1906.

the beginning of the 1900s the Republicans enjoyed a commanding influence and the fight for progressive reforms was rather widespread (Iowa, Ohio, Illinois, and others). This forced Bryan to shift the accent of his political program.

The demand for nationalization of the railroads was removed. Speaking in Madison Square Garden at a meeting of New York Democrats, Bryan first of all declared the necessity of adopting a series of measures in the area of labor legislation: rescinding injunctions in labor conflicts; creating arbitration committees of representatives from the federal government, business circles, and workers; making public the differences that arose between them, and introducing an eight-hour workday for those employed in "interstate branches of industry." In addition, he demanded the prohibition of contributions by corporations to political party funds and called for the direct election of senators.[49]

Actually, these points were not new for the Democrats. The article prohibiting the use of injunctions in conflicts between workers and employers first appeared in the party platform during the 1896 elections, and the demand for the direct election of senators in 1900.[50] But now, in the atmosphere of the comparatively strong labor movement, the fight for political reforms in the states, and the growth in the popularity of socialist ideas, they were given special significance. Bryan's placement of the labor question at the center of the party's reform program undermined Hearst's efforts to head the Democratic political organization.

Bryan's agitation for labor legislation was also directly connected with the increasing tendency in the unions by the middle of the twentieth century's first decade for independent action.[51] The integration of the demands of the labor organizations by the Democrats into their program would allow them to secure the support of the unions and guarantee a certain superiority over the Republicans. The task was eased by the fact that the leaders of the AFL, headed by Samuel Gompers, rejected the idea of independent political activities by trade unionists and resorted to a compromise with the major political parties. The appeal of the AFL to the U.S. Congress on March 21, 1906, which became famous as a bill of grievances, made the following demands: an eight-hour workday in government institutions and work related to fulfilling government contracts; limiting immigration with the goal of halting the falling value of labor in the country; prohibiting forced labor of prisoners; rescinding injunctions; and changing the makeup of the members of the committee on labor in the House of Representatives.[52] The new strategy of the AFL steadfastly prepared the way for the opening of cooperation by its leadership with one of the leading political parties in the country.

The broadening of the demands in the Democratic reform program and the appeal to labor left an indelible mark on the fight for overcoming the sectional, "agrarian" character of the party, which earlier had relied mainly on the support of voters from

49. *Commoner,* September 7, 1906, W. J. Bryan Papers, LC, MD, box 49, folder 5.
50. *National Party Platforms,* 99, 115.
51. See: S. M. Askol'dova, *The Formation of the Ideology of American Trade-Unionism* [Formirovanie ideologii amerikanskogo tred-iunionizma] (Moscow, 1976), 148–49.
52. *Democratic Campaign Text Book* (Baltimore, 1906), 184–85.

the Far West and South. This policy began to yield results as early as the election campaign of 1908, when for the first time the AFL manifested a clear orientation toward the Democratic party.[53] At the time, on a wave of growing criticism directed toward the Roosevelt administration, the Democrats managed to attract a segment of the working- and middle-class urban electorate of the Northeast and Midwest, earlier mostly oriented toward the Republicans.

Especially telling in this respect was some growth in votes supporting the party in such states as Indiana, Wisconsin, Illinois, Ohio, and Michigan, where it traditionally did not enjoy popularity with the mass of voters. In the presidential election of 1908 Bryan received 1.3 million votes more (26 percent) than Alton Parker had in 1904.[54] And despite the fact that William Howard Taft, who had come to power first of all as a successor to Roosevelt's reform policy, won the election, a very optimistic sentiment reigned in the Democratic reformist circles. "Only now, when the waste of the battle is behind, can we evaluate the worth of that tangible step forward, which the Democratic party made, in comparison with 1904. . . . For the first time in 16 years the party was able to begin to converse on an equal footing with the Republicans," wrote Henry Rainey, the Democratic congressman from Illinois in November 1908.[55]

As president, Taft radically changed the priorities of Roosevelt's program of moderate reforms. At the central place in the strategy of the new president was the issue of tariffs, which if addressed, in his estimation, could blunt the growing interest by both parties in the antitrust theme and spread discord among supporters of reform of various stripes. As a result of Taft's lobbying with leaders of the Republican majority in Congress, the Payne-Aldrich bill appeared, which called for a moderate reduction of tariffs but actually exemplified the protectionist policy of the administration.

Discussion of the bill in the Senate confirmed that reform had become an irrevocable factor that had to be reckoned with by each of the two leading parties when making policy. This applied more to the Democrats, who had endured a rather dynamic internal restructuring in the process of introducing elements of statism into their political strategy. By this time two new independent factions had been formed on the basis of the reformist wing of the party: the left, progressives, and the centrist moderate reformers. United by the idea of fighting against the power of monopolies, the progressives represented the interests primarily of farmers in the western and southern states, and also segments of the unincorporated urban middle class. During the debates over the Payne-Aldrich bill the Democrats, supporters of progressive reforms, having linked together the issues of tariffs and trusts, subsequently defended the idea of duty-free imports from abroad of products made by American corporations.[56]

The moderate reformers were oriented toward the representatives of the well-to-do urban middle class, liberal circles of the intellectuals, the more practical-minded

53. Samuel Gompers, *Seventy Years of Life and Labor. An Autobiography,* 2 vols. (New York, 1925), vol. 2, 263.

54. E. Robinson, *The Presidential Vote,* 13–14, 48.

55. H. Rainey to W. J. Bryan, November 16, 1908, *Henry T. Rainey Papers,* LC. MD, box 1, folder February 1904–May 1909.

56. *Congressional Record,* vol. 44, pt. 2, 1293; pt. 4, 3799–3800.

businessmen of the Northeast and Midwest, and landowners of the South, who had recognized the necessity of halting the more odious methods of business activities of trusts for the sake of stabilizing the economic and social situation in the country.

The tariff debates clearly drew the political lines of the factions. The moderate reformers compromised with the conservative group of Democrats for the sake of neutralizing radical trends in the party. As if to confirm this the moderates, the majority of whom supported moderate reductions of tariffs, made it known to the conservatives that they were prepared to waive their principles and recognize as expedient the establishment of a rather high duty on those imported products that contradicted the interests of the American economy. Hoping, however, to hide their true intentions behind the dialogue with the "reorganizers" in order to strengthen for themselves the role of a third sort of power capable of supporting the balance of different forces in the party, the moderate reformers simultaneously assured the progressives that they shared their position on the necessity of limiting abuses by monopolies and using for this goal a "mechanism of reasonable regulation of tariff policies."[57] The double game of the representatives of the moderate reformist group brought visible dividends and allowed them at this stage to add the predominant features of their ideological and political orientation to the Democrats.

Classical liberalism, having set deep roots down in economic and political doctrines, the social consciousness of American society, highly influenced the gradual integration of reforms into ideology and policy of the Democratic party. On the one hand, this process was slowed down by still powerful followers of the laissez-faire doctrine in the party. On the other, the intention of the moderate reformers to overcome the hostility of corporate business and to expand the electoral basis of the party stimulated their search for dialogue with the representatives of other factions of the party.

Among supporters of the doctrine of laissez-faire, the recognition was growing that changes were necessary that would allow them to defend their positions against the onset of progressivism in the party. The individual compromises and negotiations, which Bryan increasingly relied upon, created favorable conditions for forming a coalition force with the conservative and reformist camps in the fight for the party to emerge from its long period of opposition. This became urgent after the congressional elections of 1910, which dealt the ruling party a visible blow. The Democrats after a long break (since 1892), gained a majority in the House of Representatives and won seven new governorships.[58] As the Democrats' national power increased, however, it became evident that Bryan could no longer preserve his position as political leader.

Bryan's role in the formation of the moderate reformist doctrine of the Democrats is apparent. For a large number of American voters, and primarily the unincorporated,

57. Ibid., pt. 2, 1995; pt. 3, 2193.

58. After 1910 the Democrats were represented in the House of Representatives by 228 congressmen, while the Republicans had 161; in the Senate the difference was cut to 10 seats: 51 Republicans were opposed by 41 Democrats. Twenty-six Democrats held the position of governors. *Historical Statistics,* pt. 2, 1083; *A Many Colored Toga. The Diary of H. Ashurst* (Tucson, Ariz., 1962), 3.

mainly agrarian, segments, he had introduced the concept of social engineering into the party's strategy. Radical antimonopoly rhetoric, permeated by religious dogma, for a rather long time allowed him to play in their eyes the role of a sort of prophet capable of healing society of the flaws of capitalism.

Bryan skillfully shifted the accent in his credo depending on changes in the mood of the electorate. In place of silver and anti-imperialism came his criticism of trusts and railroad companies, and his fight for introducing elements of labor legislation and political reforms. Rescinding monopolies, limiting the application of injunctions in labor conflicts, the direct election of senators, the establishment of a legislative initiative and referendum—inclusion in the Democratic campaign platform of these points, which Bryan had borrowed from the program of the Populists, established an important basis for working out an alternative program of reform to the Republican policy.

On the other hand, constant defeats for the party in the presidential elections of 1896, 1900, and 1908 were connected with the name of Bryan. The lack of desire to connect himself with any ties to any of the internal party groups showed the eclecticism of his views. Preaching a return to the times of free enterprise and strict observance of the rights of states figured in with the calls to carry out a series of moderate reforms, which aimed at the strengthening of the functions of the federal government. The latter, for example, were related to Bryan's widely publicized demands for broadening the prerogative of the Interstate Commerce Commission, introducing an income tax, and establishing control over corporate financing of party election campaign funds. The place as a party ideologue, which he had prepared for himself, interfered with him making a real impact on the process of the Democratic political mechanism's functioning.

Despite Bryan's attempts, especially visible during the presidential campaign of 1908, to strengthen his position in the northeastern states, the Democrats of this region on the whole remained hostile toward him. A representative of the Midwest, extremely well-known for its populist traditions, he lobbied for a series of progressive reforms, but he was deeply alien to the "reorganizers." Democratic governors who had assumed power in 1910 in a whole series of states in the Northeast did not hide their open hostility toward Bryan. As a majority, those who had recently left the conservative camp in the party preserved strong ties with industrial-financial circles. They lobbied for reforms only to the extent that such could guarantee the safety of their interests and solidify their influence in Democratic political organizations. Thus, the governor of New York, John Dix, speaking to a meeting of the executive committee of the state in March 1911, declared that carrying out sociopolitical reforms was necessary primarily so as not to allow the progressives to assume power.[59]

Woodrow Wilson belonged to the cohort of conservative politicians of the "new wave." A southerner by descent, historian by education, a professor and from 1902 the president of one of the most prestigious schools, Princeton University, Wilson was far from practical politics. In addition, he never hid the fact that his political

59. Quoted from *Franklin D. Roosevelt State Senatorship Papers. 1910–1913,* F. D. Roosevelt Library, Hyde Park, New York, box 5, folder 7.

sympathies were on the side of the Democratic party's conservative wing. Even in 1896 he voted for the "Gold" Democrats, and in 1907 directly declared the necessity for kicking Bryan and his supporters out of the party.[60]

The radicalization of American public opinion during the 1890s and 1900s turned out to be a significant influence on Wilson's political views, which were characterized by a large amount of pragmatism and flexibility. Wilson was extremely cautious in his assessment of the political situation in the country, but even he was forced to recognize the presence of certain shifts in the public consciousness of Americans influenced by the stormy process of the formation of trusts.[61] But not wishing to compromise his own beliefs and pass himself off as a reformer, he also proposed to "revamp" conservatism, to adapt it to the real situation of the beginning of the new century. "The true conservatism," he said, "consists in reexamining old principles, seeking such a reformulation of them as will adapt them to the circumstances of a new time. There is no danger that the tested principles of government which we have derived from the long experience of our race will be discredited, if we understand their present application."[62]

Having been influenced by social Darwinist ideas, Wilson came out against spasmodic changes in society and for strict observance of legacy in leadership by government.[63] Such an approach completely conformed to the views of those representatives of the conservatives who hoped to renovate slightly the doctrine of classical liberalism with the least losses for it. Wilson's other thesis on observing the principle of party adherence in politics played right into their hands. "Party government is necessary. . . . One wing or the other will triumph in the test of strength, and that faction of the party coming out on top will fall heir to the party name and the party organization," he emphasized in an interview with a correspondent for the *Philadelphia Record* in October 1910.[64] This point created favorable conditions for the conservatives for neutralizing the left or progressive wing, and for subjugating the moderate reformers in the party and easing the fight by the Democrats for political power.

First encountering real politics in 1910 when he was elected governor of New Jersey, Wilson only then became convinced that the strategy of social engineering was the only "road from revolution." In 1911 he persuaded the legislature to pass a series of laws limiting the abuse of trusts, eliminating corruption, democratizing the electoral system in the state, and establishing compensation for work-related injuries.[65] This attracted the attention of many moderate reformers under the influence of progressive sentiments in both parties, those leaning more toward striking up a deal with conservatives. "Wilson is a novice, but he surprisingly correctly figured out the political race . . . the main danger is from the left," noted the former leader of the

60. R. Goldman, *The Democratic Party in American Politics* (New York, 1966), 78.
61. *The Papers of Woodrow Wilson,* A. Link, ed. (Princeton, N.J., 1973–), vol. 15, 14.
62. Ibid., vol. 18, 537–38.
63. Ibid., vol. 21, 190.
64. Ibid., 223.
65. J. Blum, *Woodrow Wilson and the Politics of Morality* (Boston, 1956), 49.

minority party in the House of Representatives, John Sh. Williams, elected to the Senate in 1911 after a two-year break.[66]

The double-edged goal set by Wilson and directed toward working out a flexible and differentiated approach both for conservatives and supporters of progressive reforms propelled him to the rank of a politician of national stature. The 1912 presidential election became a culminating point in the fight of the Democratic party for political power. Conservative tendencies holding sway in the Republican leadership during Taft's tenure in power somewhat eased the Democrats' task, since this gave them a real opportunity to make a successful stand before the voters as the main reform force in the country. This became particularly true in an atmosphere ripe with sharp political crisis, to a large extent hastened by the formation in 1911 of the National Progressive Republican League, which actively challenged the major parties. The leading politicians also faced the realities of the growing influence of the Socialist party, which could become a destabilizing factor in the established political order.[67]

Years of being in the opposition had definitively proven to the Democrats that victory was only possible if they were to fight the ruling party on the most important points of its campaign program. Meanwhile, various corporate leaders in the Northeast began to lean toward the necessity for putting forward a compromise candidate. Wilson, who had recently attacked Bryan during the previous presidential campaign, took steps to reconcile with him. "We are both carrying out a war for liberating our society from the undivided rule of the power of those who have," he wrote to Bryan.[68] The manifestation of loyalty to the former leader of the Democrats, who continued, despite his fall in personal popularity in the party, to preserve the image of a sort of "unselfish reformer" in the eyes of a significant segment of American voters, enabled Wilson to adopt some points of Bryan's reform program.

Key among them was the point on trusts. Judge Louis D. Brandeis, one of the visible ideologues of reform policy who had proposed to Wilson in 1912 a program of "regulated competition," became the ideological inspiration for the future president in working out the government's domestic policy as a whole, especially in the economic sphere.[69] The Democratic platform once again, as four years earlier, held that "a private monopoly is indefensible and intolerable" and demanded the use of the Sherman antitrust legislation and regulation of the activities of entrepreneurial companies to such an extent as they threatened competition.[70] Establishing free competition by means of government antitrust action—it was exactly this slogan that became the main

66. J. Williams to L. Carpenter, September 17, 1911, *John L. Williams Papers,* LC, MD, box 3, folder 2.

67. On the National Progressive Republican League see I. A. Beliavskaia, *Bourgeois Reformism in the U.S.,* 275–91.

68. "W. Wilson to W. J. Bryan," April 3, 1912, *W. J. Bryan Papers,* LC, MD, box 28, folder December 1911–April 1912.

69. On the views of L. Brandeis see L. N. Popkova, "Social-Political Views of Louis D. Brandeis" [Sotsial'no-politicheskie vzgliady Luisa D. Brandeisa], *Amerikanskii ezhegodnik* (Moscow, 1983), 254–70.

70. *National Party Platforms,* 169.

connecting link between Bryanism and Wilson's program of reforms, subsequently named "The New Freedom."

But its second part was sounded in the 1912 Democratic platform rather timidly. The future president, an advocate of a strong central authority, approved inclusion in the document of a whole section on the doctrine of states' rights meant to "protect the people from injustice at the hands of those who seek to make the government a private asset of business."[71] Thus, he gave tribute to the respective views of Bryan, who always had opposed excessive federal interference in the activities of states. Besides, during the elections this point, as well as the demand to rescind monopolies, successfully contrasted with the Roosevelt doctrine of "New Nationalism" at the base of the campaign program of the Progressive party.

It was not regulation of the activities of trusts by means of active government interference, as Roosevelt had proposed, but a fight against "dishonest" methods of competition, with the states in the leading role—on this point Bryan and Wilson appeared unified. Contradictions, which during the election campaign neither one nor the other wanted to inflame, manifested themselves somewhat later. Although both interpreted a monopoly as the absolute opposite of competition, Wilson nevertheless did not completely reject the objective character of the process of concentration of production, but at the same time he thought that the policy of disbanding the trusts would not deal a great loss to big-business interests.[72]

The labor question also held one of the central places in the Democratic platform in 1912. And once again, as in the point about trusts, the demand for "Rights of Labor" did not go outside the framework of the 1908 platform. It would limit the system of injunctions in labor conflicts, create a Department of Labor, and guarantee the employer's responsibility for safety at the workplace. It would recognize the right of workers to organize for addressing with employers the questions of salary and working conditions.[73] The atmosphere in which Wilson recognized the importance of this domestic issue played a significant role in forming the fundamental principles of the "New Freedom" and began gradually to attract the working class into the orbit of the Democrats' political influence, a process initiated by them in the 1900s during their period as the opposition party.

The articulation of the key domestic political issues such as trusts and the labor question and the schism within the Republican party brought Woodrow Wilson victory. For the first time in twenty years the opposition party won not only the presidency but also the majority in both houses of Congress. The Wilson model of reforms absorbed a series of other Bryanist demands: on perfecting the tax system, carrying out bank reform, direct elections of senators, and others.

In 1912 Bryan and Wilson appeared to agree that the fundamental authority for

71. Ibid.
72. "The development of business upon a great scale, upon a great scale of cooperation, is inevitable, and . . . desirable," since this "is a business that has survived competition by conquering in the field of intelligence and economy," wrote the president a year after the elections. W. Wilson, *The New Freedom* (New York, 1914), 165, 180.
73. *National Party Platforms,* 172.

carrying out reforms rested with the states. Only after Wilson came to the White House did there occur a split on this point: Bryan's apprehension of central government was set against the idea of strengthening the prerogative of the executive branch, which, in the president's view, was charged on the one hand with containing the "orgy of the plutocracy," and on the other with weakening the socialist movement.

The centrist moderate reform group, making up the base of the Wilson coalition, increased on account of those who had fled the conservative camp and, in such a manner, in their political strategy had shifted to the right somewhat. Having preserved the radicalism of the party rhetoric, its supporters definitively became demarcated from such reform projects as, for example, the nationalization of the railroads and carrying out general elections for federal judges, and gradually adjusted the ideas of Bryanism to the long-term interests of the corporations.

The strategy of reforms, which had been developed by the Democrats during the period of opposition, was realized in Wilson's presidency in the establishment of the Federal Reserve System, the recognition of trade unions, introduction of an eight-hour day on the railroads, and a series of other measures directed to meet the interests of the broad spectrum of the American society.

Comment

by Samuel T. McSeveney

In their essays, Larisa V. Baibakova and Alla A. Porshakova deal, respectively, with "the Genesis of the Reformist Policy" in the United States during the 1890s through the presidential election of 1896 and with "the Origins of the Reformist Ideology" in the United States during 1900–1912. Both pieces are more than a decade old, the former dating to 1987, the latter to 1986. They focus on the Democratic party during periods of considerable interest to American historians and political scientists, though understandably not always in the same ways as their counterparts in the United States. Given their emphases, the essays are complementary: essentially they illuminate the Democratic party over an epoch some two decades in duration but do not shed sustained light on the Republican party, which after all dominated national government during most of the period.

Baibakova traces the leadership of the Democratic party from the electoral successes of the Democracy during 1890–1892 through its internal conflicts during the presidency of Grover Cleveland until the Bryanites' capture of the party in 1896 and their defeat in the presidential election that same year. Porshakova deals with the Democrats as they wandered in the wilderness during the years following the Republicans' capture of national power, with the changing emphases of William Jennings Bryan as he sought to redefine his party's position under difficult circumstances and restore it to competitiveness, and with the emergence of Woodrow Wilson as a party and national figure through his election as president of the United States in 1912. Historians of various persuasions will recognize Baibakova's characterization of the 1890s as a period of interrelated national crises, even when they do not share her Marxist perspective. She sees the period as having been marked "by the evolution of capitalism to its highest, monopolist stage of development" and by "the exacerbation of the conflict between labor and capital in the U.S.A." Workers became more organized and more frequently advanced political demands. Others—farmers, the "unincorporated" bourgeoisie, the intelligentsia—joined the struggle. Confronted by this situation, according to Baibakova, "the ruling elite" began to substitute "the tactics of maneuvering and compromise" for older means of maintaining power, e.g., "violence and relentless denial of reforms." By their new adroitness they "channeled [the antimonopoly movement] in a safe direction," stabilizing "the political system and its basic institution, political parties." Baibakova sees her research filling a need in "Soviet historical science," which holds "bourgeois reformism" to be basic to

167

American political processes in the twentieth century, but which has "insufficiently" studied its genesis during the 1890s.

Divergent weltanschauungs and specific interpretations aside, I am struck that the foundations on which Baibakova rests her case are less solid than they should be. In part this reflects the author's apparent unfamiliarity with important American scholarship and her sometimes loose reading of works cited in introductory paragraphs, i.e., by W. Dean Burnham, William N. Chambers, and especially Philip Converse. (My own perspective on one point is also inadequately paraphrased.) Basic data presented in support of central arguments are (perhaps necessarily) fragmentary and (unfortunately) not always carefully chosen. Strike figures from 1881 and 1886 alone do not suffice to support the claim that the late 1880s were marked by "a growing . . . strike movement." To be sure, strikes did involve more workers during 1886–1890 than 1881–1885, but the numbers immediately fell off from their peak in 1886, which was exceeded only in 1894 over the century's final fifteen years. The Socialist Labor (not Socialist) party did increase its efforts, but 1892 and 1896 SLP votes should be presented in percentage terms, 0.18 percent and 0.26 percent (i.e., one-quarter of 1 percent), respectively, thus making clear that popular support was virtually nonexistent. One may wonder, too, whether Congress was "forced" by "the pressure of popular masses" to create the Interstate Commerce Commission in 1887; the legislation and commission are better characterized as regulatory than "antitrust," a confusion that recurs.

References to the "mass base" of support for the reviving antimonopoly movement as made up of "impoverished small farmers" and to "[t]he popular demand among the masses for 'cheap money,' " i.e., Free Silver, masses composed of "[f]armers, small businessmen, and even some workers," stand as assertions, largely unsupported by documentation. Still, Baibakova's concluding generalization with regard to the point is suggestive; one can only add that she would have benefited from access to Bruce Palmer's *Man over Money*.[1]

That party allegiances began to loosen in 1890 under the impact of a number of developments seems clear enough. Baibakova explains this portentous development insofar as Populism in the West and South was concerned. But again her reference to "strong unrest among the lower strata of the population" cries for analysis of elections or at least of reference to scholarship that identifies and seeks to explain the popular bases of support for and opposition to the People's party. (Total disregard of factors other than class conflict leads Baibakova to report Populist successes in 1892 in "core Republican states," Idaho, Kansas, Colorado, and Nevada, but to ignore Democratic victories in Wisconsin and Illinois, traditional Republican strongholds where cultural conflicts contributed to the outcome.) We are told that "increased social activity of the masses caused the split among the ruling classes and exacerbated the intrastructural conflict between the unincorporated groups of bourgeoisie and the monopolist upper

---

1. Bruce Palmer, *'Man over Money': The Southern Populist Critique of American Capitalism* (Chapel Hill, N.C., 1980); Gretchen Ritter, *Goldbugs and Greenbacks: The Antimonopoly Tradition and the Politics of Finance in America, 1865–1896* (New York, 1997), postdates Baibakova and offers a keen analysis of the subject.

strata." But these abstractions never become real because the analysis fails to go beyond the traditional view of conflict between the colonial South and West and the metropole, the Northeast. Workers and farmers in the Northeast and Midwest do not figure in such an analysis. At one juncture, Baibakova goes so far as to claim that "a part of the rapidly growing stratum of monopolists" also joined "the liberal two-party bloc," but such defectors are never identified nor is their behavior explained.

Inadequate documentation and background plague the discussion of developments during the earliest period under study, c. 1887–1892. A key point regarding the strategy advocated by "the shrewdest statesmen" during those years is supported by a single reference—to one speech, reported in the *Congressional Record,* by an unidentified speaker, delivered in 1895, by which time, of course, the political context was different. (Indeed, congressional speakers generally remain unidentified by name and party in footnotes throughout the essay.) Baibakova draws on the papers of David B. Hill of New York in her discussion of the money question in the Democratic party, but an understanding of Hill's need to undercut former President Grover Cleveland to win the 1892 Democratic presidential nomination would have enabled her to present the evidence in context.[2]

Like others before her, Baibakova understandably arraigns the Cleveland administration for its intransigence in the face of hard times and resultant political pressures during the nationwide economic depression that set in during 1893. Her account of the cross-party coalitions that fought over repeal of the Sherman Silver Purchase Act is on target, though it actually illuminates sectional conflict more than class conflict. All the same, one reference does not suffice to take seriously the claim that "[c]ontemporaries even noted that the air smelled with a new civil war" during the repeal fight, nor can Henry Adams be said to have spoken for "contemporaries." On one page southern Democrats are assigned to "[t]he right wing of Congress," on the next they are said to have formed "the nucleus of the opposition." At one point Baibakova confuses southern Democratic representatives with House Democrats as a whole. Her explanation of the Democrats' "utter defeat" in the 1894 midterm elections, that it resulted from the "pro-monopolist course of government," badly oversimplifies, inexplicably, too, for she reveals awareness of the Republicans' rhetorical appeal, at least to business.

Coverage of the Democrats' fateful change of course during the Cleveland years is acceptable, but slips weaken it at points, a bad misdating here, an undocumented political slogan ("Long live the struggle") there, reliance on Anna Rochester's obsolete Marxist *The Populist Movement in the United States* (1943) elsewhere. Baibakova sees the 1896 Democratic national platform and presidential candidate, William Jennings Bryan, as abandoning "classic liberalism" for "bourgeois reformism," but she wisely does not read too much into the shift: reformism was "moderate"; it was "the conservative leadership" of the Populists that endorsed Bryan, over the protests of "the party's left wing." Bryan's defeat at the hands of William McKinley revealed that "bourgeois reformism" had not yet become dominant. Again, Baibakova's thin research and apparently limited familiarity with recent American

2. Herbert J. Bass, *"I Am A Democrat": The Political Career of David Bennett Hill* (1961), remains basic on the New York governor, senator, and presidential aspirant.

scholarship circumscribe the value of the work she has done.[3] Marxist references to the contrary notwithstanding, her account still smacks more of sectional conflict than class struggle.

Alla A. Porshakova picks up the analysis of the genesis of "bourgeois reformism" in the Democratic party where Baibakova leaves off, with the Bryanite coalition's capture of the national party in 1896. She soundly contends that the Democrats responded earlier than the Republicans to pressures for reform because of the party's bases in the South and the West—the former traditional, the latter not so, I would add, both experiencing the Populist challenge to stand-pat politics. But though the Democratic reformers managed to co-opt Populism, one may doubt whether they fully captured "the changing mood of the electorate" and "significantly broadened their influence on the voters." Porshakova, who paints a national, rather than sectional, canvas, ignores the antidemocratic behavior of southern Democrats, who crippled their Populist and Republican opposition and reduced voter turnout, especially among African Americans, but also among disadvantaged whites. She also overlooks the decisive Republican defeat of the Bryanite Democrats, including shifts of northeastern urban and rural districts toward the G.O.P., a mood (or at least behavioral) shift that hardly demonstrated a broadening appeal by the Democracy. It strikes me that any such analysis should assess the political weakness, as well as appeal, of Free Silver as a mobilizing issue and the consequences of the absence of labor organizations comparable to farmers' organizations for the daunting task of mobilizing a national coalition across class, sectional, and cultural lines.

At the same time, emphasis on shifts in political strategy within "the ruling circles" disregards, rather than weighs (if only to reject) an alternative reading of the Democrats' leadership during 1893–1896, years of economic depression and social conflict, i.e., that the flawed policies of the Cleveland wing of the party enabled rival leaders and their supporters temporarily to capture the national Democratic party, rather than that changed circumstances finally led old leaders to accommodate to grass-roots pressures. After all, prominent Cleveland Democrats were to desert their party in 1896 for the National (Gold) Democrats or even for the Republicans, while in the other major party camp, Republican leaders were to accept the bolt of western dissidents rather than compromise with them at that year's national convention. Finally, Porshakova credits Bryanism, albeit "not a clearly defined and comprehensive doctrine," with subsequently spurring the Democratic party to consider alternatives to the policies of the Republican administration of President William McKinley and, by transcending party lines, with influencing reformism in the political system as a whole.

Porshakova provides welcome background for her discussion of Democratic reformism, 1900–1912, by sketching the consolidation of major industries at the turn of the century. Thus, even as the farmers' movement faded because of the split in the Populist party (without reference to the return of agricultural prosperity), urban

3. Such scholarship is too abundant to cite here, but Robert Cherny, *American Politics in the Gilded Age, 1868–1900* (Wheeling, Ill., 1997), provides a good synthesis and an ample bibliography.

elements ("the working class, liberal circles of the middle class, and the highly educated") came to support Progressivism, which challenged "the power of corporations
in the economic and political life of the country." Given her focus on the national
Democratic party, as well as her perspective, Porshakova does not engage American
scholars who offer different understandings of Progressivism.[4]

"The Democratic Party in Opposition" views the immediate turn-of-the-century
period as one in which the clashes between the business consolidation movement
and antitrust sentiment and between laissez-faire ideology and bourgeois reformism
(or "social engineering," as Porshakova now refers to it, without defining the term)
were unresolved, making it difficult for the party system to establish "the principles of
sociopolitical maneuvering." For the Democrats, again defeated in 1900, the problems
included achieving party unity and victory at the polls. Anti-imperialism had proven a
short-lived issue of limited utility. With the return of national prosperity and passage
of the Gold Standard Act of 1900, bimetallism had lost its appeal. Under these changed
circumstances Bryan increasingly emphasized antitrust rhetoric and policy, not that
this was inconsistent with his position during the 1890s. According to Porshakova,
Bryan's shift away from bimetallism hastened the breakup of the party's silver bloc
because its members were divided on how best to address the trust question. At
the same time, with the gold standard secure and bimetallism fading as an issue,
conservative Democrats sought to regain control of the party from Bryan and his
supporters. In this, the reorganizers, as these Democrats were called, succeeded, but
they went down to resounding defeat in 1904, when the party nominee of their choice,
Alton B. Parker, lost to President Theodore Roosevelt in a landslide.[5]

Porshakova does well to include discussions of the Republicans, especially in
the Roosevelt administration and in the Congress, for the activist president and
dominant G.O.P. largely shaped the political agenda during the period. In doing so, she
likely exaggerates what she characterizes as "the explosive situation in the country"
regarding the trust question. Her treatment of congressional discussions of important
economic issues—trusts (during Roosevelt's first term), railroad regulation (during
his second), and the tariff (during Taft's administration)—makes no reference to
differences among interest groups within the business community.[6] References to the
Congressional Record reveal primary research regarding these legislative matters, but
they fail to identify congresses by number and session and speakers by name and party;

4. A single citation of Gabriel Kolko, *Railroads and Regulation: 1887–1916* (Princeton,
N.J., 1965), aside, Porshakova fails to draw or comment on studies by American scholars who,
during the 1950s–1980s, influenced our thinking with regard to the Progressive period: George
Mowry, Arthur Link, Richard Hofstadter, Samuel Hays, Robert Wiebe, John Buenker, and for
that matter, the broader work of Kolko himself.

5. Paul W. Glad, *The Trumpet Soundeth: William Jennings Bryan and His Democracy,
1896–1912* (Lincoln, Nebr., 1960), remains standard on Bryan and the Democratic party
during this period.

6. In this connection, Porshakova's single reference (Note 38) to Kolko, *Railroads and
Regulation,* 16, 33, fails to convey Kolko's argument regarding the creation of the Interstate
Commerce Commission, to say nothing of Kolko's understanding of the role of the railroads
themselves in the formulaion of railroad rate regulation policy.

they do not indicate the inclusive pages of debate. Still, Porshakova's understanding of Theodore Roosevelt's role enables her to view Bryan's reform proposals, enunciated at the end of 1904, as a response to Roosevelt's program.

Returning to the internal dynamics of the Democratic party, Porshakova portrays Bryan as subsequently responding to the challenge of William Randolph Hearst by stressing labor issues, which undermined Hearst, drew the American Federation of Labor closer to the Democrats, and resonated (as earlier emphases had not) in urban-industrial areas. I would add only that Hearst's successive defeats in races for mayor of New York City and governor of New York State in 1905 and 1906, respectively, further contributed to the deflating of the newspaper magnate's political ambitions.

Porshakova satisfactorily explains Bryan's dilemma as titular leader of the Democratic party following his third presidential election defeat in 1908, but one wishes that she had addressed the significance of the midterm elections of 1910 for the Democrats. She notes that northeastern Democratic governors elected that year were hostile toward Bryan, but, whether or not documentation would support this contention, perhaps a more important point is that with the Democrats' capture of governorships in populous states and of control of the U.S. House of Representatives, the latter for the first time since their defeat in 1894, governors and congressional leaders fresh from the people could seek advancement in a fluid situation in which the party might be nationally competitive in 1912.

Woodrow Wilson, elected governor of New Jersey in 1910, was of course to capitalize upon the Democrats' upsurge and the Republicans' split to win the presidency in 1912. Porshakova outlines Wilson's political thinking and stance, citing four scattered passages (only one of them dated) from *The Papers of Woodrow Wilson*. Readers will recognize her Wilson even when they would have portrayed the Democratic newcomer in a different light. Reference to "various [northeastern] corporate leaders" seeking a compromise candidate in 1912 should, however, have been fleshed out and documented. Louis D. Brandeis did advise Wilson; he would become a justice of the U.S. Supreme Court in 1916, but he was not a judge in 1912. Theodore Roosevelt's "New Nationalism" and the Progressive party platform, indeed, the national campaign of 1912, merit explication and documentation.

In conclusion, I would have recommended concluding the essay with a tighter, fuller analysis of the reformist positions of Bryan and Wilson as of 1912 and deleting the bare-bones paragraph on Wilson's administration that now closes the piece. As it stands, this brief paragraph is too sketchy to be of any value, but, given Porshakova's coverage of 1900–1912, her fuller treatment of Democratic reformism during the Wilsonian presidency would be most welcome.

Response

by Larisa V. Baibakova

Professor Samuel T. McSeveney's critical remarks made the author of this article think over the essence and form of expounding the problems. Some of them can be explained by the fact that the article was written more than fifteen years ago and contained both the definitions and terminology used in Soviet historical science in those days. In spite of some categorical and rough formulas that reflect the outmoded view of the problem ("evolution of capitalism to its highest, monopolistic stage of development"), the author is convinced as before that the growth of the industrial economy increasingly dominated by giant business corporations and trusts went through difficulties and conflicts in the United States.

For a few decades, from the end of the Civil War to the turn of the new century, an agrarian country was transformed into a powerful industrial state. The rapid rates of development and modernization of American society that made "the captains of industry" the main characters of the epoch complicated the process of adaptation of Americans to new conditions of life. A transition from an agrarian to an industrialized economy was difficult and ruinous to the population, and brought commotions for the country. The United States was not a harmonious society.

Earlier the United States endured powerful political protest movements from the farmer-labor third parties of the 1870s to the Populist crusade of the 1890s. No other countries in Western Europe made "antitrust" a prime political issue to counter the growing economic and political power of "big business." Theoretically, this problem as completely worked out in both Western and Russian political science proved that in the years of the most intensive industrialization a range of orthodox values and community structures were shattered by the rapidity and extent of economic and social change. This evolution imminently brought the growth of social tension. Surely, popular dissatisfaction in the American society was shown in social strata differently. Various were their demands and forms of social protest—from strikes to formation of political parties. The fact of "the conflict of labor and capital" that raised some doubts of the respectable reviewer did take place. Meanwhile, the definition of the term "labor" involves not only workers but other categories of the working, employed population.

The genre of a small article that had another problem as its main object of research did not suggest taking a lot of sources to prove this thesis of general use. The recent works of American writers that were kindly enumerated in the comment completed the picture of strained social atmosphere in the American society. The author is familiar

173

with these researches, especially works of Fulbright Lecturer Robert Cherny, who delivered a special course in 1996 for the students and professors of the history faculty at Moscow State University.

The problem of intercommunion, the complex connection of politics and economics in one of the critical periods of history—the "turbulent 1890s"—is of peculiar importance in studying the process of working out the policy of reforms. In broad meaning it concerns the interdependence of the positions of the ruling party and the economic interests of different social classes whose crossings in the political sphere create sharp, sometimes insolvable contradictions. Perhaps the process of intercommunion of politics and economics is not going rectilinearly and unilaterally; it depends not only on interests of social strata but also the ability of the authorities to place them together. The era of "robber-barons" that used all possible means in getting wealth and power signified "big business" coming to politics. Functional economic organizations in the form of giant corporations began to make stronger policy demands than individuals ever had. Specified attention of the authorities to the needs of this segment of the electorate evoked negative reaction of Americans. Without doubt the first antitrust laws of 1887 and 1890 were adopted by "the pressure of popular masses" although the reviewer had another point of view. They had (at this point I agree with him) "regulatory" status toward monopolies, restricting the most clamorous manifestation of their corporate will. The acts both removed shortcomings in the law and created a special base for restricting negative aspects of monopolies.

At the same time the lack of reforms, as it took place in the administration of Grover Cleveland, did intensify social tension in the American society and evoke a political crisis of power. The Populist party was quoted here as a well-known example of "strong unrest among the lower strata of the population." Populists were never a single-interest party. Their program shared important concepts with the major farm and labor organizations and absorbed economic interests of many Americans. Perhaps in other times most voters responded to parties in terms of ethnicity, religion, and race, but not in the years of economic crisis of the 1890s, the most serious and hardest in the last century. This explained why a demand of silver coinage became the symbol of social protest versus gold as a concentrated expression of growing power of the rich. Of course, D. Barry's assertion that the air smelled with the new civil war would not be understood word for word, verbatim; it was used to show the seriousness and drama of the situation in the mid-1890s, when the political elite began losing its control over the electorate.

Soon the situation got more complicated because measures proposed by the Democratic administration did not correspond to the depth of the economic cataclysm. President Cleveland saw the task of leading the country out of crisis in using outmoded "laissez-faire" slogans (low tariffs and gold monometallism). More effective state regulation was on the agenda. The theoretical base of "new liberalism" was worked out by Herbert Croly, Louis Brandeis, Richard T. Ely, and other writers who in contrast to individualistic schemes held a positive view of the role of the state and government.

The logical results of such shortsighted policy were the growth of opposition headed by William J. Bryan within the Democratic party and drawing out a program of social reforms. The Democrats' turning to the "common" people and their recognition of the state's social mission was dependent on acute political strife. The Democratic program was declarative and moderate: in substance only the income tax and silver coinage were given social importance. The defeat of Bryan in the election of 1896 revealed that ideas of "new liberalism" (now this notion is considered more correct than "bourgeois reformism") had yet to gain popular support. Only in the Progressive era did the policy of liberal reforms attain stability and permanence.

In conclusion I would like to thank Professor McSeveney for his useful and valuable comments.

8

Alfred E. Smith and the Conservative Political Tradition in the 1920s–1930s

by Ilya V. Galkin

The period of Franklin D. Roosevelt's New Deal politics (1933–1938), a time when many of the fundamental principles for modern state-monopolistic policies of the ruling U.S. circles were established, has attracted constant attention by Soviet historians for more than forty years. A whole series of works of a general profile, monographs, and articles analyze the class content of the Roosevelt administration's political course and its most important reforms. A multitude of peripeteia of the sharpest sociopolitical conflicts are explicated and the characteristics of social movements are given.[1] The tension arising from the class struggle and the New Deal reforms exerted significant influence on the content and dynamics of political life in the United States. In Soviet historiography the Marxist concept of realignment of the U.S. two-party system has been formulated. This concept reflects a transition of the party tandem, setting out on the road toward statist political theory and practice. As American studies specialists asserted, this brought about cardinal changes in the role and place of the leading U.S. parties, the Democrats and the Republicans, in the American political system.

The New Deal period is related to a number of critical developments in the history of American political thought. From the last third of the nineteenth century to the first third of the twentieth century, political views of a significant contingent of the ruling circles of the country were either inextricably connected to the postulates of individualism or repelled by these postulates and modified. They outgrew this ideology and moved toward reformist ideas that had not been completely conceptualized. In the 1930s different variants of statist ideology took a very visible, and as a rule domineering, place in the political arsenal of the American ruling elite and its fundamental

1. See N. V. Sivachev, *The Political Struggle in the U.S. during the 1930s* [Politicheskaia bor'ba v SShA v seredine 30-x godov XX veka] (Moscow, 1966); V. L. Mal'kov, *The "New Deal" in the U.S.: Social Movements and Social Policies* ["Novyi kurs" v SShA: Sotsial'nye dvizheniia I sotsial'naia politika] (Moscow, 1973). On the modern conceptual level of addressing the issue of the history of the New Deal see N. V. Sivachev, "The 'New Deal' of F. Roosevelt" [Novyi kirs" F. Ruzvel'ta], *Voprosy istorii* 9 (1981); V. L. Mal'kov, "'Just a little bit left of Center': The General and Specifics of F. Roosevelt's Social Policies" [Chut-chut' levee tsentra": obshchee I osobennoe v sotsial'noi politike F. Ruzvel'ta], *Amerikanskii ezhegodnik* (Moscow, 1983); *History of the U.S.: In Four Volumes* [Istoriia SShA: V 4 t.] (Moscow, 1983–1986), vol. 3, 151–316. This essay by Ilya V. Galkin was originally published in *Problemy amerikanistiki* [Problems in American Studies] 8 (Moscow, 1980): 90–110.

parties, the Democrats and Republicans. Neoliberalism and neoconservatism became two of the most important trends in statist ideology beginning with the epoch of the New Deal.[2]

Soviet Americanists who have analyzed the evolution of liberal political thought in the U.S., such as A. V. Valiuzhenich, V. O. Pechatnov, B. V. Mikhailov, and others, consider the 1930s a critical turning point in the development of American liberalism.[3] K. S. Gadzhiev, N. N. Glagolev, A. S. Manykin, A. Iu. Mel'vil, and others share this evaluation in regards to conservatism.[4] Emphasizing the clear secondary role of conservative political views during the New Deal epoch, historians correctly explain this first of all with the incongruence of conservative postulates with the then realistic needs of American society, squeezed in the vise of an economic depression and torn apart by sharp social contradictions. Second, researchers point to the fact that the political initiative of 1933–1938 was in the hands of liberals from the Democratic party who had supported the reformist course of the Roosevelt administration. According to this point of view, the evolution of conservative ideas during the 1930s both in the Republican party, their main stronghold, and in the Democratic party was to a large extent a type of ideological reaction to Roosevelt and his heirs' liberal-reformist politics.[5] Recognizing the validity of such an interpretation, one might note that to a significantly larger extent than liberalism, conservatism represents continuity and an attraction toward preserving outdated ideological postulates. From the latter proposition it follows that the picture of the evolution of conservatism, including during the 1920s and 1930s, is somewhat incomplete without some account of the processes of internal transformation of this trend in sociopolitical thought. It goes without saying that these processes occurred within the framework of an interrelationship between conservatism and other trends in the social consciousness of the United States.

N. N. Glagolev and A. S. Manykin's works are devoted to elucidating the predominant trends and explicating the new conservative views. The focus in the studies by

2. See I. P. Dement'ev and V. V. Sogrin, "On the Role of Ideology in the History of the Two-Party System in the U.S." [O roli ideologii v istorii dvukhpartiinoi sistemy SShA], *Novaia I noveishaia istoriia* 6 (1980); N. V. Sivachev, *The U.S.: Government and the Working Class* [SShA: gosudarstvo I rabochii klass] (Moscow, 1982), 274–91.

3. See A. V. Valiuzhenich, *American Liberalism: Illusion and Reality* [Amerikanskii liberalizm: illiuzii I real'nost'] (Moscow, 1976); V. O. Pechatnov, "Reformism in Ideology and Politics of the Democratic Party" [Reformizm v ideologii I politike demokraticheskoi partii], in *The U.S.: Political Thought and History* [SShA: politicheskaia mysl'i isotoriia] (Moscow, 1976); B. V. Mikhailov, *Modern American Liberalism: Ideology and Politics* [Sovremennyi amerikanskii liberalizm: ideologiia i politika] (Moscow, 1983).

4. See N. N. Glagolev, "The Evolution of Traditionalism: Ideological Principles of the Republican Party" [Evoliutsiia traditsionalizma: ideinye ustoi respublikanskoi partii], in *The U.S.: Political Thought and History* [SShA: politicheskaia mysl'i istoriia] (Moscow, 1976); K. S. Gadzhiev, *The U.S.: Evolution of the Bourgeois Consciousness* [SShA: evoliutsiia burzhuaznogo soznaniia] (Moscow, 1981), 3–84; A. S. Manykin, "W. Willkie and the Genesis of 'New Republicanism' " [U. Uilki I genezis "novogo respublikanizma"], *Amerikanskii ezhegodnik* (Moscow, 1981).

5. *Modern Political Consciousness in the U.S.* [Sovremennoe politicheskoe soznanie v SShA] (Moscow, 1980), 131–36.

these scholars has rightly been primarily on the Republican party as the main bearer of the slogans of conservatism during the 1920s–1930s. This present article will set out to address analogical questions as applied to the history of the Democratic party, using as an example of political activists from that period one of the Democratic leaders, Alfred E. Smith.

The election campaign of 1936 is one of the most stormy of all American history since U.S. parties have existed. The Democrats' opponents on the party tandem, the Republicans, embarked upon an energetic attack against key elements of the New Deal policies under the slogans of militant individualism. In the concentrated attacks on the liberal statism of Roosevelt the Grand Old Party was supported by a host of conservative and reactionary organizations, including the Freedom League, established in 1934 by representatives of monopolies and several conservative activists from the Democratic party. Among the latter, Smith enjoyed the greatest national recognition.

In the summer of 1936, when political tempers flared, the governor of the state of New York, George Lehman, in a private conversation with Roosevelt touched on the topic of Smith extremely inopportunely. In sum, the president's interlocutor received a sharp sermon: "If it wasn't for Smith we wouldn't be in the position in which we find ourselves today. When he was governor of the state, it was precisely he who waged a battle for liberal and progressive social legislation and made it possible for the party to occupy the position in the state that it today occupies."[6] Recalling 1936, the chairman of the Democratic National Committee (subsequently Smith's enemy "out of duty"), James Farley, felt the need to note that "that political course, which FDR wanted to propose to the nation, was not invented by him until several weeks before assuming the post of president. Roosevelt's legislative proposals were of the same type and extent as those carried out in New York by Smith."[7] Similar estimates of him by Roosevelt, and especially by Farley, cannot but force us to take a closer look at Smith's political profile.[8]

Smith, making use of the constant support of the New York urban party machine, Tammany Hall, and having begun his career in politics in 1904 as a member of the lower house of the New York legislature and ascended up all the steps of the hierarchy in the state legislative assembly, and having served as sheriff of a city on the mouth of the Hudson and as head of the city council, in 1918 ran successfully in the gubernatorial elections. In 1920 he was defeated, like many of his colleagues in the party, but in 1922 he managed to return to the governor's mansion in Albany, and to remain there as its occupant until 1929, an achievement with only one precedent

6. James A. Farley, *Behind the Ballots: The Personal History of a Politician* (New York, 1939), 346.

7. Ibid., 216.

8. Farley prepared a manuscript of the book cited above for print during those days when he contemplated assuming the burden of leadership in the party from Roosevelt and that he had serious chances for the presidency from 1941. Therefore, the first memoirs of Farley are a source, exclusively loyal in regards to Roosevelt. In them he recounts rather adequately the views that FDR wanted to promulgate. The later autobiography of Farley is more biased in this respect.

in the history of the "empire state" of New York, which took place more than one hundred years earlier.

By the middle of the 1920s Smith enjoyed some national popularity and was a real candidate for the top jobs in the Democratic party. He established firm connections with a number of visible Democratic politicians, governors from New Jersey (J. Siltser), Maryland (A. Ritchie), senators Royal Copeland, Robert Wagner (both from New York), T. Baird (Delaware), and a member of the House of Representatives, John J. Douglass (Massachusetts). The governor of New York enjoyed the most support among the urban electorate of foreign extraction residing in the Northeast. At first this was explained by Smith's Catholic background and his negative attitude toward the Dry Law. But when he began to display aspirations for internal party domination, the profile of the "wet" (that is to say aligned against anti-alcohol legislation) Catholic was in need of a serious addition: the New York governor's supporters were in need of a political program. The program emerged from the ideas present in the bills worked out under Smith's leadership from 1919 to 1928, and also from various measures taken by his state administration. On the whole they came to reform the system of government and to solve several sharp socioeconomic problems.

Reforming government consisted of imposing broader prerogatives for the executive branch and for the well-known Democratic electoral system in the state. At its basis was the establishment of a so-called executive budget, that is, transferring the right to plan expenditures and income into the hands of the governor, requiring only a subsequent bill of approval of the budget by the legislators. In this manner the organs of the state's executive branch gained the opportunity to directly and energetically tamper with socioeconomic processes, using the mechanism of financial pressure, and then, as earlier, their role came to only administrative orders by the governor in accordance with petty bargaining between the executive branch and the legislators in Albany over various appropriations.[9]

A reexamination of the rights and responsibilities of the organs of the state's administration was carried out with the goal of strengthening the prerogatives of the executive branch. In place of 169 agencies to which officials were chosen and appointed in sixteen various ways (by determination of the governor, the legislature as a whole or one of its houses, general referendum, etc.), sixteen departments were created under the auspices of the governor with carefully defined functions. The heads of these organs were appointed by the governor, and a mandate by the voters became required for assuming other high official posts in the state. The state's legislature lost the right of initiative in the formation of the executive branch's apparatus.[10]

The period 1919–1920 was marked by the onslaught of monopolies against the rights of the working class. Persecution of striking workers in court, open violence, police methods in fighting the working movement became the political norm. In this period and later in the 1920s, when federal authorities supported by reactionaries in the Supreme Court and the majority of governors carried out pro-monopoly and anti-

9. A. E. Smith, *Up to Now, An Autobiography* (New York, 1929), 157–58, 187, 202, 253, 257.

10. Ibid., 253–66; *Political News* (1926), no. 1: 1–2; (1928), no. 3, 4–6.

worker policies openly, Smith chose a different path for solving labor conflicts. Under the aegis of the New York governor a special commission was created, made up of both representatives of unions and businessmen. Smith unequivocally and consistently preferred negotiations between workers and employers, and decisively opposed using the police as a tool for anti-labor policies of the monopolies. He sometimes personally mediated individual and collective complaints by striking workers.[11] The moderate-liberal approach of the New York governor toward the labor question was in general clearly not conducive to the conservative political climate at the end of the 1920s because this signified, for all practical purposes, a recognition of unions' rights to conduct negotiations with employers through official representatives using the mediation of organs from the executive branch. In addition, in the state of New York a special agency for the control of unemployment was created, and in 1928 Robert Wagner, with the consent and support of Smith, introduced for consideration in the federal Congress a bill to create a national statistical service to aid in planning measures to fight unemployment and to prepare for developing a federal system of public works in the country in the event of an economic crisis.[12]

At the governor's initiative the New York legislature carried out a series of measures in the area of social security for workers and their families. Pensions were increased for disability, temporary disability pay for the injured and their families who lost means of subsistence as a result of an accident at work was introduced, and rather progressive amendments to the state's 1914 legislation were adopted which regulated female and child labor. Despite the extreme limits of the measures enumerated above, they did not touch either upon retirement or unemployment insurance. With the complete absence in the United States of national social legislation, this side of Smith's activities was accompanied by the growth in popularity of such policies and in the number of its supporters from the working class. Among other measures in the social plan embarked upon by Smith in the 1920s, it is worth mentioning the increase in the number of elementary and middle schools, the increase in teachers' salaries, especially for rural teachers, the development of a network of medical institutions subsidized completely or partially from the state coffers, and the building of cheap apartments for low-income citizens using appropriations from the state's budget.[13]

The specifics of Smith's views are most evident in analyzing his position on the question of providing the population with electricity. The New York governor categorically protested against transferring to private hands the existing hydroelectric stations and the rights to building new energy complexes in the north of the state (at Niagara and on the St. Lawrence River), maintaining that they should be ruled by "the citizens of the state" as represented by the organs of the executive branch. Smith and his supporters in the 1920s allowed well-known interference by the

11. A. E. Smith, *Up to Now,* 189–90; *The Labor Record of Governor Alfred E. Smith* (New York, 1928), 11–14.

12. *Congressional Record,* vol. 69, pt. 6, 6811; pt. 7, 7502; Joseph Huthmacher, *Senator Robert Wagner and the Rise of Urban Liberalism* (New York, 1971), 58–60.

13. Smith, *Up to Now,* 268–69, 270–77; Matthew and Hannah Josephson, *Al Smith, Hero of Cities. Portrait, Deriving from the Papers of Francis Perkins* (Boston, 1969), 352; *Congressional Record,* vol. 69, pt. 1, 428; pt. 2, 1312–14.

executive organs of the state in social and economic processes. They allowed for their definite regulation, the scale of which was limited and which occurred as a rule not systematically as a routine form of the state's administrative activity, but rather primarily only during crisis or in extreme situations, or in capital-intensive sectors of the economy (energy and transportation construction).[14]

The legislative programs proposed by Smith during the 1920s served as the basis for the dissemination of information to his benefit, which from 1925 was conducted by the closest supporters of the New York governor. By 1927 two fundamental biographies of Smith were prepared and published, the authors of which, Norman Hapgood (writing with Henry Moscowitz) and Henry Pringle, did not lack epithets to show the "sincere progressiveness" and "natural democraticism" of the governor in Albany.[15] The propaganda efforts by Smith's close circle were supported by Tammany Hall and other urban party machines of the Northeast (Boston, Jersey City, and others), Chicago, Indianapolis, and by special emissaries of the New York governor in the South and West of the country. On January 26, 1926, in Washington, under the chairmanship of senator David Baird, the Thomas Jefferson League was established. Among the ranks of its leadership were the Democratic senators William C. Bruce (Maryland), Edwin S. Broussard (Louisiana), and the former senator Augustus O. Stanley (Kentucky). As stated in the first manifesto of this "non-partisan organization," its fundamental goal consisted in the dissemination of the theory of states' rights, which are a "counterbalance . . . to the national government." In addition the league prepared to fight "the attempts to deny anyone the natural right to election or appointment to any post in the U.S. because of religious affiliation." In its argumentation the league actively used the ideological legacy of Thomas Jefferson, including his Virginia statute on religious freedom and anti-federalist pamphlets from the 1790s. Subsequently, an informal goal of the league arose: disseminating the views of Smith and the measures of his administration directly among the legislators on Capitol Hill.[16]

Related to this period is Smith's strengthening of those close ties formed with the most powerful businessmen from New York, William F. Kenney, J. Haus, George Getz, and James Riordan, representing the newest generation of millionaires in the empire state. The New York governor consolidated ties with the "old money" and clans of financial oligarchs (Rockefellers, DuPonts) through the vice president of the General Motors corporation, millionaire John J. Raskob, who in 1925 had become a permanent member of Smith's closest circle.[17]

The New York governor began to gather supporters from among the intellectual elite of the United States. The future "first journalist of the country," Walter Lippmann, wrote about Smith thus: "He believes in the established American political institutions and carries out his reforms without breaching them. In a well-known sense . . .

14. Smith, *Up to Now,* 247, 270–73; Robert Moses, *A Tribute to Governor Smith* (New York, 1962), 26–33; *Political News* (1926), no. 6, 11–12.
15. Norman Hapgood and Henry Moskowitz, *Up from the City Streets* (New York, 1927); Henry Pringle, *Alfred E. Smith* (New York, 1927).
16. H. M. Berry to A. E. Smith, December 12, 1925, UNCA—SHC, H. M. Berry Papers; Josephson, *Al Smith,* 352; *Political News* (1926), no. 4, 12–13; no. 6, 1.
17. Josephson, *Al Smith,* 354–55.

one can maintain that governor Smith is the most influential conservative today in America. . . . He is a proponent not of barbarous revolution, but rather he is leading toward a completely respectable social movement. . . . He will manage to override all these crowds of citizens." "Affairs in the state of New York have never gone as well as they have under governor Smith," maintained the main editor of the influential liberal weekly *Nation,* Oswald Villard, noting that in his opinion, "politics conducted in Albany, without any doubt, are progressive." The evaluations of publicists are a highly subjective matter, but it would be difficult not to note that even H. L. Mencken, with all his cynical misanthropy and aggressive rejection of any bourgeois politician, considered the New York governor "honest and an upright person in . . . a crowd of amoral jesters playing out the proscenium in our political puppet show."[18]

It is impossible to evaluate categorically Smith's political views and his practical activity during the 1920s. To a well-known extent politics were a consequence of the period that America was undergoing: having rejected the state-monopolistic legacy of Wilsonism, it would have been impossible not to give some consideration to the fact that the ideological and political views of individualism from the epoch of free competition at that time did not at all correspond to that concrete historical stage of development in which American society found itself. The political views of Smith and his supporters represented more than an attempt to overcome reformist statist views, which lay at the base of the federal government's political course during the years of the Wilson presidency. They were a unique reaction to the existing need by the country for pragmatic politicians who would strive to be realists given the opportunity, yet would not desire to see the objective need to use the levers of governmental power on a national scale for deep and broad social maneuvering and regulation of economic life in all of American society. The governor of the New York and his circle figured that the new problems could be solved by using slightly renovated, but in essence old, methods. In the atmosphere of a significant strengthening of individualist views in the United States, Smith had the fortunate opportunity to work out slogans for the party as a whole. This primarily arose out of the relatively prosperous state of American industry during the years of the temporary and partial stabilization of capitalism.

Under such conditions the political views and practical activity of the New York governor were based on, first of all, the recognition of the dogma about the importance of the old adherence to the rights of states as a counterbalance to the national government. Second, the idea of the necessity for very limited social reforms, in the eyes of many Democrats who were waiting for their party leaders' proposals as alternatives to the course of the ruling Republicans, seemed valuable and realistic for the present situation. Moreover, several results achieved through extremely halfway measures were propagandized by the supporters of Smith as the "greatest" successes of the New York governor, emphasizing that they were the result of an improvement in the style and methods of ruling, and not "unnecessary centralization of power," "levying of burdensome taxes," "governmental extravagances," etc. In addition, Smith's supporters, praising the faithfulness of their leader to the old dogma of classic

18. Walter Lippmann, *Men of Destiny* (New York, 1928), 6–7; Oswald G. Villard, *Prophets: True and False* (New York, 1928), 6, 9.

liberalism—the government that rules less is the better government—wholeheartedly maintained that decentralizing power and guaranteeing freedom for entrepreneurial activity would enable the New York governor to achieve an improvement in the workers' situation.[19] In the background of an openly pro-monopoly and anti-labor policy of the Harding and Coolidge administrations, this raised the prestige of the Democratic leader, since on a series of separate questions there were some alternatives to the governmental course in the Republican party.

It is not surprising that in the first round of voting during the convention in Houston Smith received the right to head the Democratic ticket for the presidential election. During the course of the election campaign of 1928 the political profile of the New York governor was significantly distorted without the participation of Smith himself. Thus in July–August 1928, before he actually entered the race, he made it known that he would not object to reexamining the Dry Law in the heat of internal party debates. In sum, the Democratic National Constitutional Committee was created, whose main slogan became the call to "teach the Democrats to vote for Hoover and in addition candidates from the Democratic party who were fighting for elected posts in states, counties, and municipalities." The committee, a united body of politicians from southern and midwestern states, including senators Robert L. Owen (Oklahoma) and Furnifold Simmons (North Carolina), completely supported Hoover's candidacy and led a fierce campaign against Smith, spreading absurd rumors about the Democratic leader among the voters in southern and midwestern states, where anti-Catholic sentiments were especially strong and the number of self-interested proponents of the Dry Law was imposing enough.[20] In sum, Smith's political ideas, somewhat encrusted in the Procrustean bed of individualism, turned out to be entirely hidden from the voters with the help of the ballyhoo over the religious beliefs of the New York governor and his attitude toward anti-alcohol legislation.

After his defeat in the 1928 election, Smith was left with a problem: to transform formally the highest post in the party (in accordance with unwritten interparty tables of rank) to a starting platform for attempting to head the party in 1932. It should be noted that the first steps by the former governor reflected his lack of readiness to assume the burden of the permanent leadership in the party. In particular, appealing to the voters on January 16, 1929, Smith spoke out only for organized strengthening of the party and called on Democrats to follow "the progressive, active and energetic course," not mentioning how that should end.[21] And in actuality in 1929 measures were adopted for the organizational solidification of Smith's position and of his supporters in the highest echelons of the party leadership: in the National Committee a deliberative council and

19. Thomas H. Dickinson, *The Portrait of a Man as Governor* (New York, 1928); *What Everybody Wants to Know about A. E. Smith* (New York, 1928), 11, 13–15; Hans Morgenthau, *Why I Support Alfred E. Smith* (Salt Lake City, 1928), 3–4; *The Labor Record of Governor Alfred E. Smith*, 3, 11–14.

20. H. M. Berry to S. Morison, June 28, 1928, UNCA—SHC. H. M. Berry Papers; Fr. Whispering Campaign, F. D. Roosevelt Library, Hyde Park, G. B. Graves Papers; M. D. Lightfoot to W. G. McAdoo, December 15, 1928, LC. MD., W. G. McAdoo Papers.

21. Radio Address of A. E. Smith, January 16, 1929, NYSA. A. E. Smith Papers. Subject File.

a propaganda apparatus were convened. In addition, other than by releasing a series of statements about the necessity of reexamining the Dry Law, the council did not in any way add to the ideological arsenal of the Democrats. The National Committee apparatus was limited to several philippics addressed to the Hoover administration on banal themes like the losses to agriculture in the United States because of high tariffs and the timeliness for finally rejecting anti-alcohol legislation.[22] It would not be difficult to suppose that all of the enumerated ideas added practically nothing to the political profile of Smith, whose name regularly appeared in the Council newsletters and the National Committee press releases.

The economic crisis proved to be one of the most important influences on the dynamics and makeup of partisan life in the United States at the turn of the decade. The first reaction to Smith differed little from the initial one shown toward him by other Democratic leaders: they all did not take the stock market panic of the fall of 1929 seriously. By the interim elections of 1930 the scale of the crisis became such that it became impossible to ignore it. Smith stepped forward with a statement proposing a five-day work week to increase the number of temporary positions. In addition the former New York governor, in one of his few speeches, called for the expansion of public-sector jobs, cautioning in passing against "governmental handouts for the needy."[23]

The result of the interim elections was relatively unsuccessful for the Republicans. When it became clear that the Democratic party received partial control of Congress, its leading activists, headed by Smith, came out with a statement. It emphasized the "insistent necessity" in any way to facilitate "the efforts of the Republican administration to develop business activity as the main factor in fighting the Depression and in renewal of prosperity." The National Association of Manufacturers "greeted with approval" this point of view, but the liberal magazines *Nation* and *New Republic,* which had supported Smith in 1928, sharply criticized his position for its "conciliatory spirit."[24]

As mentioned, by the fall of 1930 the former governor could rely on the corresponding organizational structure in the upper echelons of the national Democratic leadership. But it was clear to Smith and his circle that without a real program it would be senseless to count on the leadership of the party. As a result a plenary session of the National Committee was planned for March 1931 to "sweep together several divisions of the party platform for the convention," that is to say, in essence, to come forward with a statement on the Democratic line for the upcoming presidential election. It soon became known that there were "several divisions" over the demand to rescind the Dry Law and to establish high tariffs on agricultural products. During the course of the session Smith met with opposition from such influential figures in the party as

22. Hugh Bone, *Committees and National Politics* (Seattle, 1959), 217; Cornelius Cotter and Bernard Hennessy, *Politics without Power: National Party Committees* (New York, 1964), 211.

23. *World,* October 26 and November 1, 1930.

24. *A Joint Statement by J. M. Cox, J. W. Davis, A. E. Smith, et al.* (Washington, 1930); *New York Times,* November 8, 1930; *Nation,* November 19, 1930; *New Republic,* December 17, 1930, 137.

Joseph Robinson, Harry Byrd, John N. Garner, Franklin D. Roosevelt, and Cordell Hull. The opposition was of a tactical nature. For example, the very conservative politician from Virginia, Byrd, during the course of the session protested against the politicization of the anti-alcohol controversy: "in the country there are economic difficulties and the party has more important matters to address." This point of view was shared by Garner and Hull. Indirect evidence allows us to suggest that Franklin Roosevelt was of the same inclination. Smith's criticism of the Dry Law, which had won him supporters during the years of prosperity, now at times had the opposite effect in conditions of depression. As an anonymous pamphleteer wrote caustically in 1931, "the nation wants to eat, but he wants to make it drunk."[25]

The plenary session of the Democratic National Committee in March 1931 ended with practically no results: no sort of decisions were taken. But, in perspective, it proved to be a negative influence on Smith's political career. As Cordell Hull and James Farley noted in their memoirs, it was exactly after this session that the decisive growth in Roosevelt's prestige occurred in the southern and western states. Emily Warner, Smith's daughter, made it understood that at this session the former governor of New York felt some unsteadiness on the political ground on which he stood.[26] In addition, it should not be forgotten that March 1931 is known as a pivotal point in Smith's life.

If Roosevelt as a personality began to win sympathy in the party, then in the capacity of a political leader the former governor more completely and more adequately expressed the ideological views that had wide support among Democrats, something confirmed by the results of surveys taken in 1931.[27] It goes without saying that Smith was informed about the mood that reigned among the functionaries. But his presidential ambitions were awakened by more than ideological considerations and an accounting of the general political situation in the party. In the Democratic party elite in 1931 a well-known reevaluation of individualistic ideopolitical values began. This is shown in particular by the measures by Roosevelt in the state of New York and the statist position of Senators Robert Wagner and Thomas J. Walsh (Montana) on the question of stimulating employment, taxation, and labor relations.[28] All this potentially threatened the "liberal and progressive" political profile of Smith, formed at the end of the 1920s. Smith, transforming his personal views into dogma, was out of touch not only with the national party organization but also with his own home state.

In addition, Smith's lack of desire (or lack of knowledge) to draw serious conclusions from the socioeconomic situation in which a crisis-ridden America had fallen,

25. *New York Times,* February 11, 1931; March 5, 6, 7, 1931; *Mirrors of 1932* (New York, 1931), 34; Charles Michelson, *The Ghost Talks* (New York, 1935), 135–37.

26. Cordell Hull, *Memoirs* (New York, 1948), vol. 1, 141–43; Farley, *Behind the Ballots,* 74–75; Emily S. Warner and Hawthorne Daniel, *The Happy Warrior: A Biography of My Father, Alfred E. Smith* (New York, 1956), 250–51.

27. Analysis of Replies from Test Mailing, November 4, 1931, NYSA. A. E. Smith Papers, Subject File, FR. 162.

28. T. Walsh to B. Baruch, October 16, 1931, LC, MD, T. Walsh Papers; T. Walsh to J. Robinson, November 7, 1931, LC, MD, T. Walsh Papers; Huthmacher, *Senator Robert Wagner,* 149–53.

and for all practical purposes his disregard for several political slogans that he had proposed at the dawn of his personal career, caused a real fall in his authority among the urban working class and the petty bourgeoisie, not to mention the intelligentsia of the Northeast. Expressing the point of view of the latter, the above-mentioned anonymous pamphlet, clearly hinting at the close not-uninterested ties of Smith to "the better houses" on Fifth Avenue and Park Avenue, maintained that the former governor "has grown fat and flabby, not only physically, but intellectually as well."[29]

From the time that Franklin Roosevelt occupied Smith's place in Albany, relations between them began to worsen. At first they had run-ins over appointments to the executive apparatus of the state, then debate flared up over their views of the Dry Law and over the procedure for the administration of the law in the state. In the first and the second case the arguments between FDR and Smith touched not on the content of those measures proposed by the former, but the methods of their realization. Smith rejected the practice of amending the state's constitution with elements of the so-called statute legislation, that is, criminal, civil, administrative, and procedural norms. Roosevelt did not see any problems with it, thinking that it yielded political dividends. In 1930, for example, in the state a real battle between FDR and Smith unfolded over the Wheat amendment to the state constitution on the use of a referendum for determining the size of appropriations for developing afforestation. Smith defended his child, the executive budget, which was considered the exclusive right of the governor to work out. Roosevelt, making use of the right to separate the budget appropriations for the summer of 1931 to establish the temporary extraordinary administration of aid, supported the amendment out of propagandistic considerations.[30] But during 1929–1931 a complete rift between Smith and Roosevelt did not occur, and the boundaries of their opposing stances were not so much of a general ideological nature as they were from personality differences and concrete political motives.

It would be completely correct to relate the aforementioned to the election campaign of 1932. In the beginning of February, two weeks after Roosevelt, Smith made an official statement: if "it should be the will of the pre-election congress," then he would enter the race for president, but "no sort of steps to win votes from the convention's delegates before its opening were planned" by him.[31] It is telling that in the statement there was not one word about Smith's views.

Up until the opening of the Democratic convention in Chicago (at the end of June 1932) the former governor of New York only once publicly criticized FDR's position, in his speech of April 7 in which he talked about the need to defend the interests of the "downtrodden . . . located at the bottom of the economic pyramid." On April 13 Smith sharply condemned Roosevelt for "demagogy" and the attempt to "inflame class prejudices, to encourage hatred of the rich against the poor and the poor against the rich." Smith maintained that it was "irresponsible" to promise work to the unemployed while "normal conditions of employment in the private sector

29. *Mirrors of 1932,* 34.
30. Samuel B. Hand, "Al Smith, Franklin D. Roosevelt, and the New Deal: Some Comments of Perspective," *Historian* 27 (1965): 377–80.
31. *New York Times,* February 8, 1932.

were not restored." At the convention in Chicago, Smith, besides introducing into the platform the demand to rescind the Dry Law and attempting through manipulation of the vote of undecided delegates to block Roosevelt's nomination, in no way proved his worth. The fundamental campaign document of the Democrats was categorically approved, and two days after the convention ended, Smith officially declared his complete support for the main Democratic ticket in the elections.[32]

After the impressive victory by Roosevelt in the elections, Smith for some time entertained the hope that he would be invited to play a key role in the new Democratic administration. But the possibility of such an appointment was never even discussed in the White House, and the only accessible form of participation in political life for Smith was working for the magazine *New Outlook* as the main editor, a position he had begun in September 1932.[33]

The Roosevelt administration's program in March and April of 1933 was rather consistently supported by Smith. He maintained his loyalty in his attitude toward the direction of the measures of the "Hundred Days" as well as in his estimation of the Emergency Banking Act of March 9, 1933. The law on reconstructing of industry [NIRA] was met with a positive note, although, in Smith's opinion, it "undermines the principles of our constitution or signifies revolution." The decision by the administration to curtail pensions for veterans of the First World War was characterized positively, and, it goes without saying, Roosevelt's initiative in the ratification process of the twenty-first amendment to the constitution, which annulled the eighteenth amendment, called forth an explosion of genuine enthusiasm on the pages of *New Outlook*. Smith also viewed favorably the recognition of the Soviet Union by the United States.[34]

The "era of good feelings" in the relations between Smith and the Roosevelt administration began to come to an end as soon as the U.S. Senate, toward the end of April, adopted an amendment by Elbert Thomas to agricultural legislation. As is known, the amendment granted the executive branch the right to determine the gold parity to the dollar. In the course of the debates, for the first time the lines were more or less drawn definitively between the supporters and the opponents of Roosevelt's liberal reform course, including within the Democratic party. Thus criticism of FDR's policies was heard from the mouth of the conservative Virginia Senator Carter Glass, whose position was laid out in a very lengthy speech on April 27, 1933, and led, in essence, to a declaration that the Thomas proposal supported by the administration was "expropriation and unconstitutional."[35] Subsequently, it became known that the given view was close to that of Smith, and from June 1933 a constant departure of the magazine *New Outlook* from support of the New Deal began. "I am for gold dollars and against dollars of air," declared Smith, commenting

32. *New York Times,* April 14, July 4, 1932; Ralph Martin, *Ballots and Bandwagons* (Chicago, 1972), 320–21, 342–60.

33. Warner and Daniel, *The Happy Warrior,* 262; J. A. Schwartz, "Al Smith in the Thirties," *New York History* 4 (1964): 317.

34. *New Outlook,* April 1933, 9; *New York Times,* December 1, 1933; Schwartz, "Al Smith in the Thirties," 318; Oscar Handlin, *Al Smith and His America* (Boston, 1958), 173.

35. R. Smith and N. Beasley, *Carter Glass: A Biography* (New York, 1939), 347–56.

on the Thomas amendment in particular and the financial policy of the Roosevelt administration from the end of April to the end of 1933 as a whole. Measures to renew industry, and especially the creation of a multitude of federal agencies in charge of various programs of aid for the unemployed, also underwent criticism in the editorial column of *New Outlook:* "The government is obliged to assure the renewal of normal conditions for the livelihood of business, and not go into business itself." Smith consistently emphasized that public work not paid back and direct monetary subsidies to the unemployed amounted to "handouts," which force the latter to think that "the government owes them something."[36]

In the end of 1933 Smith decided to put into action his criticism of the New Deal, which was previously in word only. In one of his articles, having praised leaders of the past, who, "despite mistakes . . . made our country what it is today," and having acrimoniously spoken of Roosevelt's closest circle, the so-called "brain trust" ("these callow young college teachers . . . prepared to turn Americans into guinea pigs"), he threatened the new party establishment that he "deserved the right to be independent in the party."[37]

In addition, criticizing the policies of the Roosevelt administration in the second half of 1933–1934, Smith did not take negative positions categorically. Thus, he proposed the idea for establishing programs for the poor segments of the population in the area of housing construction with an accent on municipal initiative supported by the federal government. There was a rational kernel to his criticism of the confusion that had arisen in the system of federal agencies charged with the organization of aid to the unemployed during the fall of 1933 and the winter of 1933–1934. In this, he did not dispute the principle itself of federal aid to the states for organizing self-financed "work beneficial to the public" (construction of paved roads in rural regions, recreational facilities in national parks, etc.) for the unemployed in those areas of industry in which there was no competition with the private sector.[38] But the aforementioned did not mean that Smith continued to associate his personal positions with the policy of the New Deal in 1934. Eight months after the declaration of his "independence" he became one of the founders of the American Liberty League.

In the ranks of the league's leadership were the most influential monopolists of the United States—the DuPont brothers, Ernest Weir (president of Weirton Steel), Alfred P. Sloan, Jr., and D. Brown (president and first vice-president of General Motors), D. New, and William L. Clayton—on the one side, and the top echelons of the conservative Democrats—John W. Davis, John Raskob, Jouett Shouse, Bainbridge Colby, and Senator James B. Reed—on the other side. The league was an unusual formation because it was a political organization in which the representatives of the industrial-financial elite of the United States openly and intimately worked with professional American politicians, usually not advertising their direct affiliation with monopolistic capital. The main slogan of the league's charter was the well-known call

36. *New Outlook,* December 1933, 10; July 1933, 9; Warner and Daniel, *The Happy Warrior,* 266.
37. *New Outlook,* December 1933, 10.
38. Handlin, *Al Smith and His America,* 174.

to defend the constitutional guarantees and the rights of states "as a counterbalance to the centralization aspirations of the federal government." The league perceived the measures of the New Deal within the prism of this slogan. Coming out against deficit budget planning, federal programs for aid to the unemployed, and the federal system of public sector jobs, its leaders rallied for transferring the prerogative for their realization to state governments.[39] After adopting the legislation of the "Second Hundred Days" and the move to the left in the policies of the New Deal (in the spring and summer of 1935), the league shifted somewhat the accent of their criticism, pushing forward now the fight against raising taxes on profits and attacking the federal system of social security. "The League's criticism was directed against the working class and all workers, the slogan of defending the constitution . . . was of a reactionary anti-labor character because for all practical purposes it meant the prohibition of the federal government from taking any responsibility for the fate of the lower echelons of society."[40]

Having more than generous financial resources, the league during 1934–1936 created offices in twenty states, released 135 pamphlets in a huge circulation for the United States (five million copies), and was able to recruit into their ranks between 75,000 to 125,000 people. The league maintained direct contacts with the National Association of Manufacturers and the U.S. Chamber of Commerce. Various groups of businessmen came together during the first Hundred Days of the New Deal in conjunction with the NIRA to participate in programs for encouraging entrepreneurial activity, and for all practical purposes, turned into a unique auxiliary regional branch of this organization.[41]

From the beginning of its activities, numerous points of correspondence took shape in the league's position with the views of the absolute majority of representatives of the "old guard" of Republicans. Thus, in his book *Challenge to Liberty,* Herbert Hoover cited practically all of its arguments against the New Deal. The accusation that the Roosevelt administration was tampering with the constitutional rights of Americans and states' prerogatives, arising from the Tenth Amendment to the U.S. Constitution, resounded in the so-called conference of the rank-and-file Republican party in June 1935 and from the pages of the book by the Republican candidate for president, Alf Landon, in 1936, *America at the Crossroads.* It is symptomatic that in the corridors of the above-mentioned conference the prospects for Smith's candidacy as the head of the electoral ticket of the Grand Old Party were discussed in 1936.[42]

An important element of the criticism of the New Deal by the conservatives from

39. *New York Times,* August 23, 1934.
40. N. V. Sivachev, *The Political Struggle in the U.S. in the Middle of the 1930s* [Politicheskaia bor'ba v SShA v seredine 30-x godov XX veka], 85.
41. George Wolfskill, *The Revolt of the Conservatives: A History of the American Liberty League, 1934–1940* (Boston, 1962), 61–55; Schwartz, "Al Smith in the Thirties," 322; K. McQuid, "Corporate Liberalism in the American Business Community, 1920–1940," *Business History Review* (1978), no. 3: 362–63.
42. *Literary Digest* (June 22, 1935): 11; Alf Landon, *America at the Crossroads* (New York, 1936); *The New Deal: Revolution or Evolution?* Edwin Rozweng, ed. (New York, 1949), 1, 62, 64–66, 69–70.

both parties, various associations of businessmen, and social movements on the right, was the identification of FDR's policies with socialism or communism. It should be emphasized that Smith was one of the first to resort to this in polemics with Roosevelt. As early as 1933 he wrote that the development of governmental intervention in the economy on the basis of the NIRA would lead to a situation in which U.S. citizens "would sell their rights of American primogeniture for communist hogwash." Smith, however, achieved the most odious apogee in rhetorical exercises of a similar nature in his speech at the league's banquet at the Mayflower Hotel on January 25, 1936. He declared that Americans could have only one capital, either Washington or Moscow, and could breathe only one air, "the pure, clear, and fresh air of America," or "the foul atmosphere of communist Russia." Smith presented himself and his supporters as defenders of Americanism, while Roosevelt and his administration were declared "Moscow's hand."[43]

Beginning with a campaign of so-called "red baiting," unleashed by reactionary circles in the United States from 1919–1920, the use of primitive anti-Soviet and anticommunist clichés became the norm in political discussions. Thus Smith twice had been listed as a "socialist" and as "an agent of the Third Internationale," the first time in 1919–1920, when the New York governor came out against demands to expel five socialist members from the state legislature for their membership in the U.S. Socialist party, and second, in 1927–1928, in connection with his position on property for hydroelectric resources.[44] Hoover did not escape this labeling either, as the Democrats in 1930 accused him of socialism because of his attempts to pass through Congress a bill on irrigation work in the Mississippi Valley.[45] In 1934 Hoover himself found that the New Deal legislation concerning the rights of the executive branch to regulate industrial and agricultural production were "undoubtably socialist."[46] Smith's position, as expressed in his speech of January 25, 1936, appears amidst the examples enumerated above of criticism in an even more unflattering way: if earlier anticommunist rhetoric was used by him for some concrete purpose (in regard to legislation, an executive order, etc.), then now the label was hung on all policies without exception of one of the two leading parties in the United States. Subsequently, this more than dubious polemical device would be intensively used not only by critics of the New Deal during the 1936 campaign but also in the arsenal of McCarthyism as the main weapon in the interparty struggle of 1950–1952.

On February 3, 1936, the *New York Times* attempted to bring Smith to his senses. "His declarations regarding the president being red," wrote the paper, "should seem absurd to him. Roosevelt, after all, is saving us from Communism." Anticommunist attacks in Smith's speeches lessened, which were more than made up for in the attempts of Hoover, Landon, and the Hearst press. After the latter reported in

43. *New York Times,* January 26, 1936. In the papers the speech was printed in a summary with all of its anticommunist ideas. For the complete text see Warner and Daniel, *The Happy Warrior,* 278–81.
44. Josephson, *Al Smith,* 299–300, 353; Handlin, *Al Smith and His America,* 110.
45. Michelson, *The Ghost Talks,* 32–35.
46. *The New Deal: Revolution or Evolution?* 65.

September of 1936 that Roosevelt was a presidential candidate from the "Comintern of the U.S. Communist party," Smith could not contain himself, and having reported on the "agents of Moscow" in the White House, branded the administration with a "communist planned economy."[47]

In addition, finishing up the campaign tour with a speech in Albany, Smith, to the great surprise of his listeners, declared outright the opposite of what they were used to hearing from him earlier: "Right now too much fuss is being made over Communism . . . don't allow anyone to say that Roosevelt is a Communist. . . . He is no more a Communist than I am. But something is happening in our country. What, I don't know. But I do know that something is here, and his main sin is that he isn't aware of that something."[48] Was Smith's impulsive anticommunism sincere, only a reflection of his lack of understanding of those fundamental changes in political life and in the socioeconomic sphere, spurred by the Depression of 1929–1933 and the New Deal reforms? This question can most likely be answered affirmatively.

Smith's anticommunist attacks to a great extent set a general tone for his speeches in 1936. It would be an oversimplification to tie his ideological-political views of the mid-1930s to his primitive anticommunism. The less-often-quoted first part of Smith's speech of January 25, 1936, besides the already common criticism of Roosevelt for his "attempt to set one class against another," contained other positions that were characteristic of those held by the former governor during that period. Thus Smith rebuked the administration for "laying the ground for bureaucratic methods of governing and disregard for the law." The first governmental services and agencies had been created that "pump resources from the people and redistribute them in an illegal manner, by bureaucratic whim," maintained Smith, adding that Democrats had forgotten almost completely their promises from the 1932 platform, this "the most compact, definite and wise document of all, ever adopted by the parties." Smith appealed to his colleagues on Capitol Hill, where, as is well known, from the summer of 1935 dissension over the policies of the New Deal began to be felt in Democratic factions, with the advice to "do that which is right, but not that which arises from immediate need," and, in particular, "to find the 1932 platform, to teach it . . . and follow it."[49] Smith's position regarding the platform, his demand to follow it, which was repeated in his speech eight times (!), forces us to briefly characterize this document.

In the preamble to the 1932 platform was affixed a very significant thought: "The only hope for improving the existing conditions, to renewing employment, to an easing of the despairing condition of the population and to returning the nation to its true state of internal harmony and financial, industrial, and agricultural leadership in international affairs consists in a decisive change in the governmental economic policy."[50] What concretely was this "decisive change" to consist of? The most careful analysis of the election document does not yield a definite answer to this

47. *New York Times,* October 25, 1936.
48. *New York Times,* November 1, 1936; Warner and Daniel, *The Happy Warrior,* 286.
49. Warner and Daniel, *The Happy Warrior,* 278–79.
50. *National Party Platforms,* Donald Johnson, ed. (Urbana, Ill., 1972), 331.

question. Thus, the sections in the platform that called for decreasing government expenditures, for a balanced budget, for avoiding governmental interference in the affairs of business "with the exception of those spheres in which it is necessary," gravitated toward the conservative canons of the 1920s and literally verbatim were produced in the articles and speeches of Smith from 1933 to 1936. On the other hand, recognizing the necessity for planned public sector jobs, an easing of the farmers' debt, and introduction of unemployment insurance showed the distinct liberal-reformist characteristics of the Democratic course on the eve of the 1932 elections. The essence of the enumerated slogans did not bring on particular attacks against Smith, even in the period of the apogee of his condemnation of the policy of the New Deal in 1936. In general the 1932 Democratic platform in all its "compactness" was not "definite and wise," but the opposite, very contradictory and an eclectic document, which on its face was a mixture of bourgeois-individualistic and moderate-reformist postulates with the predominance of the former. An analogous picture can, evidently, be seen in an analysis of the political views of Smith during the 1930s. But if during the period of temporary and partial stabilization of capitalism at the same time the most primitive had a big share in U.S. public life, Smith's views and his supporters looked moderately conservative, then in the epoch of the New Deal, under conditions of a noticeable shift in the political axis of the country to the left and a deep political polarization of American society, they in essence signified extreme forms of conservatism. Finally, it should be emphasized that Smith's anticommunism to a great extent was spontaneously polemical, and delivered a thick retouching of his ideological positions, hiding from the eyes of contemporaries and heirs their reactionary components.

Smith's political activity during the 1936 campaign was distinguished by his ideological positions. In the summer of 1936 he, Bainbridge Colby, James A. Reed, Joseph B. Ely, and Daniel F. Cohalan appealed to the party convention with a letter in which they insisted on the nomination of not Roosevelt, but some other "true Democrat" for president.[51] It goes without saying that the letter had no sort of effect, and on August 7–8, its authors together with representatives from twenty-two state Democratic organizations held a conference. On the basis of the "experience" of the internal party opponents by Smith in 1928 and the galvanization of the Thomas Jefferson League the National Organization of Jeffersonian Democrats was thus created, excluding Roosevelt from the Democratic party and calling on all its supporters to vote for Alf Landon.

After the defeat of the right opposition in the 1936 presidential elections, a slow but entirely distinct departure of Smith from active political activity began. He supported anti-Roosevelt forces in his own state in 1937–1938, and in 1940 he grew closer to the Republican group headed by Wendell Willkie. In the presidential election campaign of that year Smith appeared with several brief and diffuse enough speeches in favor of the candidate from the Grand Old Party. Smith's support for the foreign policy of the Roosevelt administration in the end of the 1930s to the beginning of the 1940s, in particular his approval of the proposal to reexamine the Neutrality Law and the Lend-

51. *New York Times,* June 22, 23, 1936.

Lease Law, caused some surprise in the country. Beginning in 1943 Smith grew closer to the Republican governor of New York, Thomas Dewey. In the beginning of the following year suppositions that Smith would appear on the ballot for the U.S. Senate on the Republican ticket against Robert Wagner began to circulate. Smith's serious illness (from spring 1944) and death (October 4, 1944) did not allow confirmation one way or another about these rumors, although Smith himself denied them.[52]

The influence of Alfred Smith on the U.S. conservative political tradition of the 1920s–1930s was far from constant and not very simple. During his years of "flowering" this politician made a significant contribution to the modernization of the ideological postulates of individualism, on separate issues going beyond its framework. Criticizing the policy of the New Deal from the ideological platform of the 1920s, Smith did much for working out several fundamental slogans for conservatism in the middle of the 1930s. Beginning in 1937 they began to transform, in conformity with the concrete tasks of the interparty debate, and partly went into the ideological arsenal of Willkie. It is interesting to see not only the correspondence of the concrete political steps by Smith with Willkie's line (which became evident in their uniting forces in 1940) but also the distinct ideological points of contiguity of their positions. To that in particular can be related the recognition of the active regulative role of the organs of power in the system of socioeconomic relations. True, the state level of power in conjunction with the theory of states' rights was endowed by Smith with the greater socioeconomic prerogatives than was allowed in Willkie's structure. Neither politician saw the basis for the American way of life as undermined in making labor politics the concern of government in the plan of recognizing the rights of unions and the necessity for administrative regulation of labor relations enforced by government organs. In particular, Smith, just like Willkie, considered the state authorities to be responsible for taking on social functions in the area of the struggle with unemployment, housing, and education.

Willkie's ideological political views were the first example of the so-called new Republicanism, a neoconservative statist ideology. In the opinion of A. S. Manykin, Willkie's concept, while preserving a host of traditional conservative dogmas, allowed for the use of governmental methods of a moderate character in order to regulate social and economic relations.[53] It goes without saying that it would be a mistake to see a direct and complete ideological succession between Willkie's views and Smith's views. But within a number of parameters, the political concepts of the New York governor during the 1920s were closer to the early forms of neoconservatism than the ideological postulates of the political theory and practice of the Republican party at the end of the 1920s until the middle of the 1930s.

52. *New York Times,* July 31, 1940; January 11, 1941. James Farley, *Jim Farley Story: Roosevelt Years* (New York, 1948), 204, 206; Schwartz, "Al Smith in the Thirties," 326–27; Studs Terkel, *Hard Times: An Oral History of the Great Depression* (New York, 1970), 337.

53. On the views of W. Willkie from 1938 to 1940, see for more detail A. S. Manykin, "W. Willkie and the Genesis of 'New Republicanism' " [U. Uilki I genezis "novogo respublikanizma"], *Amerikanskii ezhegodnik* (Moscow, 1981), 37–44.

Comment

by David Burner

Ilya V. Galkin's essay carrying in English the title "Alfred E. Smith and the Conservative Political Tradition in the 1920s–1930s" is a product of scholarship in the latter days of the Soviet Union. It has upon it the mark of Soviet vocabulary if not ideology: "state-monopolistic policies of the ruling U.S. circles," "political arsenal of the American ruling elite," "the urban working class and the petty bourgeoisie," not to mention "the intelligentsia." Yet its content conforms to what I once heard from an American historian of Russia: in the days of communism, Soviet scholars who made the appropriate verbal obeisance to ideological formulas had a good chance thereupon of writing respectable history, whatever its relation to their gestures of correctness.

This does not mean that Galkin's use of Marxist analysis is either pure facade or irrelevant to his real story. It happens that in the case of Smith's turn to conservatism, or rather his increasing expression of the conservatism that was already there, and in FDR's dispute with him, what Soviet historians would believe of American politics accords with the facts. It accords, indeed, with what members of differing persuasions within the Democratic party would have been quick to affirm: that in mainline American politics, reform has aimed not to destroy capitalism but to make it respectable. In defining two directions within the party, toward preservation of individualism and the restriction of reform to the state level and toward reform that accepted the centralizing tendencies of the American economy, Galkin is therefore positioned to effect a viable way of looking at Smith's place in American politics. At the very least, it aids in explaining how his early championship of progressive measures in New York might accord with his rejection of much of the vigorous employment of federal power under the New Deal.[1]

In his more specific examination of conflicts within the Democratic party, Galkin recognizes the reality of electoral politics in the United States. He takes due account of prohibition as an issue; he finds that the quarrels between conservative and progressive Democrats reflected actual and important clashes of opinion about the future course

---

1. There is no full-length scholarly biography of Smith. Still useful is the brief and cogent Oscar Handlin, *Al Smith and His America* (Boston, 1958). See also Paula Eldot, *Governor Alfred E. Smith: The Governor as Reformer* (New York, 1983); Robert Wesser, *A Response to Progressivism: The Democratic Party and New York Politics, 1902–1918* (New York, 1986); J. Joseph Huthmacher, *Senator Robert F. Wagner and the Rise of Urban Liberalism* (New York, 1968); Elisabeth I. Perry, *Belle Moskowitz: Feminine Politics and the Exercise of Power in the Age of Alfred E. Smith* (New York, 1987).

of the country; he knows that there was a voting public to which politicians had to attend. Galkin perceives, rightly and with the advantage of standing ideologically outside American politics, that conflicts between liberals and conservatives took place within a capitalism to which both were completely committed. Upon that assumption, he does American political history the service of clarifying the content of these quite genuine differences and suggesting how the ideas of each camp were addressed to the common task of fine-tuning capitalism. Yet the orthodox Marxist reduction of capitalistic politics to strategies among ruling economic classes, together with Galkin's distance from American culture, may contribute to setting the limits of his analysis.

Particularly notable is Galkin's offhand treatment of the issue of prohibition. Among the advocates of repeal, to be sure, were businessmen who both feared extensions of federal power and saw a liquor tax as an alternative to levies upon their wealth. If Galkin had gone back a decade or so in his study, he might have remarked as well that numbers of prohibitionists had thought themselves to be combating an especially noxious capitalist interest, besides contributing to a progressive—some of them were prepared to say a socialist—reordering of American society. It is curious, in fact, that Galkin overlooks these deceptively tempting reinforcements to his class analysis of why Smith ended as a conservative. But the politics of prohibition, as anyone familiar with American history and culture knows, was richly embedded in mentalities that go beyond economics and class.[2] Protestant ideas of morality along with fears of the city and its immigrant communities clashed with urban and immigrant traditions of fellowship centered in the saloon and ethnic festivities—and, of course, simple thirst. Galkin, moreover, takes only brief note of anti-Catholic hostility to Smith, and none of Smith's deep loyalty to his faith and church. He appears unaware also of Smith's wryly affectionate attachment to the big-city East, which together with his unabashedly public Catholicism led him to what a less honestly colloquial politician would have defined as public indiscretions: political calculation argued against hanging in the governor's mansion at Albany an autographed portrait of the Pope. A larger attention to the intertwining issues of alcohol, social mores, and religion could have added much to Galkin's understanding of the politics of the time before the Depression and the New Deal changed the terms of politics.[3]

Galkin's essay could be faulted too for lacking a sense of the fundamental difference between the conditions of Smith's progressive period and the circumstances of his later conservatism. In the last part of his political career, he was quite consciously attempting to defend capitalism against the New Deal—which, of course, was also

2. K. Austin Kerr, *Organized for Prohibition: A New History of the Anti-Saloon League* (New Haven, Conn., 1985); Joseph Gusfield, *Symbolic Crusade: Status Politics and the American Temperance Movement* (Urbana, Ill., 1963); James H. Timberlake, *Prohibition and the Progressive Movement, 1900–1920* (Cambridge, Mass., 1963).

3. David Burner, *The Politics of Provincialism: The Democratic Party in Transition, 1918–1932* (New York, 1968); Edmund A. Moore, *A Catholic Runs for President: The Campaign of 1928* (New York, 1962); Ruth Silva, *Rum, Religion and Votes: 1928 Re-examined* (University Park, Pa., 1962); Allan Lichtman, *Prejudice and the Old Politics: The Presidential Election of 1928* (Chapel Hill, N.C., 1979).

trying to preserve capitalism, but by more widely reformist means. During his earlier and, in fact, quite energetically progressive days, he had also been acting wholly within the basic premises of capitalism and, in putting some restraints upon it, perhaps making it slightly more attractive. But that was not his point, for aside from the presence of a quite secondary socialist movement and political movements on the radical right, capitalism was not in the least danger. Had it been, Smith might have become at that moment the outspoken opponent of the left he was later to evolve into. But then again, he might not have. People as well as times change.[4]

These flaws aside, Galkin's essay shows a remarkable range and suppleness of knowledge of American politics, and a willingness to let it speak on its own terms. Of Smith's call early in the New Deal for housing programs for the poor supported by the federal government but municipal in "initiative," the historian acknowledges "a rational kernel," for federal administration of antipoverty programs had brought inefficiencies. Galkin has admirable purchases on the time and society he examines. He is familiar, as a good historian of the twenties should be, with the scorning and cynical H. L. Mencken, who managed to credit Smith with integrity. This, Galkin observes, was in the face of Mencken's "rejection of any bourgeois politician"—a phrase that may indicate either Galkin's Marxist or Mencken's bohemian identification of the bourgeoisie as an economic class with the bourgeois culture despised by artists, and above all by Mencken.

Writing during the Soviet era and a continent away from American culture, Galkin was doubly constricted in his approach to his subject. What he managed to accomplish under these conditions makes in itself for an interesting glimpse into what Soviet scholars were able to do. Beyond that, he is worth reading by American historians for a view from outside capitalism of the bounds within which American politics works.

---

4. On the later Smith, besides Handlin, see George Wolfskill, *The Revolt of the Conservatives: A History of the American Liberty League, 1934–1940* (Boston, 1962); Frederick Rudolph, "The American Liberty League, 1934–1940," *American Historical Review,* 56 (October, 1950): 19–33; and William H. Harbaugh, *Lawyer's Lawyer: The Life of John W. Davis* (New York, 1973). Davis, the Democratic presidential candidate in 1924, was a fellow member of the Liberty League's leadership along with Smith.

9

Electoral Strategy of the Republican Party in the 1970s–Early 1980s

by Elena Ia. Borschevskaya

The modern pattern of the voters' division between the two major parties of the United States took shape to a large extent during the years of the New Deal. This period displayed a demarcation of the parties and electorate over issues of great social reforms of that time. Representatives of big business, of the more well-to-do strata, and residents of rural regions of the West and the agricultural Midwest leaned toward the Republicans. In terms of religion and ethnicity the Republicans remained primarily an Anglo-Saxon Protestant party. The Democrats, who had become the majority party, relied on the support of the bourgeoisie and enjoyed the support of the working class plus racial, ethnic, and religious minorities, who resided in the urban industrial regions of the Northeast and Midwest. Democrats also retained the support of the southern electorate. Such a distribution of power was evident on all levels of voting, from national to local elections, and could be seen in party identification (according to the public opinion polls) of American citizens up until the end of the 1940s.

In the postwar period the boundaries of party blocs, which had run along the lines of class, religion, and regional characteristics, began gradually to change. The former polarization of parties lessened as Democrats strengthened their position among the wealthier strata and among Protestant voters, while gradually losing their monopoly in the South and among blue-collar voters, a large part of whom having improved their financial positions began to support Republicans more often than previously. Nevertheless, the traditional nucleus of both parties' voting coalitions was preserved, ensuring the Democratic dominance in Congress and in local governments, as well as on the level of party identification of American voters.[1]

A different picture unfolded for the presidential elections, where there was a much greater influence of such factors as the personality of candidates, articulation of

---

1. For more detail see V. O. Pechatnov, *The U.S. Democratic Party: Voters and Politics* [Democraticheskaia partiia SShA: izbirateli i politika] (Moscow, 1980). See the data of Everett C. Ladd, Jr., and Charles D. Hardley, *Transformations of the American Party System* (New York, 1976), 234–37; Gerald M. Pomper, *Voter's Choice: Varieties of American Electoral Behavior* (New York, 1978), 28–29; Warren E. Miller and Edward I. Schnieder, *American National Election Studies Data Sourcebook, 1952–1978* (Cambridge, 1980), 374. This essay by Elena Ia. Borshchevskaia was originally published in *Problemy amerikanistiki* [Problems in American Studies] 4 (1986).

national problems, and the huge role of the mass media, which altered voting behavior from traditional party loyalty patterns. As a result, in the words of the well-known American political scientist Everett Ladd, "a two-tier electoral system" was formed in the United States in which the Republicans competed with the Democrats on an equal footing in the fight for the White House, but significantly conceded to them on the lower levels.[2]

Starting from the second half of the 1960s, with the deepening of the centrifugal tendencies in the Democratic party, the Republicans' prospects began to brighten. This had a casual connection to racial crisis, the war in Vietnam, and the growing dissatisfaction of middle-class voters with the tax and welfare system expanding at the expense of the middle class. While the influence of the first two factors waned with time, the influence of the latter only increased throughout the 1970s under conditions of economic stagnation and unprecedented growth of inflation. At the same time a process of general weakening in party loyalty developed along with an increase in the proportion of independent voters (by the end of the 1960s approximately one-third of U.S. citizens were not registered with one or the other of the country's leading bourgeois parties), thus even more contributing to the "fluidity" of the electorate.[3]

The Republican leadership took a course toward broadening the popular base of the party by wooing voting segments from the Roosevelt coalition, primarily representatives of those social groups where the growth in numbers of middle-class voters dissatisfied with the social policies of the Democrats was the most evident—i.e., blue-collar workers, Catholics, and southerners. Thus the "new Republican majority" was conceived, built not upon a traditional coalition of solid social voting blocs but rather on a coalition made up of their different segments. Economic and social conservatism supplemented by neopopulist rhetoric should have become the political foundation of this coalition.[4] All these ideas were reflected in the well-known book by Kevin Phillips, *The Emerging Republican Majority* (1969), which became the definitive conservative Republicans' manual for action during the 1970s–1980s.

According to official statistics, by the end of the 1970s "blue-collar" workers made up 33 percent of all voting Americans, and they influenced the outcome of the country's elections to a significant degree. Among them, industrial workers from the states of the Northeast and Midwest (such as Illinois, Michigan, New York, New Jersey, Ohio, Pennsylvania, Wisconsin, Missouri, and several others) played the most noticeable role in political campaigns.[5] A significant contingent of "blue-collar" workers are members of labor unions. Organized labor and their families made up roughly 40 million people of voting age, or 23.6 percent of all U.S. voters.[6]

It is not possible to place the unequivocal sign of equality on the electoral subgroups that make up "blue-collar" workers. Non-union workers, in comparison to union

2. Everett C. Ladd, Jr., *Where Have All the Voters Gone? The Fracturing of America's Political Parties* (New York, 1978), 32.

3. Gallup Poll, June 18, 1981, 2–3.

4. *U.S.: Political Thought and History* [SShA: politicheskaia mysl'i istoriia] (Moscow, 1976), 512.

5. *National Journal* (November 1, 1980): 1834.

6. Ibid., 1834, 1836.

members, are more conservative in their political views and apolitical (in the sense of participation in the electoral process), less educated, and not so inclined as union members to support candidates from the Democratic party.

The different size of "contributions" by the previously mentioned subgroups to the Democratic coalition can be explained not so much by their differences in political orientation (in essence non-union and organized labor should be viewed as one social component that holds a particular type of political psychology), but rather by moments of an organizational character.

Industrial labor, as already stressed, was a key ingredient of the Democratic coalition. These groups rendered a reliable support to Roosevelt's party in elections up to the end of the 1960s and thus did not attract much attention from the opposition party. But in connection with the Republican course noted above, which aimed at broadening its popular base and creating in the long run a "new majority" capable of transforming the minor partner of the two-party tandem into a leading political force in the country, "blue-collar" workers became a priority in the Grand Old Party candidates' strategies.

This choice was not accidental. Closely following the trends taking place in the labor force during the 1960s–1970s, Republican strategists drew a conclusion that certain forces were at work that were capable of weakening the working-class Democratic ties. Favorable conditions were being created for the GOP to make a breakthrough to the working masses. This was an opportunity that should be seized without delay.

In the first place, one of the negative influences on the relationship between the Democratic party and working-class voters as the two postwar decades passed and the labor-union movement grew was the progressive decline in union memberships. The proportion of organized labor in the U.S. labor force decreased during the period of 1966–1983, from 28 percent to 20 percent.[7] The diminishing number of registered union members during the 1970s, according to American experts, was inextricably related to the reduction in such highly unionized sectors as the automobile and steel industries, trucking, and several others, and also with the well-known difficulties the unions faced in recruiting new members. The latter can be explained on the one hand by employers resorting to more and more sophisticated methods of combating the organized labor movement; on the other hand it can be explained by the fact that the basic efforts union leadership exercised in the 1970s to attract new members were directed toward the unionization of blue-collars from the so-called "Sun Belt" states, where up to the present anti-union tradition is rather strong.

In the second place, the racial makeup of the U.S. working class changed. In the days of Roosevelt it was almost exclusively white. Today the situation is different: working-class black Americans form a large group among blue-collars, and the process of industrial enterprises absorbing Negroes is on the rise.[8] The flow of

7. *U.S. Department of Labor, National Labor Relations Board* (Washington, 1981), 66; *U.S. News and World Report* (October 17, 1983): 96.

8. For more detail see John H. Bracey, ed., *Black Workers and Organized Labor* (Belmont, Calif., 1971).

American blacks into the ranks of industrial workers did not meet with approval among a certain segment of the white workers and gave impetus to their negative reaction to the Democratic racial policies, and thus weakened their support for the Democratic party. Public opinion polls showed that the overwhelming majority of blue-collar workers accepted racial equality as an abstract idea, but when it came to desegregation in practice they treated it painfully.[9] To a large extent this kind of reaction by white Americans in the 1970s, marked by general economic decline in the United States, could be explained by their rivalry with blacks as competitors in the labor market.

In the third place, the erosion of the support of blue-collar workers for the Democrats was related to the weakening role the union leaders played in the upper echelons of the party. Leaders of the strongest unions, and the leadership of the AFL-CIO in particular, up until the end of the 1960s maintained close business relations with top Democratic party functionaries and had strong positions among the so-called party elite groupings. This gave them the real opportunity to influence the nomination of a "proper" candidate acceptable to unions. Moreover, the union bureaucracy, relying on vigorous apparatus of regional, state, and local branch organizations, was in a position to exert quite a strong pressure upon its rank-and-file members, forcing them to act in whatever direction was expedient for the union.[10] The year 1968 was the peak of the union leaders' influence and at the same time the starting point for destabilization of their positions in the party hierarchy. (Hubert Humphrey was the last candidate whose nomination was strongly attributed to the "working elite efforts"; in the following elections up until 1984 in the presidential nomination process union leaders adhered to a policy of neutrality.)

The sharp decline of the union leaders' prestige within the party was intimately connected to a decrease in the contribution the blue-collars made to the Democratic electoral coalition in the 1970s and early 1980s. The diminishing support for the party by workers and, on the contrary, increased support on the part of representatives from other key voting groups led to a change in the balance of power within the party leadership (the democratization of the selection of delegates at national conventions, which began in the late 1960s and early 1970s, also played into the hands of the "new groups," giving them access to the inner party power levers).[11] In turn, an inevitable consequence of the undermining of the union leadership within the framework of the party was the weakening of its political control over rank-and-file workers and correspondingly a narrowing of the channels of communication between the Democrats and the broad masses of workers.

The gradual increase in numbers of independent voters among the working-class

9. H. Edward Ransford, *Race and Class in American Society: Black, Chicano, Anglo* (Cambridge, 1977), 179–92.

10. *Congressional Record,* vol. 120, pt. 2, 34835. For more detail on the system of political pressure from the upper echelons of the unions on the rank-and-file members see William Kornblum, *Blue-Collar Community* (Chicago, 1974), 211.

11. For more detail on the realignment of the forces of the party elite see Richard L. Rubin, *Party Dynamics: The Democratic Coalition and the Politics of Change* (New York, 1976), 92–96.

masses in the 1970s was an indication of the destabilization of New Deal party support among workers (the number of "independent" working-class voters rose from 25 percent in 1964 to 37 percent in 1981).[12] There appeared "free" spirits, who could be attracted into the orbit of Republican influence with a certain expenditure of efforts.

Richard Nixon, who during the campaigns of 1968 and 1972 attempted to appeal to the racial stereotypes of white Americans, came out as a catalyst for drawing labor votes for the Republican side, emphasizing the consequences of the "law and order violation," and making rhetorical innuendos toward the "forgotten citizens" who suffered under the burden of federal taxes, the revenues from which funded the minorities assistance programs, etc. This, in the opinion of his campaign organizers, would have distinctly influenced working America.

The seeds thrown by Nixon fell on fertile soil. The 1968 elections demonstrated an evident weakening in the loyalty of industrial workers to the New Deal party, and was matched in 1972 with a sharp decline of its prestige. For the first time since the 1930s a Democratic candidate (George McGovern) received a minority of the votes not only among blue-collars as a group but even among union members and their families (labor favored Nixon by a margin of 5 to 4).[13]

Four years later the U.S. working class again gave preference to the representative of the party with which it was tied by strong knots since the Great Depression, largely a result of the "Watergate" scandal and a general worsening of the economic situation in the country during the Republican administration years. Jimmy Carter defeated Gerald Ford, with 58 percent of the blue-collars' votes (among members of the unions the proportion of votes given for the Democratic candidate happened to be more spectacular: 63 percent to 36 percent).[14]

Despite the failures of the Republican party in 1976, its representatives did not abandon their working-class strategy. For them the words of Nixon sounded as a sort of political will: "It seems to me that the Republican party cannot commit a bigger mistake than to write off the votes of organized labor. From this the party is growing noticeably weaker. . . . We have to win over to our side the majority of voters in the North and West, those places where trade unions and non-organized workers are a strong political force."[15]

The attempt at "chiseling off" the working-class voters from the Democratic coalition was renewed in 1980. During the early campaign the general strategic council for Ronald Reagan, which included members of the party's National Committee and representatives of the Reagan-Bush election committee, worked out the manual for the campaign, "Commitment 80," in which the task of securing the support of labor was given a central place.[16]

12. Pomper, *Voter's Choice,* 28–29; Gallup Poll, June 18, 1981, 5.

13. *New York Times,* November 8–9, 1972.

14. *Gallup Opinion Index,* December 15–16, 1976.

15. M. I. Lapitskii, "Unions and Elections" [Profsoiuzy i vybory] *SShA: ekonomika, politika, ideologiia* 3 (1981): 68.

16. Elizabeth Drew, *Portrait of an Election: The 1980 Presidential Campaign* (New York, 1981), 265, 354.

Reagan was well aware that like his predecessors, he had not much hope of attracting blue-collar voters through the unions, which had been the traditional approach of the Democrats. Therefore, the decision was made to appeal directly to the workers, bypassing the union leadership. For this end the Republican party candidate resorted to such effective methods of political self-advertising as television commercials in which the most was made out of his eight years of experience as head of the actors' guild; a wide distribution of the brochure "Choose the former president of a union for president," and personal meetings with workers from large industrial enterprises in the industrial centers of the Northeast and Midwest.[17]

Analyzing the results of a public opinion poll, one of the Reagan-Bush campaign managers noted: "They [labor] are dissatisfied with Carter, this is evident, but we still need to provide enough grounds for them to vote for Reagan. And this is not the easiest thing."[18] Speculating on the general disappointment of the blue-collar workers with the results of the Carter administration's policies, the Republican party functionaries tried to pour oil onto the fire, stressing the theme of working families' falling living standards (in the four years of Carter's administration blue-collar incomes fell by seven percentage points),[19] the growth in unemployment and inflation, Carter's inability to propose anything principally new for the country, and his "borrowing" of the Reagan "reindustrialization" plan.[20] But the main trump cards for the Republicans were undoubtedly the promise for economic recovery and individual income tax reduction, which would ostensibly lead to a noticeable improvement of the broad working masses' living standards. On the whole, the Republican campaign rhetoric in the early 1980s appeared to be appealing in the eyes of the working-class segment of voters because in their criticism of the Democratic policies, Republicans managed to reflect true signs of the crisis atmosphere in America.

As a result, in 1980 the industrial workers' votes divided almost evenly: Carter received 46 percent of the blue-collar votes, and President-elect Reagan 47 percent. Among the labor union members Carter led, with 47 percent of the votes compared to 44 percent given to the former governor of California. But support by organized labor, in comparison to previous elections, had dropped by 14 percentage points.[21]

At the same time labor secured impressive support for the GOP in the congressional elections (43 percent of the votes), and within the following year the list of workers registered as Republicans expanded.[22] While at the end of 1979 16 percent of workers identified with the GOP, by the middle of 1981 the number had increased to 24 percent, the highest indicator since 1960.[23] The blue-collar presence in Reagan's party brought about the illusion among Republicans that the industrial workers were

17. *National Journal* (November 1, 1980): 1834–35.
18. Ibid., 1833.
19. *Nation* (December 14, 1980). For more detail on the economic situation of working-class families in the United States in the 1970s to the early 1980s see *AFL-CIO American Federalist,* January 1981, 2–11.
20. *New York Times,* October 3, 1980.
21. Ibid., November 5, 1980: *U.S. News and World Report* (November 17, 1980): 28.
22. *National Journal* (November 6, 1982): 1793.
23. Pomper, *Voter's Choice,* 28–29; Gallup Poll, June 18, 1981, 5.

finally becoming a permanent part of their social base. The coming off-year elections should have either strengthened the Republicans' hopes, or destroyed them.

In 1982 those who had fled the bosom of the Democratic party were again back home. According to data from polls carried out by NBC together with the AP, 58 percent of blue-collar workers preferred to see Democrats on Capitol Hill, as opposed to 38 percent who supported Republicans, and thus the interparty rift in workers' votes increased in comparison to 1980 by 5 percentage points (according to the CBS/*New York Times* data the lag by Republicans was even greater, yielding a ratio of 62 to 35).[24] Among workers who were union members, Democrats had a twofold lead— 66 percent to 33 percent (according to the CBS/*New York Times* opinion surveys the margin was 64 percent to 30 percent).[25] In addition, the number of blue-collar workers calling themselves Republicans decreased from 24 percent to 20 percent.[26]

The basic reason for the party's fall in popularity in the eyes of the workers, according to the Republican David Gergen (the president's adviser on public relations and communications problems), was the gloomy economic situation in general, and the critical level of unemployment, in 1982 in particular. This conclusion is confirmed by the results of the public opinion polls taken right after voting. In order to

Diagram 1

The dynamics of support by representatives of the working class for candidates from the leading bourgeoisie parties in the United States during the presidential elections of 1952–1984. Sources: *Gallup Opinion Index* (December 1976), 15–16; Gallup Poll, *Public Opinion*, 1990 (Wilmington, 1981), 242–43; *New York Times*, November 8, 1984.

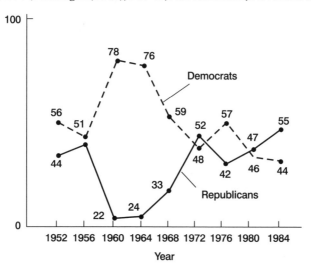

24. *New York Times,* November 9, 1980; November 7, 1982.

25. *Public Opinion* (December/January 1982): 29; *National Journal* (November 6, 1982): 1893.

26. Gallup Poll, September 22, 1983, 2.

regain the trust of the workers, the GOP, according to one Republican congressman, needed "some help from the economy." In the long run, according to Reagan, the economic boom and programs for job creation would impel the working masses to join Republicans, at least their support for the party would be not weaker than in 1980.[27]

The long-awaited economic boom began in February 1983. The sharp decrease in the level of inflation and unemployment in 1983–1984, according to the public opinion polls, came to be the decisive factor that determined the workers' electoral behavior in November 1984. In the election campaign Reagan regained the majority of blue-collar votes, defeating Mondale 53 percent to 46 percent and thus improving upon his success achieved in the previous election.

The energetic actions of the AFL-CIO leadership, directed toward mobilizing union members to support the Democratic candidate, yielded little: a significant part of organized labor and members of their families, like four years earlier, supported the president.[28] He received 45 percent of the votes from union members compared to the 53 percent cast for Mondale. The overall effect of the Republican strategy during the 1970s and the 1980s expressed itself in the noticeable evening of the support provided by workers for the leading bourgeois parties in the country.

The two-party realignment of the Great Depression era proceeded for the most part along the lines of class and religious affiliation. Now a break with the old watersheds could be viewed as a manifestation of a new emerging two-party system, in which, in the opinion of the Republicans, their party should have received the victory laurels. Attempting to stimulate the process of regrouping, the Republican functionaries dealt their first carefully planned blow to the heart of the Roosevelt coalition—the blue-collars and Catholics (on the whole, representatives of white ethnic groups of European origin—Italians, Slovaks, Poles, and several others making up at the beginning of the 1970s around 27 percent of the overall electorate in the United States).[29]

For decades Catholic loyalty to the Democrats was taken for granted. Tracing back to the Jacksonian era, Catholic immigrants, having settled primarily in the large cities along the Atlantic coast, found refuge in the Democratic party. Later on, Catholics

27. *National Journal,* June 18, 1983, 1273.

28. After the 1980 elections the AFL-CIO Executive Committee decided to put an end to the unions' neutrality in the primaries with the goal of obtaining the chance to exert a greater influence on the nomination process and thus to facilitate the restoration of the shaken consensus between the leadership and the rank-and-file members of the American unions *(AFL-CIO American Federationist,* January 1981, 19).

Taking place October 3–6, 1983, the fifteenth Congress of the AFL-CIO mobilized labor union support for Walter Mondale long before his official nomination as the Democratic presidential candidate. The Congress put as its goal to secure for him the support of 65 percent of organized labor *(Business Week,* November 19, 1984, 24).

29. Making plans for the above-mentioned voting groups, the architects of the Republican party policies considered appealing to ethnic groups as an additional means of influence on the working masses, because Americans of European origin usually live in industrial regions of the Northeast and Midwest and make up a large group of blue-collar workers in the country (36 percent of capable representatives of U.S. ethnic groups are employed in industry). *New York Times,* November 9, 1980; Miller and Schnieder, *Election Studies Data Sourcebook,* 77.

found nothing attractive in Lincoln's party, which had come into being on the eve of the Civil War, and in which prevailed the interests of Protestants and Nativists, for whom anti-Catholic sentiments were a sine qua non in their political activities.[30] In the post–Civil War period Catholic support for the Democrats was not always unanimous. Protesting against some particular aspects of the party's policies, they from time to time joined the Republicans, but their sympathies throughout remained invariably with the Democrats.[31] In 1928 a Catholic Democratic candidate, Al Smith, significantly strengthened ties between ethnic groups and his party, and then Franklin Roosevelt made Catholics the Democratic party's guaranteed source of support for a long time. A new phase in dialogue between the U.S. Catholic communities and Democrats began in 1952 and was characterized by a gradual cooling of their relations.

It should be noted that during the course of social changes within the Catholic community, economic factors gradually began to play a decisive role in determining its political behavior (previously the basic determining factor was religious affiliation). Thus, already in the 1930s the primary motivation that spurred lower-class Catholics to join the New Deal coalition was Roosevelt's policies of providing relief to the poor.

The welfare state came into being as a reliable connecting link between the Democratic party and ethnic groups. But in the post–World War II period the country's economic situation was relatively favorable, and social differentiation within the American minorities deepened: the proportion of the middle class increased. In 1952, 25 percent of Catholics could be considered middle class, while by the middle of the 1970s the number was 42 percent.[32] As a result many voters who had improved their financial situation and joined the ranks of active taxpayers began to show less willingness to support the idea of federal aid to the poor; moreover, during the 1970s, when the rate of growth in the common "economic pie" substantially slowed down, they became its open critics. The ties between the Democrats and ethnic groups began to loosen.

The emergence of a new political force in the middle of the 1960s, the black electorate, who were quickly absorbed into the structure of the Democratic party and became supposedly the main beneficiaries of a welfare state, played the role of a catalyst accelerating the process of growing discontent among white ethnic minorities. "The blacks became the favorites of the 1960s," complained the Catholics, "and ethnic minorities became the blacks of the North, and . . . the rules of the game changed. They (white minorities) were just about to score a goal when they were slapped on the shoulder and asked to pass the ball to the blacks . . . Blacks receive government aid, but we receive highways, built with our money, and we pay for both."[33]

The Republicans were preparing for the battle to woo the ethnic minorities' votes very carefully. During the 1970s, largely due to the efforts of Walter Brock (Chairman of the Republican National Committee from 1977 to 1981, who regarded the problem of the party's relationship with ethnic minorities as especially important), the work

30. Seymour Lipset and E. Raab, "The Election and the Evangelicans," *Commentary* (March 1971): 45–57.

31. Kevin P. Phillips, *The Emerging Republican Majority* (New York, 1970), 144.

32. Miller and Schnieder, *Election Studies Data Sourcebook,* 75.

33. *Time* (October 30, 1972): 25.

of a special minorities-liaison division, which had been formed during the 1950s and had established contact with representatives of thirty-two nationalities, was activated. In 1980 Reagan's advisers created a council on the ethnic groups' affairs under the auspices of his election committee to extend the campaign to twenty-six ethnic groups.

A system of communication with ethnic groups was thoroughly thought out. All the mentioned divisions as well as the party agents on the local level were supplied with lists of voters, recent immigrants from Europe, each of whom was contacted by phone. The first question the respondents were asked was whether they planned on voting for the Republicans in the upcoming elections. If the answer was negative, then the voters were no longer bothered; if positive or undecided, a second question followed about which problems were of their prime concern and what, in their view, were the best ways to solve them. The summoned information was entered into a computer, and on the basis of the final result, data letters were sent to individual voters with explanations on the party candidates' positions on this particular range of questions and information releases ("Newsletter Reports") were issued to help campaign organizers.[34]

Analyzing the political environment at the end of the 1970s, the Republicans came to the idea that it would have been most expedient for them to concentrate their efforts on wooing those voters dissatisfied with Democratic policies, the voters from the lower and middle layers of the American middle class. Recent newcomers from the underprivileged segments of society, they tried to secure their newly acquired status at all costs. Such aspirations made them conservatives in their approach to social and moral-ethical problems and skeptical toward the idea of active government. Taking into account all these considerations, Republican contenders competing in the 1970s–1980s for the right to occupy the seat in the White House hammered out their election campaign tactics.

President Nixon made the theme of getting back to traditional American values the leitmotif of his campaign speeches. He was tireless in repeating that in all times it had been the hard work of U.S. citizens and not the philanthropy of the federal government that made the country prosperous: "People who came to the American shores came not to beg, they came here in search of opportunities. And we are obliged to reject that philosophy, which preaches that he who is supported by government should receive more than he who works."[35]

Nixon's criticism of his political rival—George McGovern's platform called for legalizing abortion, securing equal rights for women, eradicating racial discrimination, and liberating the individual from the chains of out-of-date social morals—corresponded to the sentiments of white ethnic minorities. Gerald Ford's tactics in 1976 included the very same assortment of means to influence the public. Later Reagan went further with Nixon's strategy. In search for Catholic votes in 1980 and 1984, the president used the already approved methods, the essence of which C. Tawry, aide to the press-secretary of the Reagan-Bush election committee, laconically expressed in

34. Ibid. The Democrats do not obtain such a distinct system of communication with representatives of ethnic groups in the United States.
35. *Time* (October 9, 1972): 16.

the 1980 presidential campaign: "we are armed with slogans connected to traditional values (family, work, the state of minorities, and patriotic duty), we aim them at areas of ethnic group concentration and we hit the target."[36]

The Republican strategy brought the desired political dividends. If in three national campaigns during the 1960s an insignificant number of voting American Catholics gave preference to the party (respectively 22 percent, 24 percent, and 33 percent), then the following decade ushered in a spectacular shift in their vote distribution within the U.S. two-party system.

In 1972, for the first time since the 1930s the Republicans won the majority of the Catholic vote: Nixon received 52 percent to 48 percent of the votes; in 1980 the party confirmed its success, finishing with 47 percent to 46 percent, and in 1984 it won with an unprecedented margin of 11 percent (55 percent to 44 percent). On the whole, as is clearly shown in Diagram 2, in the 1970s and early 1980s the disproportion in the parties' popularity among voting Catholics noticeably evened out. Moreover, as follows from American political scientists' analyses, those voters who defected to the Republicans in the campaigns of 1972, 1980, and 1984 were largely citizens from the lower and central parts of the American middle-class income scale—exactly what the strategists of the GOP prophesied.[37]

The 1970s–1980s election statistics confirm the assumption made as far back as the early 1960s and on which the Republican strategists based their ploy—i.e., along with

Diagram 2

The dynamics of support by Catholics for the Democratic and Republican candidates in the presidential elections of 1952–1984. Sources: *Gallup Opinion Index,* **December 1976, 15–16; Gallup Poll,** *Public Opinion,* **1980, 242;** *New York Times,* **November 8, 1984.**

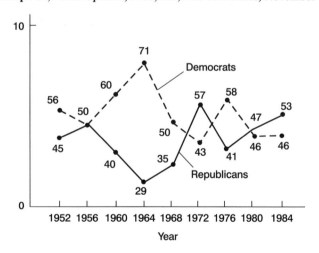

36. *National Journal* (November 1, 1980): 1834.

37. *Party Coalitions in the 1980s,* Seymour M. Lipset, ed. (San Francisco, 1981), 311: *Washington Post,* November 9, 1984.

the upward social mobility of Catholics, class considerations should finally become a more powerful factor in determining their political behavior than that of religious solidarity and this would draw them into a political alliance with the Republicans.[38]

Lately the party has devoted much attention to Spanish-speaking voters (Puerto Ricans, Mexicans, Cubans). As long as fifteen years ago none of the politicians treated Spanish-speaking Americans as an independent electoral group playing a somewhat noticeable role in the electoral process. By the beginning of the last decade they made up only 3 percent of the country's population, and, moreover, were not ranked among the active political participants.[39] But during the 1970s the rapid growth in their numbers (the proportion of Hispanics within the U.S. population doubled), and the rise of their political consciousness, one of the expressions of which was the appearance of Hispanic political organizations on the local as well as on the federal level (for example, the Hispanic Caucus in the House of Representatives), forced party functionaries to reexamine their relationship with them.[40]

The political weight of Hispanics increases if the specifics of their territorial localization is taken into consideration: they are disproportionately concentrated in the Southwest. In three of the most populous states, California, Texas, and Florida, those of Latin origin make up around 20 percent of the electorate, and in some voting districts of Utah, New Mexico, Arizona, and Colorado, their proportion exceeds 30 percent.[41] Such demographics, judging from the experience of the last decade, give Hispanics the real opportunity to influence the outcome of not only local elections but also national elections.

The difficulties of the Republican party in attracting Hispanics to its ranks are related to the fact that Hispanics represent one of the poorest social stratas in the United States (29.2 percent of Americans with Latin American origins live in poverty today).[42] They depend to a large extent on the benevolence of governmental aid programs, and thus vote Democratic in vast majorities. The level of their support for candidates from Roosevelt's party during the 1970s exceeded, as a rule, 70 percent.[43]

Nevertheless, the American Hispanic loyalty to the Democrats should not be taken for granted. In contrast to blacks, the Hispanic bloc is not monolithic. Depending on their national origin and political orientation, three groups of voters can be distinguished: Puerto Ricans, living largely in Illinois and New York, who are considered to be strong Democratic supporters; Mexicans, mostly the residents of the southwestern states, the largest cohort of Hispanic Americans, who also tend to lean toward the Democratic party, but can't be ranked among its loyal electoral groups; and Cuban immigrants to Florida, who actively vote for the Republicans.[44] Their political credo is rather contradictory. While liberal on the issues in the socioeconomic sphere,

38. S. Greer, "Catholic Voters and the Democratic Party," *Public Opinion Quarterly* (December 1961): 611–25.

39. *Statistical Abstract of the United States,* 1971 (Washington, D.C., 1971), 29.

40. *Statistical Abstract of the United States,* 1982/83 (Washington, D.C., 1983), 37.

41. *Congressional Quarterly Weekly Report,* October 23, 1982, 2707–8.

42. *Newsweek* (August 15, 1983): 29.

43. Miller and Schnieder, *Election Studies Data Sourcebook,* 374.

44. *Dun's Business Month,* October 1983, 72.

Hispanics, being Catholics by religious affiliation, are conservatives in their approach to the problems related to social ethics and morals. The starting point of Republican strategy is the reliance on the further deepening of the political differentiation of the U.S.–Hispanic electorate, as a result of the growing class polarization within the Spanish-speaking community.

For the time being Republicans do not speak of the party's total political control over the U.S.–Latin American voters. The task of the party at this stage is the gradual penetration into this electoral group by means of focusing the Hispanic Americans' attention on the ineffectiveness of the Democratic policy of social engineering and promoting traditional moral values related to the family, sex, and the status of women in society.

Reagan was the first candidate from the GOP who launched concerted efforts aimed at Hispanic voters, and in 1980 he established a record for the Republicans, getting 33 percent of their votes.[45] The Republicans, however, having become the party in power, couldn't retain the Hispanic Americans who had drifted to them for long. The dissatisfaction with the new administration's cutting of federal welfare programs under conditions of a tight economic crisis was reflected in the U.S. congressional elections of 1982 (Republicans got 17 percent of their votes while Democrats received 81 percent).[46] This discontent continued to be observed in the public opinion polls up until the middle of 1984, when signs of economic recovery appeared.

In the face of a growing wave of protest against the Reagan course, Republican strategists began to feel uneasy about the prospects for joint political actions of Hispanics and blacks in 1984; this very theme was actively debated by the National Committee of the party.[47] Also, there was the possibility that the Democratic plans (the Democrats worked in close contact with the political group Hispanic Force 1984)[48] for stimulating mass voting participation were successfully carried out (in 1984 the Democrats counted on at least one million Hispanic voters).[49]

The Reagan team prepared for the next elections more thoroughly. During 1983 Frank Farenkopf, who had replaced national committee chairman R. Richards, conducted a series of Republican leadership meetings where the principal agitational and organizational-financial measures were worked out to stimulate the party's activities among the Hispanic voters with the goal of preserving their support for the president at the 1980 level.[50] Within this framework the program "Hispanic Week" was conducted,

45. *New York Times,* November 8, 1984.

46. *Public Opinion* (December/January 1982): 29.

47. *International Herald Tribune,* July 5, 1983.

48. The governor of New Mexico, T. Anaja, headed the group, which included leaders of the leading U.S. Hispanic organizations. *(Congressional Quarterly Weekly Report,* July 23, 1983, 1507).

49. Ibid., 1506.

50. Significant organizational and financial assistance to the Reagan Reelection Committee in recruiting potential supporters of the president among Hispanic Americans was provided by the Republican National Hispanic Assembly created within the national committee of the party in the second half of the 1970s and headed by the party activist Tirso del Hunko. *Congressional Quarterly Weekly Report,* August 25, 1984, 2091.

during which Reagan made the tour to California, Texas, and Florida, speaking before Hispanic audiences; the program "Viva 1984" was successfully carried out to register new Latino voters (mainly in the voting districts of the southwestern states, where middle-class voters made up a substantial proportion of the Hispanic electorate), on which the national committee and local party organizations spent around a million dollars; significant resources were assigned for organizing a series of aggressive radio broadcasts in Spanish, widely advertising the president's successes in the economic sphere, etc.[51]

As a result of Republican efforts, supported by an economic boom in the country, in 1984 Reagan managed to attain high marks among Hispanic voters. Just like in 1980, 33 percent of Latino-American voters supported him.[52]

During the 1970s the Republican leadership also was carefully following the processes going on in the U.S. South. Vibrant economic development in the region during the previous thirty years, accompanied by its sociodemographic and political transformations, drastically changed the southern community and to a large extent influenced the behavior of its voters.

In the first place, during the twenty-year period following the Second World War the legal foundation for southern racism was torn up; the federal acts of 1957, 1960, 1964, and especially of 1965, officially declaring the removal of formal obstacles to black participation in the social life of the country, dealt a blow to the system of racial segregation in the region.[53] Beginning in the second half of the 1960s black southerners participated more and more actively in political campaigns and supported Democrats as the party of civil rights.

In the second place, the broadest social segment of the region, white southerners, underwent a significant transformation. If during the first half of the twentieth century the South continued to remain a "rural" region of the United States, then one of the characteristic features of the nation's postwar development was the partial shift of industrial forces to the South and the transformation of the region into an important economic and political center. With this the economic profile of the South began to be defined by electronics, chemistry, aerospace, and defense technologies as well as other branches of the so-called new industries. The region experienced a sharp deficit of highly qualified specialists, managers, engineers, etc. This gave impetus to a flood of migration from the old degrading industrial regions of the Northeast and Midwest—mainly the representatives of the upper middle class, who leaned to the Republican party and thus became the basis for the rising "Southern Republicanism."[54]

51. *Newsweek* (August 15, 1983): 29; *Congressional Quarterly Weekly Report,* August 25, 1984, 2091; *Business Week* (October 8, 1984): 22.

52. *New York Times,* November 8, 1984.

53. For more detail on this issue see I. A. Geevskii, *U.S.: The Black Problem* [SShA: Negritianskaia problema] (Moscow, 1974); V. O. Pechatnov, "The Democratic Party and Black Voters during the Rise in the Civil Rights Movement" [Demokraticheskaia partiia i negritianskie izberateli v usloviiakh pod'ema dvizheniia za grazhdanskie prava], in *Political Parties at the Present Time* [Politicheskie partii v noveishee vremia] (Moscow, 1982), 174–98.

54. George Tindall, *The Disruption of the Solid South* (New York, 1972); *American Political Science Review* 71 (June 1977): 481.

The mainspring for the trend toward party reorientation in the region, however, was the change in the core of the southern electorate, the native white population of the South. Data from public opinion polls from 1952 to 1974 show that white residents of the region, once an important part of the "Roosevelt coalition," were gradually leaving the Democrats. Thus in the early 1950s, 76 percent of the native white voters voted for Democrats, but by the beginning of the 1970s only 47 percent of them did so.[55] The main reason for the white electorate "desertion" from the party was the initiatives by the Democrats in the race relations sphere, traditionally considered to be the key problem in the region; but there were other reasons as well, like the change in generations of voters, the migration from the North, and the spread of "boom psychology," forming on the whole a positive attitude toward business.

It should be noted that from the end of Reconstruction the Republican party did not give up hope to be firmly established in the region, but all the attempts by its representatives to do this were built on the false idea of forming a "dichromatic" coalition of white southerners and blacks, and thus were doomed to failure from the very beginning. The only one who was able to achieve something of this kind was Dwight Eisenhower in 1952–1956, and to some extent Nixon in 1960. A decisive turn by blacks to the Democrats in the 1960s put an end to such a coalition. The new Nixon strategy, based on Barry Goldwater's notorious "Southern strategy," had as its goal attracting white southerners to the Republican camp via speculating on the aggravation of racial conflict in the region. And it was a success.

With the elections of 1972, in the view of the party's leaders, a new page in the history of the Republican penetration into the cherished land of Dixie was opened, which with pride was called "the Great Breakthrough into the South." "The solid South," sometimes giving 90 percent of its votes to Democrats, now gave 71 percent to the Republican candidate.[56]

Nevertheless, by the next presidential election the Democratic candidate—a southerner, Jimmy Carter—managed to exact revenge: in 1976 he won 54 percent of the votes in the region compared to 45 percent cast for his Republican opponent, Gerald Ford.[57] In light of the then recent "Watergate crisis," however, which still influenced public opinion, and the complex economic situation which the country had only begun to creep out from, the results of Ford's campaign in the South couldn't be called unsuccessful. They appear to be even impressive, if one remembers that this time the Republicans did not pay as much attention to the South as they had before. Working out their plans for the region, party strategists proceeded from the recognition that the appearance of Carter's candidacy on the ballot posed major difficulties for the party in the South. The opinion of the creators of the 1976 campaign on this question was expressed by the chair of Ford's campaign organization, M. Morton: "Whatever the differences between the platform of the national Democratic party and the traditional thought of the Southern Democrats, [Carter's] attractiveness of descent and personal

55. *American Political Science Review* 71 (June 1977): 484; *Public Opinion Quarterly* (summer 1976): 202–15.

56. Gallup Opinion Index, December 1976, 15–16.

57. Ibid.

characteristics for this part of the country is too complex of a barrier, which we need to overcome . . . there is no sense for the legendary 'southern strategy' this year."[58]

Taking into account that Carter was particularly popular in the Deep South (Louisiana, Georgia, Alabama, South Carolina, Mississippi), his native land, Ford decided to concentrate his efforts in the Upper South, with a special reliance on the suburbs and urban districts, where the Republican influence was the strongest. The departure from the southern strategy manifested itself in Ford's intention to get as many of the black votes as circumstances would permit (the Republican party gradually came to the understanding of the importance of this group of voters), the more so, that black southerners make up a significant part of the electorate in urban areas of the region. Later *U.S. News and World Report* wrote that "in 1976 the Republicans for the first time in 50 years made a serious attempt to win the support of blacks on the local, state, and national levels."[59]

The GOP tactics brought rewards. In 1976 Republicans received an impressive proportion of the vote. In a number of urban areas such as, for example, Mecklenburg (Charlotte) and New Orleans, Ford was supported by 30–49 percent of the black voters.[60] But more important, the president won the majority of the white southerners (55 percent), an indicator that electoral transformation of the region was not completed and that the Republicans had serious chances for success in the future.[61]

New correctives to the Republican strategy were introduced in 1980. Drawing lessons from the 1976 campaign, which clearly demonstrated that the black question had unexpectedly quickly passed the apogee of influence on U.S. social life, having given way to growing economic problems, and that to play on the racial instincts of the "white South" now was not as expedient as it had been in the mid-1960s and early 1970s, Reagan switched the emphasis to the economic sphere. In his speeches he tried to show the necessity of liberating business from excessive constraints of government. That would give the green light to business activity and thus promote American living standards—the anti-active-government sentiment, popular in the booming region. This message, combined with the rather rigid position of the Republican candidate in the question of civil rights, yielded positive results. The South once again voted for the GOP. Reagan not only beat Carter by an impressive margin (51 percent to 44 percent), he also succeeded in ten of eleven former Confederate states (only voters in Georgia favored its native son), and he managed to secure the support of 60 percent of white southerners.[62] The following elections demonstrated further interparty changes in the South favorable to the Republicans. In 1984 Reagan received 63 percent of the region's votes to 36 percent cast for Mondale, and he won in all eleven southern states. A broad new voter registration campaign aimed at blacks and Hispanic Americans was carried out by the Democrats in the region. (Especially active in mobilizing the poor

58. *Congressional Quarterly Weekly Report,* August 21, 1976, 2247.
59. *U.S. News and World Report* (April 10, 1978): 64.
60. Ibid.
61. *Washington Post,* November 4, 1976 (data from ABC).
62. *Statistical Abstract of the United States,* 1981/82 (Washington, D.C., 1982), 484; *Political Science Quarterly* 96 (spring 1981): 15.

and the nonwhite voters of the region was Jesse Jackson, campaign organizer, black leader, and one of the Democratic presidential contenders in 1984). These efforts did not undermine the president's "southern strategy."

The parallel campaign to enlist Republican supporters among the white population of the region, carried out by a number of fundamentalist organizations, played an important role in ruining the plans of the opposition as did the negative reaction by the WASP southerners to the political mobilization of the nonwhites. In some states white residents of the South gave Reagan up to 80 percent of their votes. If on the national scale white voters supported the president respectively 2 to 1, in the South they voted for the Republican by a margin of 3 to 1 (72 percent of the white southerners preferred Reagan).[63]

The results of the presidential campaigns from 1968 to 1984 made it clear that white southerners, once one of the most reliable parts of the Roosevelt coalition, in the 1970s and 1980s gradually were becoming a part of the Republican party electorate. From 1968 on, white voters of the South steadily cast the majority of their votes for Republican presidential candidates. Second, with the support of the overwhelming majority of white southerners, Republicans are practically guaranteed a victory in the region. Analyzing the results of the last elections, a well-known specialist in public opinion, Louis Harris, came to a conclusion (which for the time being probably sounds too categorical, but is not a meaningless one), that: "Probably in the future, looking back we will be able to say that in 1984 the South turned into the base of the Republican party."[64]

The main thing today that instills fear in the hearts of Democrats and, on the contrary, optimism in the hearts of their political opponents is the possible establishment by the Republicans of a political alliance of "West-South," automatically giving them 281 votes in the electoral college (270 such votes are required for election of a president).

A great source of discomfort for the Republicans in the elections was the black opposition. The party leadership spent much effort to erode it during the 1970s. In fact, since the civil rights initiatives by the John Kennedy and Lyndon Johnson administrations had bound the newly politicized black community to Roosevelt's party, the Republicans, taking the situation realistically, did not set as their goal to draw blacks from the Democratic camp. Discussion instead touched on the possible ways to deny the opposition party a monopoly over the black American votes. With the goal of splitting the black bloc of voters as a counterweight to the method of political integration of blacks used by Democrats during the 1960s, the Republicans at the end of the 1960s put forward a plan for their economic integration, the well-known Nixon "black capitalism."

In the early 1970s there was a general slowdown of the country's economic growth, thus cutting resources for financing the welfare system launched by the Democrats. Seizing the moment, the Republicans (by analogy with the case of Hispanic Americans) resorted to aggressive propaganda of their ideas. They called

63. *New York Times,* November 7–8, 1984.
64. *Business Week* (November 19, 1984): 19.

on blacks to refuse government handouts, which are of little help to those who are destitute and in addition humiliates their human dignity and condemns them to eternal passivity. In the Republicans' opinion, only the encouragement of business initiatives will help blacks break into the private sector and thus help them to occupy a well-deserved place in the American society.[65] It was clear that the Republican slogans were not intended for all black voters, but mostly for their more well-off contingents (relatively narrow, but a gradually growing social strata of a black middle class and high-income black Americans) and according to preliminary estimations could ideally secure for the GOP durable support of approximately 30 percent of black Americans.

Reagan emerged with such a line. In his election campaign he stubbornly adhered to the statement that blacks had become victims of "the new form of slavery," invented by big government, and that the way to "economic emancipation" should be sought in reviving the private sector and integrating blacks into the country's economic life.[66]

In 1972 and 1980 Nixon's and Reagan's appeals found response from 13 and 14 percent of the blacks, and in 1984 from only 9 percent.[67] These were largely citizens associated with the politically active group of "black conservatives" (they call themselves "Jeffersonian liberals"), who are the proponents of the interests of well-off and middle-class members of the black community in the United States. They stand for low taxes and cutting the federal aid programs, which in their opinion facilitate "filling stomachs, but emptying spirits," regarding economic "self-help" as the primary means for eliminating all forms of racial discrimination.[68] The majority of black conservatives call themselves Republicans, and many of them are members of the National Black Republican Council, the political unit used by the party's national committee as the main means of contact with black America and a mouthpiece for disseminating their ideas within the black milieu.[69]

So, despite the fact that the Republican party in the 1970s and early 1980s made energetic attempts to broaden the black strata in their electorate, support for the party by the black American population remains at a very low level. Actually, blacks did not and do not vote for Republicans. The idea of economic integration of blacks according to the Nixon-Reagan plan for the time being has been a failure. Black voters feel uneasy about the actual Republican political course, the cutting and freezing of programs blacks are the most interested in (aid to the poor, retraining, providing work to the unemployed).[70]

65. Today 33 percent of black Americans make up the black middle class. *U.S. News and World Report* (January 31, 1983): 62.

66. *National Journal* (July 11, 1981); *Newsweek* (July 13, 1981): 22.

67. Gallup-Opinion Index, December 1976, 15–16; *Gallup Poll. Public Opinion,* 1980, 242; *New York Times,* November 8, 1984.

68. *Newsweek* (July 13, 1981): 22.

69. *New York Times,* November 19, 1982. In the spring of 1981 the black conservatives created the Black Alternative Association, which was to put forward alternative proposals for emancipation of blacks to the programs of traditional liberal organizations fighting for civil rights. *National Journal* (March 14, 1981): 435.

70. Blacks continue to be one of the most impoverished groups of the U.S. population: 30.9 percent of the country's black residents live under the poverty line, in comparison to 8.9 percent of their white counterparts.

In the 1980 elections for the first time political commentators were drawn to the phenomenon of unexpectedly sharp differences in voting behavior by males and females, the so-called gender gap. While Reagan captured 54 percent of the male vote to Carter's 37 percent, female votes divided almost equally, 46 percent for Republicans to 45 percent for Democrats (according to Gallup the gap is wider, 49 percent to 44 percent).[71] The results of public opinion polls conducted not long before the elections showed that female U.S. voters were not pleased with Reagan's position on the question of equal rights for women. His foreign policy platform also had a distinct impact on the mindset of female Americans: many of them feared that the militaristic course of the Republicans could lead the country to a military disaster.

Yet, after all, the dissatisfaction by women with the general worsening of the economic situation in the country under the Democratic administration prevailed and made them vote for Reagan.[72] Nevertheless, the strategists of the GOP understood that in case Reagan was not successful in establishing relations with female voters (in 1980 they made up 49 percent of the whole U.S. electorate) some very undesirable complications could arise, and lately this was proved correct. In 1982 public opinion services fixed the increasing inclination of female voters toward the Democrats. While in the elections for the House of Representatives in the 1970s the difference in the level of the Republican party support by men and women made up only an insignificant 2 percent, by 1980 it increased to 4 percent, and in 1982 to 6 percent.[73]

The shift by American female voters to Democrats was attributed to the neglect of the Republican administration for the feminist movement's aspirations and to the failure of the attempts to ratify the constitutional amendment on equal rights primarily due to Republican opposition in Congress. Also impacting the political behavior of women were such factors as the failure by the Reagan administration to negotiate with the Soviet Union on controlling nuclear weapons and the growing threat of a nuclear war. The main catalyst, however, of the polarization process along the lines of men versus women in the 1980s was the deepening of differences in the assessment of the president's economic policies.[74]

There is the opinion that the move by female voters to the Democratic camp is a long-term trend. "This shift is the most important party reorientation in American politics," asserted the head of the political department of the Democratic National Committee, Ann Lewis.[75] The mass involvement during the 1970s in the production process and women's inferior position in the labor market in comparison with men, along with the growing political activity, turned females into an important reserve for the Democratic party. Similar to other underprivileged social groups, women tended to support economic and social liberalism. This long-term factor could have been strengthened with their heightened concern for the dangerous adventuristic course of the Reagan administration.

71. *Gallup Poll. Public Opinion,* 1980, 242.
72. *New York Times,* November 5, 1980; *U.S. News and World Report* (November 17, 1980): 28; *New York Times,* December 3, 1982.
73. *National Journal* (November 6, 1982): 1893; *Public Opinion* (December/January): 34.
74. *National Journal* (November 6, 1982): 1893.
75. *New York Times,* November 10, 1982.

In the light of the upcoming presidential elections the gender gap was a source of trouble for the Republicans. First, in 1983 women constituted a majority of the U.S. electorate (53 percent).[76] Second, according to the data from the Bureau of the Census on the voter turnout rates, beginning in 1964 the level of participation by women in political campaigns by the 1980s had reached that of the men.[77] Thus, as the next off-year elections showed, in some districts and states women could emerge as a political force, capable of turning the political scales in favor of the Democrats.[78]

It is not surprising that after the 1982 elections the White House hastened to launch its own efforts directed at rehabilitating the party in the eyes of female voters. In particular F. Farenkopf, representative of the Republican National Committee, together with Paul Laxalt (then holder of the newly created position of general chairman of the Republican National Committee) conducted special conferences to find out "what sort of problems . . . need to be addressed in order to secure the support of women."[79] Under the auspices of the White House a Coordination Council on women's affairs was established. It presented a series of desirable legislative initiatives to "pacify the women."[80]

Reagan's tactics in regard to female voters in the 1984 campaign were built on the basis of the council's recommendations. It pointed to appointment of a number of women to governmental posts, legislative measures on improving the situation of working women, easing the system of social security payments, liberalization of pension legislation for women and some other steps; campaign discussions focusing the voting women's attention on the economic achievements of Republicans; appeals primarily to the well-off female voters, i.e., mainly married working women up to forty-five years old.[81]

As a result, in November 1984 Reagan broadened his support among women by 10 percent in comparison to 1980 (57 percent of women voted for Reagan, 42 percent for Mondale); consequently the gender gap among those voters preferring Reagan decreased from 8 percent to 4 percent.[82]

Beginning with the realignment of the 1930s, the Republican party played the role of "minor partner" in the American two-party system, and from time to time appeared in the White House, taking advantage of the splits inside the Democratic coalition. These splits appeared to be more frequent from the late 1960s on, when the Republicans adopted a new electoral strategy. If in the presidential elections from 1948 to 1964 on the whole the Democrats gained the upper hand (in three of five occasions), then in the following period the Republicans have clearly led, winning in four of five elections (and in three of these, in 1972, 1980, and 1984, by significant

76. Gallup Poll, October 30, 1983, 1.
77. *New York Times,* November 3, 1982.
78. *Public Opinion* (December/January 1982): 34.
79. *Christian Science Monitor,* February 7, 1983.
80. *National Journal* (May 3, 1983): 490; *New York Times Magazine,* June 24, 1984, 72.
81. *Dun's Business Month* (October 1983): 70–71; *New York Times Magazine,* June 24, 1984, 76.
82. *New York Times,* November 8, 1984.

margins). Actually, the GOP on the presidential level is beginning to look like the majority party.

The reasons for the noticeable progress by the Republicans cannot be explained only in terms of political practice, i.e., elaboration and carrying out of social strategy and tactics of the party in the campaigns taking place in the late 1960s to 1980s. Nevertheless, these initiatives could be considered to be an important component of their success since at one and the same time they proceeded from and enhanced those long-term tendencies favoring Republicans, which were matched in the United States throughout the postwar period. The last three decades have been characterized by the weakening of the Democratic positions in the electorate: a desertion of the middle-class voters out of the Democratic ranks was observed, of those disappointed with the old values of the New Deal to which the party leadership was still too attached. Consequently, the party has been losing its influence among the traditional groups of its voters, many of whom, having improved their financial positions, reinforced the ranks of the middle class. Simultaneously, major demographic shifts have been observed, showing migration of well-off Americans from pro-Democratic old industrial regions of the Northeast and Midwest to the fast-developing states of the West and South, where Republicanism has been on the rise.

During the 1970s to 1980s the Republican party strengthened its position within a substantial number of voting groups previously oriented toward the Democrats, mainly by means of broadening zones of its influence among their middle-class representatives, which on the whole has allowed the party to attain substantial predominance in the "political center" of the American electorate. The duration of such domination will depend on how effective the opposition is in their already ongoing search for the ways to the hearts of the middle-class voters.

Comment

by Theodore J. Lowi

Foreigners love to analyze America, especially American politics. Analyzing America was an international cottage industry for a long time before we became the world's sole superpower, when they had to study us for their own defense. From Tocqueville through Ostrogorski to Sir Denis Brogan and Godfrey Hodgson, there were those who dedicated much of their intellectual lives to "democracy in America."[1] There were still larger numbers who, like Engels and Weber, used various aspects of American political culture as key pieces in a larger argument about democracy, or capitalism, or whatever else might have been unique about America and therefore instructive about their own systems. Whether for praise or blame, moral lessons or inspiration, almost every social critic in almost every country had to take a crack at the American ideal, the American paradox, the American myth, or the American dilemma. Many, like Weber, never even made it to the United States at all. But that did not deter them. It might not even have weakened their insight. Who doubts the validity of Weber's wonderful essay, "Politics as a Vocation"?[2]

And, by and large, Americans love to be analyzed by foreigners. Tocqueville is the most celebrated of all Americanists, even including Americans themselves who specialize in American studies. Hardly a book or article by an American, especially on American politics and political culture, can get underway without a Tocqueville epigram or longer observation as the text of the piece. Louis Hartz is not the only notable domestic Americanist whose most notable work rested upon a foreigner's observation.[3]

But the reverse is not true. The Japanese praised and purchased Ezra Vogel's *Japan as Number One,* for obvious reasons. But as for the more probing and critical works, even when on net positive, foreigners are not so receptive when Americans or other alien observers write about their history, their traditions, their institutions or cultures. For example, I have been able to locate only one book by an American on France that

---

1. Alexis de Tocqueville, *Democracy in America* [1835], Phillips Bradley, ed. (New York, 1955); James Bryce, *The American Commonwealth* (London, 1889); M. I. Ostrogorski, *Democracy and the Party System in the United States* (New York, 1910); Gunnar Myrdal, *An American Dilemma* (New York, 1944); and Denis W. Brogan, *Politics in America* (New York, 1954).

2. For the views of Marx and Engels, see S. M. Lipset, "Why No Socialism in the United States?" in Seweryn Bialer and Sophia Sluzar, eds., *Sources of Contemporary Radicalism* (Boulder, Colo., 1977), chap. 2; Max Weber, "Politics as a Vocation," *From Max Weber,* ed. and trans., Hans Gerth and C. Wright Mills (New York, 1958), 77–128.

3. Louis Hartz, *The Liberal Tradition in America* (New York, 1955).

had been wholeheartedly embraced by all French intellectuals who read this sort of thing. That book is Laurence Wylie's *Village in the Vaucluse.*[4]

Although I have not encountered any recent classic on the United States by a foreigner, I continue to search and read hopefully, and in the process I have found much to be learned about us from many of those efforts, even if they fall short of the monumental or the immortal. One good example is before us here, Elena Borschevskaya's "The Electoral Strategy of the Republican Party in the 1970s and early 1980s." (I have been informed that she is now Elena Kortunova.) I have found her piece to be most worthy of attention. We must, however, proceed with care and restraint so as not to impose our years of hindsight on her effort, which was published in 1986. It is lamentable that a scholar of her learning and ability could provide us with no update, even as an epilogue. But there is much to be gained from the piece as it stands—if we read it at more than one level: (1) What does it tell us about ourselves as a nation and how others see us? (2) What does it tell us about the character of the knowledge Russian scholars can bring to the task? (3) What does it tell us about ourselves as social scientists? What are the kinds of data we make available for domestic and foreign scholars, and how does that shape the questions we and they ask?

This is the story about two bourgeois political parties, how one dominated the electorate and the government for thirty to forty years, and how it declined and was displaced from its hegemonic position by the other party. As bourgeois parties, they differ from each other only at the margins of constituency support and public policy, but enough of a difference exists to provide for genuine electoral competition. The Democratic majority, a product of the last great realigning election of 1932, was composed of some bourgeois interests plus the racial, ethnic, and religious minorities of the urban/industrial North, plus "[having] also retained the support of the southern electorate." Democratic support began to weaken and fragment in the postwar period as the "polarization" between the two parties lessened, presumably in policies as well as demographics. A "two-tier" electoral system emerged in which Republicans competed on an equal footing for president while remaining a distinct minority at the lower levels of government. In the 1960s, the change was accelerated and deepened as Democrats promoted civil rights and wealth distribution at home and the Vietnam War abroad. This alienated certain "voting segments from the Roosevelt coalition." Out of these detaching segments a "new Republican majority" was conceived: not by appealing to whole classes of voters but to different "segments" of each—for example, whites within the working class, the unorganized, nonunion workers, South and East European ethnic segments of the Catholic Church, and the same segments within labor and the middle class. All of this would of course be facilitated by the low to barren American economy of the 1970s.

Presidential candidate Richard Nixon had capitalized successfully on this "centrifugal tendency" in the Democratic party. The author calls this the Republican party's "working class strategy," to which I shall turn in a moment, but she quickly adds that

---

4. Ezra F. Vogel, *Japan as Number One: Lessons for America* (Cambridge, Mass., 1979); Laurence Wylie, *Village in the Vaucluse* (Cambridge, Mass., 1974).

it turned out not to be a stable base, something for which the Republicans would have to wait until the 1980s and Ronald Reagan. Although the "R-word" (realignment) was not used, the author analyzed herself into that expectation: a post-1984 realignment, driven largely by bourgeoisification of blue-collars in general and South and East European Catholics in particular, plus special stress on lower-status ethnic minorities within the church, the so-called "blacks of the North." Being newly arrived as lower middle class, these segments would not only switch to the Republican party but would become conservative on race and on welfare:

> The 1970s–1980s election statistics confirm the assumption made as far back as the early 1960s and on which the Republican strategists base their ploy—i.e., along with the upward social mobility of Catholics, class considerations should finally become a more powerful factor in determining their political behavior than that of religious solidarity and this would draw them into a political alliance with the Republicans.[5]

This contention was supported by any number of opinion surveys and exit polls— as cited in the author's footnotes. But whether this was the Republican electoral strategy in the 1970s or the 1980s is another matter entirely.

At almost exactly the halfway point in the piece, the author turns from review of the survey data to an explicit focus on the strategy of the Republican leadership. A digression on Hispanics turned out to be a link to the more general strategy of "carefully following the processes going on in the U.S. South." Recognizing the "death blow" dealt to legal segregation in the 1960s, she turns to the economic transformation of the South from a rural region into an important economic center fed by "a flood of migration from the old degrading industrial regions of the Northeast and Midwest— mainly the representatives of the upper middle class, who leaned to the Republican party and thus became the basis for the rising 'Southern Republicanism.' " The data so strongly backed this kind of transformation that it must be the reason that she continued thereafter to stress the economic factors in the political change: even though "the main reason for the white electorate 'desertion' from the party was the initiatives by the Democrats in the race-relations sphere . . . ; there were other reasons as well, like the change in generations of voters, the migration from the North, the spread of 'boom psychology,' forming on the whole a positive attitude toward business." This, plus a decisive turn by blacks to the Democrats in the 1960s, set the Nixon Republicans on the course that Nixon, drawing from Goldwater, called the "southern strategy."

Republican "penetration into the cherished land of Dixie" was the great break-through of 1972. Jimmy Carter's election in 1976 was a mere Watergate-inspired interruption. By 1980, the Republicans gave up on trying to attract southern blacks into the Republican camp. They returned to the "white South" but, according to the author, with an emphasis on the economic sphere. This essentially economics message

---

5. In one of her more prescient moments, the author immediately adds that Hispanics (Puerto Ricans, Mexicans, Cubans) might soon be added. They are of particular importance in three strategic states, California, Texas and Florida, and, according to her data, they have all been overwhelmingly Democratic, largely for the economic reason of their low income and the employment and welfare programs of the Democratic party. "Nevertheless, the American Hispanic loyalty to the Democrats should not be taken for granted" (208–10).

produced the great Republican success of the 1980s: ten of eleven southern states, with a popular vote margin of 51 percent to 44 percent against the southerner Carter in 1980, and eleven of eleven southern states with a 63 percent to 36 percent popular vote margin against northerner Walter Mondale in 1984.[6]

Almost hidden within her stress on "class considerations" was the observation, almost a concession, that economics was "combined with a rather rigid position of the Republican candidate [Reagan] in the question of civil rights." It returns on the following page with a brief recognition that a "parallel campaign to enlist Republican supporters among the white population of the region" was carried out by "a number of fundamentalist organizations." But she does not identify any of them by name, and she does not define what is meant by "fundamentalist organizations," neglect of which must have left all of her Russian readers completely in the dark. But worse, by not going into these any further, she not only missed an opportunity to enrich her analysis of the Republican strategy but also allowed her story and her argument to slip back into the racial aspect of Republican strategy and southern developments without looking at religion and religious-based political ideology at all. The only observation she does make is that these fundamentalist organizations must have contributed to the southern white support of Reagan—3 to 1 in the South compared to 2 to 1 outside the South.

The author closes her assessment of the Republican strategy with a quote from the famous pollster Louis Harris: "Probably in the future, looking back we will be able to say that in 1984 the South turned into the base of the Republican party." She immediately adds a revision of the Harris prediction that the future of the Republican majority is a political alliance of "West-South." But for her it has a strongly economic basis with a white coloration, and even that is economically defined within her version of the Republican strategy. For example, appeals to black voters originating with President Reagan were to a "black middle class" on the grounds that blacks had become victims of "the new form of slavery," invented by big government in the welfare state. This may have had some effect on black middle-class voters, just as the Republican strategists had hopes that it would also have a positive effect on many of the white ethnic voters. What she overlooks here is that there had to be a much more profound incentive than economic for these white ethnic voters to go Republican, considering that Republican tax policies of the 1980s damaged middle- and lower-income Americans more than any other stratum. They absolutely had to fall in love with the Republican party for reasons other than economics.

Some of these things the author could have seen and should have seen even in 1985 when she was preparing this article for publication. One of these is the salience of race to the lower and lower-middle white strata of the United States. The other is the rising salience of religion and religious-fed government policies as carried by the so-called fundamentalist organizations that were already present but not identified in 1986. Adding these to economics, we can then talk about Republican strategy.

---

6. Walter Dean Burnham, *The Current Crisis in American Politics* (New York, 1982); Nelson Polsby, *The Consequences of Party Reform* (New York, 1983); and John L. Palmer and Isabel Sawhill, eds., *The Reagan Revolution* (Cambridge, Mass., 1994).

Economic objectives are always present in the strategic thinking of any political party. But it is never the whole story, and on this occasion economics must share to an unprecedented degree with other influences, specifically three: race, religion, and the ideological right. To simplify the matter, we might also say that economic objectives are in partnership with right-wing objectives, which are fueled by race and religion.

After an inconclusive digression on the gender gap, the author concludes her account with three tantalizing observations which, if slightly refocused, could be considered prescient. Her first conclusion is that the Republican party "on the presidential level is beginning to look like the majority party." Thus, 1984 could well have been the realigning election every American political scientist has been waiting for! Second, the Democratic party position in the electorate is weakening by desertion of middle-class voters either through their disappointment with the old values of the New Deal or simply their improved financial situations. Third, the duration of the Republican majority will depend upon their ability to maintain their predominance in the "political center" of the American electorate.

Despite eight years of the 1990s with a Democratic presidency, the author certainly has a point about the national strategy of occupying the "political center." Bill Clinton had obviously agreed with this and as a New Democrat beat the Republicans at their own game. This part she might have imagined, but neither she nor anyone else could have imagined that the Republicans would prove to be the majority party in Congress. She did not see this because we did not see it, and we are the ones who should have, because there were signs of it well before 1994, with the steady increase of Republican majorities in state governments and in the mayoralties of the middle and larger cities. Republicans were picking up governorships, moving, albeit modestly, from 13 in 1975 versus 36 Democrats (there was one independent) to 16 versus 34 in 1985. Reagan's substantial presidential victory in 1980 was followed by a landslide victory in 1984, and Republicans took control of the Senate in 1980 and kept it through the election in 1986. All of this means that in the twenty years between 1968 and 1988, Republicans held the presidency for sixteen of the twenty years. And, although Democrats continued to control the House of Representatives until 1994, their hold on the House was weaker and weaker, first because of the many "Reagan Democrats," and second because electoral margins were growing thinner as the New Religious Right came together in a coalition then called the Moral Majority.

Unlike so many social movements of the Left and the Right that concern themselves with moral and ideological issues, the Moral Majority concentrated on local elections and local issues to a very large extent. This was not going to pay off to its absolute fullest until later in the decade, but it should have been much more clear and explicit to American political scientists by 1982 and 1984 that (1) the Religious Right was not going away, (2) it was going to continue to make gains at local levels not only in the South but in other regions, and (3) they were going to begin electing conservatives, who had eventually found the Republican party more comfortable than the Democratic. Finally, when the Republicans took the entire Congress in the 1994 elections, a very large proportion of the freshman class of 1994 were Republicans who owed their election to the newly named Christian Coalition. These later results were certainly beyond the knowledge of observers in the early 1980s; but there were many indications that some kind of fundamental realignment was in the works. This was being talked about by a few political scientists, but not much was available in published form for foreign observers to read and analyze. The presidency has turned out to be something of a fight for the center, wherever that may be, and that is precisely why Republican strategy failed at the presidential level, once it lost the inestimable Ronald Reagan, but could succeed in Congress and in state and local elections.

How so? It is because Republican strategy was far less economically oriented than our author, along with so many American observers, had believed. The economy does count, stupid, as one of Clinton's advisers put it. For the Republicans, economics means classical economics, and it has been immensely successful in the national politics of the 1980s and the 1990s. But the real Republican strategy was only in part economics—and, ironically, that part was *liberal*. This strategy was so effective at the national level that Republicans succeeded in virtually stigmatizing the national government and its politics. The enormous annual deficit growth—created largely by immense Republican tax cuts and their refusal to cut expenditures proportionately— was used as the great weapon against any new public policies proposed in Congress. The policy of Republican strategists, all the way up to Presidents Reagan and Bush, was a policy of no policies. Running *for* Congress while running *against* the very government in which the elected members of Congress would serve was the governing strategy of the Republican party, and so powerful it was that it influenced a large proportion of Democratic members and candidates as well. When I say Clinton beat them at their own game, this is precisely what I had in mind. Thus, at the level of presidential politics and national public policy, our author was not far off at all, even if we have to change the name of the victorious party in the White House.

But as it turned out, the Republican party and its strategists were far more in tune with the politics of Congress and the states because of the other dimensions of its own party strategy. Along with stigmatization of the national government (in favor of free markets, etc., etc.) was devolution—devolution of the maximum number of national government programs and services downward to the states and to the local governments. Already we can see that Republican ideology was not truly anti- government but only anti-*national* government, because all this devolution meant that state governments and their creatures—the local governments—would have to expand in order to take on the devolved programs. But devolving welfare programs, job and vocational education programs, civil rights provisions, and many others to state and local governments also meant moving their orientations rightward. And that is exactly what happened.

This is very far away from anything we could have expected our foreign author to have sensed, much less articulated with any precision, without some help from us. But what she could have seen in the mid-1980s was the emergence of very important "fundamentalist" organizations, their unprecedented presence in the corridors of Congress and the Executive Branch, and their unprecedented presence in policy debate through the formation of well-financed "think tanks." The Moral Majority was already an important movement in the early 1980s, and considerable credit has been given to them for the role they played in elections and in the policy agenda. All the more significant is the fact that the Moral Majority succeeded in bringing into "common cause" conservative Catholics along with conservative Protestants, especially evangelical Protestants. This, too, is unprecedented. It was because of their presence that the Republican party platforms became increasingly polarized from the Democrats on abortion and other issues of morality policy that had always been the concern of state legislatures. The Republican party had always had a bit of a right wing, but once all those southern white leaders became Republicans, the Republican right wing became an equal wing. It was not necessarily equal in numbers of voters, but it was certainly equal—if not sometimes superior—in intellectual and policy influence. This made the Republican party far more ideological than it had ever been, and after Ronald Reagan, it actually inhibited the Republican party strategists from embracing fully enough the political center.

Strategy? There were undoubtedly some Republican tactics. In fact, Democrats in the late 1970s were quite jealous of the successful use by Republicans of the new information technology in locating their best electoral opportunities and in finding the ideal means of reaching their voters and potential voters. The executive director of the Democratic National Committee during that time once confessed to me that he used a significant amount of his staff time in "industrial espionage," trying to find the Republican secrets and to imitate them. Nevertheless, most of the Republican gains— even those attributable to their rational electoral efforts—came not from their own efforts as much as from the actions of the Democratic party. The so-called centrifugal forces to which the author refers early in her paper were the direct result of the strategy of the Democratic party during the 1960s to complete the New Deal agenda and to fulfill promises to the two or three significant organized minorities within the party, namely blacks, women, and Hispanics.

This isn't a question of virtue being defeated by opportunism. The Democrats made some terrible choices in the policies they adopted to meet their electoral obligations. Nevertheless, virtually every major issue they confronted during that decade turned out to be a "wedge issue," meaning that each step along the way was another cut in an existing cleavage within the party coalition. The most important chips off the old New Deal block were located in the southern states, and that is basically what the Republican party incorporated on the way to their own 1980s successes.

One important historical point that the author missed was that the Democratic party had been a southern party; the New Deal did not simply add the South to its coalition. The southern core in effect added the other elements to the coalition that became the New Deal coalition. There were tacit agreements all through the 1930s as to the sorts of policies the New Deal could adopt without alienating the southern core. What other way could the Democrats have had it? Virtually all of the major Congressional committees and other leadership posts were held by southerners. The main strategy of the Democratic party at that time was to respond to the obvious requirements of the Depression but at the same time to do so in a manner that would not upset the race, class, and gender status quo in the South. This North/South contract prevailed until the 1960s, when civil rights and other policies literally broke the contract. The Republicans rose out of the wreckage of the New Deal coalition.

In fact, although the Republican party did have strategies and did pursue them especially during the first four years of the Reagan administration, their strategies after that were pursued with increasing frequency within ideological blinders established and maintained by their right wing.

Virtually from the outset, I began asking if the author could not have seen something or other even in 1984–1985 when she was preparing this chapter. She could have, but she did not, and she did not because American political scientists did not prepare her or provide the empirical basis for her. During the era covered by her chapter, the United States went through some political changes as fundamental as any changes we have ever gone through in any comparable period of time. In fact it was an epoch when there was not only a social revolution but a revolution in federalism that deeply altered the relationship between the national government and the state and local governments. The accompanying table at the end of my commentary is a bird's-eye view of the key national actions that were the policies enacted in that period and became the "wedge issues" within the majority Democratic party. Yet, if one approached the United States as a foreigner with all the information and data contained in the bibliography listed and cited in this chapter, one would not know there had been a sea change in American politics during the twenty years covered in this chapter.

This is not the author's fault. This is entirely a product of the type of knowledge American political science produces and projects to political scientists and other social scientists throughout the world. Mind you, there are many other published sources, including excellent books and articles precisely on the policies, issues, and conflicts that did contribute directly to the fundamental transformations of that epoch. But they show up least of all in the systematic, behavioral electoral studies on which this chapter is almost entirely based. We got what we gave. We are what we published.

This is not to say that those students of elections who designed the research and published the results were totally and completely unaware of what was going on around them. It is to say that they *as professional social scientists* put on intellectual blinders just as influential in affecting their behavior as the ideological blinders were in affecting the behavior of the Republican political strategists.

Even though these materials are the product of what came to be called the "behavioral revolution," once the revolution was completed, the survey scientists became extremely conservative about their research designs and interview and questionnaire strategies. First, there is a well established science, with well established conventions of question-asking and index construction. Once these conventions of research are established, there is not only a methodological reason for conserving them, there are psychological and intellectual sunk costs as well as scientific commitments to the continuation of a successful survey instrument. Another reason for conservatism here is the need to preserve comparability, cross-sectionally and over time. How could one possibly have a dependable time series or a comparison from state to state or country to country unless the categories of data were kept consistent? But these categories are precisely the intellectual blinders that can easily steer students away from vital, fundamental social and political changes.

There is still another reason for reluctance to alter the data categories, and it may be the most influential because it is the social scientist's equivalent of ideology— theory. *There is implicit as well as explicit theory underlying every research design and every survey instrument.* Moreover, when other social scientists pick up that instrument to do their survey, and when still other social scientists come along and use in a secondary analysis the data generated by the survey instrument, they are, wittingly or unwittingly, committing themselves to the theoretical assumptions and terms of discourse of the original designers. Every hypothesis embodies some theory, and the collection of hypotheses in any survey instrument is an agenda not only of the necessary questions to be asked to meet the designer's theoretical needs but is also a commitment against all the hypotheses and all the questions not asked. The same with the actual categories that make up the survey questions. They may scientifically be called the variables, but the choices of categories arise out of prior preferences and prejudices, and the way they are operationalized can be highly idiosyncratic. The next user takes the whole baggage, not just a few selected lines of data.

What, for example, is the "political center"? What is the Left/Right, the liberal/conservative that defines the boundary of the center? And where in the ideological geography are they located? This is in fact the *reductio ad absurdum* of the whole survey enterprise. Left and Right, as operationalized for attitudinal and scaling purposes, were defined as belonging to a unidimensional scale moving from a position favoring full government intervention or control (Left) to one favoring minimal control or a free market.[7] Forty years later, ideology was still conceived as unidimensional on an equivalent scale of degree of anti-government sentiment.[8] This bottles up everything with a particular (and particularistic) definition of ideology, puts a special cast on the interpretation of attitudes, and minimizes recognition of substantive ideological change and variation outside that particular rubric. If the country made a big shift in ideology, a shift sufficient to say that the public had made a paradigm shift of its own, shouldn't the surveys also have to make an appropriate paradigm shift? The fact is that the United States had an ideological realignment (a paradigm shift?) somewhere in the 1980s that survey research did not catch and keep pace with. We still cannot say with certainty that we had an electoral realignment, although a solid Republican South is surely a realignment for that region. But we did have an ideological realignment, which brought most if not all the genuine moral conservatism of the country into the Republican party. And that brought about the entrance of at least one very different dimension of Left and Right, one much more akin to lineups in the last two centuries of Europe. If that isn't the time for a paradigm shift in behavioral and electoral studies, when is?[9]

What more could our single Russian scholar have known if the American researchers had not provided the knowledge first? Credit is due her for catching what she did; and credit is also due the American researchers because she had to have learned what she displayed largely from our researchers and what they made available. Indeed, what we make available is far, far more than is made available in any other

7. Anthony Downs, *An Economic Theory of Democracy* (New York, 1957), 116.
8. Gerald Pomper, ed., *The Election of 1996* (Chatham, N.J., 1997), 10, 109.
9. On the 1990s, see Theodore Lowi, *The End of the Republican Era* (Norman, Okla., 1996); Byron E. Shafer, ed., *Present Discontents—American Politics in the Very Late 20th Century* (Chatham, N.J., 1997); John C. Green and Daniel M. Shey, eds., *The State of the Parties—The Changing Role of Contemporary American Politics,* 2d ed. (New York, 1996); Benjamin Ginsberg and Martin Shefter, *Politics by Other Means,* 2d ed. (New York, 1998).

country. But because everybody missed so much, we have to ask if anything can be done to improve on what we provide.

One of the greatest needs in the social sciences is to institutionalize our capacity to study what we study—to evaluate what we study by being able to ask systematically and regularly what questions we ask, why we ask them, and what are their conceptual and theoretical underpinnings. And we need more than that. Given the vast amount of self-interested survey/electoral research being done by private consultants and by party and corporate organizations, we could also use some independent capacity to assess their questionnaires, their sampling methods, their reporting procedures, and the basis of the claims they make about their findings.

All of these needs point in one direction, toward the establishment of an "information utility"—a TVA of knowledge about all information vital to democracy. Yes, it is a proposal for regulation, but of a very special type, which is the reason why I compare it to TVA. The original theory of setting up an independent energy utility was called "yardstick regulation." The purpose of yardstick regulation was to influence the energy industry not by laying down rules and backing those rules by sanctions but to regulate by competition, by example, and by exposure—to provide, in other words, an independent and disinterested body of knowledge by which to judge the output of the private, for-profit companies in that industry. As applied here, such a utility would make more and better data available—better in the specific sense that it covers a broader range of empirical experience and it permits more than one theoretical perspective. And we could consider that a mere by-product of a still more important objective—protecting the integrity and credibility of random sample polling, an immense industry and also the most recent institution of democracy.[10]

Many years ago, one of the most imminent students of parties and elections, E. E. Schattschneider, observed that the most important contribution made by political science was to provide the basis for recognition of the political party as the newest institution of democracy and one that was so important that no theory of democracy could be successful without taking political parties into account.[11] We can now say the same thing of public opinion polling: it is no longer possible to construct a meaningful political theory, especially a democratic political theory, without taking this institution into account. Both the strengths and the weaknesses of this essay by Professor Borschevskaya-Kortunova are testimony in favor of this proposition and in favor of the establishment of an information utility. The only change I would propose making in this concept is that the information utility would be international, not merely American.

10. For a thorough and favorable treatment of TVA and "yardstick regulation," see David Lilienthal, *TVA: Democracy on the March* (New York, 1944).

11. E. E. Schattschneider, *Party Government* (New York, 1942), especially chapter 1.

Wedge Issues in the Nationalization of American Federalism, 1954–1974

Type of Action: A Selection of Major Initiatives	Initiative Taken by	Date of Initiative	Unit Acted on	Restrict (R) or Expand (E)
1. Civil rights-school segregation	Supreme Court	1954	State	R
2. Civil liberties-sedition	Supreme Court	1956	State	R
3. Civil liberties-rights of accused	Supreme Court	1961,1963, 1964, 1966,1969	State	R
4. School prayer	Supreme Court	1962	State	R
5. Civil rights-voting	Congress and Supreme Court	1957,1960	Federal State	E R
6. Food Stamp Program	Congress	1964	Federal State	E E
7. Reapportionment	Supreme Court	1962,1964	Federal	E
8. Civil rights-schools, public facilities, employment, etc.	Congress	1964	State Private	R R
9. Welfare-Medicare, Medicaid	Congress	1965	Federal State	E E
10. Elementary and secondary education	Congress	1965	Federal	E
11. Civil rights-voting	Congress	1965	Federal State	E R
12. Birth control	Supreme Court	1965	State	R
13. Comprehensive health services	Congress	1965–1966	Federal State	E E
14. Welfare rights and entitlements	Congress and Supreme Court	1970–1972	Federal State	R R
15. Privacy rights-women and abortion	Supreme Court	1973	State	R

Response

by Elena Ia. Borschevskaya

First of all, let me express my sincere gratitude to Dr. Lowi—one of the notable and widely read American scholars—who found time and went beyond the customary role of reader to carefully analyze and provide broad comments on my modest piece. In this sense it happened to be productive and stimulating. Taken as a whole, these comments represent a brilliant "blitz" (eleven pages) investigation of the main modern trends in American politics—both on the mass consciousness and on the party politics' levels. Moreover, a considerable part of the review is devoted to the ever vital problem of building up a reliable and pertinent database and making it available to all interested scholars inside the country and especially to foreigners studying American experience abroad.

Dr. Lowi makes numerous concrete and theoretical remarks of disagreements on the points stressed in the paper and in most cases is absolutely right. Still, in reading his comments I could not get rid of the feeling that there are some misunderstandings which at least should be somehow touched upon. First, and the most principal, one proceeds from the difference in the interpretation of the main idea of the paper. Dr. Lowi treats the article (as follows from his comments) as an attempt of more or less comprehensive study of the transformation of Republican politics and its electorate in the late 1960s to mid-1980s with a desirable epilogue. Actually, the original task of the paper presented was much more modest. My purpose was to show that during the last two decades (bearing in mind that the article was written almost fifteen years ago), the two-party system was marked by the intensive dealigning processes of the electorate, in general, and the loosening of the Democratic party coalition, in particular. Republicans, gaining a lot from these processes, tried to accelerate them by adhering to an absolutely pragmatic strategy for all presidential campaigns taking place in the period observed. The latter could be spelled as specific wooing plans or tactics targeted at the groups of voters traditionally constituting the backbone of the Democratic party coalition—i.e., blue-collars, Catholics, Hispanics, blacks, the South (plus women who in recent years proved to be strong Democratic party supporters).

The conception of the article predetermined its structure and justified the principle according to which these very voting groups, and not others, were chosen for examination. The criteria for drawing division lines within the electorate are numerous. It could be, for example, earnings—low-, middle-, high-income groups; geographical location—southern, western, northeastern, midwestern residents; political

229

philosophy—the right, middle-of-the road, liberal . . . with all possible intermediate gradations, and many, many others.

In the mid-1980s, when I was preparing my article, I considered it *very important* to know whether the Republican strategy was successful or not (and if successful, then to what extent). Why so? At that time I could not find a definite answer to the question: whether the realignment in the United States (which had been much talked about) did actually occur or not. The opinions diverged and could be roughly reduced to three main approaches. One group of scholars gave the negative answer. A second (mainly conservative or leaning to the Republican party) believed that definitely we were witnessing a realignment, which was in the process and gaining momentum, but an *abnormal one,* lacking those traditional features we were used to. Finally, there were those researchers standing on the position that for the time being (1970s to mid-1980s) we could speak only about a deep and intensive process of dealignment.

The latter argument seemed to be the most common and articulated one. So, if the diagnosis was dealignment, it tells much and tells little at the same time. Because the hypothesis that there is a centrifugal process at work, that the old party coalitions are falling apart, is never enough. There immediately arises the question of what direction does it take: or simply, if voters leave their party, where do they go—do they switch to the main rival, to the third party, become independents, nonvoters, etc. In one article it is hard to address all these questions adequately. That is why I set myself a limited task—to examine to what extent the traditionally pro-Democratic groups were ready to be allured by the Republicans. In case they demonstrated evident signs to be receptive, we could speak more or less confidently about a new balance of power inside the two-party system in favor of the GOP.

The second misperception concerns the conclusion of the article. According to Dr. Lowi, it is quite clear that "although the 'R-word' (realignment) was not used, the author analyzed herself into expectation: a post-1984 realignment."

Actually the "R-word" was not used exactly because I was not expecting the realignment in the nearest future. My findings concerning the behavior of the chosen electoral groups give grounds for assertion that the preconditions for the next realignment are here, but still we can speak only about dealignment or very slow realignment. Why? Because as it is noted in the paper, during the 1970s–1980s the Republican party strengthened its positions among certain previously pro-Democratic groups thanks to the salience of its ideas to the middle class. But to confirm the success and to capitalize on it is not an easy task for the parties operating within the two-party system mainly because of the counterreaction by the opposing party, usually quick enough to borrow the ideas (of course, in some transferred form) from its vis-à-vis and adapt them to the existing political realities. One of the conditions essential to realignment is the polarization of the parties' positions. But these very conditions could not be, and still are not seen, in the United States. On the contrary, from the mid-1970s the opposite situation is on hand: we have been witnessing the rapprochement tendency in the interparty relations. Following the Republican party, the Democrats (after the unsuccessful McGovernite left liberal bend in the early 1970s) also drifted rightward, and since that time there is much talk about a "two-party conservative consensus." It does not exclude the differences, even sharp differences in the parties' positions on some problems. In the 1980s–1990s these were, for example, abortion and prayer at schools, but they have not proved to be powerful enough to draw new watershed lines within the electorate and to push realignment.

Until the two parties polarized their positions, there would be a kind of creeping realignment with its characteristic attributes—fluctuations of the electorate, and short-time shifts of the voters from one party to another. Talking about the modern situation, I think that, theoretically, there are bright prospects for realignment in the post-Clinton era. The examples of the Reagan and the Clinton administrations each proved that the "conservative consensus" built on essentially transformed but still traditional approaches does not appear to be functional. This kind of ideological and political instrumentation is fully exhausted and does not fit the coming realities of the new century.

In my opinion, modern America badly needs absolutely fresh, nontraditional political recipes and solutions, if you like, breakthroughs. And I hope the American political parties will be inventive enough (Republicans, Democrats, or maybe some third party) to cope with this enormously difficult task and offer their society a eureka-like program to meet the need of the third millennium. Any initiatives of such kind could produce a realignment.

One more point of misunderstanding. Speaking about the prospects of the Republicans, I noted in my paper that much will depend upon their ability to maintain their positions in the *"political center" of the American electorate,* meaning nothing else but the *middle-class voters.* In every civilized country the middle classes constitute the broadest social stratum of the society (of the electorate) and could be called the vital center of the system. Dr. Lowi concentrated on the first part of the term, i.e., the "political center," which without its ending acquired a different meaning. Dr. Lowi read it as the *presidency* and gave interesting comments on this point, alas not related to the points stressed in the paper.

In the essay, much attention is paid to the *South as one of the historical strongholds of the Democrats.* This consideration does not only follow from the contents of the paper, but also was directly expressed in it.

> . . . White residents of the (southern) region, once an *important part of the Roosevelt coalition,* were gradually leaving the Democrats.
> . . . *The "Solid South," sometimes giving 90 percent of its votes to Democrats . . .*
> . . . The results of the presidential campaigns of 1968–1984 made it clear that . . . white southerners, *once one of the most reliable parts of the Roosevelt coalition,* in the 1970s–1980s gradually were becoming a part of the Republican party electorate.

In my experience with Russian reviewers there were never any misunderstandings on this point. It is worth mentioning that for Russian students and scholars specializing in American political history, an expression such as "Solid South," "pro-Democratic South," or "cherished Dixieland" sounds like a kind of cliché that does not need explanation.

That is why I was embarrassed reading in Dr. Lowi's comments that "one important historical point that the author missed was that the Democratic party had been a southern Party," and further, "the New Deal did not simply add the South to its coalition. The southern core in effect added the other elements on the coalition that became the New Deal coalition."

Yes, the *Democratic party had been the southern party.* The emergence of the Democratic "Solid South" could be traced back to the Reconstruction period, namely to the 1870s. Before this, up to the 1850s, within the then existing Democrats-Whigs two-party system the South had been a highly competitive political territory; in the 1850s it shifted to the Democratic party. For the southerners defeated in the Civil War the Democratic party, with its flexible position on such painful regional problems as race relations or the rights of the states, became the only possible political shelter. And indeed here they felt comfortable and politically secure for quite a long period of time, but not forever.

Quite naturally, as time passed and the socioeconomic and political situation changed, the Democratic party found it more and more difficult to maintain in balance the interests of the conservative southern electorate and those of the other voting groups, whose support was becoming increasingly meaningful for the party (especially new immigrants and blue-collars in the northern big cities and industrial centers).

The situation drastically sharpened in the 1930s. The New Deal marked the decisive shift of the Democratic party to the left and the new (and for the time being the last) realignment with the consequent birth of the Democrats-Republicans two-party system, where the Democrats became the majority party and in the political spectrum found their place in the "center and left-of-center," while the minority Republican party occupied the position of the "center and right-of-center."

The South proved its loyalty to the Democratic party and remained as a part of the New Deal coalition, but never since that time has it felt at home in the Democratic ranks. It is true that the southerners continued to vote in overwhelming majorities for the Democrats in the 1930s, 1940s, 1950s, but doing so they were driven by historical habits and deep-rooted psychological attachments to the party rather than by the feeling that they supported their like-minded brothers-in-arms sharing their sacred interests.

So what all this implies is that it is not quite an accurate contention that " . . . the southern core in effect added the other elements of the coalition that became the New Deal coalition." It leaves the impression that the Democratic party is "southern in its soul," that the South (up to the 1960s) was its main part to which all other social components were auxiliary. And thus was the ideological center of the party. But if it had been so, one can hardly imagine how the Democratic party could have given birth to New Deal politics. Still, the region could be called the core of the New Deal coalition or the Democratic coalition, taking into consideration that it was the oldest and one of the most loyal components of the Democratic party.

Here arises a question: how could it be that a vast social group whose political and cultural values lie aside the ideological mainstream of the party (and quite often contradict it) for a whole historical epoch remained its stable component? To understand this phenomenon one should refer to the unique nature of the American parties (stemming from the specifics of the U.S. political system as a whole). They represent by themselves wide, diverse, loose, very elastic and flexible political organisms. The party organizations in the states, though operating within the national party frames, are not strictly bound to the national platform. They display a high degree of independence, demonstrate remarkable adaptive capacities, attuned to the prevailing local interests and spirits. It is no wonder that Democratic party branches in southern states were run by conservatives and contributed a great deal to the promotion of the acceptable (to the southerners) candidates to the political positions at stake. What is the use of changing the party label, if your interests are well represented in the state legislatures or in the Congress?

Still, since the end of the 1960s, as broadly confirmed by the data, southerners in increasing numbers began to desert from the Democratic party to vote for Republican candidates. Dr. Lowi explains this phenomenon mainly by two reasons. First, until the late 1960s the Democratic party leadership adhered to the politics of compromise and there existed some kind of the North/South contract which was broken by the civil rights initiatives. Second, and more significant, the Republican party, under strong pressure from the unprecedentedly powerful right-wing organizations, shifted to the right. Its politics, especially meaningful for the public in areas such as religious and moral issues, corresponded well to the political moods of the southerners.

This is true, but it seems not to be the whole truth. The southerners lived through similar hard situations more than once during their long hundred-year marriage with the Democratic party and did not abandon it. As for the Republican party (I mean the modern Republican party, not Lincoln's Republicans or Progressive Republicans), its ideological image was always closer to the southerners than was that of the Democrats. But this factor had been for a long time not powerful enough to make them leave the Democrats.

Changes in the region's voting patterns in the 1970s and 1980s look even more surprising if we recall that exactly at that time the Democrats also drifted rightward.

All in all, it is obvious that for a mass reorientation such as that which the American South is now living through, there should be much more fundamental reasons than the "fundamentalist organizations," even if taking into consideration the unprecedented scope of their activities in the United States in the 1970s, 1980s, and 1990s.

In my paper I tried to show, alas unsuccessfully, that by the 1960s the region changed along many meaningful lines. Economically, socially, demographically, and psychologically, the South of 1970s and 1980s differs greatly from that "traditional South" we got used to. It lost its unique features, making it an "artificial entity," and it acquired characteristics similar to that of the American society as a whole. No surprise, then, that when in the 1960s the Democratic party no longer advocated southerners' interests in maintaining the race relations status-quo, they began to act the same way as the rest of the country—splitting their support between the two major American parties.

10

Several Conclusions from Studying the History of the U.S. Two-Party System

by A. S. Manykin, V. A. Nikonov, Iu. N. Rogoulev, and E. F. Yazkov

Two hundred years ago in 1787, after the U.S. Federal Constitution was adopted, the process of development of a government system for the young trans-Atlantic Republic began. Those holding social and class power in America at that time, the merchant and financial bourgeoisie of the Northeast and the planter/slave-owners of the South, rapidly began to broaden their arsenal of tools that would enable them to exert their political hegemony. It was exactly then, during the course of the sharpest political collisions, that the prerequisites were created for the emergence of an institution, the existence of which had not been predicted in the theoretical construct by the "founding fathers" nor in the text of the Constitution. Our discussion pertains to political parties, which formed over the subsequent decade into a two-party system.

Characterizing the significance of this political institution in the arsenal used for class hegemony by the financial oligarchy of the United States, Vladimir I. Lenin called it "one of the most powerful means of hindering the emergence of an independent workers' party, that is a truly Socialist party."[1] In the course of the entire two-hundred-year history of the United States the two-party system played and continues to play an exceptionally important role in the life of American society.

No other class in history has demonstrated such a talent for maintaining and using power as the bourgeoisie. "If in the course of already several centuries it [the bourgeoisie] has preserved power over society," comments Soviet researchers, "then this is explained not only by these or other economic, social, and additional factors, but also (this aspect is often overlooked) by the most rich arsenal of methods, means, and manner of dominance amassed."[2] This quote fully applies to the American bourgeoisie as well, which possesses, perhaps, the greatest "potential for maintaining

1. Vladimir I. Lenin, *Complete Collected Works* [Polnoe sobranie sochinenii], vol. 22, 193. This essay by Alexander Manykin, Viaycheslav Nikonov, Yuri Rogoulev, and Eugene Yazkov was originally published in *Novaia I noveishaia istoriia* [Modern and Contemporary History] 1988, no. 2, 18–33.
2. *Capitalism at the Turn of the Century* [Kapitalizm na iskhode stoletiia], A. N. Iakovlev, ed. (Moscow, 1987), 289.

power." In its development, political parties made a highly significant contribution from the outset. The flexible and complex mechanism of the two-party system, acting together with the ramified apparatus of the bourgeois government, dependent upon the powerful economic potential of the country, allowed up until this time and still allows the U.S. ruling circles to withstand, although not without some losses, the numerous sociopolitical crises, to adapt itself to the conditions of intensified class struggle, and to withstand various manifestations of social conflict within the framework of the bourgeois-democratic political process.

An analysis of the history and of the contemporary state of the U.S. two-party system is one of the most important and continual problems of American historiography. Among the large number of works on this theme are many serious and valuable studies that help to construct an objective picture of the evolution of the two-party system. But on the American book market many works of a purely apologetic character have appeared and continue to appear in which the American two-party system is depicted as a unique political institution capable of effectively solving any economic and social problem in an evolutionary way, as a power existing beyond class and which functions in the interests of "the social good and progress," and as a unique sociopolitical standard to which all other countries and peoples can and should be compared.

The problems in the development of the two-party system at different stages of the political history of the United States in the last one and a half decades has been attracting increased attention by Soviet scholars. Historians, legal scholars, and political scientists who work in the system of the USSR Academy of Sciences and in a number of the country's institutions of higher learning are actively engaged in the study of these problems. In 1977, at the initiative of Professor Nikolai V. Sivachev from M. V. Lomonosov-Moscow State University, a special laboratory for the study of the United States was created in which the central theme of scholarly work became the study of the history of the two-party system.[3] As a result of the efforts of a large array of Soviet scholars a series of studies was published that permits an evaluation of the role of this political institution in the history of American society.

The combined experience of the study of the peculiarities in the functioning of the American two-party system allows us to draw conclusions from the work in this area. A paper dedicated to exactly this topic was written by a group of Soviet historians and presented at the eightieth meeting of the Organization of American Historians in Philadelphia in April 1987. A lively debate ensued during the course of discussion, illuminating several important facets of this topic and giving fodder and new thoughts for further work. It prompted the authors of the paper, after making certain amendments to it, to present it as an article for the judgment of the Soviet scholarly community.

Not attempting an analysis of the entire complex of questions connected with the evolution of the partisan-political system in the United States, the authors focused

3. For more detail on the work of this group see I. V. Galkin and E. F. Yazkov, "Laboratory of American Studies at Moscow State University" [Laboratoriia amerikanistiki MGU], in *S.Sh.A. -ekonomika, politika, ideologia* 1987, no. 8.

their attention on such important aspects of the problem as the reason for its emergence and the factors of its stability within the U.S. two-party system, and its function during various stages of the historical development of American bourgeois society.

The fundamental reasons for the formation and growth of bourgeois political parties in the United States and other capitalist countries are connected with the character of the interrelationship between the ruling social strata and the masses in a capitalist society. In the socioeconomic structures preceding capitalism, the oppression of some classes of society by others was based on methods of extraeconomic constraint and the class privileges of the propertied strata were strengthened by means of religious and legal norms. With the emergence of the bourgeois system a different situation came about. "Normal capitalist society cannot successfully develop without a well-entrenched system of representation, without certain well-known political rights for the population that cannot help but be distinguished by its comparatively high exactingness in regards to 'culture'," wrote Lenin.[4]

Proclaiming formal and legal equality for citizens, granting voting rights to more or less broad segments of society, and transferring part of the functions in governing the country to representative organs of power introduces fundamentally new features into the mechanism of class hegemony by the wealthy minority, first and foremost in terms of at least the partial involvement of the exploited majority into the political process and its incorporation into the partisan-political structure of bourgeois society. It should be added that the ruling class itself, as a rule, is by no means united in its aims. The necessity for regulating conflicts among the ruling elite and for working out a political course that responds to the combined interests of the bourgeoisie also stimulated the appearance and development of the partisan structure of bourgeois society.

The bourgeois parties are a relatively new phenomenon in comparison with the narrowly elite political factions characteristic of the pre-bourgeois era. In contrast to this previous era, as a rule parties have a long-term program, rely on a rather large voting corpus, and create a ramified organizational structure to control the electorate. Political parties of bourgeois society characteristically present a stable systemic element both in the interrelationship between them and in relations between parties and other structural components of the political organization of society. The systemic element in turn determines an exceptionally important characteristic of that institution as well. Experiencing a serious influence on the part of the surrounding social milieu, parties also "preserve an autonomous character in regard to one another and to other socio-political organizations."[5] This creates the possibility for the well-known asynchronicity that occurs in the development of the partisan system and remaining components of the superstructure, increasing the role of adherence to the law inherent in this particular complex.

4. Lenin, *Complete Collected Works*, vol. 20, 68.
5. N. N. Marchenko, *Essays on the Theory of Political Systems of Modern Bourgeois Societies* [Ocherki teorii politichseskoi sistemy sovremennogo burzhuaznogo obshchestva], (Moscow, 1985), 146.

The peculiarities in the development of bourgeois society in various countries has predetermined the appearance of concrete models of the partisan-political structure in each of them. The primary reasons for the emergence of the two-party variant in the United States are rooted in the objective socioeconomic and political situation that took shape there at the end of the eighteenth century.

A significant peculiarity of the historical development of American society was the absence of feudalism as a structure on the territory of that country. "The United States," wrote Friedrich Engels, "was modern and bourgeois even from its inception."[6] This created especially favorable conditions for the development of capitalism, comparative purity of bourgeois relations in the United States. The presence of the class of planter/slave-owners was intimately connected to the needs of capitalist production and did not change the general bourgeois path of the country's evolution. All of this significantly limited the number of possible alternatives for the development of American society.

The political situation arising in the United States at the end of the eighteenth century also was favorable to this. The definitive defeat of the Loyalists during the course of the first American Revolution on the one hand, and the resounding defeat of independent outpourings by the popular masses on the other hand, did not leave a social footing for the somewhat successful political activities of groups and organizations that supported a different nonbourgeois path for the development of American society.

One should also consider that the political-juridical vision of the U.S. "founding fathers" was formed under the strong influence of the English experience, English political traditions carried over in the colonial period onto North American soil. And in this political tradition the principle of the two-party system was embedded already quite solidly.

It goes without saying that the principle of the two-party system in the political system of American bourgeois society was not affirmed immediately.[7] The fundamental reason for its consolidation during the nineteenth century was that it had withstood the test of practice and seemed exceptionally convenient for the U.S. ruling classes. From undeliberate approval of this principle and its elemental use it gradually changed, and was deliberately incorporated into political philosophy and concrete political practice.

The effectiveness of these efforts can be explained by an entire complex of factors, born of the specifics of the social-class and governmental-legal environment in which the foundation and development of the U.S. partisan-political system took place. So, for America of the nineteenth century a relatively high degree of social mobility in society was characteristic, and in many ways in connection with this was the relative weakness of the labor movement as well. This enabled the leaders of both bourgeois parties to maintain control over the "diverseness" in terms of its social class makeup, and through coalitions of voters. They took advantage of the tradition

6. Karl Marx and Friedrich Engels, *Works* [Sochineniia], vol. 39, 128.

7. See I. V. Galkin, A. S. Manykin, and V. O. Pechatnov, "The Two-Party System in the Political History of the U.S." [Dvukhpartiinaia sistema v politicheskoi istorii SShA], *Voprosy istorii* 1987, no. 9.

of voting for bourgeois politicians that had appeared even among the proletariat.[8] The formation of persistent stereotypes of political behavior by voters made possible both such peculiarities in the development of the U.S. political system as the relatively high level of acceptance of the primary institutions of bourgeois-democratic governmental strata created on the basis of the 1787 Constitution. The establishment of the majority voting system with individual representatives from each voting district in the opinion of the majority of political scientists led to the shaping in the country of the two-party and not a multiparty system.

Finally, the strengthening of traditional stereotypes of political behavior by voters was accompanied by such peculiarities of social psychology within Americans as pragmatism and practicality, characteristic to the majority of them, and the relatively low level of their political consciousness. The strong adherence to certain principles often is seen as the appearance of impracticality. The successful resolution of ongoing personal problems, and most important, the achievement of victory in elections, was considered about the only criteria for the effectiveness of political action. Naturally, in this situation the rather detached two-party mechanism "maintains for the political elite a convenient predictability" in the political process.[9]

In this manner, the relatively formed character of American society as a society purely bourgeois, following the political traditions of England, a series of peculiarities of the governmental structure in the nation, and the political culture and social psychology of Americans, created favorable ground for the manifestation of a two-party system in the political arena of the young American government and its gradual acceptance in political practice in the United States. In addition, the effectiveness of this institution in preserving and defending the interests of the bourgeoisie turned it into an inalienable attribute of the political system in American society.

During the course of historical development of the two-party system as one of the important instruments of class hegemony by the bourgeoisie, completely distinct and interconnected primary functions were strengthened. In our opinion, the following functions can be distinguished:

Programmatic-goal-oriented function. On the basis of agreement and uniting ideo-political interests of various segments and groups of the ruling class, taking into account the distribution of class forces in society as a whole, parties form and enact a political course that consolidates bourgeois legality and alienating factors that undermine its stability. The interrelationship between bourgeois parties in the two-party system is built upon the base of their initial agreement (consensus) on the question of the general direction in development of society and simultaneously on the basis of each of them presenting distinct alternatives which reflect differences between them in methods of attaining common political goals. The consensus-alternative principle makes up one of the most important functional bases of the livelihood of the two-party mechanism. "Without consensus the two-party system could not effectively defend the common interests of the ruling class. Without alternatives the

8. Lenin, *Complete Collected Works,* vol. 15, 235.
9. *The American Party Systems, Stages of Political Development,* William D. Burnham and William N. Chambers, eds. (New York, 1967), 6.

parties would completely lose their individuality," notes a Soviet scholar of the U.S. political system, A. A. Mishin.[10] In the process of the interparty struggle and the reconciliation of contradictory interests of separate political groups an approbation of new strategic and tactical ideological lines, new recipes for solving problems born by the development of bourgeois society, is produced.

An *Electoral Function,* which consists of the mobilization of the voting electorate to support programs and candidates of bourgeois parties. Parties nominate candidates for election to organs of governmental power in the center and in localities, secure for them support by the electorate during the course of mass electoral campaigns, integrate and interpret in a bourgeois-reformist spirit popular ideas and slogans of popular masses, direct political activity of various social class groups of society into the stream of the interparty struggle, impart to the masses norms and skills for this activity beneficial to the bourgeoisie, and hang the label "popular approval" onto the political course being carried out by the bourgeois government. However successfully the parties attract broad contingents of the electorate into the bourgeois-democratic political process, the degree they succeed in maintaining amorphous coalitions in the orbit of their influence, which are grouped around programs and candidates upholding bourgeois values, to a great extent depends on the strength of the rule of big capital and the stability of the bourgeois political system in the United States.

An *Adaptive Function,* which manifests itself in the fact that the two-party system acts as a mechanism for bringing elements of the political superstructure into accordance with the changing socioeconomic environment, with changes in the foundation of bourgeois society. Of course, the two-party system itself is an element of the superstructure, and this means that it emerges also as an object of adaptation, the type of activity and the structure of which also is brought into accordance with changes in the base processes. But, as with other elements of the political superstructure, the two-party system has relative independence and because of its special flexibility and mobility more often than not becomes the subject of processes of adaptation, actively affecting the whole political system of bourgeois society and in many respects determining the direction of changes taking place within society.

The most distinct adaptive function of the two-party system manifests itself during stages of partisan-political regroupings. Every regrouping that has occurred in American history had its own special look, and unfolded in its own individual "scenario," as far as it was realized under various conditions and in various stages

10. A. A. Mishin, *The Principle of Division of Power in the U.S. Constitutional Mechanism* [Printsip razdeleniia vlastei v konstitutsionnom mekhanizme SShA] (Moscow, 1984), 153; see also A. S. Manykin and N. V. Sivachev, "The U.S. Two-Party System: The Past and Present" [Dvukhpartiinaia sistema SShA: istoriia I sovremennost'], *Novaia I noveishaia istoriia* 1978, no. 3; I. P. Dement'ev et al., "Several Principles of the Functioning of the Two-Party System" [O nekotorykh printsipakh funktsionirovaniia dvukhpartiinoi sistemy], *Vestnik MGU, seriia "Istoriia"* 1981 no. 6; V. I. Borisiuk and N. V. Sivachev, "Problems in the History and Methodology of the Study of the U.S. Two-Party System" [Problemy istorii I metodologii izucheniia dvukhpartiinoi sistemy SShA], in *The Role of Bourgeois Political Parties in U.S. Public Life* [Rol' burzhuaznykh politicheskikh partii v obshchestvennoi zhizni SShA] (Moscow, 1981).

of development of bourgeois society. At the same time there are general moments that characterize all regroupings. Each of the regroupings was aimed at adaptation of the outmoded partisan-political structure to the changing socioeconomic atmosphere, to the new phase in the development of bourgeois society. In conjunction with this, during the course of partisan-political regroupings new ingredients in the mass base of the parties appeared. Traditional coalitions of the electorate were washed away, parties alone replaced others at the helm of power for an extended period, and political figures of the new generation assumed key posts in the parties and in government. These politicians of the newer generation held qualitatively different ideo-political views in comparison with their predecessors. Important changes in government policy occurred as well as noticeable shifts in the political structure and of the socio-psychological stereotypes of the population.

Emerging in the capacity of an instrument for solving intensified conflicts that occur periodically during the development of bourgeois society, regroupings objectively have rigid boundaries for breaking the outmoded party-political structures. These structures are distinguished by the nature of private property in bourgeois society. Allowing well-known superstructural innovations, regroupings helped the "U.S. ruling class to break the outdated, now dangerous social structures and ideological schemata on time, and legitimate new ones in their place and give a legal outlet for mass protest," and at the same time they "touch only the superstructure, and that is why their potential with each time diminishes."[11] It follows from this that a cardinal break of the whole system of relations between antagonistic classes cannot take the form of a partisan-political regrouping, since in this case a revolutionary reform of the whole socioeconomic and political structure of society would be necessary. An example of such a revolutionary break in the history of the United States was the Civil War of 1861–1865, which destroyed the system of plantation slavery. In the framework of the functioning of the two-party system, fulfilling this task turned out to be impossible.

It goes without saying that all of the noted functions of the two-party system are not realized automatically, not by themselves, but through concrete activity of people in the concrete historical situation. As a result, the process of the functioning of the two-party system cannot be unchangeable, since it occurs during a definite historical epoch and depends on people's awareness of their goals and interests, and the role in the societal process, and on the correspondence of class forces in society at one or another stage of its development. In addition, the two-party system itself undergoes a long process of evolution, developing from its initial birth to the modern structure through stages of formation, establishment, and maturity. It takes on new qualities and roles during this evolution. At each stage of the development of the two-party system the principles of its functions, the character of its connections and interaction that make up its parties, the ideological-political conceptions that they defend, the configuration of voting coalitions that has unfolded around them, and

11. S. B. Stankevich, "Modern Tendencies in the Development of 'the New Political History' in the U.S." [Sovremennye tendentsii v razvitii "novoi politicheskoi istorii" v SShA], *Amerikanskii ezhegodnik, 1983* (Moscow, 1983), 225.

the structure and organization of the parties has been realized and manifested in various ways.

In the development of the partisan-political system in the United States one can distinguish three important periods: 1) the end of the eighteenth century to the beginning of the 1870s; 2) the 1870s to the beginning of the 1930s; 3) the 1930s to the present day.

The first of these is characterized by the formation of the two-party system: an unfolding of the persistent principle of a two-party system occurs in concrete political practice and political culture of American society. During this period rapid development of a capitalist socioeconomic structure was proceeding. The bourgeois parties played an important and, on the whole, constructive role in the life of the country, making a weighty contribution toward solving a number of cardinal tasks that were facing the young Republic. Thus, they facilitated the abandonment of political particularism, which had reigned in the former English colonies, and helped consolidate sociopolitical life in the country within the framework of a single national government. They contributed greatly to working out and realizing the programs for socioeconomic development of the country, and attained a significant democratization of the political process.

Nevertheless, in the initial period of its development, the U.S. partisan-political system was distinguished by great instability. Parties arose and disappeared from the political arena, making way for new ones. The systemic ties that had unfolded and the interrelationship between them were relatively weak and were often broken. The two-party system had not yet become an axiom of political life in the country. Stages of relatively stable functioning of the two-party system were very short-lived (the first decade of the nineteenth century, the end of the 1830s to the first half of the 1840s), changing with years of a one-party system, as for example during the "era of good feelings," or a multiparty system, especially characteristic for the 1850s.

During the first decade of the existence of the young American state (the end of the eighteenth century to the beginning of the 1800s) the partisan-political system in the United States only began to be formed. The first U.S. parties, the Federalists and Jeffersonian Republicans, which had arisen in the 1790s, were characterized by relatively weakly formed political groups, to a significant degree still not standing apart from the organs of government. They by no means were a recognized element of the American political system. And the "founding fathers" of the American Republic, and many political figures of the first decade of its existence, as a rule looked on this emerging institution of American society extremely negatively. They completely shared the view expressed in the famous "farewell address" of George Washington in which he warned against "the perilous consequences of the partisan spirit."[12] And only during the course of concrete political practice among government figures in the United States did the conviction spread gradually of the necessity of parties.

At this initial stage of the formation of the U.S. partisan-political mechanism the systemic connections between parties were very weak. Although the general aim of

12. *Documents of American History,* Henry S. Commager, ed. (New York, 1945); vol. 1, 172.

the ruling political groups in the country of strengthening and developing bourgeois relations on the grounds of the articles of the 1787 Federal Constitution was the basis for interparty consensus, in the real interrelationships between the parties of the Federalists and the Jeffersonian Republicans, especially in the 1790s, the clearly expressed alternative dominated.

Programs of the first political parties in the United States reflected two fundamental conceptions in developing American bourgeois society put forward at the time. One of them, formed by the leader of the Federalists, Alexander Hamilton, was the conception of forced commercial and industrial development of the country. At the basis of Hamilton's views lay the thesis about the necessity for creating a national bank and broadening the regulatory functions of the bourgeois government in order to "protect national industry from competition from foreign goods, overcome the economic disconnection of the states, facilitate the flowering of manufacturing, and to secure a favorable balance of trade for exports over imports."[13] In response to this the leader of the Jeffersonian Republicans put forward the concept of creating a bourgeois-democratic farmers' republic, allowing for the free development of agriculture and requiring maximum restriction of the prerogatives of the federal government and the broadening of the rights of local self-government up to "direct democracy" for petty property owners, primarily landowners. Only gradually, in the concrete political practice of the period of Jeffersonian Democracy, did a well-known modification of the ideological stands of both parties occur, drawing their respective programs closer to one another, so that this facilitated a diminishment in the level of an alternative program and enabled the elemental unfolding of a consensus. As a result, a distinct strengthening of systemic ties between constituent elements of the two-party mechanism occurred.[14]

The first U.S. political parties functioned in conditions of relatively low political activity by the country's population. Solving fundamental political problems was the sphere of a narrow elite group of representatives of the landed aristocracy and the commercial-financial bourgeoisie. True, already then, the Federalists and the Jeffersonian Republicans had support among farmers and masses of the urban population. This support was significantly broader in comparison with the only European parties that had formed by that time, the English Tories and Whigs. But, nevertheless, the social base of the early bourgeois U.S. parties was still very limited. They did not have the need to create firm and constant organizational structures to connect with the voters. Therefore, they preserved their existing elitist character.

The stormy processes of economic development in the United States of the first decades of the nineteenth century, which included the deepening and widening development of capitalism during the course of the beginning of the Industrial

13. V. V. Sogrin, *Ideological Trends during the American Revolution of the 18th Century* [Ideinye techeniia v amerikanskoi revoliutsii XVIII veka] (Moscow, 1980), 293.

14. See G. N. Sevost'ianov and A. I. Utkin, *Thomas Jefferson* [Tomas Dzhefferson] (Moscow, 1976); M. O. Troianovskaia, *The Ideo-Political Evolution of the Jeffersonian Republican Party (1800–1810)* [Ideino-politicheskaia evoliutsiia partii dzheffersonovskikh respublikantsev (1800–1810 gg.)] (Moscow, 1983) (diss.); V. O. Pechatnov, *Hamilton and Jefferson* [Gamil'ton I Dzhefferson] (Moscow, 1984).

Revolution in the North, the incorporation of new territories in the West, and the rapid growth of plantation slave-based agriculture in the South, introduced significant changes in the socioeconomic and political atmosphere in the country. New social segments such as the industrial bourgeoisie, owners of large cotton plantations, and capitalist farmers actively made themselves known in the political process and demanded a reevaluation of the course of governmental policies so that new policies would take into consideration their interests as well.

After the demise of the Federalist party, contradictory interests of all these social groups could temporarily fit into the framework of one party, the Jeffersonian Republicans. But, characteristic for the "era of good feelings," the condition of an unstable balance could not continue because in the framework of one political organization in the 1820s several factions became ever more distinguished. These factions expressed the views of various social groups and supported such a path of development for American society that would respond exactly to their interests.

Thus, for example, one of the factions, headed by Andrew Jackson and Martin Van Buren, expressed the views of a complex conglomerate of social forces. The new planter groups and western farmers and also a portion of the bourgeoisie and rather broad segments of the working urban population of the Northeast put forward a more or less broad program for democratization of sociopolitical life in the country. Another political group, headed by John Quincy Adams, Henry Clay, and Daniel Webster, attempting to address the broadest segments of the bourgeoisie and a part of the planters, worked out a doctrine of the so-called American System, proclaiming slogans for protectionism and stimulating development of industry, domestic trade, and transportation. Finally, representatives of the planters of the old slave states of the South, led by John C. Calhoun, propounding the thesis about "Southern exceptional status," took the Jeffersonian idea of defending states' rights to the extreme in slogans calling for the exit from the Union if the system of plantation slavery would be threatened.[15]

On the basis of deep shifts in the social structure of society in the United States of the 1820s–1830s brought on by the beginning transition from a manufacturing stage of capitalist development to an industrial stage, the first partisan-political regrouping took place. As a result, during the time of Jacksonian Democracy a second variant of the two-party system arose, the system of Democrats and Whigs, which held sway until the mid-1850s.

During this new stage in the formation of the U.S. two-party system important changes in the methods of its functioning manifested themselves. The system of ties and interaction between its constituent parts significantly broadened and became more complex. Both the Democratic party and the Whig party, remaining under the control of the bourgeois-planter bloc, captured with their influence all the major social groups of the period: farmers, planters, the commercial-financial and industrial bourgeoisie,

---

15. See V. I. Terekhov, "Conflicting Trends within the Republican Party during the 'Era of Good Feelings' (1815–1824)" [Bor'ba techenii vnutri respublikanskoi partii v "eru dobrogo soglasiia" (1815–1824)], in *U.S. Political Parties in Modern Times* [Politicheskie partii SShA v novoe vremia] (Moscow, 1981).

petty urban property owners, and a newly formed proletariat. The inevitable need for compromise under these conditions in the ideo-political positions of both parties made them much more diffuse, and less ideologized than those doctrines that had held sway in the first national parties. Preserving differences, in many cases very significant ones, in the concrete programs for socioeconomic development of the country, and continuing under the new circumstances previous arguments about two paths of development for American bourgeois society, the Democrats and Whigs to a much greater extent than previous U.S. parties managed to work out a general system of political values. The system included the belief in the unlimited possibilities of capitalist free enterprise, a recognition of the utmost importance of the colonization of the West, espousal of the program for well-known democratization of life in the country, but under the necessary condition of preserving the system of slavery in the South.

The social mobilizing function of the two-party system significantly widened during this stage, and a more solid and ramified organizational structure of the parties was created, something necessary for attracting a significantly growing contingent of voters. In such a manner, as a result of the partisan-political regrouping of the 1820s and 1830s replacing the earlier structure, in many respects, archaic party-clubs, the Democrats and the Whigs arrived. In their functioning the characteristics of a new, bourgeois-democratic party (more liberal or more conservative) could be felt. These parties attracted rather wide segments of the electorate. Under conditions of expansion of the scale of activity of the parties, the growth in the number and significance of national problems, the existence of political parties and national institutions became an objective necessity for effective work of the whole U.S. political system, and politicians of the new generation, in contrast to their predecessors, considered the existence of two competing parties to be completely natural.[16]

Up to the middle of the 1840s the two-party system of Democrats and Whigs remained balanced enough to act effectively as a political institution that reliably defended the interests of the bourgeois-planter bloc and created favorable conditions for the development of capitalist relations. But at a certain stage the Democrats and Whigs, intimately connected with not only the new, rapidly developing social forces but also the old, outmoded ones, primarily slave-owners, turned out to be unable to fulfill the tasks standing before the two-party system. The emergence of the issue of slavery into the center of the country's political life and the gradual growth of the "irrepressible conflict" between the North and South became the main

16. See N. N. Bolkhovitinov, *The U.S.: Problems in History and Contemporary Historiography* [SShA: problemy istorii I sovremennaia istoriografiia] (Moscow, 1980); A. S. Manykin, *History of the U.S. Two-Party System* [Istoriia dvukhpartiinoi sistemy SShA] (Moscow, 1981); G. A. Dubovitskii, "The Two-Party System of the 'Democrats and Whigs': Peculiarities and Its Role in the Political Development in the U.S. during the 1830s-1850s" [Dvukhpartiinaia sistema "demokraty-vigi": osobennosti I rol' v politicheskom razvitii SShA v 30–50-e gody XIXv.], in *From the History of the Internal Political Struggle and Public Thought in the U.S.* [Iz istorii vnutirpoliticheskoi bor'by I obshchestvennoi mysli SShA] (Kuibyshev, 1981); M. A. Vlasova, *The Formation of the Whig Party in the U.S. (1828–1840)* [Obrazovanie vigskoi partii v SShA (1828–1840)] (Moscow, 1986) (diss.).

reason for the deep crisis that gripped the Democratic and Whig parties in the mid–nineteenth century. The decomposition of these parties and the appearance in 1854 of the Republican party, which united under its banner opponents of the system of plantation slavery, signified the beginning of a new era in reconstruction of the two-party system. But resolution of the fundamental contradictions between the capitalist North and the slave South, having gone to the extreme, occurred not in the form of partisan-political regrouping but rather as a revolutionary break in the system of plantation slavery during the course of the bloody Civil War of 1861–1865, a time when the evolutionary development of American bourgeois society was interrupted.[17]

The second partisan-political regrouping in the history of the United States was completed in the 1870s. At this stage of the development of capitalism, which was characterized by its gradual development into monopolistic capitalism, in the United States a new variant of the partisan-political system arose and began to develop, based on the functioning of two purely bourgeois political parties, the Republicans and Democrats. The second important period in the history of the two-party system began, having continued until the 1930s.

The confirmed hegemony of big capital, the growth of monopolies, and the transfer from "free" capitalism to imperialism unified the political process in the country. It facilitated a definitive strengthening of the principle of the two-party system in the U.S. partisan-political system and confirmed the viability of the system in the interrelations between its constituent elements. At this stage of the history of the two-party system its development was realized not in a broken form characterized by the disappearance of some and the appearance of other fundamental bourgeois parties, but rather by way of the gradual transformation of the acting parties in the process of intensification and the subsequent partial resolution of antagonisms and conflicts both between themselves and between the two-party complex as a whole and third parties.

Having set as their main goal defending the interests of big capital, both components of the two-party system, the Republicans and the Democrats, turned into a conservative force striving to prevent cardinal changes in the socioeconomic and political structure of bourgeois society. It is telling that even American political scientists, for example, William Chambers, in evaluating the nature of the two-party system's influence on the course of political development in the country cannot but indirectly admit this shift in the role of the party from "innovation" to "patching up and accommodation."[18]

In the last quarter of the nineteenth century a more distinct formation of the party mechanism occurred within the framework of the U.S. political system. First, the parties once and for all stood apart from other components of the political structure in American society. At the end of the nineteenth and the beginning of the twentieth century a transition from self-affirmation of the parties to their institutionalization, that

17. See A. A. Kormilets and S. A. Porshakov, *The Crisis of the U.S. Two-Party System on the Eve and during the Civil War (End of the 1840s-1865)* [Krizis dvukhpartiinoi sistemy SShA nakanune I v gody Grazhdanskoi voiny (konets 1840-x-1865 g.)] (Moscow, 1987).

18. Burnham and Chambers, *The American Party Systems,* 22–23.

is to say formal recognition and juridical strengthening, and also to the well-known regulation of their activity in the electoral right of the states, took shape. The "party machines" headed by bosses became widespread. This was a new organizational basis for the structure of bourgeois parties. With their help a higher degree of mobilization of the electorate was achieved.[19]

But, from the point of view of the long-term interests of the ruling circles in the United States, the two-party system of Republicans and Democrats resolved far from all of the problems standing before it. The ideological-political positions of both parties at this time, a period known as the "Golden Century" of American capitalism, for all practical purposes was based on individualistic conceptions in their extreme social Darwinian form to the same extent as before. The interrelationship between constituent elements of the two-party system was founded on a clear predominance of consensus, with sharp restriction of the scale of alternatives to the reigning views.[20] New important problems, which had arisen then in connection with the appearance and growth of big monopolistic corporations, did not find expression in the political course of both bourgeois parties. In perspective, this inevitably led to the undermining of their influence among the masses and to diminishing the degree of effectiveness of the two-party system.

In such a manner, the stage of relative stability in the functioning of the two-party system of Republicans and Democrats turned out to be very short-lived. The conservative character of this model of the two-party mechanism, its lack of attention to new socioeconomic and political conditions connected with the transition of the country to the stage of monopolistic capitalism, already in the 1890s provoked a powerful wave of mass democratic movement, which culminated in the formation and activity of the Populist party. In its program were affixed such important demands by labor and farmers as nationalization of the railroads and communication, regulation of the operation of monopolistic intermediary firms, establishment of the eight-hour workday, introduction of workman's compensation, easing of conditions for credit and relief of farmers' debts, and broad democratization of the electoral system. Having actively entered the political process, the Populist party spread its influence across

19. See A. S. Manykin, "Several Aspects of the Development of the Organizational Structure of the Bourgeois Parties" [Nekotorye aspekty razvitiia organizatsionnoi struktury burzhuaznykh partii], in *U.S. Political Parties in Modern Times* [Politicheskie partii SShA v novoe vremia] (Moscow, 1981); G. G. Bovt and I. P. Dement'ev, "The Phenomenon of the Boss and Corruption in the Two-Party System in the U.S. during the Second Half of the Nineteenth Century" [Bossizm I korruptsiia v dvukhpartiinoi sisteme SShA vo vtoroi polovine XIX v.], *Novaia I noveishaia istoriia* 1985, no. 4; I. V. Galkin and V. A. Nikonov, "Urban Party Machines in U.S. Political Life" [Gorodskie partiinye mashiny v politicheskoi zhizni SShA], in *Problems in American Studies* [Problemy amerikanistiki] (Moscow, 1986).

20. During the first years of its existence, especially during the 1880s, the two-party system of the Republicans and Democrats was a very effective political institution in certain aspects of its activity. Thus it secured the necessary governmental-legal conditions for development of big industry and achieved integration of a large army of immigrants into the political structure of American bourgeois society. It was precisely then that the peak of mobilization of the electorate was achieved.

rather broad layers of the electorate and its members won elections to Congress and various organs of power in a series of states.[21] In the beginning of the twentieth century the program for democratic reforms put forward by the U.S. Socialist party was extremely popular among voters. All of this gave rise to deep crises in the partisan-political system in the country.

With the goal of overcoming these crises, at the end of the nineteenth and the beginning of the twentieth century the first attempts at transforming the two-party system in the United States to the positions of bourgeois reformism occurred. Already during the course of the 1896 election campaign the Democrats and their candidate for president, William Jennings Bryan, managed to appropriate from the Populist party a series of its more moderate demands and return those voters who had supported the Populists back to the fold of the two-party system. An even stronger incentive for developing the reforms was given during the years of the "Progressive era" in the concrete practical activity of the Republican administration of Theodore Roosevelt and the Democratic administration of Woodrow Wilson. Through the efforts of activists from both parties the petty-bourgeois radicalism of the Populist movement and the radical program of the Socialists were transformed into the theory and practice of very moderate bourgeois reform, which included measures for the consolidation of the financial system in the country, limited regulation of trusts, and for suppression of the more scandalous incidents of arbitrariness by the railroad companies, food-processing firms, and firms that produced medical goods, and calls for formal recognition of trade unions, etc.[22]

In such a manner at the end of the nineteenth and beginning of the twentieth century in the United States the tendency toward a new partisan-political regrouping became clearly defined. This became evident first in the attempts by activists from both parties to use methods of governmental regulation of economics and social relations, and to adapt the two-party mechanism to conditions of the monopolistic stage of capitalism.

The transition of the two-party system to the State-Monopolistic course became even more of a necessity after the Great October Socialist revolution in Russia led to the appearance of a government that espoused the goal of building a society of true social justice and eliminating exploitation of individuals by individuals. The more far-sighted political activists in America called upon the leaders of both leading parties to come to terms with the new realities and introduce the necessary changes into the ideological positions of the two-party system. The movement for independent political activity, finding its brightest expression in the nomination of the independent candidate, Senator Robert La Follette, who emerged in the 1924 elections with a

21. See L. V. Baibakova, "Protectionism or Free Trade? The Problem of Tariffs in the Policies of the U.S. Bourgeois parties (1880s-Beginning of the 1890s)" [Protektsionizm ili svobodnaia torgovlia? Problema tarifov v politike burzhuaznykh partii SShA (80-e nachalo 90-x godov XIX v.)], *Problemy amerikanistiki* (Moscow, 1986).
22. See G. P. Kuropiatnik, *The Farm Movement in the U.S. from Grangers to the Populist Party, 1867–1896* [Fermerskoe dvizhenie v SShA ot greindzherov do Narodnoi partii, 1867–1896] (Moscow, 1971).

progressive antimonopoly platform, showed the growth in the crises of the two-party system's development.[23]

But the tendency toward a partisan-political regrouping that cropped up at the turn of the twentieth century was not for all practical purposes realized either during the time of the "Progressive era" or during the first decade after World War I. Moreover, during the 1920s an even clearer movement backwards was observed. On the basis of a significant strengthening of the position of the American monopolistic bourgeoisie as a result of the war, there occurred a significant weakening of the State-Monopolistic tendencies and a return of the two-party system of the Republicans and Democrats to the course of traditional individualistic ideology. The atmosphere of "prosperity" characteristic for most of the 1920s created in the ruling circles and in the electorate the illusion that American capitalism and its main moving force, big business, were capable by their own forces of solving all of the problems facing the country and therefore were not in need of any sort of interference on the part of government.[24]

Activists from both parties, in particular leaders of the ruling Republican party, forcefully cultivated these ideas. Calvin Coolidge in one of his presidential addresses declared: "The essence of our system of rule consists of the fact that it is based on the principles of freedom and independence of the individual. In his activities each individual depends only on himself. Therefore he cannot be denied the fruits of his ingenuity. . . . That, which is accumulated through his personal efforts should not become the source for government waste."[25]

Nevertheless, the concrete historical experience in the functioning of the two-party system in the United States showed the impossibility of resolving the most important problems arising from the development of monopolistic capitalism on the basis of "strict individualism." This was demonstrated with special force during the course of the deepest economic crisis of 1929–1933, which, according to the justified comments by Nikolai V. Sivachev, became for the United States "the decisive accelerator for the growth of monopolistic capitalism into state-monopolistic capitalism."[26] The crisis gave birth to unusually bitter class conflicts and threatened the principles

---

23. See I. A. Beliavskaia, *Bourgeois Reformism in the U.S. (1900–1914)* [Burzhuaznyi reformizm v SShA (1900–1914)] (Moscow, 1968); V. V. Sogrin, *Sources of Modern Bourgeois Ideology in the U.S.* [Istoki sovremennoi burzhuaznoi ideologii v SShA] (Moscow, 1976); B. D. Kozenko, *"New Democracy" and War: Domestic U.S. Politics (1914–1917)* ["Novaia demokratiia" I voina. Vnutrenniaia politika SShA (1914–1917)] (Saratov, 1980); A. A. Porshakova, *Bourgeois Reformism in the Activity of the Democratic Party of the U.S. at the Beginning of the Twentieth Century (1901–1912)* [Burzhuaznyi reformizm v deiatel'nosti demokraticheskoi partii SShA v nachale XX v.] (Moscow, 1983) (diss.).

24. See E. F. Yazkov, *The Farm Movement in the U.S. (1918–1929)* [Fermerskoe dvizhenie v SShA (1918–1929)] (Moscow, 1974).

25. See G. L. Kertman, *The Struggle of Tendencies in the Republican Party of the U.S. (1924–1928)* [Bor'ba techenii v respublikanskoi partii SShA (1924–1928 gg.)] (Moscow, 1981) (diss.); I. V. Galkin, *The Socio-Political Course of the Democratic Party in the U.S. during 1921–1929* [Sotsial'no-politicheskii kurs demokraticheskoi partii SShA v 1921–1929 gg.] (Moscow, 1982) (diss.).

26. N. V. Sivachev, "State-Monopolistic Capitalism in the U.S." [Gosudarstvenno-monopolisticheskii kapitalizm SShA], *Voprosy istorii* 1977, no. 7, 84.

of American private-property capitalism. The extraordinary atmosphere urgently called for new approaches in solving the most important socioeconomic and political problems facing the country at that time. In the political atmosphere electrified by the Depression, Franklin Roosevelt's words during the heat of the election campaign of 1932 rang true: "The country is in need of change, and if I understand the nation's mood correctly, insistently demands brave experiments. . . . Millions of the needy will not be patient forever when all that is required for satisfying their needs is on hand."[27]

The stormy events of political life at the beginning of the 1930s gave impulse to a new third partisan-political regrouping in the history of the United States, which turned the Democratic party into the leading component of the two-party mechanism and placed the Republicans in the role of the minority party, and in a significant way betrayed the ideological positions of both parties, the balance of power between them and in each of them, the spheres of their regional influence, and their electoral base. The adaptation to the process of forced development of State-Monopolistic Capitalism during Roosevelt's "New Deal" and during the years of World War II, first by the Democrats, and then by the Republicans, marked the entry of the U.S. two-party system into a third important period of development, the modern stage of its historical evolution.

The main distinguishing factor of this phase in the functioning of the two-party system in the United States is the conscious use by both of its constituent components of the apparatus of the bourgeois government for regulating socioeconomic processes. The realization of this political course, meant first of all to strengthen class hegemony by the monopolistic bourgeoisie, has been conducted up to the present time primarily by two fundamental methods. Already during the years of Roosevelt's "New Deal" the doctrine of neo-liberalism was worked out and had received its first test in practice as it was adopted by the Democrats. This doctrine called for the active interference by the federal government in the economic life of society and for carrying out a series of liberal reforms with the goal of liquidating the more stinging wounds of the bourgeois structure and recognition for workers of fundamental democratic rights within the social sphere.[28]

The liberal-statist approach to resolving socioeconomic problems, successfully assimilated by the Democrats, allowed this party to seize solidly the political initiative and made it the main moving force in the mechanism of the two-party system. After World War II the doctrines of neoliberalism received the furthest development at the end of the 1940s in the policies of the "fair deal" of the Harry Truman administration and especially during the 1960s, in a new series of liberal reforms by the administrations of John Kennedy and Lyndon Johnson.[29]

As a counterbalance to the bourgeois-reformist conception of neoliberalism the

27. *The State of the Union Messages of the Presidents of the United States,* Fred L. Israel, ed. (New York, 1966), vol. 3, 2691.
28. *The Public Papers and Addresses of F. D. Roosevelt,* S. I. Rosenman, ed. (New York, 1938–1950), vol. 1, 646.
29. See N. V. Sivachev, *The Political Struggle in the U.S. during the Middle of the 1930s* [Politicheskaia bor'ba v SShA v seredine 30-x godov XX v.] (Moscow, 1966); V. L. Mal'kov, *The "New Deal" in the U.S. Social Movements and Social Policies* ["Novyi kurs" v SShA.

Republicans gradually worked out a doctrine of neoconservatism, which proposed significantly more moderate interference by the government in socioeconomic relations. Its defenders placed the fundamental portion of responsibility for solving deep-seated problems of life for American society not on the federal government, but on the authority of states and municipalities. They concentrated the power of the government apparatus first on limited regulation of the activity of trade unions and other labor organizations. The first hints of this conservative variant of state-monopolistic regulation of economics and social relations appeared at the end of the 1930s,[30] but the main test of the doctrine of neoconservatism in practice came during the administrations of Republican presidents Dwight Eisenhower and Richard Nixon.[31]

The combination of two fundamental methods of state-monopolistic regulation replacing each other with the administrations of the Democrats and the Republicans, the adoption by both parties of the idea of social responsibility of bourgeois government, the creation of a ramified social infrastructure of contemporary American society, all allowed during the course of a significant part of the postwar years a rather solid integration of broad masses of workers, farmers, middle layers of the urban population, the intelligentsia, blacks, and other racial-ethnic minorities into the structure of the U.S. two-party system. This helped for a time to fend off the threat of the emergence of a mass third party and even more strengthened the principle of the two-party system in the political culture and mass consciousness of the United States.

The postwar model of the party system was characterized by not only broad reform programs periodically carried out by the ruling party to integrate the protest movements, but also pseudo-populist rhetoric, actively used by the ultra-right, and a two-party approach preached by both parties toward working out a foreign policy strategy. Perhaps never before had foreign policy been used by the bourgeois parties to such an extent and as successfully to consolidate their positions in the political process.[32]

Sotsial'nye dvizheniia I sotsial'naia politika] (Moscow, 1973); N. N. Iakovlev, *Franklin Roosevelt, The Man and Politician. A New Reading* [Franklin Ruzvel't, chelovek I politik. Novoe prochtenie] (Moscow, 1981); A. S. Manykin, *Fundamental Directions in the Ideo-Political Evolution of the Two-Party System in the U.S. during the Years 1933–1952* [Osnovnye napravleniia ideino-politicheskoi evoliutsii dvukhpartiinoi sistemy SShA v 1933–1952 gg.] (Moscow, 1987) (diss.).

30. See I. A. Geevskii, *The U.S.: The Black Problem. The Policies of Washington on the Issue of Blacks (1945–1972)* [SShA: negritianskaia problema. Politika Vashingtona v negritianskom voprose (1945–1972 gg.)] (Moscow, 1973); A. A. Fursenko, *The Critical Decade for America. The 1960s* [Kriticheskoe desiatiletie Ameriki. 60-e gody] (Leningrad, 1974); V. A. Savel'ev, *The U.S.: Senate and Politics* [SShA: senat I politika] (Moscow, 1976); V. O. Pechatnov, *The U.S. Democratic Party: Voters and Policies* [Demokraticheskaia partiia SShA: izbirateli I politika] (Moscow, 1980).

31. See A. S. Manykin, "W. Willkie and the Genesis of 'New Republicanism' " [U. Uilki I genezis "novogo respublikanizma], *Amerikanskii ezhegodnik, 1980* (Moscow, 1981).

32. See V. I. Borisiuk, *The U.S.: At the Roots of the Modern Anti-Labor Policies* [SShA: u istokov sovremennoi antirabochei politiki] (Moscow, 1982); K. S. Gadzhiev, *Evolution of the Fundamental Trends of American Bourgeois Ideology* [Evoliutsiia osnovnykh techenii

In conditions of a significant rise in the level of education and awareness of broad masses of the population, in an atmosphere of growing politicization of public life in the country, to a great extent leaders of both parties tried to reflect their ideo-political positions in the preelection party platforms with the goal of strengthening their influence on the voters. The volume and detailed elaboration of such platforms grew sharply during the 1980s.

In the postwar period the process of institutionalizing the parties and strengthening their place and role in the political system of contemporary American society hastened significantly. This found expression in the biggest regulation of the parties' activities by the organs of the federal government in the introduction of government financing for election campaigns of candidates from the leading bourgeois parties, in the development of the ideology of a "partisan government" and "partisan democracy" and other activities directed primarily at increasing the parties' effectiveness.[33] These measures became an insistent necessity after World War II in conditions of a sharp worsening of all the contradictions of capitalism and the rapid growth of the forces for social progress in the world.

But the measures taken during the postwar years to strengthen the bourgeois political parties had a limited effect. From the beginning of the 1970s in the partisan-political system of the U.S. a growth in destabilizing tendencies could be seen. In the atmosphere of intensified economic crisis and the upsurge of mass movements of social protest, a crisis in methods of state-monopolistic regulation of the economy and social relations emerged by that time and began to manifest itself ever more distinctly. An obvious discrepancy became clear between the traditional demarcation of parties. It had cropped up during the years of Roosevelt's New Deal over the question of the socioeconomic role of the bourgeois government and the new problems and contradic-tions of contemporary bourgeois society like "stagflation" (stagnation accompanied by inflation), a fall in the effectiveness and competitiveness of American industry, a weakening in the international position of the United States, and intensification of social problems. Democrats and Republicans during the 1970s not only failed to put forth realistic ways for solving these problems but also could not even come up with clear alternatives to them. The attempt to put forth an alternative program, by the Democratic candidate, George McGovern, during the 1972 election campaign, turned

---

amerikanskoi burzhuaznoi ideologii] (Moscow, 1982); V. I. Terekhov, *The Republicans in Power: Socio-Economic Policies of the D. Eisenhower Administration (1953–1960)* [Respub-likantsy u vlasti: sotsial'no-ekonomicheskaia politika pravitelistva D. Eizenkhauera (1953–1960)] (Moscow, 1984); V. A. Nikonov, *From Eisenhower to Nixon. From the History of the U.S. Republican Party* [Ot Eizenkhauera k Niksonu. Iz istorii respublikanskoi partii SShA] (Moscow, 1984).

33. See A. S. Manykin and E. F. Yazkov, "The Role of Third Parties in the U.S. Partisan-Political System" [Rol' tret;ikh partii v partiino-politicheskoi sisteme SShA], *Voprosy istorii* 1981, no. 2; A. S. Manykin, V. A. Nikonov, and E. F. Yazkov, "Bourgeois Political Parties and the Formation of Foreign Policy in the U.S." [Burzhuaznye politicheskie partii I formirovanie vneshnepoliticheskogo kursa SShA], in *Bourgeois Political Parties in the U.S. and American Foreign Policy (19th-20th Centuries)* [Burzhuaznye politicheskie partii SShA I amerikanskaia vneshniaia politika (XIX-XX vv.)] (Moscow, 1986).

out to be unsuccessful. All of this taken together, on top of the Watergate scandal, gave birth to a crisis of trust by voters in the two-party system, weakened the electoral base of both parties, led to an end to traditional voting coalitions, and significantly lowered the degree of mobilization of the electorate.

The growth in crisis-ridden phenomena in the process of the two-party system during the 1970s and beginning of the 1980s manifested itself also in the weakening of "party machines" and in general of the role of the party apparatus in such important spheres of the parties' activities as control of voter behavior, nomination of candidates, and conducting election campaigns. The parties began to experience competition to an ever greater degree in these directions from various nonpartisan sociopolitical organizations: the mass media, pressure groups of business associations, political action committees, and professional firms of political consultants. The emergence and development of these organizations was the result of the increased need by leading circles in the United States for additional means of controlling political behavior of the masses in conditions in which the bourgeois parties cannot manage in full with the functions bestowed upon them.[34]

At the basis of these processes lies the growing inadequacy of the ideo-political course of both bourgeois parties in the United States. This course has been based during the postwar years on Keynesian recipes and on the postulates of the "Cold War," which have been inadequate for the objective realities of the modern stage of the development of capitalism and for the new relationship of forces in the international arena.[35] The ruling circles in the United States have attempted to find a way out of this situation by changing the ideo-political positions in the direction of creating a conservative right model of state-monopolistic capitalism, activating an aggressive foreign policy course, and inflaming chauvinistic sentiments in the country.

On this basis, noticeable changes in the two-party system occurred in the 1980s; tendencies toward a new partisan-political regrouping have become distinct. Reflecting a shift to the right in the sentiments of monopolistic circles and bourgeois-everyday America, and speculating on the crisis of liberal statism and using a temporary improvement in the economic state of the market and a weakening of democratic forces, Republicans managed to strengthen their electoral base and secure a victory in the elections of 1980 and 1984.[36] The period during the Republican administration of Ronald Reagan was known for important shifts in the socioeconomic policies of the American government, a reorientation of its course and a sharp change of the whole

34. See M. N. Marchenko, "Regulation of the Activity of Bourgeois Parties in the Political System" [Regulirovanie deiatel'nosti burzhuaznykh partii v politicheskoi sisteme], *U.S. Political Parties Today* [Politicheskie partii SShA v noveishee vremia] (Moscow, 1982).

35. See V. O. Pechatnov, "Several New Tendencies in the Functioning of the Two-Party System from the 1970s to the beginning of the 1980s" [Nekotorye novye tendentsii funktsionirovaniia dvukhpartiinoi sistemy v 70-kh-nachale 80-kh godov], *Problemy amerikanistiki* (Moscow, 1983).

36. See *Modern U.S. Foreign Policy, In Two Volumes* [Sovremennaia vneshniaia politika SShA, v 2-kh t.], G. A. Trofimenko, ed. (Moscow, 1984); S. M. Plekhanov, *Right Extremism and U.S. Foreign Policy* [Pravyi ekstremizm I vneshniaia politika SShA] (Moscow, 1986); *History of the U.S.* [Istoriia SShA], vol. 4, 1946–1980, G. N. Sevost'ianov, ed. (Moscow, 1987).

system of national priorities in favor of monopolies, the military-industrial complex, and the prosperous segments of society.

The Republicans' policies, however, not only failed to solve the fundamental problems of the country but also led to a fall in the standard of living for millions of workers, to the intensification of socio-class polarization of American bourgeois society, and to the growth of contradictions unique to itself. The militaristic, openly reactionary direction of modernized American conservatism enters into a discrepancy more than ever with objective long-term tendencies of internal development in the United States and with the real demands of the modern world.

Only the future will show whether the new restructuring of the U.S. partisan-political system will become realized, and if so, then what will be the result. For the time being one can only agree with the conclusion of American Communists that the contemporary two-party system will remain the instrument of class hegemony by the U.S. monopolistic bourgeoisie. It is the "vise in which state-monopolistic capitalism desires to squeeze the class struggle and social problems, securing with this the stability of their power."[37] Further perfecting of the system of the U.S. bourgeois two-party mechanism can lead to only a temporary and partial solution to the most pressing class contradictions tearing apart contemporary American society.[38]

37. See E. Ia. Borshchevskaya, "Electoral Strategy of the U.S. Republican Party from the 1970s to the Beginning of the 1980s" [Elektoral'naia strategiia respublikanskoi partii SShA v 70-e-nachale 80-kh godov], *Problemy amerikanistiki* (Moscow, 1986).

38. *The New Program of the U.S. Communist Party. The People Versus Monopolies* [Novaia programma Kommunisticheskoi partii SShA. Narod protiv monopolii], 23d National Congress of the U.S. Communist Party (Moscow, 1985), 267.

Comment

by Joel H. Silbey

The American two-party system has existed for more than two centuries. Its organizational structure of loyal members, bosses, and consultive structures such as committees and conventions, and its elemental purpose, to organize and manage the political landscape on behalf of different political perspectives, have changed little since the beginning, even as the parties' role in the nation's political life and their effectiveness in shaping and directing the political realm have varied significantly over time. During its lifetime the two-party system has accomplished a great deal, hesitated about or failed to do some important things, and has too often ignored many matters that deserved attention if American politicians were to live up to their claims about their contribution to the evolving democratization of American life. Its history is interesting, complicated, and often difficult to come to terms with and fully understand.

"Some Results from Studying the History of the U.S. Two-Party System," written by a formidable quartet of Russian scholars, was first presented, in an earlier version, to a meeting of the Organization of American Historians. It is an attempt to get an interpretive handle on that—party centered—aspect of the nation's political past and to draw some summary conclusions from their, and their colleagues', extensive research efforts into the subject. This is very much an in-house effort, the four authors are all veteran scholars in Moscow University's Laboratory for United States Studies; most of their citations are to works by other Russian scholars from that research center (only Chambers and Burnham's *The American Party Systems* appears in the essay's footnotes to represent this side of the Atlantic—it appears twice, in thirty-eight footnotes, most of them with multiple citations).[1]

Manykin, Nikonov, Rogoulev, and Yazkov's story is a long one, clearly told. Their description of the way that the American parties originated and evolved from the Constitution through the 1790s and beyond, and their identification of the important marking points in their history along the way to the present, is unexceptional and fairly congruent with the usual description by American historians of these same matters. The Russian scholars, as they have revealed so often, are well read in the relevant literature from both sides of the Atlantic, and they have digested the standard fare with very few surprises for anyone who knows the basic literature. In addition, they

---

1. William Nisbet Chambers and Walter Dean Burnham, *The American Party Systems: Stages of Party Development* (New York, 2d ed., 1975).

254

have themselves engaged in effective research, some of it in American archives. They know a good deal about the subject.

More problematic is what the authors then proceed to do with these facts, that is, the nature of the particular history that they construct from their extensive file of note cards. Specifically and unsurprisingly, they cast the story of American political parties within traditional Marxist-Leninist terms. At the center of America's two-party history, they argue, have been the continuous crises and persistent contradictions of capitalism, and the ability of the bourgeoisie (until lately) to use political parties to meet and overcome them and effectively undergird their own extensive power.

In the view expressed here, the political parties were not only instruments of bourgeois hegemony in the United States but also one of the latter's main weapons in that endeavor:

> The flexible and complex mechanisms of the two-party system, acting together with the ramified apparatus of the bourgeois government, dependent upon the powerful economic potential of the country, allowed up until this time and still allows the U.S. ruling circles to withstand, although not without some losses, the numerous sociopolitical crises, to adapt itself to the conditions of intensified class struggle, and to withstand the framework of the bourgeois-democratic political process.

The way that the bourgeoisie operated, in this view, was often subtle, and quite agile. It allowed the "partial involvement of the exploited majority into the political process," for example. But this right to participate, and, apparently, to be listened to, of course, was not all that it seemed to be. Parties operated to reinforce bourgeois purposes. All of their apparent opening to large numbers of American citizens, to participate in their nominating and campaign activities, and to vote, were really effective weapons that maintained bourgeois hegemony. As a result of this single-mindedness, the parties survived over two hundred years because their success was "exceptionally convenient for the U.S. ruling classes."

All aspects of America's two-party history is fit within this rubric. When things change over time, and they have done so, it is because the parties, that is their elite leadership, are adaptive to the shifting needs of the bourgeoisie even (or especially) as the elements comprising the substructure of society shift. Electoral realignments are mechanisms of this adaptation to social transformations. They are never self-driven, by voter eruptions, for example, but are part of a process of moving with the tides of history. In the course of American history, as a result of these shifting tides, that is, changes in the dominant forms of economic organization and activity, these scholars delineate three distinct eras: from the beginning of the nation to the 1870s, from there to the 1930s, and a third, since the 1930s. American realignment theorists, and others, would shift these dates somewhat and think in different terms about the origins and nature of the process.[2] But there is also an acceptable argument for the way these different turning points are described here, a nonbehavioral, nonquantitative

---

2. Bruce A. Campbell and Richard J. Trilling, eds., *Realignment in American Politics: Toward A Theory* (Austin, Texas, 1980); Byron Shafer, *The End of Realignment?: Interpreting American Electoral Eras* (Madison, Wisc., 1991).

one, rooted in a basic systemic shift, that is close to one offered by Theodore Lowi, for example.[3]

It is no surprise to anyone that, within each era, political parties both promoted internal conflict in the United States and also controlled its excesses in the name of maintaining a stable society. Whether that stability was promoted on behalf of a single, hegemonic class each time, or was less deterministic than that, remains more of an open question than is allowed here. Political parties in American historiography have been primarily about conflict, less about system maintenance or class protection. American historians have expended a great deal of effort delineating what they usually see as important differences between the parties, the different social groupings that attach themselves to each coalition, and the different policy agendas that each party espouses.[4]

Messrs. Manykin et al. accept that such social differences existed, but suggest that the parties, at best, were manifesting different variations of the overall bourgeois political domination. Thus, in the 1830s, "both the Democratic party and the Whig party, remaining under the control of the bourgeois-planter bloc, captured with their influence all the major social groups of the period." Or, "having set as their main goal defending the interests of big capital, both components of the two-party system, the Republicans and the Democrats [in the 1870s] turned into a conservative force striving to prevent cardinal changes in the socioeconomic and political structure of bourgeois society."

In this view, American politics have not been particularly open, nor American society all that pluralistic. Rather, manipulation and control has been the hallmark of both, and many opportunities ignored, or overcome, to attend to the interests of those who remained outside bourgeois comfortableness. When an opportunity was presented to change things, in the third party, Populist and Socialist struggles of the late nineteenth and early twentieth centuries, and, most particularly, "after the Great October Socialist revolution in Russia led to the appearance of a government that espoused the goal of building a society of true social justice, and eliminating exploitation of individuals by individuals," American party leaders, as was to be expected, went the other way, safeguarding and increasing their control on behalf of conservatism, a process culminating in the emergence of a particularly pernicious form of bourgeois domination, "state monopoly capitalism," in reaction to the Depression after 1929.

These defensive attacks and superficial accommodations all worked effectively enough, according to the authors, to keep the lid on potential protest from below until the contradictions and the pressures grew too much even for this adaptable system to continue to handle matters as effectively as it had always done. It ultimately proved

3. I have in mind Lowi's notion of the emergence of a second republic in the 1930s. See, among other places, Theodore J. Lowi, *The Personal President: Power Invested, Promises Unfulfilled* (Ithaca, N.Y., 1985).

4. See, as one example of this, a work well known to Russian scholars, Robert Kelley, *The Cultural Pattern In American Politics: The First Century* (New York, 1979). Kelley taught at Moscow University as Distinguished Lecturer in the Fulbright Program and kept in touch, thereafter, with some of the Russian scholars.

inadequate in the crisis of capitalism that began to be manifested in the late 1960s, characterized by "the most pressing class contradictions tearing apart contemporary American society." The result, however, was not the expected popular revolution, but, rather, mass alienation from politics and from the parties, and the latter's decline as important political forces on the American landscape.

None of this story of cyclical adjustment within long-range decline is presented in full detail, nor could it be in a short essay. What the authors do present, however, underlines how much fresh overviews and a different interpretative gloss applied to the elemental facts, of the kind offered here, are always welcome, and often quite useful as a route to advancing our common knowledge. And, so far as their interpretation goes, there are American historians who would agree with much that is presented here, perhaps with some of them asking that the Marxist-Leninist trappings be muted or dropped altogether, others perhaps accepting only aspects of the offered interpretation (especially about the last, declinist, phase of the story), and not the whole.[5]

Nevertheless, the problems that "Some Results . . ." pose to American scholars are obvious. The authors' single-minded Marxist-Leninist superstructure raises critical questions of understanding and difficulties of fit. This is simply not the way that most American historians of the subject read the evidence. There have been always been attempts, in their view, to assert hegemony, to be sure. But these were never as complete nor as uncontested as suggested here. New Deal measures, for example, provoked rabid opposition from capitalists as its derivatives do today from their descendants. To be sure, as is argued here, some capitalists supported aspects of the New Deal in the interest of maintaining their control, but the wide differences over policy and the intense political battles continued as well. The era needs to be described, I would suggest, as do others, in more mixed terms than are offered in this essay.

(On the other hand, the situation described covering the period from the 1870s to the 1930s needs less mixing of different perspectives—it fits closest to a common interpretative framework).[6] The point is that a standard, stable claim remains largely untouched by the efforts made here, that the often messy disorderliness of party operations was not usually only on behalf of a hegemonic class. America's political party culture was never as democratic as its adherents claimed. But it contained enough such elements that notions of systemic hegemonic control need to be used with caution.

Beyond that, the Russian scholars' interpretation leaves no room in which to fit much of the important discoveries and fresh interpretative forays that have emerged among American scholars in recent years: the interest in the importance of different group cultures within the same political system, the crosswinds set off by ideologies such as republicanism and its battle early in the nation's political history to retain

---

5. Walter Dean Burnham, *The Current Crisis in American Politics* (New York, 1982).

6. See Martin J. Sklar, *The Corporate Reconstruction of American Capitalism, 1890–1916: The Market, the Law, and Politics* (New York, 1988). But there are also caveats to this construction. A good place to start is Samuel P. Hays, *The Response to Industrialism 1885–1914* (Chicago, 2d ed., 1995); and in the many works of Louis Galambos on the organizational revolution.

dominance against the emerging bourgeoisie; the presence and importance of ethnore-
ligious conflict between the parties and their supporters, the constant prebourgeois
political stirring among mid–nineteenth century workers.[7]

Surprisingly, neither African Americans nor women receive much attention in this
overview, although both groups, and their efforts to achieve political empowerment,
have been getting a great deal of attention from political historians. No history of
American political parties can ignore the rather innovative and informative material
that is coming out about these ultimate outsiders in the American political experience.
And, at the same time, there is much room, given the enlarged factual base, to consider
different understandings of, and engage in debate about, the experiences of these
oppressed groups within a two-party dominated political system.[8]

Northern-southern differences in American society is another area of some interest
that does not get the attention here that it deserves. When discussed in this essay, the
subject is approached quite conventionally, and in too limited a fashion, since the role
of sectional impulses in the history of American political parties extended well beyond
the antebellum and Civil War years. The political history and recent transformation
of southern politics from long-standing commitment to agrarian racialism and the
Democratic party to following the course of petite bourgeois racialism into the
Republican party is a significant story for the American experience, one that has
received much attention by political historians and will, and should, receive more.[9]

Finally, there are other matters that would have been welcome if they had been
addressed by Messrs Manykin and his colleagues. The authors do not ask new
questions about all of this material, they are not intellectually adventurous, generally
content, as I have argued, with the existing questions about parties, and for the use
of conventional categories in understanding their history. On another plane, although
acknowledging that there were differences within the bourgeois hegemony, the authors
neither elaborate on them nor see such as critical to our understanding as most
American scholars would—and should.

At the end of the day, this essay is a monument, first, to the efforts pushed so
hard and so effectively years ago by the late Professor N. V. Sivachev for Russian
historians to learn what American historians were doing concerning the history of

---

7. Daniel Rodgers, "Republicanism: The Career of A Concept," *Journal of American
History* 79 (June 1992): 11–38; Richard Hofstadter, *The Idea of a Party System: The Rise of
Legitimate Opposition in the United States, 1790–1840* (Berkeley, Calif., 1969); Paul Kleppner,
The Third Electoral System: Parties, Voters and Political Cultures, 1853–1892 (Chapel Hill,
N.C., 1979); Sean Wilentz, *Chants Democratic: New York City and the Rise of the American
Working Class* (New York, 1984).

8. Elizabeth Varon, *We Mean to Be Counted: White Women and Politics in Antebellum
Virginia* (Chapel Hill, N.C., 1998); Rebecca Edwards, *Angels in the Machinery: Gender in
American Party Politics from the Civil War to the Progressive Era* (New York, 1997).

On African Americans and the political system, one can usefully begin with Steven F.
Lawson, *In Pursuit of Power: Southern Blacks and Electoral Power, 1965–1982* (New York,
1985). Also see Lawson, *Running for Freedom: Civil Rights and Black Politics in America
Since 1941* (Philadelphia, 1991).

9. Among many other studies of the South, see James M. Glaser, *Race, Campaign Politics
and the Realignment of the South* (New Haven, Conn., 1996).

political parties, and to explore, along with them, as much of that subject as time and opportunity offered.[10] Second, it is a monument in its own right, as the summing up of the Russian scholars' thinking as it has evolved since Sivachev's early efforts. All well and good. But, in the end, Professor Manykin and his colleagues present a perspective that originated in, and matured throughout, the "period of stagnation," and one that is fundamentally shaped by that fact, a shaping that locks them into an interpretation that, while containing some useful insights, also has too narrow a focus to encompass all that they claim for it.[11]

All of which raises an interesting question as to what Russian scholars of American political parties might say now about their understanding, given the sharp and extensive changes that have occurred in their country's intellectual life since 1989, and given the apparent deviation of so many Russian historians from the Marxist-Leninist interpretative structure, a deviation so powerfully manifested at the landmark 1991 conference on American history held in Moscow.[12] The answers seem fairly clear given what so many of the Russian scholars argued then—and fairly different from the kind offered in this interesting essay—ultimately, a monument to another time.

10. See my comments about Professor Sivachev and his efforts in the general introduction to this volume.

11. Vadim Kolenko, "American History Abroad: North American History in the USSR before Perestroika and Today," *OAH Newsletter* 19 (August 1991): 4.

12. Marcus Rediker, "The Old Guard, The New Guard, and the People at the Gates: New Approaches to the Study of American History in the USSR," *William and Mary Quarterly*, 3rd ser., 48 (October 1991): 580–97. See my brief comments about this conference in the introduction to this volume.

Response

by Iu. N. Rogoulev

The comment by Professor Joel H. Silbey exhibits no discontent on the role of American political parties among historians of this field. Nonetheless, there is yet a significant variety and difference in how to interpret even infamous facts in American political history. Inevitably, this might impede future dialogue between followers of various historical schools.

Professor Silbey dealt with a complicated task. He had to evaluate an essay by Soviet historians who mainly summarized numerous articles on the history of American political parties. Most of these works were published over a prolonged period of time and were exclusively aimed at Soviet historians and Soviet readers. In order to comment on such an essay, one must have a clear understanding of the peculiarities of Soviet historiography, theoretical excursions, terminology and jargon adopted by Soviet historians. Much remains to be thoroughly explained to an American reader. Marxist theory, which this essay is based on, and the so-called stagnation period are not to be blamed for certain scholarly confusion. To a considerable extent, it is mostly the matter of language and terminology taken upon by Soviet historians when faced with isolation from their colleagues and readers abroad alike.

This article encounters more challenges, for the authors attempted to offer a new theoretical overview, and even more so, a new Soviet historiographical systematic concept of American political parties from their emergence to their present existence. The authors analyzed the functioning of major political parties as a two-party system. There can be found main ideological differences between Soviet historians and their colleagues in the West.

American historians, as it follows from Professor Silbey, consider a long-time dominance of two parties on the political arena as a given. The consistency of the major parameters of the U.S. political system doesn't arouse any questions in their minds either. Consequently, as Silbey acknowledges, American scholars pay more attention to conflicts and differences between the parties rather than to problems of "system maintenance."

On the contrary, Soviet historians are more interested in the preservation of the two-party system and its perseverance over the last two centuries. Similarly, comparative study of American political history and, for instance, that of European states with their diverse political specter, past and present, is of greater interest to Soviet Americanists.

In the United States, however, any attempts to effectively organize farmers, labor, trade unions, socialists, communists, reformists, ethnoculturalists, religious believers, or environmentalists into political coalitions, and movements into independent political parties, invariably failed. Newly emerging political parties were scornfully coined by American historians as "third parties," which, in fact, emphasized their weakness and inability to compete with the two major parties.

Soviet historians are fully aware of the openness and pluralism of American society as well as of differences between political parties. But ideological and public pluralism in real political life were constantly being limited to fit into the ideological-political mainstream. The latter was represented by the two major independent—yet similar in their type, character, and social basis—parties. Is it possible then to avoid mentioning the two-party system's dominance in U.S. political history?

It is beyond argument that American political history had experienced periods of fierce competition that led the parties to depart from each other and fight bitterly. There also were periods when the parties came closer again and even formed partisan, interfactional coalitions on a legislative level. Parties traded their roles and went back and forth between being a majority and an opposition party. At the earliest stages of their existence, they were elite political organizations. In the era of mass politics, parties began to represent far-flung interests and to form mass electoral coalitions. Achieving this goal was considerably eased due to the fact that American political parties have never practiced individual membership and have been amorphous electoral unions.

From then on, however, party bureaucrats and political candidates were recruited from the political elite, which in turn transformed into a "ruling" one. One may choose to call or not to call it "bourgeois," but the latter doesn't cease to rule the American political arena.

Political power in the United States, as we know, is formed in a democratic way through wide involvement of the population in the electoral process. It became possible thanks to long and unrelenting struggle to assert rights and freedoms for American citizens. But even nowadays in elections, Americans delegate their authority to representatives of the political elite, which realizes this political power. These are the ABC's of the American political system, and Professor Silbey cannot be unaware of that.

Parties ensure democracy in the electoral process, and this constitutes one of their major progressive functions. At the same time parties fight for political power and manipulate and control the electorate. No wonder most politicians, with few exceptions, did not enjoy profound trust among Americans. The popularity rate of political parties never rose above the medium level, and politics itself was considered immoral business, to put it mildly.

We agree with Silbey that such terms as "bourgeoisie," "bourgeois parties," "ruling circles," and "class struggle" are applied by the authors indiscriminately to all periods of the parties' history, and do not necessarily reflect objectively the essence of an ongoing process. This is the above-mentioned case of using special, "Soviet" language in historical literature.

Thus, the authors occasionally use the term "bourgeoisie" as a synonym for "capitalist" or "political elite." Regardless, they agree that the political elite neither did nor does consist of capitalists only, but has a wider social basis and is not monolithic in nature. Clearly, the character, social composition, and ideology of the political elite has changed over time. In the same fashion the authors use the term "class struggle" to describe social unrest with the understanding that unrest can have a place within the ruling elite as well.

Politics reflect a constant process of struggle for power that features clashes of various factions of the political elite dependent on mass electoral support. Evaluating reasons for the two-party system's stability, the system emphasized the firmness of the political elite's stand, its intentions to use every available means, including illegal manipulation and tight control, to weaken positions of their opponents. In the same vein, the article pointed out the political flexibility of such a system, its ability to adapt to changing conditions, to initiate progressive social reforms and to democratize the political process.

In this regard Professor Silbey mistakenly interprets the authors' position as allegedly denying the objective nature of partisan transformations. Surely, partisan transformations and shifts in political favors of the electorate testified to fundamental changes in American society, in its cultural and social structure. Another mistake would be to bluntly overlook the role of political parties. For instance, it is hard to decide what in fact prompted the transformation of such scale in the 1930s: objective processes rooted in the previous decades or the New Deal implemented by Franklin Delano Roosevelt.

In describing the New Deal, the authors are using a common Soviet historiographical term: "state-monopolistic capitalism." It is also known that in American scholarly literature the term "monopoly" and its derivatives are not welcomed, since monopoly is illegal in America. Perhaps, references to "state-monopolistic capitalism" provoked such a negative reaction from Dr. Silbey. But the meaning of this term, no matter how threatening it might appear, is not confined to describing "a particularly pernicious form of bourgeois domination," as he writes. It marks the advent of an epoch for big business and big government, state regulation and the welfare state. So, the authors are far from calling this politics conservative or, even more, reactionary, as it seems to Professor Silbey. Franklin Delano Roosevelt's New Deal no doubt was a progressive step forward in the development of American society on the whole. Roosevelt, being an experienced and shrewd politician, succeeded in containing potential threats either from the Right or from the Left, and ensured certain superiority for himself and for the Democratic party.

Excessive theorizing, an abundance of special "Soviet" terms, and a systematic approach and thus inevitable schematizing make this article more politological rather than simply historical. This surely poses difficulties for comprehension by Americans. Besides, such an article requires firsthand familiarity with Soviet historiography, something that we cannot demand of American historians.

In my opinion, this is the main source of criticism by Professor Silbey, who analyzes the article according to criteria common in American historiography. One can hardly agree with such an approach. It is impossible to criticize historians for adhering to a different national school of historiography. Surely, Soviet historians interpreted many facts differently. Surely, they embraced themes within the realm of their interest and not necessarily those that might be popular among American historians. In addition, many obstacles and limitations to study and research in archives and libraries in Russia and in the United States are now being encountered.

Hopefully, a broadening of contacts and ties, and also joint publications and projects, will bring historians of both countries together to achieve better understanding and to overthrow a barrier of alienation. In conclusion, there are now no more ideological or political obstacles existent at the time when this article was first written. Otherwise, they would have slowed down productive cooperation between the two countries.

Contributors

RUSSIAN

Larisa V. Baibakova, Moscow State University

Elena Ia. Borschevskaya, Institute of U.S. and Canadian Studies, Russian Academy of Sciences

Ilya V. Galkin, Moscow State University

Alexander A. Kormilets, Moscow State University

Alexander S. Manykin, Moscow State University

Viaycheslav A. Nikonov, Moscow State University (1988), from 1994, member of the Duma

Sergei A. Porshakov, Institute of World Economy and International Politics, Russian Academy of Sciences

Alla A. Porshakova, Moscow State University

Yuri N. Rogoulev, Moscow State University

Nikolai V. Sivachev, Moscow State University

Vladimir V. Sogrin, Institute of General History, Russian Academy of Sciences

Marina A. Vlasova, Institute of General History, Russian Academy of Sciences

Eugene F. Yazkov, Moscow State University

AMERICAN

Allan G. Bogue is Frederick Jackson Turner Professor of American History Emeritus at the University of Wisconsin, Madison

David Burner is Professor of American History at the State University of New York at Stony Brook

Phyllis F. Field teaches American History at Ohio University

Theodore J. Lowi is the John L. Senior Professor of American Institutions at Cornell University

Samuel T. McSeveney is Professor of American History at Vanderbilt University

William G. Shade is Professor of American History at Lehigh University

Joel H. Silbey is the President White Professor of History in Cornell University

Index